BIBLICAL ARCHAEOLOGY

BIBLICAL
ARCHAEOLOGY

G. ERNEST WRIGHT

THE WESTMINSTER PRESS

Philadelphia

First published 1957
New and revised edition 1962
Reprinted 1966, 1970 and 1974

LIBRARY OF CONGRESS CATALOG CARD NUMBER: 57–5020
ISBN—0—664—20420—1

Printed in Great Britain by
REDWOOD BURN LIMITED
Trowbridge & Esher

CONTENTS

LIST OF ILLUSTRATIONS

LIST OF ILLUSTRATIONS

LIST OF ILLUSTRATIONS

LIST OF MAPS

FOREWORD

THE purpose of this volume is to summarize the archaeological discoveries which directly illumine biblical history, in order that the Bible's setting in the ancient world and its relation to its environment may be more readily comprehended. The framework of the volume is thus the biblical story and the subject matter is treated chronologically. Yet the book is not meant to be a biblical history; it is simply a supplement thereto. At various places in the text, and especially in Chapter VII, a small attempt is made to introduce the reader to the large world of comparative theology in ancient times. Yet in neither theology nor history does the volume pretend to be exhaustive. It is introductory and selective, the purpose being simply to introduce the main areas of inquiry and discovery. The greatest freedom has been used in quoting from biblical translations. I generally began with the A.V. but usually revised it. In most instances, therefore, the translations correspond exactly with none of the modern versions. Thomas Nelson & Sons have granted permission to quote from the R.S.V. in some twenty-three instances where I used its readings.

I am greatly indebted to the following people, to whom grateful acknowledgement is here made: Professors W. F. Albright, John Bright, Frank M. Cross, Jr., and Floyd V. Filson, who read various portions of the manuscript and gave me the benefit of their wise counsel; Miss Nancy Renn who rendered valuable assistance in the preparation of Chapter XIV; Mrs. G. Kenneth Shafer and Mrs. Lawrence A. Sinclair who typed the manuscript with such care and accuracy; and Mr. Charles F. Stevens whose skill as artist and draftsman was employed in a number of drawings. I am particularly grateful to Mr. Herbert Rees for his careful work on the manuscript in order to make it clear and consistent, and for compiling the index.

McCormick Theological Seminary,   G. ERNEST WRIGHT
      Chicago

June 4, 1955

FOREWORD TO THE SECOND EDITION

No changes in the structure of the volume have been introduced into this revision. Minor changes have been made throughout, and substantial additions have been added to Chapters V, VIII, IX, and X, the only purpose being to bring the discussion up to date. I feel particularly humbled by, and grateful to, the many readers who have expressed their appreciation of the first edition, not merely by their extensive purchase of it, but especially by word, letter and suggestion. I am deeply indebted also to Gerald Duckworth & Co. Ltd. for their interest, understanding and patience, and also to Dr. Paul Meacham and the Westminster Press who have so successfully handled the volume in the U.S.A., in spite of the great expense occasioned by the many pictures.

Harvard Divinity School   G. ERNEST WRIGHT

April 18, 1962

CHAPTER I

BIBLICAL ARCHAEOLOGY

" Remember the days of old ; consider the years of generation upon generation ; ask thy father and he will show thee ; thy elders, and they will tell thee " (Deut. 32 : 7).

BIBLICAL archaeology is a special " armchair " variety of general archaeology. The biblical archaeologist may or may not be an excavator himself, but he studies the discoveries of the excavations in order to glean from them every fact that throws a direct, indirect or even diffused light upon the Bible. He must be intelligently concerned with stratigraphy and typology, upon which the methodology of modern archaeology rests and of which more will be said later in this chapter. Yet his chief concern is not with methods or pots or weapons in themselves alone. His central and absorbing interest is the understanding and exposition of the Scriptures.

BIBLICAL ARCHAEOLOGY AND BIBLICAL THEOLOGY

The Bible, unlike the other religious literature of the world, is not centered in a series of moral, spiritual and liturgical teachings, but in the story of a people who lived at a certain time and place. Biblical man, unlike other men in the world, had learned to confess his faith by telling the story of what had happened to his people and by seeing within it the hand of God. Faith was communicated, in other words, through the forms of history, and unless history is taken seriously one cannot comprehend biblical faith which triumphantly affirms the meaning of history. The biblical student must be a student of ancient life, and archaeology is his aid in recovering the nature of a period long past. In reconstructing the history of biblical times one comes upon many periods which are not well known from the surviving written records. One illustration is the Patriarchal period of Israelite life as we know it from the Book of Genesis. Who were these Hebrews ? When did they live and how is their movement to be fitted into ancient history ? Genesis in itself only hints at the answers to these questions. The material within it was passed down orally for many generations before it was committed to writing, and it is necessary for

us to recover its original background if we are to answer the historian's questions. This can only be done by archaeological investigation, the results of which we must carefully sift and use because we have no other means of getting into the period in question.

Of course one might ask : " Why is all this historical effort necessary when all we need to get from the Bible is its faith and religious ideas ? " Yet what is biblical faith but the knowledge of life's meaning in the light of what God did in a particular history ? In the biblical sense there is no such thing as a knowledge of God apart, or somehow separated, from the real events of this human scene and from the special responsibilities he has given us within it. Faith and knowledge in the Bible are founded in a complete commitment to the God who rules history and in the loyalty, obedience and hope which are anchored in him but which necessitate one's personal and responsible involvement in, not retreat or removal from, the events of history. Furthermore, biblical man could express his faith so confidently because he understood that the events he describes really happened. If we are to take him seriously, we must also take his history seriously ; and the more we know about it, the more we shall be enlightened by what he says concerning it. The intensive study of the biblical archaeologist is thus the fruit of the vital concern for history which the Bible has instilled in us. We cannot, therefore, assume that the knowledge of biblical history is unessential to the faith. Biblical theology and biblical archaeology must go hand in hand, if we are to comprehend the Bible's meaning.

Yet the study of archaeology leads the theologian to a considerable and unavoidable risk. What if one should find that the biblical events did not occur at all ? That this may happen is the risk that must be taken, for again we must say that we cannot understand the nature of the Bible completely unless we know all that we can know about its background. For the most part archaeology has substantiated and illumined the biblical story at so many crucial points that no one can seriously say that it is little but a congeries of myth and legend. No longer is the situation what it was 150 years ago, when " from the chaos of prehistory the Bible projected as though it were a monstrous fossil, with no contemporary evidence to demonstrate its authenticity and its origin in a human world like ours ".[1] Yet numerous historical problems have arisen, as we shall see in the pages which follow, and in addition there is in the Bible an interpretation of events and of experience which is not subject to historical or archaeological testing. That a violent wave of destruction occurred in southern Palestine during the course of the 13th century B.C. is clear from the excavations. That this was caused by the Israelite invasion is a reasonable historical inference. That the warfare was directed by God for his own righteous ends in history is, however, an interpretation by faith which is not subject to historical testing. The resurrection of Christ was an inner certainty to early Christians but it is something which archaeology can do nothing to illuminate. Hence the biblical archaeologist is definitely limited in the work which he can do. He cannot prove that the Bible is " true ", but he can and has illuminated the historical setting, the events and the cultural background with which biblical faith is concerned. In doing so, however, he has found that while for the most part he has played a positive role in biblical exposition, he has also had to play a negative part on a number of occasions. Perhaps the clearest illustration of this negative role is to be found in the archaeologist's discovery of the antiquity of man's past. Since this discovery is so intimately tied to the development of biblical archaeology, it is necessary that we here say a few words about it.

When early Christian scholars reconstructed a history of the world, their chief source was the Old Testament. How old was the earth and the life upon it? Here was a record concise and precise, which told them what they wanted to know. The great Fathers of the first three centuries, knowing little if any Hebrew, used the Septuagint or Greek translation exclusively, and from it they learned that the creation of earth and man was to be placed some six thousand years before their day. This was indeed interesting to some, for did not God create this world in six days, and is not one day with the Lord as a thousand years?

Later scholars, Eusebius and Jerome, studying the Hebrew text itself, were inclined to lower the figure to four thousand years, but within those limits all were agreed. The history of man is not shrouded in obscurity. It is definite and confined, having begun with the creative act of God between four and six thousand years B.C. And most were agreed also that this creative act was confined to six days of twenty-four hours each.

Such was the view commonly held throughout Christendom until the middle of the last century. Luther in his *Commentary on Genesis* declared: " We know, on the authority of Moses, that longer ago than six thousand years the world did not exist." Calvin agreed; but Melanchthon, wishing to be more exact, set the actual date of creation at 3963 B.C., a figure varying only a few years from that of Jerome. It was a saintly Irish clergyman, Archbishop Ussher, however, who established himself as the greatest authority in the matter with the publication of his *Annals of the Old and New Testaments* in 1650. His calculations showed that man was created in 4004 B.C., and his opinions were accepted as final. An enterprising publisher included this chronology for the convenience of the reader in the margin of the Authorized or King James Version of the Bible; and, like many a marginal note in history, it was soon invested with almost as much sanctity as the text itself, only being omitted with the publication of the Revised Version in 1885.

With the Renaissance, however, had come a new interest in pagan antiquity and during the succeeding centuries an increasing number of travellers brought reports of ruins still standing in the East. The traditional theory of the age of man could not remain unchallenged by such antiquarian interest. Sir Walter Raleigh's *History of the World*, published between 1603 and 1616, contained a premonition of what was to come, when it informed the reader that " in Abraham's time all the then known parts of the world were developed . . . Egypt had many magnificent cities, . . . and these not built with sticks, but of hewn stone, . . . which magnificence needed a parent of more antiquity than these other men have supposed ".[2] Succeeding generations saw the development of many branches of science, and,

---

[1] W. F. Albright, " Recent Discoveries in Bible Lands ", Supplement to Young's *Analytical Concordance* (20th ed., New York, 1936), p. 1.

[2] Quoted by A. D. White, *A History of the Warfare of Science with Theology* (New York and London, 1923), Vol. I, p. 254.

during the last century, various lines of investigation were converging to drive man's origin back into the dim obscurity of millennia upon millennia.

THE DEVELOPING SCIENCES

Two of the first of these lines of investigation to be mentioned are the developing sciences of geology and biology. When comparatively few species of fauna were known, there was no difficulty in supposing that Noah's Ark was large enough to preserve them all. Sir Walter Raleigh, allowing for some one hundred different kinds of animals, was able to show that one floor of the Ark could have held them. Another floor, he believed, could have held the food; a third the birds; and ample room would still remain for the human occupants. In the succeeding centuries, however, the number of species was increased by the thousands, and the matter of the Ark became more and more troublesome.

But worse was yet to come. William Smith, known as "the Father of English Geology", had proved by 1799 that rock is apparently stratified, and that the chronological order of the strata can be determined by the character of the fossils contained in them. The problem of the fossils was, of course, not new. The early Church Fathers had held that fossils were the remains of animals which had been drowned in the Flood of Noah. Securing a wealth of information from William Smith, one Joseph Townsend published a book entitled, *The Character of Moses established for veracity as an historian, recording events from the Creation to the Deluge* (1813). A standard textbook for the study of Scripture in America during the 19th century, Horne's *Introduction to the Study of the Bible* (first edition, 1827), informed the student that "the Mosaic narrative of the Deluge is confirmed by the fossilized remains of animals belonging to a former world, which are found in every quarter of the globe, frequently on the summits of the most lofty mountains; and it is worthy of remark, that the remains of animals, belonging to *one* part of the globe, are often found in *another part very distant*". Many fossils were believed, further, to be proof of the Scriptural giants, for which there was also warrant among the Church Fathers. Augustine believed that a fossilized tooth discovered in North Africa belonged to such a giant. This belief was further elaborated to include all of our antediluvian ancestors, one scholar giving the height of Adam as 123 feet 9 inches, and that of Eve, 118 feet 9 inches plus !

The problem soon became too complicated, however, for such simple explanations. It was observed that the older the rock stratum, the larger was the number of the remains of animal species now extinct. In addition the distribution of the species was by no means uniform over the globe. These were problems not easily explained by the early chapters of Genesis alone. Finally, the publication of the great work, *Principles of Geology* (first edition, 1830–3) by Sir Charles Lyell, the most eminent geologist of his day, presented a mine of factual information, indicating that the earth was evidently not formed in six days, and that the presence of fossils in the various rock strata could scarcely be explained by a single, forty-day, universal deluge.

THE "THUNDER STONES"

Another line of investigation was concerned with the "thunder stones". For centuries men had been discovering pieces of chipped or polished stone, the larger of which were thought to be thunderbolts and the smaller, arrows. They were venerated because they were believed to have been used as weapons in the heavenly war during which Satan and his cohorts had been driven from the presence of God. Such divine implements were naturally thought to be possessed of great magical value and were presents worthy of royalty. During the 11th century the Emperor of the East in Constantinople sent one of these "heaven axes" as a present to the Emperor of the West in Rome. In the following century a bishop claimed that such stones were a divinely appointed means of insuring success in battle and security on sea or land against the heavenly thunder. Even in the 17th century a French ambassador presented a stone hatchet to the Prince-Bishop of Verdun, claiming that its virtues in the matter of health were said to be of some importance.

It was not until the 18th century that various dissertations were written upon the origin and uses of these "thunder stones", showing that they had been made and used by early races of men. During the early part of the last century it was further discovered that many of these implements were associated in geological strata with the bones of long extinct animals.

One of the most important of these discoveries was made by a French geologist, named Boucher de

Perthes, and published in 1847. For some years a force of men under his direction had been digging into the terraces of the Somme valley, near Abbeville, France. Thousands of flint implements were discovered in the various terraces, buried in geological debris, high above the present level of the river Somme. Boucher at first believed that these implements belonged to men who were drowned in the Flood, but it was soon seen that they were proofs of something quite different. While his discoveries were greeted with skepticism and violent opposition, committees of prominent and respected scholars visited the valley and were convinced that his results had been correctly described. Other discoveries in England, America and on the Continent corroborated the natural inference, that the history of man is vastly longer and more complicated than the Old Testament record had led men to believe. The publication of Lyell's *Antiquity of Man* (1863), Huxley's *Man's Place in Nature* (1863), and Darwin's *Descent of Man* (1871) summarized the evidence, and added a new theory regarding the origin and history of man which shook the religious and intellectual worlds to their very foundations. New vistas of the past and future were opened and it was difficult to make the necessary mental adjustments.

THE RECOVERY OF LOST CIVILIZATIONS

Still another line of investigation, and one with which we are here most concerned, was the archaeological recovery of the ancient civilizations of the biblical world. The literary survivals of the great Near Eastern nations were few and fragmentary, preserved here and there among the Greek and Latin authors. Much of that preserved, however, gave erroneous information, and the picture of the Ancient Orient presented was dim and badly distorted.

During the 17th and 18th centuries a succession of travelers returned to Europe with reports of the wonderful ruins still standing in Persia, Mesopotamia, and Egypt. Shortly after 1600 the first copy of some wedge-shaped (today called "cuneiform") characters from the ruins of Persepolis, the capital of the Persian kings, reached Europe, together with a few inscribed bricks from Babylon, and the traveler who brought them, Pietro della Valle, believed that they were a queer kind of ancient writing. The work of two of the greatest scholars of the 16th and 17th centuries, Joseph Scaliger and Athanasius Kircher, may be mentioned as revolutionizing the current knowledge of the history and chronology of the pre-Greek world. Indeed, it seems to have been Kircher who first called attention to Egyptian hieroglyphic writing. In 1798 Napoleon Bonaparte set off with his army for Egypt. While the primary purpose of his expedition was military conquest, he took along with him the finest scholars in France, who, while the army was doing its duty, pursued more peaceful pursuits, traveling through Egypt, copying and describing everything they saw. Shortly thereafter were published the tremendous volumes of the work, *Description de l'Egypte* (1809–13), a magnificent publication, befitting the patronage of an emperor. Thus Europe first became acquainted with the artistic and monumental treasures of ancient Egypt, and it was surprised at the splendor of this vanished civilization.

The most important single object recovered by this expedition was not discovered by the scholars, however, but by the army. A French artillery officer, while directing the excavations for a fort near Rosetta in the Nile Delta, came across a slab of black granite covered with writing. This was the now famous Rosetta Stone which furnished the key needed for the decipherment of the Egyptian hieroglyphics (picture writing). It proved to be a monumental stone set up by the priests in honor of a decree issued by the king about 195 B.C., conferring certain honors upon them and exempting them from the payment of taxes. It was divided into three registers, and written in two languages. The topmost register gave the inscription in the old hieroglyphic; the middle in demotic, the ordinary Egyptian handwriting; and the third in Greek, which was the language of the government at that time. Despite the fact that it never reached France but was captured by the British when the latter took Egypt from the French in 1801, and was deposited in the British Museum, it immediately attracted the attention of several scholars. By 1822 the Frenchman, Champollion, had solved the mystery of hieroglyphic with the aid of the Greek translation, and a wealth of information about that remarkable people was gradually collected and studied. Indeed, it is astonishing what a quantity of facts was rapidly gathered together. Wilkinson's *The Ancient Egyptians* (1836) is still fascinating and informative reading, since details regarding Egyptian life were assembled from every available source.

Events moved more slowly in Mesopotamia. A series of brilliant guesses began the decipherment of Old Persian, but Akkadian (the name given today to the Assyrian and Babylonian cuneiform or wedge-shaped writing) was a troublesome and difficult puzzle to solve. Finally, by means of inscriptions written both in Old Persian and Akkadian the decipherment was accomplished. The most important of these inscriptions was the Behistun Rock, which has been called the "Rosetta Stone" of Persia. On a steep rock face at Behistun in Persia, some three hundred feet above the plain, Darius the Great (522–486 B.C.) carved three inscriptions recording his triumph over all enemies in the revolt following his coronation (Fig. 1). One was in Old Persian; another was a translation into Elamite; and the third was a translation into Babylonian. An English army officer, Major Henry Rawlinson, at great risk to his life, copied the first and third of these inscriptions between 1843 and 1847, and in his hand they proved to be the master key for the unlocking of the secrets of the Assyrian and Babylonian literatures.[3] Of course, many were skeptical, but the correctness of the decipherment was finally established by an impressive demonstration on the part of the Royal Asiatic Society in 1855. Copies of one of the inscriptions which had recently been excavated were sent to four prominent Akkadian scholars. Each prepared an independent translation; and, when the Society published the results, all four were seen to be in substantial agreement. The Germans were the last to be convinced, but by 1880 all were persuaded that these peculiar signs could really be read.

In the meantime French and British excavators were at work in the Assyrian ruins of Nineveh, Khorsabad, and Calah, where the great palaces of the Assyrian kings, who played such an important part in the history of Israel between the periods of Elijah and Jeremiah, were unearthed. Soon the British Museum in London and the Louvre in Paris were exhibiting to a surprised and enthusiastic public the statuary and sculptured reliefs which once adorned these palaces. Without reading a single cuneiform character people were introduced to the customs and habits of the ancient Assyrians, who had caused such trouble to Israel, to the life and exploits of the kings, and at the same time to the whole civilization of Western Asia during the days of the Hebrew prophets, since the sculptors carefully depicted all peoples with whom they came in contact through war or otherwise.

By far the most important single discovery was that of the great library of King Asshurbanapal (669–ca. 633 B.C.) by the English digger, Layard, and his associate, Rassam. This king had collected and copied thousands of documents of all sorts, and stored them away in two of his palaces at Nineveh. They dealt with practically every field of learning and science known to the scholars of the time. Among them were historical treatises and chronological lists of events, astronomical reports, tables of measures, and mathematical treatises, revealing a knowledge of mathematics unequalled by any other ancient oriental people. There were religious epics, hymns, and prayers, sometimes disclosing a depth of religious feeling scarcely inferior to that in Israelite psalms. There were cuneiform sign lists, grammatical exercises, tables of synonyms, texts in two languages, lists of plants, stones, animals, cities, temples, gods, countries, months, and years, which have been the main source for the preparation of grammars and dictionaries. Letters and addresses of kings and high officials tell us about the administration of the government and about the life of private individuals. We are informed about revolts, taxes, tribute, the repairing of buildings and canals, for upon the latter the stability of the country depended. Most of the tablets were concerned with medical subjects; we are even told about a summons given a physician to prescribe for one of the court ladies. Astrology seems to have been one of the most popular pursuits of a large number of the learned men, and it is one of the least meritorious of our many inheritances from this remarkable people.

While studying this literature, one of the assistants in the British Museum, George Smith, discovered the Babylonian stories of the Creation and the Flood, and dealt a death-blow to the traditional view of these events in an entirely unexpected manner. Prominent scholars of the latter half of the last century were immediately convinced that the ultimate sources of the biblical narrative of the Creation and the Flood are to be found in the same cycle of ancient tradition that inspired these vastly more crude and polytheistic accounts of the Babylonians.

[3] The Elamite inscription was not copied by Rawlinson because of the difficulties. This has been done recently by Professor George Cameron of the University of Michigan. See his eloquent account, "Darius Carved History in Ageless Rock", *National Geographic Magazine*, Dec. 1950, pp. 825–44.

1. The Behistun Rock in Iran

2. Air view of the mound of Megiddo, after excavations. Area AA is that of the city gate and Canaanite palaces. Area BB is that of the eastern stables of Solomon and of Canaanite temples. Area CC is that of the southern stables

THE DEVELOPMENT OF ARCHAEOLOGICAL METHOD

Such discoveries, important and startling though they were, merely foreshadowed what was to come. In 1870 the German journalist, Heinrich Schliemann, began work at Homeric Troy, and for the first time learned the true nature of the peculiar mounds in the shape of a truncated cone which are scattered throughout Western Asia. The Semitic name for such a formation is *tell*, and it means a mound made up of the ruins of many cities, long since destroyed (Fig. 2). Just as William Smith had observed that English rock is stratified, so it was now discovered that these mounds were filled with successive strata of destroyed cities. The Authorized Version of Josh. 11 : 13 reads : " But as for the cities that stood still in their strength, Israel burned none of them, save Hazor only." The Hebrew word here translated " strength " is *tell*, and the passage really means, " the cities that stood on their tells ", that is,

on the mounds of ruins which had been centuries in accumulating. This was of course not understood by the translators in the 17th century, and the progress of discovery is illustrated by the fact that the scholars who revised the Authorized Version in the eighteen-eighties were able to translate the passage correctly. No more eloquent description of the common fate which befell the civilizations of the Ancient East has ever been given than that in Josh. 8 : 28 : " And Joshua burnt Ai, and made it a tell forever, even a desolation unto this day."

But what was to be the means of dating the archaeological strata uncovered ? Digging in the ruins of the palaces and tombs of Assyria or Egypt presented comparatively few chronological problems, since inscriptions or reliefs telling us to whom they belonged were usually abundant. But what about poorer countries like Palestine where inscriptions mentioning some datable king are rarely found in positions which date the level in which they are found? Here is a house or a tomb with nothing in it of a spectacular character. To whom did it belong and when? That was a difficult problem which troubled many an early archaeologist. One of them decided that the ruins of King Saul's fortress at Gibeah were of no importance because they dated from the Crusader period of the Middle Ages. Herodian masonry around the Temple Area in Jerusalem, actually dating from the latter part of the 1st century B.C., was said to have been hewn by Solomon. A series of tombs belonging to the 1st century A.D. was thought to have been the necropolis of the kings of Judah.

The clue which was needed to solve the problem of chronology was discovered in 1890 by the great patriarch of Near Eastern archaeology, Sir Flinders Petrie (Fig. 3). After several years of experience in Egypt, he began the examination of a mound in southern Palestine called Tell el-Hesi, perhaps the site of the biblical Eglon. Here he discovered the interesting fact that the styles and fashions of pottery differed in the various levels of the mound, and that a study of the pottery was therefore significant.

He recognized some of the pieces found as of the same types he had previously unearthed in Egypt, where he could date them by means of inscriptions. Thus he was able to make his famous prophecy: "Once settle the pottery of a country, and the key is in our hands for all future explorations. A single glance at a mound of ruins, even without dismounting, will show as much to anyone who knows the styles of the pottery, as weeks of work may reveal to a beginner."

Since that day our knowledge of the pottery styles has increased tremendously. Given a sufficient quantity of broken or whole pieces from a given stratum, the date of that stratum can be established (cf. Fig. 4). Great attention has also been paid to methods of excavating. Before 1910 the vast majority of excavations can be characterized in no other way than as mere "treasure hunts". Trenches were dug here and there over a mound for the purpose of finding interesting and exciting buildings and objects. Today archaeology has become an exceedingly careful and meticulous procedure. Photography, surveying, drawing, recording, and classifying have been developed into a system, so that when the excavation is completed, a paper reconstruction of the mound could be prepared wherein all the objects could be placed in their proper places. Then it is possible to tell the story of the town, its cultural relations, the life of its inhabitants, and the destructions it suffered. Such careful excavation has made it possible for us to note the difference between early Israelite towns and those of the Canaanites whom the Hebrews

3. Sir Flinders and Lady Petrie, in the garden of the American School of Oriental Research, Jerusalem, May, 1939

4. Père L. H. Vincent (*left*) and W. F. Albright (*center*), examining the pottery of the last Canaanite occupation of Bethel in order to date the Israelite conquest of the city

could not drive out, to trace the evidences of the Israelite Conquest of Canaan, to follow the fortunes of the Chosen People in the centuries which followed, and to observe the ravages of the Babylonian army of Nebuchadnezzar, when in 587 B.C. the Kingdom of Judah was brought to an end.

The initial shock which the developing sciences caused the student of biblical chronology was now replaced by a growing confidence. As a result of the work of the scientists, it was increasingly understood that the early chapters of Genesis were not to be taken as a literal and factual account of prehistoric man, but were instead a theological interpretation of the world in relation to God which was presented in the world-view common to ancient times. The validity of what these chapters teach is thus unaffected by their " science ", and they are now generally read as a kind of theological poetry which is more " true " and enduring than anything which a scientist who sticks to known facts might write. Furthermore, the actual excavations in biblical lands rapidly restored a degree of confidence in the Bible, for people could now see with their own eyes the portrayals of persons and events which the Bible reflects or mentions. In II Kings 18–19, for example, we have the biblical account of the Assyrian emperor Sennacherib's siege of Judah, including its capital city, Jerusalem, and its major fortress, Lachish. As a result of the British excavations at Nineveh, one could read the actual story which Sennacherib himself wrote of the same event and view the stone-carving on the wall of his palace in which he had an artist picture the siege and surrender of Lachish, with Judean men and women of the time of the prophet Isaiah being led into captivity (Figs. 115–17).

The increasing number of excavations, particularly in Palestine itself, and the development since the First World War of more rigid archaeological and linguistic methods of study have served further to increase our confidence in the biblical story within known historical periods. The discovery of numerous ancient documents and the increased knowledge of the grammar of the ancient languages has made it possible to penetrate deeply within the ancient mind and to understand biblical man more fully than ever before. The study of biblical geography has identified most of the places which the Bible mentions. The pioneer in this field was Edward Robinson, the results of whose trips to Palestine in 1838 and 1852 as published in his *Biblical Researches* (3 vols.) were revolutionary in the accurate identification of biblical sites. No explorers before 1920 were his equal, though since that date much has been done to correct, refine and supplement his work and that of others by the use of the pottery criterion in identifying places. W. F. Albright and Nelson Glueck are the greatest of the modern explorers who have followed in his steps, but with a knowledge of the pottery they have been able to say whether old ruins are really ancient and to what period they belong.

Reference has already been made to the unsatisfactory nature of early excavations. Of first importance from the standpoint of both history and archaeological method was the Harvard Excavation at Samaria (Figs. 100–5), the capital of northern Israel, between 1908 and 1910, as directed by the Americans G. A. Reisner and Clarence S. Fisher. The important discoveries made by these men and by another expedition to the same site under the direction of the British archaeologist, J. W. Crowfoot, between 1931 and 1935, will be described in subsequent chapters. Here we may pause to comment on the archaeological method which they evolved and which under the inspiration of C. S. Fisher has been used on all important diggings in Palestine since that time, though others have introduced numerous refinements. Among the most important of the subsequent excavations which have followed and developed the Reisner–Fisher methods we may mention the following in particular : the work of the American School of Oriental Research (Fig. 5) under the direction of W. F. Albright, especially his excavation at Tell Beit Mirsim in southwestern Judah between 1926 and 1932 ; the

5. The American School of Oriental Research in Jerusalem

6. A section of the mound of Megiddo, showing the levels of occupation

work of the Oriental Institute of the University of Chicago at Megiddo between 1925 and 1939 (Fig. 6), of the University Museum in Philadelphia at Beth-shan (Figs. 58-9) between 1921 and 1933, of the British expeditions to Lachish (1932-8; see Figs. 47-8, 118) and to Jericho (1930-6, and especially that of Kathleen Kenyon, 1952-58; see Fig. 44), of the Hebrew University at Hazor (1955-8), and of the Drew-McCormick Expedition at Shechem (since 1956).

In simple terms we may describe the methods of the excavator somewhat as follows: By surface exploration he has located the mound or *tell* on which he wants to dig and has collected the necessary equipment, including an adequate staff, surveying instruments, hoes, baskets, record books and the like. He hires laborers and begins to dig. A short distance below the surface he will usually encounter walls of ancient buildings. These he uncovers, watching carefully for floor levels which seal the objects below from those above. The typical mound is composed of several layers or occupational levels of these buildings, one below the other down to virgin soil or bedrock, and it is of vital importance that they be distinguished. The various rooms or find-spots are numbered, drawn on maps and photographed. Every significant object discovered is labelled and recorded so that its level and place are not forgotten. Intrusive objects that are out of place, having fallen down from above or come up from below, must be recognized wherever possible. Thus when the work is done, it is possible by the plans and records to put everything back together again on paper just as it was found. This in brief is the stratigraphical method, the careful excavation by levels or strata and the collection or assemblage of all objects found within the strata. The mound containing the ruins of Beth-shan (Fig. 58), for example, contains

eighteen different strata within about seventy-nine feet of debris, accumulated during four thousand years of intermittent occupation. The smaller Judean mound of Tell Beit Mirsim (biblical Debir or Kiriath-sepher) contains ten strata in about twenty feet of debris, accumulated over a period of two thousand years. The average size of these Palestinian mounds varies considerably because cities were small and large. Tell Beit Mirsim, for example, comprised only some seven acres within its walls. The neighboring Lachish was very large for an ancient Palestinian city, covering about eighteen acres, while the mound of Megiddo (Fig. 2) includes thirteen acres within its circumference.

During the excavations at Samaria, 1931-5, and at Jericho, 1952-8, Kathleen Kenyon has introduced into Palestine certain refinements in the method of digging which are of particular importance. Especially significant is the analysis of debris, its coloration, striations in type and texture, and precise relation to existing structures. This involves the careful cutting of " baulks ", that is, of sections in the debris, the digging of exploratory trenches at right angles to walls instead of horizontal to them, and the recording on paper of the sections by sketches and photography. This has revised the understanding of a stratum. It is a floor level or occupation surface together with the walls and debris both above and below which belong to it. Other material between floors must be analyzed because it may be a leveling fill for new building and theoretically of any earlier period.

No ancient city can be correctly excavated nor its history interpreted, however, without a knowledge of typology. The latter is simply the classification of the various types of objects which are discovered and the study of their history. A piece of jewelry, an arrowhead, a lamp or pitcher must be seen as belonging to a certain type or class, and one must know as much as he can from all other excavations about the history of this class and the way in which its style has changed or evolved during its history. In possession of this knowledge the excavator can observe the classes of objects which are found in a given stratum and date the assemblage because their particular forms occur together only within a certain period. Modern excavation has so refined its stratigraphical methods and so increased its typological knowledge that in using the two together the good excavator knows precisely what is going on, is able to interpret what he finds and is not forced to resort to elaborate guesswork.

By the use of these methods in Palestine and elsewhere in the lands of the Bible the last half century has witnessed a remarkable revolution in our understanding of the ancient world and of the Bible's place within it. Scholars are now able to tell the story in great detail of man's first major effort to erect a complex civilization. Whereas the center of his second effort lay in Greece and Rome, the earlier drama centered in the lands of Egypt, Syria and Mesopotamia. This is the region where the earliest development of agriculture took place, where the first towns were established (*ca.* 7000 B.C.), where methods of writing were invented (beginning *ca.* 3500 B.C.), where the first great states were formed (*ca.* 3000–2000 B.C.), and where the resources of those states were first used for empire-building. Possessing new power in knowledge, in community organization and in natural resources, man promptly set about the task of attempting to control as much of the earth's surface as he could.

This, then, is the epoch in human history when the nation of Israel lived in Palestine, when it was destroyed and scattered among the nations, when it wrote a magnificent testimony to its faith, now preserved as our Old Testament, which in the fulness of time became the soil in which the Christian Church found its roots. The Bible is the testimony to the especial work of God in man's first great age, by which its meaning and his Lordship over all ages is affirmed.

In this perspective the biblical scholar no longer bothers to ask whether archaeology "proves" the Bible. In the sense that the biblical languages, the life and customs of its peoples, its history, and its conceptions are illuminated in innumerable ways by the archaeological discoveries, he knows that such a question is certainly to be answered in the affirmative. No longer does this literature project from the chaos of prehistory "as though it were a monstrous fossil, with no contemporary evidence to demonstrate its authenticity". Yet the scholar also knows that the primary purpose of biblical archaeology is not to "prove" but to discover. The vast majority of the "finds" neither prove nor disprove; they fill in the background and give the setting for the story. It is unfortunate that this desire to "prove" the Bible has vitiated so many works which are available to the average reader. The evidence has been misused, and the inferences drawn from it are so often misleading, mistaken, or half true. Our ultimate aim must not be "proof", but truth. We must study the history of the Chosen People in exactly the same way as we do that of any other people, running the risk of destroying the uniqueness of that history. Unless we are willing to run that risk, truth can never be ours.

It can be stated emphatically, however, that to those who have been willing to run this risk the literature of Israel and of the Church appears more distinctive than ever before. We are now in a position to evaluate it, because we have something with which to compare it in its time. We can now see that though the Bible arose in that ancient world, it was not entirely of it; though its history and its people resemble those of the surrounding nations, yet it radiates an atmosphere, a spirit, a faith, far more profound and radically different than any other ancient literature. The progress of archaeology, of textual, literary, and historical criticism has never obscured the fact that the biblical writers were the religious and literary giants of ancient times, though they themselves would never have said so. They claimed that they were simply bearing witness to what God had done, and that whatever was accomplished through them was God's work, not their own.

The problems that troubled our fathers during the last three centuries no longer seem serious to a modern generation of Bible students. Few scholars trouble themselves with "proving" the Bible, because they believe that it can stand by itself, that in some respects it has suffered more "from its well-intentioned friends than from its honest foes". As Professor Albright has so well written: "Climaxing and transcending all ancient religious literatures, it represents God's culminating revelation to man at the latter's coming to the age of maturity. At least a hundred thousand years had elapsed since man first learned to make artifacts—less than two thousand years have passed since the close of the Canon. Yet some ask us to believe that the Bible reflects so primitive a stage of cultural and even biological evolution that it no longer has a meaning for modern man!" [4] We owe to the biblical scholars and archaeologists an everlasting debt for the perspective in which we are able to view and use this sacred literature.

[4] *Op. cit.*, p. 43.

FURTHER READING

A. D. White, *A History of the Warfare of Science with Theology* (New York, D. Appleton and Co., 1896), contains a mine of stimulating information about the subjects treated in the first part of this chapter.

For the story of the excavations in Bible Lands during the last century, H. V. Hilprecht, *Explorations in Bible Lands During the 19th Century* (Philadelphia, A. J. Holman and Co., 1903), is undoubtedly the best. For a briefer survey covering Mesopotamia alone, see the fascinating account of Seton Lloyd, *Foundations in the Dust* (London, New York, Toronto, Oxford University Press, 1947). Note also A. Parrot, *Discovering Biblical Worlds* (London, SCM Press, 1955).

To supplement these the following are recommended : W. F. Albright, " Recent Discoveries in Bible Lands ", a supplement in *Young's Analytical Concordance* (New York, Funk and Wagnalls Co., Revised ed. 1955), and published separately as a small monograph by The Biblical Colloquium, 731 Ridge Ave., Pittsburgh 12, Pa., U.S.A. By the same author, *From the Old Stone Age to Christianity*, Chap. I (Baltimore, Johns Hopkins University Press, 3rd ed., 1946).

As special treatments of the history of Palestinian excavation, the following are recommended : C. C. McCown, *Ladder of Progress in Palestine* (New York and London, Harper & Bros., 1943) ; W. F. Albright, *The Archaeology of Palestine and the Bible*, Chap. I (New York, Fleming H. Revell Co., 1932) ; W. C. Graham and H. G. May, *Culture and Conscience*, Appendix, pp. 314–37 (Chicago, University of Chicago Press, 1936) ; R. A. S. Macalister, *A Century of Excavation in Palestine* (London, The Religious Tract Society, 1925) ; F. J. Bliss, *The Development of Palestine Exploration* (New York, Charles Scribner's Sons, 1906) ; G. A. Barton, *Archaeology and the Bible*, Chap. IV (7th edition ; Philadelphia, American Sunday School Union, 1937).

To answer the question " What is Biblical Archaeology ? ", see the interesting discussion of Nelson Glueck, *The Other Side of the Jordan*, Chap. I (New Haven, American Schools of Oriental Research, 1940).

The question " How does one excavate ? " is well answered by Kathleen M. Kenyon, *Beginning in Archaeology* (New York, Frederick A. Praeger, 1952).

CHAPTER II

GIANTS IN THE EARTH

" There were giants (*Nephilim*) in the earth in those days " (Gen. 6 : 4).

THE Israelites had certain traditions about the aborigines of their country. They believed them to be giants and called them by various names : Nephilim, Rephaim, the descendants of Anak, the Emim, and the Zuzim or Zamzummim. The Emim and Zuzim were localized across the Jordan, and the children of Anak were believed to have lived in the neighborhood of Hebron. Og, king of Bashan, to the east of the Sea of Galilee, was reported to be one of the last of the Rephaim, and his famous iron bed, the Israelites said, was $13\frac{1}{2}$ feet long and 6 feet wide (Deut. 3 : 11). Israel's spies, sent out by Moses from the wilderness to look over the " land of milk and honey ", returned with the frightening report :

The land through which we have passed in spying it out is a land that eateth up the inhabitants thereof; and all the people that we saw in it are men of a great stature. And there we saw the Nephilim (the sons of Anak are from the Nephilim). And we were in our own eyes like grasshoppers, and so were we in their eyes (Num. 13 : 32–3).

Unfortunately, archaeology has unearthed no evidence of any of these people, with possibly one exception. That is the children of Anak. A large number of broken pottery vessels have been found in Egypt, dating within two centuries after 2000 B.C., on which had been written the names of the enemies of the Crown. After the lists were completed, the vessels were broken. This was done for magical reasons. Just as the pots were shattered, so it was believed that the rebels would be crushed. Among the rebels a Palestinian tribe bearing a name practically identical with Anak is mentioned, a tribe composed of at least three clans since three chieftains are named. Whether the two are to be connected, however, is not certain, but it is the only evidence ever discovered for the aboriginal names preserved by the Israelites.

As for giants it must be said that no trace of a people of abnormal stature has ever been found in the Near East, though there is ample evidence as to the reasons for such a tradition. The Israelite spies complained that the Canaanite cities were great and

walled up to heaven (Deut. 1 : 28 ; Num. 13 : 28). We now know that the unhappy men were not indulging in illegitimate exaggeration. Having lived a simple nomadic life in the wilderness of Sinai-Midian, and then having come suddenly upon Canaanite cities " standing on their mounds ", they were obviously justified in thinking in terms of giants. For these cities possessed walls sometimes as thick as 15 or more feet, and at least as high as 30 to 50 feet, and often built of huge masonry. Small wonder then that they became in their " own eyes like grasshoppers " ! Israelites were no exception in this regard. Early Greeks had the same idea. Looking upon the great walls of some of their oldest cities, they came to the conclusion that only giants could have built them ; and they had a tradition that the walls had been constructed by the Cyclopes, not the one-eyed race of Homer, but giant artisans brought to Greece from Asia Minor (whence our term " cyclopean ").

PREHISTORIC MAN

Palestinian highlands, especially those in Transjordan, still contain today great tombs called dolmens (Fig. 7), and huge standing stones, sometimes almost 15 feet high, known as menhirs. It is difficult to date them, though the menhirs are at least as old as 2000 B.C., and perhaps the same age as the dolmens which are probably to be dated from the end of the Stone Age, *ca.* 9000–5000 B.C. Such structures are not confined to Palestine, however, but are also found in Syria, Asia Minor, Armenia, Kurdistan, and in a number of European countries such as Ireland, England, France, and Sardinia. The interesting point is that wherever traditions are preserved about them, they have to do with giants. In Europe dolmens are still known popularly as tombs of the giants, giants' houses, or giants' beds or tables. Israelites and other inhabitants of Canaan who looked upon such great structures undoubtedly believed that giants built them, just as did the people of Europe. Scandinavians, for

7. A dolmen in the Jordan Valley, looking west with the hills of western Palestine in the background

example, have traditions about a mythical race of giants, called Jöten, and one biblical scholar some years ago aptly said that the Rephaim were to the Israelites what Hünen were to the Germans and Jöten to the Scandinavians. As mentioned in the preceding chapter, one of the very old traditions of the human race is that we have descended or degenerated from mythical giants, statues commemorating which have been standing for centuries in such cities as London, Antwerp, and Douai.

What archaeological evidence is there for a race or races of prehistoric giants? The question is simply answered; there is none. Before 3000 B.C. Near Eastern man seems to have been somewhat smaller on the average than he is today. After that time, undoubtedly owing to better food, he grew a little until he was about the same size as we are to-day. Of course, there were exceptions just as there are in modern times, and we hear of huge men like Og and Goliath and his brethren, but excavation has shown that we can no longer speak of a *race* of giants.

The first men to live in Western Asia, as far as we know, did so in the early part of the Old Stone Age, at least 200,000 years ago, and probably much more. We know very little about them because only a few of the stone implements which they once used have been found. It was the time of the glaciers and, while the ice did not reach as far south as Syria and Palestine, men in these countries took to caves for protection and continued to live there even during warm periods. The excavation of several of these caves has made Palestine one of the

great centers of the search for Early and Middle Stone Age man. In two caves in a valley leading to the sea south of Mt. Carmel were found a dozen skeletons of a mixed " race " related to Neanderthal man (Fig. 8). They belong to the Middle Paleolithic (or Old Stone) Age.[1] These people lived by hunting and gathering food which grew wild; but most interesting is the fact that as early as this they had certain religious beliefs about an after-life, as is indicated by the care they took in the burial of their dead. Since they show racial mixture, we must be on guard in the use of the term " race "; pure-bloods in historical times have never existed.

The last glacier had retreated by about 8000 B.C., and the period between about 10,000 and 8000 B.C. is a transitional one which has been rather inadequately called the " Mesolithic Age ". At that time men began to shift from a food-gathering to a food-producing economy. This period is now better known from the Palestinian caves than from anywhere else in the world. A large number of skeletons have been found belonging to a slender, long-headed people who were 5 to 5 feet 4 inches in height, very much like the earliest historical peoples known in Egypt, Syria and Palestine. They were perhaps members of the group from which the Semites descended. They are called Natufian man, from the Wadi Natuf northwest of Jerusalem where they were found, and they were far advanced over their predecessors. While they still hunted, killing large numbers of such animals as the gazelle which by that time had become quite common, they had added fishing to their accomplishments, and, far more important, they had learned how to grow and reap cereals of which one was probably the earliest known variety of wheat. They may have domesticated the dog, perhaps using it in hunting. They knew how to make vessels out of stone, and to carve in bone. Indeed, one example of their workmanship, a reclining fawn, is superb, even according to modern standards. Great care was still taken in the burial of the dead. The ornaments worn in life were worn in the grave, and this would indicate a belief in physical survival.

The Late Stone or Neolithic Age, now to be dated in the Near East between the 8th and 5th millennia B.C., is the time when the first villages were founded and the first experiments in a more complex community life were undertaken. Some of the most interesting and important discoveries of this

[1] D. A. E. Garrod and D. M. A. Bate, *The Stone Age of Mount Carmel* (Oxford, 1937).

8. Prehistoric caves in the Wadi Mugharah

period have been made at the famous biblical city of Jericho. It was a sizable village then with the world's oldest buildings and massive stone fortification wall (Fig. 9). One building was apparently a temple, for around it were religious objects including clay statues, presumably idols, occurring in two groups, each containing a man, woman, and child. The earliest known clay modelling may be said to occur here also, because several skulls have been found which had faces modelled upon them in clay (Fig. 10).[2] This is the period when it was discovered that clay will harden in fire, and consequently, we have the invention of pottery, the first appearance of man's commonest possession.

The next age is transitional to historical times and is called the Chalcolithic, from *chalcos*, "copper" and *lithos*, "stone". While stone and bone were the two materials most commonly used for implements of the period, the secret of copper smelting had been discovered by 4000 B.C. or shortly thereafter, and the first "boom" age in Bible Lands began. In North Syria and Mesopotamia a beautiful and elaborately decorated pottery was made in a succession of styles which were not surpassed and rarely equalled before the days of the great Athenians of the time of Socrates and Pericles in the 5th century B.C. In Palestine some houses have been discovered which were plastered and decorated with elaborate scenes (Fig. 11). It is impossible to interpret them, but they indicate a surprising degree of complicated imaginative activity. By 3500 B.C. the earliest great public buildings had been built in Mesopotamia and picture writing was being developed, which in the course of centuries soon lost most of its resemblance to its pictorial origin. Religion developed and flourished; temples were institutions of great power and influence; and the intellectuals of the time were able to speak about such abstract things as "soul", "divine",

<hr />

[2] For a summary of the important recent work at Jericho, see now Kathleen M. Kenyon, *Digging up Jericho* (London and New York, 1957), and *Archaeology in the Holy Land* (London and New York, 1960).

9. Late Stone Age city walls at Jericho. The earliest at the bottom of the photo is still standing to a height of over 18½ feet

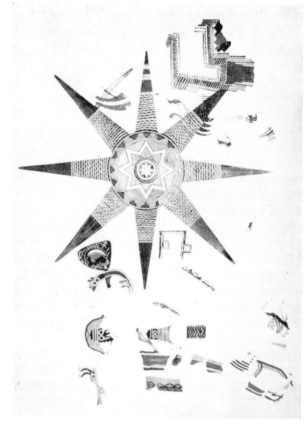

11. A painting on the wall of a building excavated at Teleilat el-Ghassul in the Jordan Valley (*ca.* 36th–33rd centuries B.C.)

10. The late Stone Age skull, with features modelled in clay, as found at Jericho

"mankind", "holiness", "goodness", "purity" and "truth". The civilization of this age has been called an "irrigation culture", since it was chiefly confined to valleys and plains where irrigation was possible. To construct and maintain an elaborate system of canals and dams meant that the people must organize to regulate life and protect their rights. This is probably one reason for the emergence of the first organized states in Mesopotamia and Egypt.

There is some evidence also which indicates that most people became somewhat taller during this period. The reason for this may well have been improved diet, for we know that by this time the basic cereals, fruit, and vegetables had been "tamed" and were being grown: wheat, barley, grapes, olives, figs, dates, onions and garlic, lettuce, melons, beans, peas and many others were cultivated. Since that time the species have been refined and improved, but here is the first extensive development of them for domestic purposes.

It is apparent that even if early man did not attain gigantic physique, he can certainly be said to have reached a high level of intellectual attainment. We have been accustomed to think of people before the time of the Athenians in Greece as " primitive ", a conception not true to the facts. If we mean by " primitive " the inability to fly an airplane or to understand that the earth moves round the sun, then the term is justified. But if we mean by " primitive " the inability to read and write, to think abstractly, to build cities and architectural " wonders ", to attain profound religious and moral insights, to develop great art and literature, and to be proud of such intellectual attainments for their own sake, then we are scarcely justified in using the term until we go back at least to the 4th millennium B.C.

EARLY " GIANTS "

About 3250 B.C. we have the beginning of a new age. It is called the Early Bronze Age, though bronze was rare before the 2nd millennium B.C. There was a sudden burst of prosperity. In Palestine a large number of fortified cities were built ; Jericho, Ai and Megiddo among others were supplied with great city walls (Fig. 12). The evidences of world trade and of material prosperity are manifold. In Egypt and Mesopotamia we have the beginning of the Dynastic Ages, and from now on we hear of a succession of kings, great and small, who established the first great empires. Monumental architecture, statuary, and inscriptions occur, and great personalities who stood head and shoulders above their fellow men begin to emerge. We shall mention a few of these " giants in the earth " as examples of their respective civilizations.

Our first " giant " is perhaps the first great humanitarian of whom we know. He was a king of the city of Lagash in Southern Mesopotamia by the name of Urukagina (25th century B.C.). He was a Sumerian, a member of a people who are the earliest known inhabitants of Mesopotamia. They were

12. City wall of Megiddo, Stratum XVIII, *ca.* 2800 B.C. (Early Bronze II)

organized in a series of city-states, of which Lagash, Ur, Kish, and Erech were the chief. These cities were constantly at war with one another. Though politically weak, Lagash flourished agriculturally and commercially; and priests and officials became very corrupt. When Urukagina came to the throne, he started an administrative reform, bringing to a halt the unjust oppression of the poor by the priests and evildoers who had violated the " righteous laws " of the god Ningirsu. It was from these " righteous laws ", among others, that Hammurabi, many years later, was able to construct his famous code. This was but one contribution of the energetic Sumerians, whose culture became the basis of the later Babylonian civilization. Their literature was extensive, and a great deal of it is being recovered from the ruins of the city, Nippur. Their system of writing, their language, religious beliefs, and great epic poems, such as those of the Creation and the Flood, became the classical inheritance of later Mesopotamian peoples, just as Greek culture has become the classical heritage of the Western World.

Our second " giant " was the first empire builder of history. He was a Semite named Sargon (cf. Fig. 13), the founder of the Dynasty of Akkad (*ca.* 2360–2180 B.C.), and Mesopotamia's greatest king during the 3rd millennium. The Sumerians and the Semites had lived side by side in Babylonia for a long time, and during the Dynasty of Akkad the Semites had come to dominate the country. Sargon extended his rule over the whole of Mesopotamia and, for a time at least, over Syria. He is even credited with expeditions as far away as southern Arabia and Asia Minor. So famous were his exploits that he became the Charlemagne of his day. An epic was written about him, entitled " The King of Battle ". This epic was circulated for centuries and was read and copied as far away as Assyria, Asia Minor, and Egypt. Curiously enough, a story told about him at a much later time is strikingly similar to that of the childhood of Moses. We are informed that he had a lowly birth, that his mother bore him in secret, placed him in a reed basket, and set him adrift on the Euphrates. He was rescued by a gardener, adopted, and grew up to become king. The dynasty founded by Sargon brought about a revolution in artistic standards, and the quality of workmanship was scarcely surpassed even by the Egyptians during the two succeeding millennia.

Our third " giant " is the builder of the Great Pyramid in Egypt. Khufu (or Cheops as the Greeks

13. A bronze head of a prominent person, probably Sargon of Akkad, found at Nineveh

called him) was his name, and he reigned as Pharaoh not later than about 2500 B.C. He became even more famous than Sargon, for the Greeks regarded his pyramid as one of the seven wonders of the world. The Egyptians were exceedingly conservative people. Habits and customs were preserved for centuries with very little change. One of the astonishing things about them is that the wealthy seem to have spent so much of their time preparing for an honorable death and burial to ensure their well-being in the hereafter. At least such was the case with the kings and nobles, and the upkeep of the elaborate tombs became a major economic problem as well as the occasion for the great tomb-robbing " racket " of later times.

Cheops and the other Pharaohs of the Pyramid Age were absolute monarchs, perhaps the most absolute the world has ever seen. They were deified to increase their prestige and were as unapproachable as formerly was the Emperor of Japan. The energy and wealth of the whole country were concentrated on one thing—the building of a structure which would forever house the king's remains. One tradition informs us that it took one hundred thousand men twenty years to build the Great Pyramid, and we can well believe it when we consider its size. It was 481 feet high and composed of over two million blocks of limestone, each weighing 2½ tons on the average. The stones were laid without benefit of the modern crane, but solely by manpower. After a course was laid, a ramp was built up to it, and the stones were dragged up the ramp and put in place. In spite of the difficulties, however, the stones and the granite casing on the outside were fitted with such precision as still to arouse the admiration and wonder of our ablest engineers. It could have been done only by a king who was considered a god and at whose disposal the entire resources of the country were placed. So astonishing is Cheops' accomplishment that there are those today who see in the Pyramid the key to the unlocking of the mysteries of life. It should be stated, however, that Egyptologists of our day are not willing to go that far, for they believe that the " Secret of the Pyramids " has been solved without resort to mysteries.

Imhotep, or Imuthes as he was called by the Greeks, was a " giant " in scholarship. Indeed, he was the world's first known scholar. Surprisingly enough, he was not a king but merely the prime minister of a Pharaoh who lived shortly before Cheops. Imuthes was so learned a man in such subjects as architecture and medicine that he left a reputation which was not diminished but rather increased as time went on. A beautiful temple constructed by him for his master has recently been excavated and is the oldest building of hewn stone which has ever been found, for it was Imuthes who took the earlier mud brick and wattle structures and converted them into stone. Centuries later the people still remembered his proverbs, and two thousand years later he had become a god of medicine whom the Greeks identified with their own Asklepios.

Next in order we should mention a series of Egyptian " giants " whose names are unknown, but who have immortalized themselves in their remarkable literary compositions, as the late Professor James Henry Breasted brought to our attention in his book, *The Dawn of Conscience*. One of them has been called " the first great poet of world literature "; his poem is a dramatic dialogue between himself and his soul. The poor man, like Job, has been overtaken by a series of misfortunes, as a result of which he determines to give up the struggle and commit suicide, for the beautiful hereafter is more

to be desired than life. His soul attempts to dissuade him. There follows a long argument, each forcibly presenting his case. The man complains of the bitterness of life, and of the fact that " there are no righteous; the land is left to those who do iniquity ". In contrast to the bleakness of this existence is the bliss of the life with the gods hereafter. Life is a long sickness from which one recovers at death to enter into a beautiful garden. To all of this the soul replies that an after-life is but a vain hope, and the only solution to the problem of existence is not suicide but the drowning of trouble in pleasure. Live life to the full while you are here; there is nothing hereafter. So the argument progresses, until finally the soul is convinced, for the picture of the beauty of the life beyond wins the day.

Our author wrote this shortly before 2000 B.C. at a time when Egypt, and for that matter the whole of the Near East, was passing through a period of disorder and hard times—a veritable dark age. There was civil war, and the way was left open to invaders. In Mesopotamia these invaders were called " Westerners " or Amorites, and some of them undoubtedly caused trouble in Egypt. This was the soil out of which the despair and pessimism of the poet arose. As so often happens, when the foundations of civilization are shaken, men begin to re-think older views and to challenge the accepted thought-forms of the day.

From the same period are other writings which give expression to many noble ideas. One father bids his son to remember: " More acceptable is the virtue of the upright man than the (sacrificial) ox of him that doeth iniquity." Another writer by the name of Ipuwer wrote a series of " Admonitions ". Most of them are an indictment of the horrible conditions of his day. The land is absolutely lawless; government has ceased to function; " a man regards his son as his enemy " and " a man smites his brother of the same mother ". " Woe is me for the misery of this time! " But Ipuwer does not leave his readers without hope. Out of the misery of that day will come a better time when the noble and good, now displaced by the ignoble and bad, will be restored in the land, and invaders repelled.

Others of this period write about social justice, to the end that the poor and oppressed may be treated with equity and righteousness. Best known is the story of the Eloquent Peasant, a poor man who is cruelly robbed by an official, but who takes his case to court and so eloquently defends himself that the king grants him justice. The long court-room dialogue contains a timeless indictment of corruption, and a vivid description of the responsibilities of those who hold public office. It is a most interesting fact that such pleas for social justice follow the age of absolute imperialism in Egypt. It is also interesting to remember that the Great Pyramid represents man's greatest attempt to secure eternal preservation by purely physical means. The attempt was a failure and it was apparently soon recognized as such. In any event during the Pyramid Age itself the tombs began to be filled with the " Pyramid Texts ", magical hymns and spells designed to aid the dead person on his journey to heaven—as though physical means would not suffice to get him there, but all the congeries of magic must also be employed. In the work of the men which we have just been discussing we have the implication that neither piles of stone, nor magic (nor both together) are sufficient, unless there also has

been goodness and uprightness in the character of the deceased.

Entering the Middle Bronze Age about 1900 B.C., we encounter a large number of " giants " of whom we can mention but a few. We should by no means omit Zimri-Lim, king of the city of Mari on the Upper Euphrates in the 18th century B.C. His palace has been excavated (since 1936), and in the first campaign at the site his archives were uncovered, consisting of over 20,000 clay tablets, some 5000 of which were letters written to him by kings, officials, and commoners from all parts of Mesopotamia. These documents have revolutionized our knowledge of Western Asia during this period, including the reduction of the date of the great Babylonian, Hammurabi, by some two hundred years.

Mari at that time seems to have been the most important state of this area, extending some 300 miles from the frontier of Babylon to the border of Syria. And Zimri-Lim's palace, consisting of

14. Air view of the ruins of the palace of Mari

nearly 300 rooms and covering more than 15 acres, was one of the show places of the world (Fig. 14). Indeed, one of the letters in the library, written to the king from a certain Hammurabi who was king of Aleppo, reads as follows : " To Zimri-Lim say : Thus saith Hammurabi, thy brother, the Prince of Ugarit [Ras Shamra on the Syrian coast] hath written me as follows, Show me the house of Zimri-Lim. I would see it. Now, behold, I am sending thee the prince his son."

Zimri-Lim had constructed a remarkably efficient state. Accurate and detailed records and reports were kept ; for example, there are two large tablets, about a foot in length, each of which contains almost 1000 names of craftsmen belonging to different guilds. The country was unsettled and great attention was paid to defense. An elaborate system of fire signals was developed, and in this way news could be flashed throughout the state in a very few hours, a practice known to have been used later in the Kingdom of Judah. Certain tribes giving trouble to Zimri-Lim bear the same name as a later Hebrew tribe, Benjamin. The name meant " children of the right hand (i.e. of the south) ". For many years it was thought that the name " David " appeared in these texts as a title, meaning " chieftain ". In 1958, however, the great Accadian linguist, B. Landsberger, appears to have proved this to be a mistaken interpretation. One letter tells Zimri-Lim of an oracle by an ecstatic seer or " prophet ". This seer said that a deity had commanded him to write to Zimri-Lim to the end that meals be presented to the " shade " of the former king, his father. The correspondent adds ; " I write it to my lord in order that my lord may do what seems good to him." (See further Chap. VI.)

Of great interest is a group of clay liver models found in one room of the palace. These were used in divination, a practice to which great attention was paid in the court. Mesopotamians were not as concerned about life hereafter as were the Egyptians. Apparently they were not quite sure that there was such a thing as immortality for the ordinary mortal. One of their great epics was about the adventures of the hero Gilgamesh who, at one time, was overtaken by a morbid fear of death and became interested in the pursuit of immortality, but was never quite able to find it. Consequently, the Mesopotamian (and the Israelite as well) was primarily interested in living this life as successfully as possible. To do this meant the development of techniques to pierce the veil of the future and to learn the will of the

gods. Divination by various means was therefore highly developed, and Babylonian diviners were soon scattered all over the civilized world. The Old Testament Balaam is a good example. Modern astrology goes back ultimately through the Greeks to this same source.[3]

Mari was conquered during Zimri-Lim's day by our next " giant ", Hammurabi of Babylon (ca. 1728–1686 B.C.; cf. Fig. 15). He became the second great Semitic ruler of Southern Mesopotamia, the first having been Sargon, as we have seen. He was at the head of an empire which lasted over a century and a half, finally to be destroyed

15. A diorite head, dating from the First Dynasty of Babylon ; perhaps representing Hammurabi (life-size)

[3] For a review of the discoveries at Mari, see George E. Mendenhall, *The Biblical Archaeologist*, Vol. XI, No. 1 (Feb 1948), pp. 2–19, and A. Parrot, *Mari, une ville perdue* (Paris, 1948).

about 1550 B.C. by the Hittites of Asia Minor. Under his rule Babylon, which had been a comparatively unimportant town before this time, became a second wonder city of Western Asia, probably even more impressive than Mari, for it was the commercial center of a rich empire.

The god of Babylon, Marduk, extended his sway with the conquests and became the patron deity of the whole country. The most famous building of Babylon was his temple-tower, a temple built on top of a great tower (Fig. 16). Its name was *Etemenanki*, which meant "The House of the Foundation Platform of Heaven and Earth". Even at this early date it was one of the wonders of the world. It was still standing a thousand years later when Nebuchadnezzar repaired and finished it, giving us its dimensions. It was in seven stages, the bottom one being 300 feet square, and the top one being some 300 feet above the ground. Babylon, being the polyglot city that it was, and possessing this tremendous tower second in size only to the Great Pyramid, was the perfect setting for the Israelite story of the Confusion of Tongues, for indeed it was "a city with a tower whose top shall reach the heavens" (Gen. 11 : 4).

16. A model of the temple-tower of Babylon as it stood in the time of Nebuchadnezzar (after Unger)

Besides the efficiency of his administration Hammurabi's most notable achievement and greatest claim to fame lies in his code of laws, engraved on a shaft of diorite. Keeping in close touch with all parts of his realm, the great king saw the necessity for uniform administration of justice. He is pic-tured on the monument as he is commissioned to establish the code by the sun-god Shamash. In reality he collected and systematized the older Sumerian and Akkadian laws and customs, adding to them and improving them in order that they might better fit his empire. This code has long interested students of the Bible, for, like older and later legal collections in Western Asia, it contains the same type of formulation and even certain provisions which occur in some early Israelite laws.

Many more "giants" might be mentioned, as, for example, Mayor Kushshiharbe (about 1500 B.C.) of the Horite city of Nuzi in Northern Mesopotamia. The mayor's claim to fame lies solely in the fact that he was one of the first great racketeers now known from Western Asia. We are astounded, however, not so much at his gangsterism, but at the fact that he could be, and was, brought to trial for his misdeeds by the people of his city![4] This is not the first example of democracy in ancient times, for earlier evidence of primitive democratic institutions in Mesopotamia has recently been pointed out.[5] We may also mention the first "Walt Disney" of history, who seems to have operated in Palestine about 1500 B.C. one or more large pottery workshops. He decorated his distinctive vases with cleverly drawn animals, fish, and birds, and exported his wares as far away as Cyprus and Tarsus.[6]

And so the procession of "giants" continues. We have said enough, however, to set the stage for the first Hebrews. While the people of Bible Lands before the days of Israel were not of gigantic stature, they had certainly developed a civilization which was far from primitive, in the ordinary sense of that term. When Israel appears upon the scene of history many great civilizing minds had preceded them. We cannot assume, therefore, that the Old Testament arises from so "primitive" a stage in the history of man that it can mean little for our modern day. In religion it was radically revolutionary, but at the same time it assimilated and refined and added to the best which the ancient world produced. It thus became the noblest product of that world.

[4] See R. H. Pfeiffer and E. A. Speiser, *One Hundred New Selected Nuzi Texts* (*Annual of the American Schools of Oriental Research*, Vol. XVI, New Haven, 1936), pp. 59 ff.
[5] Thorkild Jacobsen, "Primitive Democracy in Ancient Mesopotamia", *Journal of Near Eastern Studies*, Vol. II, No. 3 (July 1943), pp. 159–72.
[6] See W. A. Heurtley, *Quarterly of the Department of Antiquities in Palestine*, Vol. VIII (1938), pp. 21 ff.; G. Ernest Wright, *The Biblical Archaeologist*, Vol. II (1939), pp. 16–20; and *The Bible and the Ancient Near East* (New York, 1961), p. 91.

FURTHER READING

For summaries of pre-Israelite history in the ancient Near East see Chap. III of W. F. Albright, *From the Old Stone Age to Christianity* (3rd ed., 1946; Anchor Books of Doubleday and Co., 1957), to which this chapter is greatly indebted. Here will be found references to the technical treatments of the subjects discussed. See also his article on " The Old Testament World ", *The Interpreter's Bible*, Vol. I (New York, Abingdon-Cokesbury Press, 1952), pp. 233–71 ; his Pelican Book, *The Archaeology of Palestine*, 1949, Chaps. III and IV ; John Bright, *A History of Israel* (Philadelphia, Westminster Press, 1959), pp. 17–37.

The reader may also be referred to Henri Frankfort, *The Birth of Civilization in the Near East* (London, Williams & Norgate Ltd., 1951) ; Robert J. Braidwood, *Prehistoric Men* (Chicago Natural History Museum, 3rd ed., 1957) ; *The Near East and the Foundations for Civilization* (Eugene, University of Oregon Press, 1952) ; and G. Ernest Wright in *The Bible and the Ancient Near East*, pp. 78–88. In these works will be found reference to primary sources and data.

CHAPTER III

THE FOUNDING FATHERS

"Now the Lord said unto Abram: ' Get thee out of thy country, and from thy kindred, and from thy father's house, unto a land which I shall show thee ' " (Gen. 12 : 1).
"Thy servants have been keepers of livestock from our youth until now, both we and our fathers " (Gen. 46 : 34).

WHAT do the archaeological discoveries have to say about Hebrew origins, about the founding fathers of Israel, Abram, Isaac and Jacob ? Needless to say, no records of these men have ever been found outside the Bible. What has been accomplished is the lifting of the veil which previously hid their times. As a result, we now know more about the type of people they were, where they came from, how they lived, what they believed, where and how they are to be fitted into the histories of the great nations of ancient times, than did the later Israelites themselves.

We must admit at the outset, however, that there is still much we should like to know, but which cannot be known. The stories about the Patriarchs, like the Homeric tales about the Trojan War, were historical epics which were not written down for centuries. Instead, they were passed on from generation to generation in semi-poetic form. They were polished by centuries of telling and re-telling until they became beautiful sagas, very different from the histories of David and the later kings of Israel in the books of Samuel and Kings. The various narrative units, however, have been fitted into a comprehensive theme, so that they together form a confession of the acts and promises of God in relation to the nation's founders. The past events were later seen to have the promise of the future embedded in them.

The early Hebrews were organized in a patriarchal system of society. They naturally assumed, therefore, that all peoples, themselves included, could trace their lineage back to a common ancestor, that every people and every tribe had a patriarch who originated it. Often, too, in speaking of a people the Hebrew story-teller personified the group : i.e. used the name of the supposed patriarchal father of the group for the people itself. Thus, today, when reading the stories about Jacob and Esau, for example, it is difficult to be quite certain in a given instance whether the original narrator meant the men themselves, or whether he was talking about the tribes which they were believed to have started. So difficult is it to separate tribal history from personal history that some scholars have gone so far as to assume that the whole narrative is tribal. To other scholars this is an extreme view, but it is a subject which archaeology cannot settle.

In the process of polishing, occasional historical details were modernized. For example, there are a number of references to the camel in Genesis, as in the story of Abraham's servant who takes a camel caravan back to Aram in search of a wife for Isaac (Chap. 24). Archaeology now informs us, however, that the camel had not been generally domesticated as yet, and we should, therefore, substitute " donkey " for " camel ". Another example is the mention of the Philistines as living along the southern coast of Palestine (21 : 34 ; 26), but we now know that the settlement of the Philistines did not occur until five or six hundred years later (see Chap. VI). Both the camel and the Philistines are examples of modernization. Later Hebrews were simply bringing the stories up to date, and what modern teller of tales does not do the same ?

We shall probably never be able to prove that Abram really existed, that he did this or that, said thus and so, but what we can prove is that his life and times, as reflected in the stories about him, fit perfectly within the early second millennium, but imperfectly within any later period. This is an exceedingly important conclusion, one of the most important contributions which archaeology has made to Old Testament study during the last four decades. It is one which was not widely appreciated by former generations of biblical students. Some had felt that archaeology could do little with the Patriarchal stories ; others went to the other extreme in assuming that every detail had been substantiated. Neither position is correct, and it is important to keep in mind just what archaeology has and has not done.

THE ORIGINAL HOME OF THE PATRIARCHS

Where was Abram's original home? Later Israelites tell us it was the country of Paddan-Aram, which means "Field of Aram". Still another name for it in Genesis is "Aram-of-the-Two-Rivers" (in Hebrew, Aram-naharaim, Gen. 24 : 10). We gather that the chief city of this area, in and around which Abram's kin were settled, was Haran (Gen. 11 : 31 ; 28 : 10).

Where was this country? It is the land between the Euphrates and the Tigris rivers in their upper courses, between Carchemish on the west and Nineveh on the east. Two tributaries of the Euphrates can be seen in this area, the Balikh and the Habur (Khabur). The chief city on the Balikh was Haran; that on the Habur was Gozan or modern Tell Halaf (II Kings 17 : 6). To be more exact, therefore, Paddan-Aram was the region around these two tributaries, especially around the Balikh on which Haran was situated.

Here, then, was the home of the Patriarchs. Not only did Abram come from there, but when he reached the land of Canaan, he and his descendants kept close touch with their relatives around Haran. The present text of our Old Testament tells us in Gen. 11 : 31 that Abram's father, Terah, migrated to Haran from Ur of the Chaldees, a great Sumerian city near the Persian Gulf; but the reference is a very obscure one. The oldest text of the Bible which we now have, the Greek translation of the 3rd century B.C., contains no reference to the city at all. Consequently, many scholars believe that "Ur" here represents some textual corruption or late addition. In any event, we are safe in saying that the home with which the Patriarchs were most closely connected was Haran, and there is little evidence of any south Mesopotamian influence upon their traditions.

What was the ethnic background of the Patriarchs, according to the Old Testament? Israelite children of a later day were taught to say: "A nomadic (or fugitive) Aramean was my father" (Deut. 26 : 5). The name of their home, as already mentioned, was "Field of *Aram*" or "*Aram*-of-the-Two-Rivers". Jacob's cousins, Bethuel and Laban, are called Arameans, that is men of Aram (Gen. 25 : 20 ; 28 : 5 ; 31 : 20, 24). The biblical tradition, therefore, is that the Patriarchs were Arameans, a people who later became very famous in ancient history as great traders and who were able to build a state with its capital at Damascus. Now what does archaeology have to say about this homeland and about the ethnic background of the Patriarchs?

1. *Names of towns in Paddan-Aram.* First is the interesting fact that the names of several of Abram's ancestors who are listed in Gen. 11 : 10 ff. are now known to be names of towns in the vicinity of Haran. The name of one of Abram's brothers was Haran, almost the same as the city itself except that the two words begin with different kinds of *h* in the original. Haran was a flourishing community during the 19th and 18th centuries, and is frequently mentioned in contemporary letters and documents.

The second of Abram's brothers is Nahor, to whose city Abram sent for Rebekah (Gen. 24 : 10). Nahor also is now well known from the Mari texts (see below) and Assyrian documents. Though its mound cannot be identified as yet with certainty, it was a town in the neighborhood of Haran. The same can be said for the name of their father, Terah, which appears in the name of the town, Til-Turakhi. Their great-grandfather was Serug, the name of a town (Sarugi) west of Haran. Still further back in their ancestry was Peleg, a name which has been identified with a town named *Phaliga* on the Euphrates just above the mouth of the Habur.

Here, then, is a remarkable situation. The identification of one name with an ancient town might be mere coincidence, but here are several identifications in the precise area from which Abram came. These biblical names of the brethren and ancestors of Abram were probably patriarchal clan names which were either given by the clans to towns which they founded, or borrowed by them from cities and villages which they seized during the disturbances around 2000 B.C.

2. *The "Amorite" Invasion about* 2000 B.C. What were these disturbances which have just been mentioned? An explanation of them will throw light upon the question, Who were the Patriarchs? Shortly before and after 2000 B.C. there were "barbarian" invasions in every settled country of the Near East, bringing to a temporary halt the flourishing cultures of every country, including that of the Pyramid Age in Egypt. From the obscurity of the resulting dark age certain facts are being assembled. The invaders secured their greatest foothold in Northern Syria and Mesopotamia, where they were called "Westerners" by the Babylonians, a name

preserved in the Old Testament as " Amorites ". In all probability, though, there were several closely related groups included, one of which may well have been early Arameans who settled in Paddan-Aram, or at least a group from which the later Arameans descended. Shortly after 2000 B.C. we hear of " Amorite " states all over that area. Mari, Haran, Nahor, Qatna, Ugarit all appear as " Amorite " cities with " Amorite " kings. Babylon became the capital of an Amorite state to be ruled about 1700 (according to the latest chronology) by the great Hammurabi. It seems probable that Amorites and their kin pushed into Palestine and Egypt, causing disturbances in each country.

Who were these invaders ? They were evidently Semitic nomadic peoples who lived along the desert fringes of the great Fertile Crescent. Through ancient history and into modern times there has been a constant struggle between such people and the civilized communities within the Crescent, as has been well phrased by Nelson Glueck :

The struggle between the Desert and the Sown seems to be a perpetual one. The moment that the central political authority weakens or is destroyed, that moment the Bedouins sweep in, carrying all before them. . . . Like the waters of the ocean, the Bedouins may be held in check, but the moment the barriers are weakened, in they sweep with a destructive force that cannot be stemmed. . . . They can always retreat into the desert whither few can follow, and they are always prepared to break into the fertile lands at the first appearance of weakness there. They can live on next to nothing, and have the patience of the ages. Of the Bedouins it may be said that it is the weak who shall inherit the fruits of the earth. It is only when the Bedouins seize the acres of the Sown, and become by the force of circumstances agriculturists in their own right, that they are subject to the forces of growth and decay, from which in their native state they are secure. There are, however, always enough of their original kind left behind them to enable the eternal struggle to continue, with the chances for final victory inevitably weighted in favor of the Bedouins.[1]

The " Amorite " movement is one of the first of these great Semitic invasions known in history.

What interests us about it is that the Haran area whence the Patriarchs came was one of the centers of the new Semitic settlements precisely at the time when the Patriarchs are supposed to have been there. In addition the names Abram (in the form *Abam-ram*) and Jacob (in the form *Jacob-el*) are known as

personal names among the " Amorites ". There is even frequent mention in the Mari library of a tribe of Benjaminites which was causing some trouble in the area. The name is the same as that of the later Israelite tribe of Benjamin, though, of course, the two are to be identified only in name.

Another troublesome group at Mari was the Hapiru. People called by this name frequently appear in early documents. They figure in various ways : as raiders, mercenary soldiers, captives, government employees, rebels, and slaves. In times of peace they worked in various capacities for the settled people. In unsettled periods they might raid the urban areas or hire themselves out as soldiers to the highest bidder. It is probable that the term does not apply to any particular nationality, religion, or language, but rather to a social or legal status. At the moment it is difficult to define that status more accurately. According to one scholar, George E. Mendenhall, the various occurrences are best explained as applying to a people existing outside the bounds of a given legal community and not completely controlled by its laws and mores. While we cannot be certain, it seems likely that the term was used for the unsettled, nomadic people, among others, who continually haunted the civilized communities around the Arabian Desert.

In Gen. 14 : 13 Abram is referred to as " the Hebrew ", the first appearance of that term in the Old Testament. In the past scholars have been practically unanimous in their identification of " Hapiru " with " Hebrew ". Recent evidence complicates the problem, but it still seems probable that, since the two are so much alike, we are fairly safe in assuming at least an indirect connection between them. It has also been pointed out that most references to " Hebrews " in the Old Testament belong to the Patriarchal period and the period of the Sojourn in Egypt. In examining the occurrences it is interesting to observe that the term is usually employed, (1) when an Egyptian speaks to an Israelite, (2) when an Israelite identifies himself to an Egyptian, or (3) when the Israelites as a group are named along with some other people or group. An Israelite speaking to one of his own group would not use the term, but in speaking to an Egyptian he would. The word " Hebrew ", in all probability, like *Hapiru* did not refer originally to a particular racial group, but rather to a status which ranked him as a foreigner. The matter is by no means certain, but it seems probable that we have here another indication that the Patriarchal " Hebrews " of the

---

[1] Nelson Glueck, *The Other Side of the Jordan* (New Haven, American Schools of Oriental Research, 1940), pp. 6–7.

Old Testament came from the nomadic or semi-nomadic peoples who occupied Northern Mesopotamia before and after 2000 B.C. The Patriarchs themselves as they moved south into Palestine were a part of this same movement. Presumably they spoke the same dialect as did their cousins in Mesopotamia, though at some later time in Canaan, they adopted closely related local dialects.

3. *Patriarchal Customs and the Nuzi Tablets.* There is still other evidence for the North Mesopotamian origin of the Patriarchs. Even more interesting than anything mentioned so far is the illumination thrown upon Patriarchal customs by the archives uncovered in the city of Nuzi, a town southeast of Nineveh. A number of the customs about which we read in Genesis have been very obscure, and it seems likely that they were not understood even by the later Israelite story-tellers. The new evidence from the Nuzi tablets (Fig. 17) helps to explain them, for these tablets reveal a customary law similar to that of the Patriarchs, but not like that of any later period. The Nuzians were Hurrians, a people mentioned in the Bible as Horites, who until recent years were commonly explained as Palestinian " cave-dwellers ", perhaps to be listed among the aboriginal " giants ". We now know that they were a non-Indo-European, Armenoid, people who pushed into Northern Mesopotamia and founded a great state in the " Amorite " area during the 16th and 15th centuries, taking over much of the older " Amorite " culture, including in all probability the customs in question.

In Gen. 15 : 2 Abram complains to God that he has no son, but that the man who is to be his heir

is one Eliezer, who apparently was " the elder of his house, that ruled over all that he had " (24 : 2). God replies : " This (servant) shall not inherit thee, but the one that shall go out of thine inwards, he shall inherit thee."

Now what does this mean ? How is it that an outsider, a trusted servant, is to be the heir of Abram ? Some of the Nuzi tablets explain the matter. It was a custom for a couple who had no children to adopt someone as their son. This adopted son was to take care of them as long as they lived and see to it that they received an honorable burial. In return for this service he inherited the property. The bargain was nullified, at least in part, however, if a son was born. Apparently Eliezer was the adopted son of Abram, but the birth of Isaac changed his status as heir.

In the story of Jacob the main concern of his wives seems to have been the production of children. When one failed to bear, she supplied her handmaid (Gen. 30 : 3). Sarah, Abram's wife, once said to him : " Behold now, the Lord hath kept me from bearing. Go in, I pray, unto my maid. Perhaps I shall be built from her " (16 : 2). We now know this to have been the custom of the time. Marriage was for the purpose of bearing children, not primarily for companionship, and in one way or another it was absolutely necessary that the family should multiply.

Esau's sale of his birthright to Jacob is also paralleled in the Nuzi tablets where one brother sells a grove, which he has inherited, for three sheep ! This would seem to have been quite as uneven a bargain as that of Esau : " Esau said to Jacob : ' Give me, I pray, some of that red pottage to eat . . .' And Jacob said : ' Sell me first thy birthright.' And Esau said : ' Behold I am about to die (of hunger) ; what is a birthright to me ? ' And Jacob said : ' Swear to me first.' And he swore to him and sold his birthright to Jacob. Then Jacob gave Esau bread and a mess of lentils and he ate and drank " (25 : 30–4).

Oral blessings or death-bed wills were recognized as valid at Nuzi as well as in Patriarchal society. Such blessings were serious matters and were irrevocable. We recall that Isaac was prepared to keep his word even though his blessing had been extorted by Jacob under false pretenses. " And Isaac trembled with a very great trembling and said : ' Whoever it was that hunted game and brought it to me and I ate . . . even he shall be blessed ' " (27 : 33). Custom decreed that Isaac must keep his word even

17. A Nuzi tablet

though the blessing may have been received by some impostor outside the family. Jacob on his death-bed designated Judah as the next head of the family: "Judah, as for thee, thy brethren shall praise thee . . . the sons of thy father shall bow down to thee" (49 : 8). At Nuzi there was one case when such an oral "blessing" was upheld in court, reflecting standards much higher than we observe even today.

Perhaps most interesting of all is the explanation of the relations between Jacob and Laban by means of the Nuzi tablets. This story (in Gen. 29–31) has been difficult to understand heretofore, but it is now easily explained by means of Nuzian customary law. Laban, it seems, had no male heir, so he adopted Jacob as his son and gave him his daughters, Leah and Rachel, for wives. The rule was, however, that if Laban should beget a son in the future, that son was also to share in the inheritance and receive the family gods or *teraphim* (Fig. 18). Only if no son was born, was Jacob to take the *teraphim*. Another rule was to the effect that Jacob could marry no other women under penalty of forfeiting his rights.

In the course of time it seems that Laban was fortunate enough to have sons born to him (Gen. 30 : 35). As time went on also, Jacob was able to accumulate a sizable fortune by practices, which, though legal, were certainly morally "shady" (cf. 30 : 31–31 : 12), whereupon he decided to leave and go back to Canaan. This he did by stealth, Rachel meanwhile stealing the family gods or idols.

While there has been some discussion as to what the *teraphim* were (31 : 19, 34, 35), there can be no doubt that they were the family gods because they are called "gods" in Chap. 31 : 30, 32. Apparently, according to the Nuzi records, the possession of these idols was most important. Not only did they help to secure a successful life, but also ensured the possessor of the family inheritance. Small wonder, then, that Laban was far more excited about the loss of his *teraphim* than he was about the loss of his daughters, their husband, and live-stock. And according to Nuzi law he was justified in demanding indignantly: "Wherefore hast thou stolen my gods?" (31 : 30).

When once we think of Jacob as Laban's adopted son in accordance with the law as known at Nuzi, we can understand why Laban could say: "The daughters are my daughters and the children are my children and the flocks are my flocks and all that thou seest is mine!" (31 : 43). As the Patriarchal father, Laban had every right to exercise his authority over all members of his family. That he allowed them to continue on their flight to Canaan was probably because he was either glad to be rid of his clever son-in-law, or else because the latter was now stronger than he. The whole story, as understood with the aid of the Nuzi archives, shows us a group of crafty Arameans, each partly in the right but partly in the wrong, constantly in search of loop-holes in the law!

4. *Patriarchal Conceptions of Human Origins.* What the Founding Fathers of Israel thought about human origins is a problem about which we do not have satisfactory information. The Old Testament properly begins with a discussion of this subject, informing the reader about many questions dealing with the beginnings of the world and man. But to what period or periods of Israelite history do these discussions belong? That they reflect the faith and beliefs of Israelite leaders of opinion from the 10th to the 5th century, there is no doubt. But do any of these beliefs go back to the period of the Patriarchs?

It is an interesting fact that the Hebrew stories of the Creation and the Flood in Gen. 2 and 6–9 do not resemble anything in either Egyptian or Canaanite literature. This is very curious since Israelites lived for so many years as neighbors of both people. Both had a great influence on the literature and religion of Israel, but that influence did not extend to the beliefs in question. On the other hand, ever since George Smith's publication of *The Chaldean*

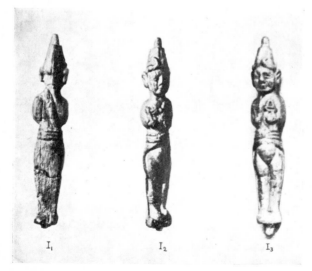

18. Household idol (of a class called *teraphim* in the Bible) from Nuzi

Account of Genesis in 1876, the many close similarities between the Mesopotamian and Hebrew stories have been evident to all. Why is it that the country farthest away from Israel in the Near East should have had the greatest influence upon her ideas about beginnings?

Most biblical scholars have assumed that Israel borrowed the conceptions during the time when the Assyrian power was making itself felt in the world between the 9th and 7th centuries, and during the Babylonian captivity of the 6th century. The Israelites in Exile were certainly influenced to some extent by Babylonian conceptions, but the most important result of the Exile, however, was not the borrowing but the growing tendency of the Israelites to *separate* themselves from their Gentile captors. As for the preceding period, we may recall that the Assyrians were great adepts of the art of war but hardly of the quieter arts of the mind in which the Babylonians excelled. Consequently, an increasing number of scholars have been coming to the conclusion that many of these ancient traditions regarding origins must go back to an earlier period. In fact, it seems most probable that some of the traditions about the Creation, the Garden of Eden, the Flood, the stories of Nimrod (Gen. 10 : 8 ff.) and of the Tower of Babel (Gen. 11) were brought from Mesopotamia by the Patriarchs themselves. How else explain why Israel had them but Canaan did not?

We shall reserve comparisons between the biblical and Babylonian conceptions until Chap. VII, and need only remark here that the story of the Tower of Babel must have originated at a time when Babylon and its great Temple-Tower or *ziggurat* were flourishing and well known : that is, at least between 1800 and 1530 B.C. before the city was destroyed by the Hittites, though the ziggurat may have been erected as early as the 24th century B.C. (Fig. 16). In addition, it is interesting to note that the mountains on which the ark landed in the Babylonian story of the Flood were just east of Mesopotamia, while in the Hebrew story they are the mountains of Ararat or Armenia, just north of Haran. The story of the Tower, then, gives its approximate age, while the story of the Flood indicates that we are dealing not with a Babylonian but with a North Mesopotamian tradition.

It is evident, therefore, that the archaeological facts are in agreement with the biblical tradition that the original home of the Patriarchs was in the area of Haran. Consequently, we are able for the first time to answer such questions as : " Who were the Patriarchs and whence did they come ? "

THE PATRIARCHS IN CANAAN

The Founding Fathers are represented in Genesis as making their living from their herds of cattle and their flocks of sheep and goats, wandering in the hill country of Palestine between Dothan and Beersheba, and constantly concerned about pasturage and springs, for the latter especially were none too plentiful in a country in which the surface rock is a soft and absorbent limestone. They were not primarily peasants, therefore, but nomads. In using the term " nomad " to describe them, however, we may be inclined to think of them as a dirty, uncouth, uncivilized people of the type which are common in the Syrian and Transjordanian semi-desert land today. Such a conception is probably not true to the facts, since the nomads or semi-nomads of the Patriarchal type are now fairly well known to us from ancient documents and pictures. Perhaps it would be better to think of them as breeders of live-stock, half-way between the modern nomad and the American ranchers and cowboys of the last century.

Their type of life is well illustrated by a contemporary Egyptian story (about 1900 B.C.) of the adventures of a man named Sinuhe. The latter was a high official in the Egyptian government who had to flee the country for reasons of state. After numerous adventures and hardships he reached the country of the " East " (Kedem) in Syria, which in all probability is approximately the same as " the land of the children of the East (Kedem) " to which Jacob went (Gen. 29 : 1). While the Kedem or " East " to which Sinuhe fled may not have been precisely the same as Paddan-Aram, it is certainly in the general region. Here Sinuhe met an Amorite chieftain of the same kind as Laban, Abram, and Jacob. This sheikh was delighted to see him (for other Egyptians who were there identified him) and made him a member of the tribe by giving him his eldest daughter in marriage. To Sinuhe the country was one of " milk and honey " :

It was a good land. . . . Figs were in it, and grapes. It had more wine than water. Plentiful was its honey, abundant its olives. Every (kind of) fruit was on its trees. Barley was there, and emmer [an early type of wheat]. There was no limit to any (kind of) cattle [livestock]. . . . Bread was made for me as daily fare, wine as daily provision, cooked meat and roast fowl, beside the wild beasts of the desert, for they hunted

19. A caravan of Asiatics entering Egypt, led by " the Ruler of a Foreign Country Abi-shar "

for me and laid before me, besides the catch of my (own) hounds.[2]

In the rest of the story Sinuhe tells us how great a man he became, and how in his old age homesickness overtook him, whereupon he returned to Egypt and made his peace with Pharaoh.

What interests us here about the story is the contemporary description of " Amorite " tribal life, for we may be sure that the life of the Patriarchs was somewhat similar. The story also reveals the close relations which existed between Syria–Palestine and Egypt at this time. Messengers went to and fro. The Egyptian language was understood by at least certain of the people associated with the " Amorite " sheikh. Sinuhe was not the first Egyptian to reside in that region; others were there before him. Such conditions would render a trip by Abram to Egypt (Gen. 12) certainly not impossible but quite in the order of the day.

A contemporary Egyptian relief (about 1900 B.C.)

gives us further information about Patriarchal life. It depicts a family of Semitic semi-nomads, thirty-seven in number, entering Egypt (Fig. 19). First to be noticed are the donkeys. Neither camels nor horses were yet sufficiently domesticated to be in common use. The donkey, therefore, was the beast of burden, just as it is today, but without help from the horse or camel. We may note also the appearance of the people : the long straight noses, the cut hair and beards of the men, the long hair of the women held in place by a band, and the elaborate, many-colored woolen clothes. The men wear short skirts and sandals, the women shoes and long dresses fastened by a single shoulder-clasp. The spear, composite bow, and throw-stick or mace are their weapons. One man carries a skin water-bottle on his back and an eight-stringed lyre in his hands.

This relief is most interesting in that it is approximately contemporary with Abram and shows how he and his family must have looked. It also indicates that we are not to think of Patriarchal life as too primitive, though to highly civilized Egyptians, Syrians, and Mesopotamians such people may well have been wild, savage, and primitive enough.

[2] Translation by John A. Wilson in J. B. Pritchard, ed., *Ancient Near Eastern Texts* (Princeton, Princeton University Press, 1950), pp. 19–20.

Indeed so despised were the Amorites to the old settlers of Mesopotamia that the following derogatory remarks are made about them in an old poem:

> The weapon is (his) companion. . . .
> Who knows no submission,
> Who eats uncooked flesh,
> Who has no house in his life-time,
> Who does not bury his dead companion.[3]

It is interesting to note that Abram, Isaac, and Jacob are associated with certain areas of the Palestinian hill country. Abram is most closely associated with Mamre, south of Jerusalem: " And Abram moved his tent and came and dwelt by the oaks of Mamre, which are in Hebron " (Gen. 13 : 18). Here was the cave of Machpelah which Abram purchased and which became the patriarchal burial chamber (cf. Fig. 20). Isaac, on the other hand, seems to have spent most of his life further south in and around Beersheba (Gen. 26 : 23 ; 28 : 10), while Jacob was most closely associated with the area north of Jerusalem, especially Bethel and Shechem (33 : 18 ; 35 : 1). His flocks even roamed as far north as Dothan in search of pasture (37 : 17). At all these sites there were apparently old holy places, where altars and pillars were set up by Abram and Jacob for purposes of worship.

20. A tomb at Jericho from about the 17th century B.C., showing the remains of a wooden table (*left*), bier (*right*), bowl, baskets and pottery

There are several things in this picture which are of interest archaeologically. For one thing, all these sites are located in the hill country of Palestine, which we now know to have been rather sparsely populated at that time and thickly wooded but

with areas profitable for grazing. If the Patriarchs were to follow their nomadic habits of life anywhere in the land of Canaan between the Mediterranean and the Jordan, the thinly populated hill country or central ridge was precisely the place for it. In fact, the towns with which they were associated were the main settlements in that area during the period between 2000 and 1700 B.C. Dothan, Shechem, and Bethel were all in existence. At Shechem " Jacob's Well ", a main source of water for the area, is now a holy place, and at least as old as the time of Jesus (cf. John 4), but how much older it may be is impossible to say.

No archaeological investigation has determined how old Hebron and Beersheba are, though the wells at the latter site are certainly very ancient. Hebron, we are told in Num. 13 : 22, was founded " seven years before Zoan in Egypt ". Zoan was a city in the Nile Delta which had a number of names in its history, probably including that of Raamses, the store-city built or re-built by the Hebrews in bondage (Exod. 1 : 11). It has been excavated and is now known to have been re-built by the Hyksos about 1700 B.C. Hebron, therefore, having been founded about the same time, probably under the name of Kiriath-arba (Gen. 23 : 2 ; 35 : 27), was evidently not in existence in the time of Abram, a fact which accounts for the association of the Patriarch with Mamre. In the narrative we are informed only by two explanatory notes that Mamre is Hebron, indicating that though Abram settled there, the city itself was not yet in existence.

What about the Canaanites who are said to have been in the land at that time ? Unfortunately, we do not know a great deal about them, except what we can learn from the material remains in their cities. During the period just before and after 2000 B.C. there would appear to have been very little urban activity in Palestine, whereas during the 19th century a whole new era began (Middle Bronze II); the number of towns and the quality of the material culture increased rapidly. Some Egyptian figurines and pieces of pottery have been found which list Asiatic enemies of Egypt during this age. The earliest group, the Berlin texts, date from the 20th century B.C. These give evidence that Palestine was in a nomadic or semi-nomadic state at the time, and the only Palestinian cities mentioned are Jerusalem and Ashkelon. The second group, or Brussels texts, date from the second part of the 19th century (Fig. 21). In them many cities and their kings are mentioned, reflecting the increased urban

---

[3] Translated by W. F. Albright, *From the Old Stone Age to Christianity*, p. 121.

21. An inscribed figurine from Egypt, purposely smashed in a cursing ceremony

by a very strong city wall, and the Egyptian statues and other objects dating about 1900 B.C., which were found there by the English excavator, Macalister, between 1902 and 1909, indicate that this city may have been an Egyptian outpost early in the Patriarchal period. This important discovery informs us that at least the Palestinian coastal plain was probably controlled by the Egyptian government at that time.

A second great city of Canaan was Megiddo (Fig. 2), guardian of the pass through Mt. Carmel from the Plain of Sharon to the great Esdraelon Plain. The most important discoveries for the Patriarchal period were made at the site by the Oriental Institute of the University of Chicago in 1938–9. Of great interest are a number of Egyptian objects and a series of three temples (Fig. 23), all of the same shape : a portico with columns in front and a rectangular room which once contained the statue of the deity worshipped. The temples were side by side and presumably were the " houses " of three different deities. Behind the temples was the great High Place, a circular structure, 29½ feet in diameter at the base and 6½ feet high (Fig. 24). One ascended to the top of it by a flight of steps on the east, at the base of which was found a large quantity of animal bones. The High Place was for great burnt offerings and the bones were the remains of animals thus offered. Here is contemporary evidence for the religion of Canaan about the time of Abram. In all probability it was much the same as at later periods, and its nature will be described in a subsequent chapter.

Besides the coastal plain and Esdraelon there was another area which was flourishing and dotted with towns early in the Patriarchal period. That was eastern Transjordan and the Jordan Valley. We hear something about this in Gen. 13 : 10–13 : " And Lot lifted up his eyes, and beheld all the Plain of the Jordan, that it was well watered everywhere, before the Lord destroyed Sodom and Gomorrah, like the garden of the Lord (Eden), like the land of Egypt, as thou goest unto Zoar . . . and Lot dwelt in the *cities of the Plain* and tented as far as Sodom."

This is an interesting tradition, for Genesis is here informing us that before Sodom and Gomorrah were destroyed, the Jordan-Dead Sea Valley was well watered like the garden of Paradise (Eden) and the land of Egypt. Subsequently we are told about the destruction of Sodom and Gomorrah and the civilization of the Plain: " Then the Lord

activity. Among the cities listed are : Jerusalem, Shechem, Accho (Acre), Achshaph (near Acre), Tyre, Hazor (in Galilee), Ashtaroth (in Bashan), Pella (across the Jordan from Beth-shan), etc. Also the term *Shutu* appears, which is probably the ancient name of Moab, east of the Dead Sea, a name which seems to occur also in the Hebrew text of Num. 24 : 17.

Excavations show us that one of the great Canaanite cities of the country at this time was Gezer, situated on one of the foothills bordering the coastal plain southeast of Jaffa (Fig. 22). It was guarded

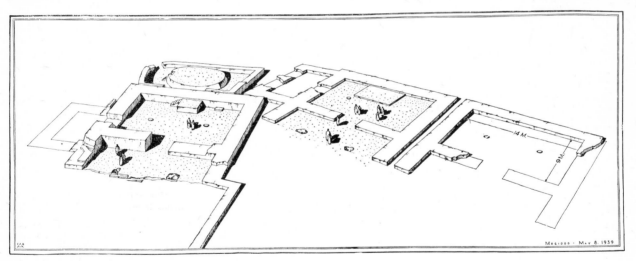

22. (*top*) The mound of Gezer, from the north

23. (*center*) Three temples with altar for burnt offering found in Stratum XV (about 1900 B.C.) at Megiddo

24. (*left*) A large altar for burnt offerings found at Megiddo

D

49

rained upon Sodom and upon Gomorrah brimstone and fire from the Lord out of heaven, and he overthrew those cities and all the Plain and all the inhabitants of the cities and that which grew upon the ground. . . . And Abraham . . . looked toward Sodom and Gomorrah and toward all the land of the Plain, and beheld, and lo, the smoke of the land went up as the smoke of a furnace " (19 : 24-8).

This description sounds very much as though there was a tremendous earthquake, perhaps the only explicit reference in the Bible to an earthquake in the Jordan valley, though we know that such earthquakes have been fairly common in history, some of them exceedingly serious, killing hundreds of people. It is well known that the Jordan valley is well below sea-level, the deepest rift of its sort in the world. It was formed as a result of a great geological fault extending from Asia Minor through Syria and Palestine into Africa, and disturbances of the earth along it are not uncommon. If there were volcanos in the Valley, we might think of the " brimstone and fire from the Lord out of heaven " as referring to volcanic eruption. But, since there are none, we are probably to think in terms of an earthquake, unless the whole story is mythical. And at this point archaeology enters the discussion.

Nelson Glueck while Director of the American School of Oriental Research in Jerusalem made a thorough survey of Southern Transjordan east and south of the Dead Sea (between 1932-9) and discovered that the nomadic peoples settled down in villages there in the centuries before 2000 B.C., just at the time when a dark age was settling over Palestine and Egypt, due to the " Amorite " eruption. But suddenly about the 20th or 19th century the villages were abandoned for some mysterious reason, and the people apparently returned to nomadic pursuits. The same situation existed in the Negeb (Southern Palestine), through which Abraham journeyed on his way to Egypt.[4]

In addition, W. F. Albright has succeeded in solving the problem of the location of Sodom, Gomorrah, and Zoar. He has shown that they are now in all probability beneath the shallow waters at the southern tip of the Dead Sea. Thus it is impossible to excavate them or to learn more about them. He did excavate two sites near by, however, and found that they were abandoned about the 20th century, as were the other towns in southern

Transjordan. Examining the length of the Jordan Valley to the north of the Dead Sea, both he and Glueck found that it was a flourishing center of civilization throughout this period, but thereafter the density of its occupation steadily diminished.

These discoveries furnish the only objective date which archaeology is able to supply for Abram. If the latter was contemporary with the fall of the cities of the Plain, then he would probably have lived about the 20th or 19th century B.C. We cannot be entirely certain of this date, however, since it is possible that the cities of the Plain fell somewhat later than the abandonment of the towns in southern Transjordan. Yet it is difficult to understand the raid of the eastern kings, as narrated in Gen. 14, if the area were unoccupied and if the copper mines south of the Dead Sea were not being worked (see below). Meanwhile we have an approximate figure upon which we can fix, which, interestingly enough, is in accord with late biblical traditions. The figures preserved by Judean priests inform us that Abram left Mesopotamia a little more than 600 years before the Exodus of the Israelites from Egypt, that is, about 1900 B.C.[5]

Ultimately it is probable that the 14th chapter of Genesis will throw still more light on the date of the Patriarchs. Here we have an old story of the raid by four Mesopotamian kings into Transjordan and the defeat and plunder of the cities of the Plain. The route taken by these kings is now well known, for it is an old road through Transjordan, called by later Israelites " the King's Highway " (Num. 20 : 17; 21 : 22). Formerly, many scholars identified one of these kings, Amraphel, with the great Babylonian king, Hammurabi, but this identification can no longer be held. At the present none of these kings can with certainty be identified, but we may

---

[4] See now Nelson Glueck, " The Age of Abraham in the Negeb ", *The Biblical Archaeologist*, Vol. XVIII, No. 1 (Feb. 1955), pp. 2-9.

[5] This date for Abram is, of course, extremely tentative. The contention of this chapter is simply that the Patriarchal stories are best understood in the setting of the early 2nd millennium B.C. For a very different view which dates the Patriarchs some centuries later, see the detailed and closely reasoned treatment of H. H. Rowley, *From Joseph to Joshua* (London, Oxford University Press, 1950), also Cyrus H. Gordon, *Introduction to Old Testament Times* (Ventnor, N.J., 1953), pp. 103-4. On the other hand, D. N. Freedman in an unpublished paper has reasoned that the argument from the genealogies on which these scholars base much of their case is unsound because the genealogies preserve no information regarding ancestry before the Conquest of Canaan other than the general designation of clan and tribe. For example, when Num. 16 : 1 speaks of " Korah the son of Izhar, son of Kohath, son of Levi ", it only means that a man named Korah ben-Izhar belonged to the Kohath clan of the tribe of Levi. One cannot argue from such a passage, therefore, that there were only three generations between the Patriarchal period and the Conquest because no precise genealogical information is preserved before the time of Moses.

be confident that we shall learn more about them in the future. The reason for the raid may well have been the copper mines south of the Dead Sea, for these were being worked and explain the prosperity of the inhabitants of the region before the sudden and mysterious abandonment of village life some twenty centuries before the time of Christ.

There are many other things in the Patriarchal narratives which are illustrated by the archaeological discoveries, but we must limit ourselves to two. The first is the Cave of Machpelah at Mamre (Hebron), the Patriarchal burial chamber. Such family burial caves are now well known to us through excavations (Fig. 20). Many of those which have been excavated had been used for generations. It was the custom to bury the dead with large quantities of pottery and other objects used by the deceased in life. The pottery vessels contained food for use by the shades of the dead in the after-life.

The story of Abraham's purchase of the cave from Ephron the Hittite (Gen. 23) has usually been interpreted as a shrewd manoeuvre on Ephron's part by which he obtained an excessive price. Recently, however, the incident has been examined in the context of Hittite law by Manfred R. Lehmann.[6] The Hittite Code of laws, found in the Hittite capital at Boghazköy in Turkey, specifies that if a buyer purchases all of the seller's property, he must render certain feudal services, the exact nature of which we do not know. The transfer of Hittite land carried with it the obligation of these feudal duties, unless only a portion of the seller's property were purchased. In Abraham's second request before the town council, he specifies that he desires only the cave at the edge of Ephron's field (Gen. 23 : 9). Ephron, however, sees the opportunity of ridding himself of his obligations and replies : " I sell you the field, and I sell you the cave which is in it " (vs. 11). He refused to divide his property so that Abraham was forced to become feudatory for the entire field. The mention of trees in vs. 17 is also interesting because Hittite business documents consistently list the exact number of trees in each real estate transaction.

A second custom has also to do with Patriarchal beliefs. On at least three occasions Jacob set up pillars at places where he had had a religious experience. After his dream at Bethel, he erected such a pillar, made a vow to God, and named it " Bethel "

⁶ For reference see Bibliography at the end of this chapter.

meaning " House of God " (Gen. 28 : 18 ff.). When he and Laban made their covenant of peace and called in God as a witness and party to the covenant, a pillar was set up (31 : 44 ff.). A third pillar was set up at Shechem and was named " God, the God of Israel " (33 : 20 where we are to read " pillar " instead of " altar "). The significance of this custom is not entirely clear. Such pillars are very familiar to us, however, since many of them have been discovered (Fig. 25). They appear to have been erected chiefly as memorial stones to commemorate a theophany, a vow or sacred covenant rite, or even an ancestor or important official.

25. Pillars at Lejjun in Transjordan

Concerning the religion of the Patriarchs very little can be said in detail with certainty. Tradition has preserved, however, the general name applied to the patriarchal family deity. He was known as " the God of the Fathers ", or " the God of Abraham, Isaac, and Jacob ". Albrecht Alt and Julius Lewy have brought together a large number of illustrations from pagan antiquity of this type of family deity whom a patriarch would consciously choose as his personal God and with whom he would enter a special contractual or covenantal relationship. This deity took special charge of the family or clan, and successive generations would choose and enter into the relationship anew. In all probability we have here one portion of the background of the later covenant between God and Israel. " The God of the Fathers " was identified with Yahweh (Exod. 3) ; he became Israel's God and Israel by free choice became his people. The ideology of the patriarchal family continued to govern the thought of the people centuries later when they had become a nation and had adopted into the covenant unity many groups of extraneous origin.

The proper name of the Patriarchal deity is not

known with certainty, but one of his titles has been preserved. It is "Shaddai" (Gen. 17 : 1 ; Exod. 6 : 3), a name which W. F. Albright has shown to be a Mesopotamian word, meaning "mountaineer". The symbol of a mountain was often used in antiquity to point to the might and awe-inspiring majesty of a particular deity. The translation "almighty" for Shaddai is thus not far from the original thought contained in the title. Shaddai as the family God of the Patriarchs does not necessarily mean, however, that monotheism is to be dated this early in Hebrew history. Abram's worship of El Elyon (" God Most High ") in Jerusalem

(Gen. 14) would appear to indicate that the contrary was the case. El was the head of both the " Amorite " and later Canaanite pantheons of deities, and we have no reason to suppose that he is anything else in the original tradition behind Gen. 14.

So we take leave of the Founding Fathers of Israel. While we have not begun to exhaust the evidence, enough has been written to indicate that the past thirty years of archaeological discovery enable us to understand the life and times of Abram, Isaac, and Jacob in a way which has hitherto been impossible. A new chapter has been added to Israelite history, a most important contribution to biblical study.

FURTHER READING

Since most of this material is the result of recent scholarship, it is not to be found in the majority of our textbooks. The most important treatments are those of Professor W. F. Albright, to whose work many of these discoveries are due :

From the Old Stone Age to Christianity (Baltimore, Johns Hopkins University Press, 3rd ed., 1946), Chap. IV, Sections A and B.

" Recent Discoveries in Bible Lands ", Supplement to *Young's Analytical Concordance* (New York, Funk and Wagnalls Co., 1955 edition ; published as a separate monograph by The Biblical Colloquium, 731 Ridge Ave., Pittsburgh 12, Pa.), Chap. XI.

The Archaeology of Palestine and the Bible (New York, Fleming H. Revell Co., any of the three editions—1932, 1933, 1935), Chap. III, Section 2.

Other references, the footnotes of which will lead into other literature, are :

John Bright, *A History of Israel* (Philadelphia, Westminster Press, 1959), pp. 41–93 ; R. de Vaux, " Les patriarches Hébreux et les découvertes modernes ", *Revue Biblique*, LIII, (1946), pp. 321–48 ; LV (1948), pp. 321–47 ; LVI (1949), pp. 5–36 ; H. H. Rowley, " Recent Discovery and the Patriarchal Age " in *The Servant of the Lord and other Essays* (London, 1952), pp. 271–305.

C. H. Gordon, " Biblical Customs and the Nuzu Tablets ", *The Biblical Archaeologist*, Vol. III, No. 1 (Feb. 1940). This is the fullest discussion in one place of the Patriarchal customs referred to in the first section of this chapter.

J. P. Harland, " Sodom and Gomorrah ", *The Biblical Archaeologist*, Vols. V, No. 2 (May 1942) and VI, No. 3 (Sept. 1943). The best and most detailed discussion of the problem of the location and destruction of these cities.

M. G. Kyle, *Explorations in Sodom* (New York, Fleming H. Revell, 1928), is an interesting popular account of the expedition made by Professor Albright and himself in search of Sodom, Gomorrah, and Zoar in 1924, the result of which was the decision that the ruins must now be beneath the waters of the southeastern end of the Dead Sea.

Nelson Glueck, *The Other Side of the Jordan* (New Haven, American Schools of Oriental Research, 1940), Chap. V ; *The River Jordan* (Philadelphia, Westminster Press, 1946), Chap. III, and *Rivers in the Desert* (London and New York, 1959).

Albrecht Alt, *Der Gott der Väter* (Leipzig, 1929).

Julius Lewy, " Les textes paléo-assyriens et l'Ancien Testament ", *Revue d'Histoire des Religions*, CX (1934), pp. 29–65, especially pp. 50 ff.

Manfred R. Lehmann, " Abraham's Purchase of Machpelah and Hittite Law ", *Bulletin of the American Schools of Oriental Research*, No. 129 (Feb. 1953), pp. 15–18.

For an entirely different viewpoint towards the Genesis traditions, one which insists that archaeology can be of little assistance in dealing with traditional material of this type, see Martin Noth, *The History of Israel* (London and New York, 1958), pp. 120–6; and " Het die Bibel doch recht ? " *Festschrift für Günther Dehn* (Neukirchen, 1957), pp. 16–19.

For a critique of this approach see John Bright, *Early Israel in Recent History Writing* (London, 1956) ; and G. Ernest Wright, " History and the Patriarchs", *The Expository Times*, July 1960, pp. 3–7. For reply see G. von Rad, " History and the Patriarchs ", *ibid.*, April 1961, pp. 213–16, and M. Noth, " Der Beitrag der Archäologie zur Geschichte Israels ", Congress Volume, Oxford, 1959 (Supplements to *Vetus Testamentum*, Vol. VII, Lieden, 1960).

CHAPTER IV

SOJOURNERS IN EGYPT

" And the patriarchs, moved with envy, sold Joseph into Egypt.   But God was with him, and delivered him out of all his afflictions, and gave him favor and wisdom in the sight of Pharaoh, king of Egypt.   And he made him governor over Egypt and all his house " (Acts 7 : 9–10).

" Marvelous things did He in the sight of their fathers, in the land of Egypt, in the field of Zoan " (Psa. 78 : 12).

THE Exodus from Egyptian slavery was the dominant and dominating event in Israelite history and faith.   This was the unique event in which God had revealed himself as the Sovereign Lord of history and had brought Israel into being, as a nation, for his own purposes in history.   From it Israelites learned to understand God's nature from historical events and to confess their faith by reciting God's works in the forms of history.   The mighty acts of God in Egypt and in the wilderness were a sign, a wonder, giving evidence of a Power greater than all the powers of this world.   Here was One who could make both nature and the recalcitrant heart of Pharaoh serve him.   Yet he was also One who for a reason known only to himself had set his love on a defenseless people and had chosen them as his own.   The knowledge of God was thus believed to have been revealed in what had actually happened.

Yet the events which were so important to Israel were so unimportant to the Egyptians that no record of them was preserved outside the Bible.   Nevertheless, the tradition must have an historical basis. In the first place, there suddenly appeared in the biblical record a number of Egyptian names, belonging especially to the tribe of Levi : *Moses*, an abbreviation of a longer name, is from an Egyptian verb meaning " to bear, beget ".   The same verbal element occurs in such Egyptian names as Thutmose and Rameses (cf. Fig. 30), the first syllables of which are god-names while the remainder indicates that the god is the begetter of the person named.   Other Levite names apparently acquired from the Egyptian language are Phinehas, Hophni, Pashhur, and perhaps Hur and Merari.

In the story of Joseph, however, scholars have observed that some of the Egyptian names were evidently changed in the course of time.   Thus, for example, the names *Potiphar* (born by the captain who purchased Joseph, Gen. 37 : 36), *Potiphera* (Joseph's father-in-law), *Asenath* (his Egyptian wife), and *Zaphenath-paneah* (Joseph's Egyptian name, Gen. 41 : 45), were not used in Joseph's day, as far as we know, but only came into common use from the time of David on.   In other words, there was a tendency to modernize the narrative, just as in the earlier patriarchal stories ; and it is interesting to note that the same thing occurred again in the Greek translation of the Pentateuch during the 3rd century B.C.

In the second place, it has often been pointed out that the Egyptian coloring in the story of the Sojourn is very good, and must have been given to it by those who knew Egypt well.   Thus we know that dreams were indeed regarded by Egyptians as extremely significant when interpreted.   Potiphar made Joseph " overseer over his house ", a title which is a direct translation of an office in the houses of great Egyptian nobles.   Pharaoh gave him an office with similar title in the administration of the realm (Gen. 41 : 40), and it has recently been shown that the Israelite official title " the one who is over the house ", corresponds exactly to the office of Prime Minister, or Vizier, of Egypt, who was the actual ruler of the country, second in power to no one but the Pharaoh.

The titles " chief of the butlers " and " chief of the bakers " (Gen. 40 : 2) occur in Egyptian inscriptions.   The birthday of Pharaoh is known to have been an occasion for feasting, and possibly for the release of prisoners, which recalls the feast which Pharaoh made for his servants on his birthday, at which time the chief butler and the chief baker were released from prison, the one to life and the other to death (Gen. 40 : 20).   We know also that magicians (41 : 8) were plentiful in Egypt, that " every (Asiatic) shepherd is an abomination to the Egyptians " (46 : 34 ; cp. also 43 : 32) ; that seven-year famines were otherwise known in Egypt ; that Joseph's lifespan of 110 years (50 : 22) was considered the traditional length of a happy and prosperous life in

Egyptian inscriptions; and that the embalming or mummification of Jacob and Joseph (50 : 2, 26) was the customary Egyptian preparation of the body of an important person for burial. Pharaoh's gifts to Joseph upon the latter's induction into the office of Prime Minister would be quite in keeping with Egyptian custom : " And Pharaoh took off his signet ring from his hand and put it on Joseph's hand, and arrayed him in vestures of fine linen, and put a gold chain about his neck. And he made him to ride in the second chariot which he had ; and people cried before him : ' Bow the knee ! ' " (41 : 42-3).

It has also been pointed out that the ten plagues (Exod. 7-12) are based on natural scourges which are still troublesome in Egypt. After the Nile reaches its height in August, it often becomes dull red in color, due to large numbers of tiny organisms. Under certain conditions the water might easily become foul and undrinkable. Plagues of frogs have occurred a number of times, generally in September, and such a plague would be more frequent, it is reported, if it were not for the ibis, a bird which feeds upon vermin and frees the country of them. The decomposition of dead frogs easily explains the third and fourth plagues, those of lice and flies ; and such conditions would certainly bring pestilence to cattle and men (fifth and sixth plagues). Hail storms, while rare, have been known to occur, and locusts have caused damage of plague proportions in the Near East on many occasions. The thick darkness (ninth plague) can be explained as a terrible sand and dust storm, brought in by the *Khamsin*, the hot desert wind which is one of the most disagreeable features of the Egyptian spring. The *Khamsin* blows for two to four days at a time, while the " thick darkness " is said to have lasted for three days (Exod. 10 : 22). These natural Egyptian " terrors ", occurring in particular severity at one time, may indeed have appeared to both Moses and Pharaoh as witness to the wrath of the God of Israel.

During the course of centuries the story of Joseph may have attracted occasional details from other popular stories which had nothing to do with Joseph. The Egyptian Tale of Two Brothers is the story of Anubis and Bitis. Bitis was the younger, and was entrusted with all the older brother's property, just as Joseph was entrusted with all the affairs of Potiphar, the captain of the guard. The affectionate relation between the two brothers was disturbed, however, by the wife of Anubis. One day when Bitis went to the house to get some seed, the wife tried to seduce him. He angrily resisted, but said

nothing to his brother. That evening, fearful of the consequences to herself, the wife complained to her husband that she had been mistreated by Bitis, whereupon the latter was forced to flee for his life. This story corresponds so exactly to the biblical tale of Joseph and the wife of Potiphar (Gen. 39 : 7 ff.) that scholars have generally taken it as a mythological accretion to the life of Joseph. Other elements in the Genesis story have been explained in a similar fashion, but none are as clear as this.

THE HISTORICAL BACKGROUND OF THE SOJOURN

As already pointed out, the position to which Joseph attained in Egypt is well illustrated by inscriptions and reliefs. Joseph not only was second in power to none but Pharaoh, but in view of the approaching famine he was placed in control of all grain and granaries. From Egyptian records we should judge that he therefore combined in his person two offices : that of " governor " or Prime Minister at the head of the government, and that of " superintendent of the granaries " (cf. Fig. 26).

26. Tomb monument of an Egyptian official of the Eighth Dynasty, dating shortly before 2000 B.C., illustrating the typical manner in which such officials were represented

The duties of the Prime Minister were various; he was not only minister of the interior and chief magistrate, but occasionally minister of public worship also. The office of " Superintendent of the Granaries " was especially important at all periods in Egypt, for the real wealth and stability of the country lay in its grain (Fig. 27). The Superintendent had to see to it that the supply was plentiful, and it was a great day in the realm when the Superintendent in solemn audience presented to Pharaoh the " account of the harvests ". If there

had been " a better harvest than for thirty years ", then the official would be given special honors by the king, anointed and decked with valuable necklaces.

Some have thought it peculiar that a foreigner like Joseph should have risen to such a position of authority in Egypt. A study of Egyptian officials, however, reveals that this was probably not an unusual occurrence. Slaves of the New Empire (after 1570 B.C.) became the favorites of the kings, and often rose to positions of great power. Like many powerful monarchs (for example, Turkish Sultans of the Middle Ages) the Pharaohs apparently felt some distrust of their own subjects and sought to surround themselves with trustworthy people whom they knew well. Besides, we shall indicate later that Joseph may have lived at a time when foreigners were ruling over Egypt, and his rise to power would not have been unusual.

The biblical story of seven years of famine in Egypt is likewise not unusual. Various inscriptions speak about famines in the land, and at least two officials, giving laudatory summaries of their good deeds on the walls of their tombs, tell of distributing food to the hungry " in each year of want " (cf. Fig. 28). One inscription, written in the second or early first century B.C., preserves a tradition that

27. Egyptian granaries, represented as full of grain in the top register, and as being filled in the lower register

28. An Egyptian relief, showing starving people. From Sakkarah, Fifth Dynasty (*ca.* 2500–2350 B.C.)

Pharaoh Djoser of the Third Dynasty (about 2700 B.C.) appealed to the God Khnum because of a serious famine which had lasted seven years, and was promised years of plenty. Said the king:

I was in distress on the Great Throne, and those who are in the palace were in Heart's affliction from a very great evil, since the Nile had not come in my time for a space of seven years. Grain was scant, fruits were dried up, and everything which they eat was short. . . . The infant was wailing; the youth was *waiting*; the heart of the old man was in sorrow. . . . The courtiers were in need. The temples were shut up. . . . Every(*thing*) was found empty.[1]

During the biblical famine we are told that Joseph's brethren along with many other people came to Egypt from Canaan for food (Gen. 41 : 57). Finally, at Pharaoh's request Jacob and his family of seventy moved their belongings into Egypt and settled in the land of Goshen (Gen. 46 : 27 ff.). It was once thought that Goshen was mentioned in Egyptian records, but this is now known to have been a mistake. Another name for it was probably " the land of Rameses " (Gen. 47 : 11), and still another " the field of Zoan " (Psa. 78 : 12). The last mentioned frequently occurs in Egyptian records as the name for the area around the city Zoan or Tanis in the eastern part of the Nile delta. The " Rameses " here referred to was the name given to the same town, not in Joseph's day, but after 1300 B.C. when the city was rebuilt by the great Pharaoh, Rameses II (*ca.* 1290–1224 B.C.). While we cannot be certain that Goshen covered exactly the same territory as these two geographical terms, we are sure that it was in this area, and comprised at least the region now known as the Wadi Tumilat. This Wadi (the Arabic name for a river bed which is usually dry except in the rainy season) is a narrow valley between thirty and forty miles long, connecting the Nile with Lake Timsah. In both ancient and modern times the area around the Wadi Tumilat, especially to the north of it, was one of the richest sections of Egypt, truly " the best of the land ", as it is described in Gen. 47 : 11. The great American explorer, Edward Robinson, reported in 1838 that it yielded more revenue at that time than any other province in Egypt, and that there were more flocks and herds there than elsewhere. The population was half migratory, large numbers of people still retaining their nomadic habits. This was exactly the situation in Joseph's day, as we infer both from the Bible and from Egyptian texts. If there is any place in Egypt where the Hebrew shepherds should have settled, this is the region.

Two Egyptian inscriptions indicate that it was the customary thing for frontier officials to allow Bedouin from Palestine and Sinai to enter Egypt during hard times and live in the Goshen area. One, dating about 1350 B.C., informs us that such a group, " who knew not how they should live, have come begging a home in the domain of Pharaoh . . ., after the manner of your (that is, the Pharaoh's) fathers' fathers since the beginning . . ." Apparently, therefore, it was a long-standing custom for Pharaohs to allow them to enter the land.

The second is a communication from a frontier official to his superior dated about 1230 B.C., informing him that certain Edomite Bedouin have been allowed to pass the fortress in the district of Succoth (*Theku*) in the Wadi Tumilat, to pasture their cattle near Pithom, " in order to sustain them and their herds in the domain of Pharaoh . . ." The Egyptian word " sustain " is regularly used to indicate preservation in time of famine, so we may take it that the entry of the family of Jacob into Egypt was under exactly similar circumstances at an earlier period. We note with interest the mention in this text of Succoth and Pithom, towns mentioned in the Bible, the location of which has been much discussed; but we shall return to them later. The nomadic family of Abi-shar which is pictured as entering Egypt about 1900 B.C. (see Fig. 19) was thirty-seven in number, and during the course of the subsequent centuries the number of such families must have been very large. It is scarcely surprising, therefore, that no record of Jacob and his family has been preserved in Egypt.

Is it possible to say just when Joseph was in Egypt? Unfortunately the answer must be in the negative. There are certain hints, however, and we should say something about them.

Shortly before 1700 B.C. a dark age settled over Egypt which was to last some one hundred and fifty years. This was caused by the invasion of Asiatics whom the Egyptians called *Hyksos*, " Rulers of Foreign Countries ". These foreigners, whom the Egyptians so despised and hated, were able to build a great empire, including at least Palestine and southern Syria (cf. Fig. 29). Objects belonging to one of their greatest kings have been found as far away as Crete and Mesopotamia. They were finally driven out of Egypt, after a siege of their

---

[1] Translation by J. A. Wilson in J. B. Pritchard, ed., *Ancient Near Eastern Texts*, p. 31.

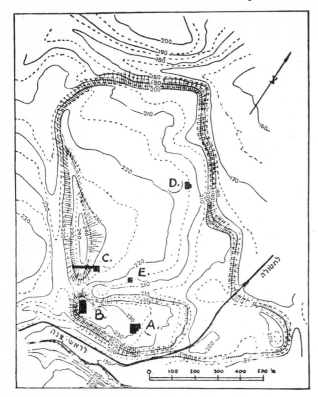

29. Plan of Hazor in Galilee, showing the citadel (*below*), and a one hundred and fifty acre enclosure to the north which was probably constructed originally as a huge Hyksos army camp

of the city by a Hyksos ruler. Thus Avaris was founded 400 years before the date on which the anniversary fell. This date has been fixed somewhere between 1320 and 1300 B.C., the establishment of Avaris as the Hyksos capital having occurred, therefore, about 1720–1700 B.C.

Now in the book of Numbers (13 : 22), in the midst of the story of the spies sent out by Moses to look over Canaan, a scribe has inserted this astonishing bit of information : " Now Hebron was built seven years before Zoan (Tanis) in Egypt." Thus Hebron must have been founded not far from the year 1720 B.C., which may account for the frequent mention of " the oaks of Mamre " in the Patriarchal stories, instead of Hebron, even though the writers knew that the two referred to the same locality. But the question which several scholars have asked is this : " How does it happen that the later Hebrews in Palestine came to fix the founding of Hebron by the Hyksos establishment of Avaris ? Why should Israel be concerned about Tanis ? " The natural inference is that there must have been Hebrews who were connected with Hyksos activity and who were in Egypt when Tanis was founded ! [2]

Further, we are told in Exod. 12 : 40 that " the time that the children of Israel dwelt in Egypt was 430 years ". Gen. 15 : 13 reduces this to the round number 400 years. These figures, when examined together with the passage in Num. 13 : 22 have reminded some scholars rather forcibly of the Tanite era of 400 years. It will be shown later that at least some Israelites were in Egypt at the time of the Tanite anniversary, so we are left with the suspicion that the Era of Tanis may have been known to the Hebrews.

These and other reasons have caused the majority of scholars to place the entry of Joseph, his father, and brethren into Egypt in the time of the Hyksos. With the seat of the government at Avaris in the Delta we can understand the impression given in the story of Joseph that the land of Goshen was not far away from the capital, and that the Hebrews had ready access to the court. Both before and after the days of the Hyksos the Egyptian Pharaohs used as their capital the city of Thebes in Upper Egypt. The site of Avaris in the eastern Delta was used for the capital only by the Hyksos (about

capital, Avaris, and chased into Palestine, where for three years they were besieged at the fortress of Sharuhen (probably the modern Tell el-Far'ah, southeast of Gaza). Indeed, several Palestinian cities which, excavations show, were destroyed during the 16th century, furnish evidence of the intensity of the Egyptian campaign to recover the Asiatic empire of former times.

For many years the exact location of the Hyksos capital, Avaris, was the subject of much discussion. But excavations seem recently to have settled the matter for most scholars, though the discussion continues. It was probably located at San el-Hagar in the Delta, a site which is now thought to have possessed the successive names of Avaris before 1500 B.C., " Houses of Rameses " from about 1300–1100 B.C., and finally Tanis (which is the same as *Zoan*) after 1100 B.C. Some of the tremendous Hyksos fortifications at Avaris have been unearthed, but one of the most important objects found at the city of Avaris-Rameses-Tanis was the *stele* or monumental stone of the year 400. It was erected by an official of Rameses II by order of the Pharaoh to commemorate the 400th anniversary of the founding

[2] There are some scholars who do not accept this viewpoint. They believe that Rameses was located, not at Tanis, but at Qantir, a few miles to the south. Furthermore, some are doubtful as to the interpretation and historical value of the " 400 yr. *stele* ".

1700 to 1575 B.C.) and by Pharaohs of the Nineteenth Dynasty after 1300 B.C. If, therefore, the family of Jacob entered Egypt either before or after the Hyksos period, we should be at a loss to explain the obvious implication concerning the location of the capital, other than to assume that in this respect the tradition was mistaken.

Another hint as to Joseph's date may be contained in the story of his buying up all the land for Pharaoh during the years of the famine (Gen. 47 : 13 ff.). Before the Hyksos Egyptian land was largely owned by powerful nobles. After the foreigners had been driven from the country, we find in the state erected by the Pharaohs of the new Eighteenth Dynasty that the old landed nobility had disappeared, and their place had been taken by a bureaucracy of government officials. The masses who worked the fields and estates were the serfs, the virtual slaves, of the Pharaoh. While, of course, we cannot be certain, it is probable that this social revolution had been aided, or perhaps even accomplished, by the Hyksos who had brought about an equally great social upheaval in Palestine. In any event it is very difficult to believe that this great change in the social structure is not reflected in the story of Joseph :

And Joseph bought all the land of Egypt for Pharaoh ; for every Egyptian sold his field, because the famine prevailed over them. So the land became Pharaoh's. And as for the people he made them bondmen from one end of the border of Egypt to the other. Only the land of the priests bought he not, for there was a subvention for the priests from Pharaoh and they lived off their portion which Pharaoh had given them. . . . (Gen. 47 : 20–2).

These are some of the hints which point to the Hyksos period as the time when Joseph lived. For purposes of dating the best are the possible connection between Israelite tradition and the Tanite era (especially Num. 13 : 22) and the implication of the Bible story that the Egyptian capital was in or near the Nile Delta in Joseph's day.

Yet it must be admitted that these do not furnish the certainty that we like to have. If it were possible to establish a date for the Exodus, then we should be able to count backward some 430 years (Exod. 12 : 40) and thus arrive at a tentative conclusion. We shall now turn to the Exodus and see what archaeology has to say to us about this subject.

WITH MOSES AND THE EXODUS

The book of Exodus begins by telling us that after the death of Joseph and his generation, the Hebrews were fruitful and multiplied until " the land was filled with them ". Then, " there arose up a new king over Egypt, who knew not Joseph ", and who, becoming worried over the minority problem which was on his hands, forced the people to go to work on government building projects. Thus two store-cities, Pithom and Raamses, were built (Exod. 1 : 11).

From various inscriptions we now know that on the borders of every civilized country in the Near East there were ever-shifting groups of nomadic peoples who in times of peace worked in various capacities for the settled people. Egypt was no exception, and we are occasionally told by the texts about a foreign group called *Apiru* (see above, Chap. III), some of whom, for example, are represented as engaged in dragging up stone for temples built by Pharaoh Rameses II (1290–1224 B.C.) in whose reign, as we shall see, the cities of Pithom and Raamses must have been built by the Hebrews.

After many years of debate and uncertainty, the cities of Pithom and Raamses which the Israelites are said to have been forced to build have been located. Pithom may now be identified with an ancient site in the Wadi Tumilat which is known today as Tell er-Retabeh (or Ertabeh). After the great patriarch of archaeologists, Sir Flinders Petrie, had excavated this site in 1905–6, he identified it with Raamses but the latest research has finally shown that this was a mistake. Pithom was found to have been an old town, but the finest structure on the site was the temple built by the great builder, Rameses II (1290–1224 B.C.). No other royal building of an earlier Pharaoh was found there, so we must conclude on the basis of our present evidence that if the Israelites worked on royal projects at the site, it must have been in the time of Rameses II.

Far more positive evidence, however, comes from the city of Raamses or Rameses. It has long been recognized that this city must be the same as the great capital of Rameses II, named by him " House of Rameses ". While this city was known to have been situated somewhere in the eastern Delta, the exact site had been unknown until recent excavations have shown it probably to have been situated at Tanis.[3]

We have already noted that this was also the site chosen by the Hyksos as their capital. But the

---

[3] If it was situated at Qantir, a short distance to the south, it would make no difference for the argument which follows.

30. The child, Rameses II, guarded by the falcon-god Horus; found at Tanis. The Egyptian words for the sun-disk (above the child's head), child and the plant which the child holds compose the name " Rameses "

great Pharaohs of the Eighteenth Dynasty (after 1570 B.C.) moved back to Thebes in Upper Egypt so that the site was deserted by royalty for almost four hundred years, as both inscriptions and excavations have indicated. About 1290 B.C. Rameses the Great came to the throne and moved his capital to the Delta site (Figs. 30 and 31). We are not sure of the reason, but presumably it was either to be in a better position to control his Asiatic empire, or to live in a city with which his family had had connections for some generations, or both. In any event, the city was renamed after him, and began its career as one of the greatest cities of Egypt, second to none but Thebes. This we know from an Egyptian poem which refers to it as the city which " none resembles in its likeness to Thebes ". Here was the seat of the government where all the records of the state were deposited. Here great building operations were carried on, as quantities of inscribed stones at the site inform us. A splendid temple was erected to the old Hyksos god, Seth, who remained the lord of the city. Flanking the approach to the temple, towering high above its massive pylons, were two colossal statues of the Pharaoh, over forty feet in height, and visible miles away. Numerous obelisks were erected, and poets wrote of the beauties of the new capital and of the richness of the country around, which became known as " the land of

31. Colossal statue of Rameses II at Memphis

59

Rameses ", a name so completely identified with this region in the eastern Delta that Israelite scribes read it back into the days of Joseph long before a Rameses came to the throne (Gen. 47 : 11).

Now the point which must be stressed is this : if the Israelites worked in labor battalions on the construction of the city of Rameses, it must have been during the reign of Rameses II (1290–1224 B.C.) and perhaps that of his father, but not before. Previously, when the identification of this city was still in doubt, many scholars have believed that the " store-cities " of Exod. 1 : 11 might have been built earlier, perhaps under Queen Hatshepsut or Pharaoh Thutmose III, just before and after 1500 B.C., and that the writer of Exod. 1 : 11 was merely giving us the later name of the city of Rameses and not the earlier name. Taking their cue from the statement in I Kings 6 : 1 that the Exodus occurred 480 years before Solomon built the Temple in Jerusalem, these scholars came to the conclusion that the Exodus took place about 1440 B.C. or just before. Now that the site of Rameses has been located at Tanis, we are forced to conclude that this figure must be explained in another way, a discussion of which we shall postpone until the next chapter. We now know that if there is any historical value at all to the store-city tradition in Exodus (and there is no reason to doubt its reliability), *then Israelites must have been in Egypt at least during the early part of the reign of Rameses II.* After much digging at Tanis by the archaeologists Mariette, Petrie, and Montet, not a single object of the Eighteenth Egyptian Dynasty has been found there. The city was destroyed by Pharaoh Amosis I (1570–1546), and was probably not reoccupied before the end of the 14th century.

We shall see in the next chapter that the Israelites under Joshua were evidently in Palestine, carrying on the main phase of the Conquest, by the third quarter of the 13th century. This means that Rameses II, who reigned during the greater part of that century, must have been the Pharaoh of the Mosaic Exodus. The Book of Exodus seems to imply that the " new king over Egypt who knew not Joseph " (1 : 8) died before the Israelite flight from Egypt, which took place under his successor (2 : 23 ; 4 : 19). Hence the father of Rameses II, Seti I (1308–1290 B.C.), would appear to have been the Pharaoh of the initial oppression. This ruling family came from the region of Tanis. Seti I began the reorganization of the empire in Palestine and southern Syria, and we know from the " 400-

year " *stele* (see above) that he was the one who began the rebuilding of the old Hyksos capital to make it his own. His son, Rameses II, continued his work, named the new city from himself, restored the empire and fought with the Hittites in Asia Minor until a treaty of peace was drawn up about 1270 B.C. From that time on his direct intervention in Asian affairs became increasingly rare.

THE ROUTE OF THE EXODUS (Fig. 32)

Under the energetic leadership of Moses permission was finally secured for Israel to leave Egypt. Where did they go ? What route did they take ? Where did they cross the sea ? What is manna ? Is there anything to the quail stories (Exod. 16 : 13 ; Num. 11 : 31) ? Where is Mt. Sinai ? Some of these questions can now in part be answered. The Exodus from Egypt is recounted to us as follows :

And the children of Israel journeyed from Rameses to Succoth. . . . And a mixed multitude went up also with them . . . (Exod. 12 : 37–8). And it came to pass, when Pharaoh had let the people go, that God led them not by the way of the land of the Philistines, although that was near. (For God said " Lest the people repent when they see war, and return to Egypt.") But God led the people around by the way of the wilderness by the Reed Sea (13 : 17–18). . . . And they set out from Succoth and encamped in Etham on the edge of the wilderness (13 : 20). . . . And the Lord spake to Moses, saying : " Speak to the children of Israel that they turn back and encamp before Pihahiroth, between Migdol and the Sea, before Baal-zephon. Before it ye shall encamp by the Sea " (14 : 1–2).

Can we trace this itinerary on the map ? Before Rameses was located this was impossible, and several prominent scholars objected to the historicity of the account on the ground that its geography was in error. With our present knowledge of the Delta these objections for the most part have been withdrawn. Starting from Rameses, the Israelites wisely decided not to attempt a direct route toward Canaan or the Sinai Peninsula (see Fig. 32). This would have taken them past the great frontier fortress of Zilu (Thel), near the modern Qantarah where travelers between Egypt and Palestine now cross the Suez Canal, and thence on to the well-traveled, and well-guarded, commercial and military road to Canaan, " the way of the land of the Philistines ". The long line of Egyptian fortifications along this route has actually been described by Pharaoh Seti I in his Karnak inscription in Upper

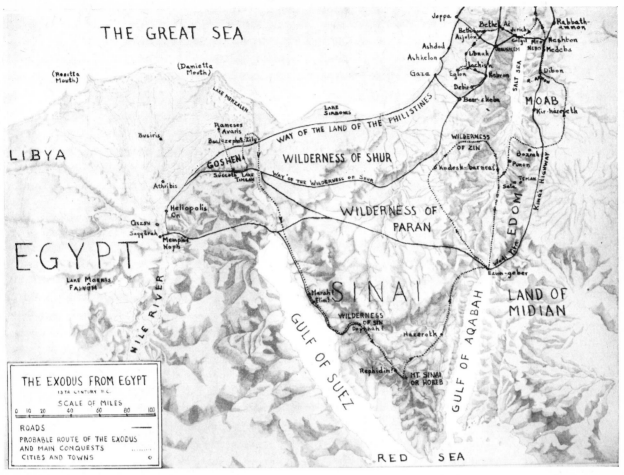

32. Map illustrating the route of the Exodus and the Conquest

Egypt. Hence Israel headed southeastward to Succoth, about thirty-two miles away, and thence to a Sinai route on which they would not be so easily followed : " the way of the wilderness by the Reed Sea ". Succoth was situated at the modern Tell el-Maskhutah, about eight and one half miles east of Pithom in the Wadi Tumilat. When it was excavated in 1883 by Naville, it was identified with Pithom and several store-chambers were thought to have been found. From numerous inscriptions found at the site it is now generally believed that this mound contains the ruins, not of Pithom, but of Succoth, and that the " store chambers " which Naville discovered are actually the foundations of a large fortress which we know to have existed there.

It is now apparent that modern translators of the Old Testament are mistaken in their rendering of the Hebrew name *Yam Suph* as Red Sea. It really should be translated as Reed or Marsh Sea, and it is highly improbable that we should identify it with

the northern arm of the Red Sea known today as the Gulf of Suez. In the first place, there are no reeds in the Red Sea. In the second place, the account implies that the Reed Sea formed the barrier between Egyptian soil and the desert wilderness. As soon as the Sea was successfully crossed, the terrifying, waterless desert was before the fleeing Hebrews, and soon the murmurings of fear and discontent arose. If the Red Sea were meant, then it would have been necessary to cross a considerable tract of desert to get to it.

But if the Reed Sea is not the Red Sea, where was it ? The Exodus account assumes a journey over Egyptian territory to the desert (from Succoth to Etham), then a trek in a backward direction which placed the Reed Sea between the Israelites and the desert, and finally the miraculous crossing of the Sea, followed by the three waterless days in the desert before the bitter waters of Marah were reached (Exod. 15 : 22). In a text describing the wonders of Rameses-Tanis we learn that there were two bodies of water near that city. One was " the water of Horus ", which is the same as the *Shihor* of two Old Testament passages (Isa. 23 : 3 and Jer. 2 : 18). The other was " the Papyrus Marsh ", a name which immediately recalls the biblical " Reed Sea ". (In fact the Egyptian word is the same as the Hebrew *Suph*.) Thus the crossing of the Sea was made at a point not far from Rameses. Since the Suez Canal was constructed, the topography of the district between the Gulf of Suez and Lake Menzaleh on the Mediterranean has been changed somewhat, and at least one lake, the former Lake Balah, has disappeared. The Reed Sea which the Israelites crossed was probably in this area, perhaps at a southern extension of the present Lake Menzaleh.

In biblical times the Pharaohs guarded their eastern frontier with a string of fortresses, none of which can be located with any certainty with the exception of Zilu (Thel), guarding the entry from the main highway to Palestine, " the way of the Land of the Philistines ". The narrative of the crossing of the Sea suggests that the problem of Israel was precisely that of passing safely through these fortresses. After arriving at Succoth and then mov-

ing to the edge of the wilderness at Etham (a place not yet identified), Israel turned back northeastward and encamped " before Pihahiroth, between Migdol and the Sea, before Baal-zephon ". Pihahiroth and Migdol are mentioned in Egyptian inscriptions but are not yet identified with certainty. Baal-zephon, on the other hand, has been located. A Phoenician letter published during World War II mentions the god " Baal-zephon and all the gods of Tahpanhes ". The latter was located at modern Tell Defneh (Greek Daphne) ; it was the Egyptian town to which Jeremiah was taken after the fall of Jerusalem and the murder of Gedaliah (Jer. 43 : 7–9). Baal-zephon was a Canaanite god, and the letter proves that a temple of his existed in this place. The occurrence of the name in the Exodus account is thus in all probability a reference to this temple and to the town which contained it—an additional proof of a northern location of the crossing of the Sea.

The route which Israel followed across Sinai is not entirely clear, and scholars are not agreed as to where Mt. Sinai (or Mt. Horeb) was. Sinai is a triangular peninsula some 260 miles long and 150 miles wide at the north. Along the Mediterranean shore there is a sandy belt of country some fifteen miles deep. To the south of this is a high gravel

33. Mt. Sinai

and limestone plateau stretching southward about 150 miles. Below it is the apex of the peninsula with its mass of granite mountains, the highest of which rise nearly 8000 feet above sea level. Among these mountains are the ancient copper and turquoise mines to which the Egyptians sent regular expeditions. Here also is the traditional site of Mt. Sinai (Figs. 33 and 34), where Moses received the Law and bound the people together into a nation in covenant with its Lord.

A number of scholars today are of the opinion that Mt. Sinai is to be located in ancient Midian, southeast of Edom in Arabia. The chief evidence for this view is the belief that Exod. 19 reflects volcanic activity and that the sacred Mount must be located in a volcanic region. This would lead us to Midian, the only area where such activity is known to have existed. Yet the same data can be viewed as being derived from a great mountain storm, and in any event the Old Testament

34. St. Catherine's Monastery at Mt. Sinai

35. Wadi Feiran in Sinai, showing a palm and tamarisk grove—a site where Israel probably encamped on the way to Mt. Sinai

frequently describes God's appearances in terms taken from such awesome natural phenomena that it is impossible to use them to depict a precise geographical location. Psa. 29 : 6 says that the mountains of Lebanon and Sirion dance like a wild bull at the voice of the Lord, and yet one could not assert on this basis that they must have been volcanic. Indeed we know that they were not.

According to Deut. 1 : 2 the journey from Kadesh-barnea to Mt. Horeb (Sinai) took eleven days, a tradition which may well have been derived from the time needed to traverse an old pilgrimage route. The stations along this route are perhaps preserved in Num. 33, and Elijah may well have followed them (I Kings 19 : 1–8). The traditional location of Mt. Sinai agrees with this route very well indeed. Furthermore, it is extremely difficult to understand why the early Church would have located the sacred spot in the most inaccessible and dangerous area imaginable for pilgrims, especially at a time when the tendency was to do just the opposite, unless the

tradition was so old and firmly fixed that no debate was permitted about it. Finally, a few of the stations can be identified with some degree of probability along the route (cf. Fig. 35) to the southern mountains of Sinai : thus Elim (Exod. 15 : 27 ; Num. 33 : 9) with the oasis of Wadi Gharandel, some sixty-three miles from Suez ; Dophkah (Num. 33 : 12) with the Egyptian mining center at Serabit el-Khadem, because the name seems to mean " smeltery " ; Rephidim near the sacred Mount (Exod. 17 : 1 ; Num. 33 : 14) with Wadi Refayid, etc.

Several details of the story of the wandering in the wilderness have been illustrated by explorers of the peninsula. Thus manna is still produced today in the tamarisk thickets of the valleys of central Sinai. One man may collect over a kilogram a day at the peak of the season in June. It is a honey-like substance, ranging in size from pinhead to pea. It is produced by two species of scale-insect which must suck in large quantities of sap in order to secure the nitrogen they need and then give off what they do not need in the form of a honeydew excretion. Rapid evaporation changes the drops quickly into sticky solids which may be gathered. Needless to say, this manna could not have formed the basic diet of the Israelites, but it did provide needed sugar, the discovery of which in the desert would have been an exciting event.

On two occasions or in two versions of the same occasion the hungry Israelites are said to have fed on flocks of quail which came up from the sea and covered the camp (Exod. 16 : 13 and Num. 11 : 31). Every fall, in September and October, large numbers of quail cross the Mediterranean from Europe to winter in Arabia and Africa. After crossing the sea, they land on the Sinai shore completely exhausted and are easily caught. Presumably, therefore, the " sea " from which they are said to have come in Num. 11 : 31 should be the Mediterranean. During their travels, then, the Israelites must have been along the Mediterranean, unless some unusual climatic circumstance could have forced the birds to land in other areas, as, for example, on the Gulf of Suez or the Gulf of Aqabah.

On occasion also Moses obtained water from a rock by striking it with his rod (Exod. 17 : 6 and Num. 20 : 11). Major C. S. Jarvis, a former British Governor of Sinai, has reported that he has actually seen such a thing happen! The Sinai Camel Corps had halted and were digging for water in the rocky sides of a valley where a slow trickle was coming through the limestone rock. While digging, a lusty blow intended for the gravel struck the rock. The polished hard face of the limestone crumbled, exposing the soft porous rock beneath, whence came a great gush of clear water, much to the astonishment of the whole camel corps. Moses, having lived in Sinai for a considerable time before the Exodus, may well have understood the peculiarities of the limestone rock in certain areas of Sinai.

According to Israelite tradition, Moses married into the family of a Midianite priest, named Jethro by one document, Reuel by another (Exod. 2 : 16 ff. and 18 : 1 ff.). The family of Reuel's son, Hobab, subsequently became Israelite (" come thou with us and we will do thee good "—Num. 10 : 29 and Judges 4 : 11), a family which was called " Kenite ". This name means " smith ", so we take it that some of the Midianites were coppersmiths. Midian was located east and southeast of the Gulf of Aqabah in a region known to abound in copper ore. Copper mines have also been found in the Arabah, the valley leading south from the Dead Sea, as well as in the area of the traditional Mt. Sinai. These mines were worked far more intensively in ancient times than they are today, so we may assume that apart from pastoral pursuits a chief source of livelihood for the inhabitants of Midian and Sinai was the profitable copper business. By 1500 B.C. these semi-nomadic smiths, in the employ of the Egyptian government at the Sinai mines, were using the earliest known alphabet. This was the alphabet which was invented and developed by the Canaanites in Syria, from whom it was subsequently borrowed by both Israelites and Greeks. The smiths of Sinai and Midian, therefore, are not to be considered as a poor and ill-fed people like most of the modern inhabitants of Sinai. They were certainly more prosperous and in closer commercial contact with Egypt and Palestine. In this connection it is interesting to recall that, according to a theory held by a number of biblical scholars during the past half-century, Yahweh (Jehovah), the God who appeared to Moses in the burning bush and declared His intention to become the God of Israel, was originally the tribal God of the Kenites or Midianites, from whom Moses learned the name. The evidence for the theory is, however, very tenuous.

In Israelite encampments in the wilderness after Sinai had been left behind, the focus of attention, we are told, was the portable Tent or Tabernacle wherein was placed the Ark of the Covenant (cf. Fig. 36). Here, it was thought, was God's dwelling-place; here petitions were offered and the assembly met. The descriptions of the Tent and Ark have long been regarded as idealized by the late priestly authors who described them, and it would be most interesting to know more about them. Unfortunately, however, archaeology is unable to help us, since nothing of this sort is known among contemporary peoples. We know very little, though, about the life of such nomadic peoples as the Midianites and Kenites at that time, or for that matter about the life of any of the people in very ancient Arabia. About all we can say is that the predominant use of acacia (rather than the cedar and olivewood used in the Temple of Solomon), goat's hair tent-cloth, ram-skins, and lamb-skins in the construction of the Tabernacle point to nomadic life, and probably represent authentic tradition. In addition, we now know that early Arabs, before the days of Mohammed, possessed sacred portable tents quite comparable to the Tabernacle (cf. Fig. 37). Survivals have persisted until modern times, and

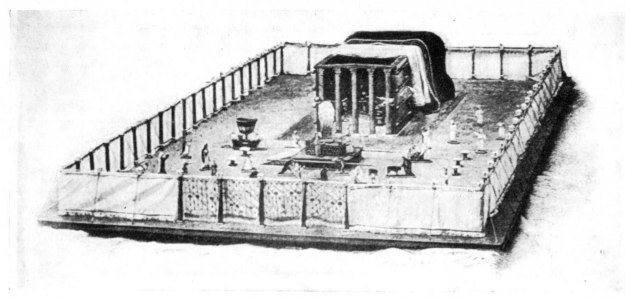

36. A reconstruction of the Tabernacle by Conrad Schick

we hear of certain Arabic tribes possessing a portable object, the function of which was similar to that of the Ark. It is the visible focus of the various clans possessing it, because the god Allah is thought to take pleasure in abiding in it. One explorer reports that if the camel bearing it begins to move, the entire tribe follows it. Where it becomes stationary, the camp is set up. Whenever the tribe is threatened by a powerful enemy and fears defeat, then the sacred object is brought to the battle and with it at the head of the tribe the enemy is attacked.[4]

This description is almost a perfect account of the function of the Ark among the Israelites in the Wandering. It, too, was the visible focus of the tribes. Whenever it moved, Israel moved. When it rested, Israel rested. In battle, the Ark was in the thick of the fray, the rallying point and inspiration of the fighters. Thus we are informed by Num. 10 : 35–6 : " Whenever the ark set forward, Moses said : ' Rise up, O Lord, that thine enemies may be scattered, that those who hate thee may flee before thee.' And whenever it rested, he used to say : ' Return, O Lord, to the many thousands of Israel.' "

Nothing has been said thus far about the number of people involved in the Exodus and the Wandering.

In Num. 1 and 26 are two census lists, the first of which is said by the compiler to be the enumeration made by Moses directly after the Exodus, and the second an enumeration made after the forty years in the wilderness. It has been pointed out that both are probably variations of the same list, originally, and both record the number of males as slightly over 600,000. If women and children are added to this figure, the total population listed by this census would have been between two and three million. It is well known that the Sinai Peninsula could not possibly have accommodated such a tremendous number. Three to five thousand would appear to be a more reasonable figure. The size of the population of Egypt at that time is unknown, though a writer in the 1st century B.C. informs us that in his day it was about 7,000,000. In the greatest battle of his career, that against the Hittites at Kadesh in Syria, Pharaoh Rameses II had an army of four divisions, totalling scarcely more than 20,000 men. If the figures in the book of Numbers, therefore, really represented the actual number involved in the Exodus, the Israelite army of 600,000 warriors should have been able to overcome anything which the Pharaoh put into the field by sheer weight of numbers ! We are faced with the necessity, therefore, of assuming that either the numbers were completely made up by later historians in Israel, or else they represent a census which became misplaced in the records and which really belongs to a later age.

[4] For a possible reference to a portable palladium for the god El of Canaan, see W. F. Albright, " The Furniture of El in Canaanite Mythology ", *Bulletin of the American Schools of Oriental Research*, No. 91 (Oct. 1943), pp. 39–44.

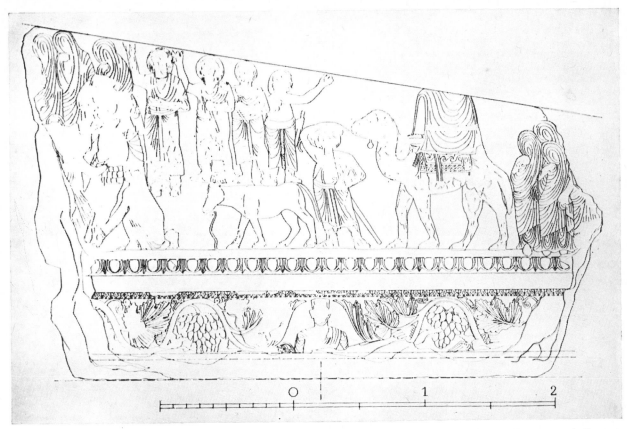

37. A bas-relief portraying a portable tent-shrine, from the temple of Bel at Palmyra (Roman period)

The latter view is the more probable. The one census of all Israel recorded elsewhere is that of David (II Sam. 24). W. F. Albright pointed out some years ago that these lists in Numbers more probably represent the census of David than that of Moses.

Sir Flinders Petrie has offered a very ingenious explanation of the numbers which would solve the problem, if it could be accepted. Instead of translating the Hebrew word for " thousand " as a numeral, he would translate it as " family " or "tent". Thus the number in the tribe of Manasseh in the first list, 32,200, would really mean, he explains, 32 tents for 200 people, or six people per tent or family. The total number involved in the Exodus would thus be reduced to between five and six thousand people, a reasonable figure. This explanation is often quoted by those who seek to retain the reliability of the census lists for the period of Moses. While it is an attractive hypothesis, experts in the Hebrew language have been unable to accept this interpretation of the Hebrew word in question. We must seek another explanation, therefore, as has been suggested above.

We shall reserve a discussion of Mosaic law and religion until Chapter VII, and turn immediately to the Conquest of Canaan.

FURTHER READING

The basic work on the geography of the Nile Delta is that of the British Egyptologist, A. H. Gardiner, for the most part to be found in the *Journal of Egyptian Archaeology*:

" The Delta Residence of the Ramessides ", Vol. 5 (1918), pp. 127–38, 179–200, 242–71.

" The Geography of the Exodus, an answer to Professor Naville and others ", Vol. 10 (1924), pp. 87–96.

See also " The Geography of the Exodus ", in *Recueil d'études égyptologiques dédiées à la mémoire de Jean-François Champollion* (Paris, 1922), pp. 203–15.

FURTHER READING (*continued*)

While these references are not generally accessible except in large libraries, the general results of Gardiner's work can be found summarized in Peet, *Egypt and The Old Testament*, London, 1922.

Since the publication of these works, the city of Raamses has been located by most scholars at Tanis, so that a portion of the results must be modified, as Gardiner has done in part in " Tanis and Pi-Ramesse : a Retraction ", *Journal of Egyptian Archaeology*, Vol. 19 (1933), pp. 122–8.   See also W. F. Albright, *Bulletin of the American Schools of Oriental Research*, No. 109 (Feb. 1948), pp. 15–16, for new information.

For interesting information about Sinai, see :

A. Lucas, *The Route of the Exodus of the Israelites from Egypt*, London, 1938.

C. S. Jarvis, *Yesterday and To-day in Sinai*, Edinburgh and London, 1931.

W. M. F. Petrie, *Researches in Sinai*, London, 1906.

Among older works which are still valuable, Palmer's *The Desert of the Exodus* (1871) and Robinson's *Biblical Researches*, Vol. I (1841), may be mentioned.

For Egyptian background Breasted's *A History of Egypt* (New York, 1912), and Erman's *Life in Ancient Egypt* (London and New York, 1894) are recommended.   The new edition of the latter is more up to date, but it has not been translated from the German into English.

For recent surveys see Albright, *From the Old Stone Age to Christianity* (Baltimore, 3rd ed., 1946), pp. 169, 183–4, 193–6 ; *Archaeology of Palestine and the Bible* (New York, 1935), pp. 143–51 ; John Bright, *A History of Israel* (Philadelphia, 1959), pp. 97–118).

Note, too, Frank M. Cross, Jr., " The Tabernacle ", *The Biblical Archaeologist*, Vol. X, No. 3 (Sept. 1947) ; and F. S. Bodenheimer, " The Manna of Sinai ", *ibid.*, Vol. X, No. 1 (Feb. 1947), pp. 2–6.   Both of these are reprinted in *The Biblical Archaeologist Reader* (ed. by D. N. Freedman and G. E. Wright, Doubleday Anchor Books, 1961), pp. 76–80, 201–28.

CHAPTER V

CONQUEST

" Hear, O Israel : Thou art to cross over the Jordan this day to go in to possess nations greater and mightier than thyself, cities great and fortified up to the heavens. . . ." (Deut. 9 : 1).
" And the Lord was with Judah and he drove out the hill-country people, but he could not drive out those who lived in the plain because they had chariots of iron " (Judges 1 : 19).

THE deliverance from slavery in Egypt and the gift of a good land in which to dwell were to Israel God's greatest acts on her behalf. They were celebrated in song and story and the thrill of them is still to be caught from that small portion of the literature which recalls them from the mists of the past. Moses before Pharaoh, the drama at Mt. Sinai, the continual recalcitrance of the divinely led but doubtfully faithful people, the fall of Jericho, the conquest of Ai, the defeat of the Canaanite alliance, all contain exceptional material for narration, no matter what the historical and theological problems involved.

The books of Joshua, Judges, and Samuel carry the story from triumph to triumph, until even the greatest of Canaanite walled fortresses were destroyed (Lachish about 1220 B.C., Megiddo, Bethshan, Jerusalem, and finally Gezer shortly after 1000), until in the reign of David the prophecy of Noah was fulfilled : Canaan was the " servant " of Shem (Gen. 9 : 25-6). Jacob's blessing and Balaam's prophecy had both been realized : the stars of Jacob had prevailed ; David ruled in the midst of the nations (Num. 24 : 17 and Gen. 49 : 10)!

The Book of Joshua is one part of a History of Israel in the Promised Land which extends through the books of Judges, Samuel and Kings. Because the compiler of this great work was heavily influenced by the theology of Deuteronomy and incorporated that book in his work as an introduction to his history, he has been called the " Deuteronomic Historian ". When older documents were available, he quoted from them extensively, as in I and II Samuel. In other places, he composed freely from such sources of information and tradition as he had. The story of the Conquest of Canaan in Joshua is largely his own composition, though it has been seen to rest on still older written, and perhaps oral, material. His view of the Conquest was that a long and drawn-out struggle took place, but that ultimate success was possible only

because of an initial, spectacular and successful campaign led by Joshua. This campaign was carried out in three phases : (1) the securing of a foothold in the central hill country, accomplished through the capture of Jericho and Ai, and the Gibeonite alliance (Josh. 6-9) ; (2) the campaign in the south which avoided Jerusalem but took the rest of the territory later occupied by the tribe of Judah (Chap. 10) ; and (3) a campaign in Galilee which, though successful in gaining territory, actually destroyed none of the fortified cities except Hazor (Chap. 11).

The impression given is that the whole country was completely devastated and subjugated. Scholars have long pointed to Chap. 1 of the Book of Judges, however, as providing an entirely different picture, in which the individual tribes bear the responsibility for conquering their respective territories. Instead of a single, united campaign under Joshua, the seizure of the land was a long process, accomplished not by Joshua but by a series of struggles on the part of the individual tribes. In choosing between the two versions, most scholars in the past have assumed that the older material in Judges 1 is the more reliable, while the later account in Joshua must be largely discredited as an exaggeration, to say the least.

It has now become necessary, however, to modify the common scholarly view. For one thing, a closer reading of the Deuteronomic historian's work in Joshua makes it quite clear that while he claims spectacular success in overrunning the country for Joshua, he is quite aware of much left to be done (cf. 11 : 13, 22). In fact, in Chap. 13 he lists the chief areas left to be conquered. He believed that by the power of God great deeds had been accomplished ; yet many of the inhabitants had been left in the country in order to test Israel (Judges 2 : 20-3), and perhaps in order to keep the wild animals from multiplying until they got out of control (Deut. 7 : 22). Furthermore, it is now apparent that Judges 1 is not an old, unified account of the original Conquest. From the standpoint of territorial history it must be seen as a collection of miscellaneous fragments of varying dates and of varying reliability.

In any view of the Conquest which we reconstruct it is now necessary to take into account two different groups of archaeological data. One group suggests a major and violent disturbance in 13th-century Palestine which brought an end to several important Canaanite cities. The other group of data is from the period of the Israelite " Judges " during the 12th and 11th centuries. It indicates that this age was one of the most disturbed and chaotic in the country's history. Every town thus far excavated was destroyed from one to four times, at least, during these two centuries. Yet so far few of the destructions can be correlated with one another ; and this suggests precisely what the Book of Judges implies : namely, that the fighting was continuous and largely local in nature.

When we put the historical and archaeological data together, we arrive at a view somewhat as follows : There was an Israelite campaign of great violence and success during the 13th century. Its purpose was to destroy the existing Canaanite city-state system, weakening local power to such an extent that new settlement, especially in the hill country, might be possible. In the centuries that followed, however, there was not only the necessity of reducing unconquered city-states but also of continuous struggle with many of the inhabitants who, though their major centres of power had been reduced, still were able to offer resistance to Israelite clans encroaching on their territory. Actually, it is difficult to conceive of the Conquest and settlement as having taken place in any other manner, for the historical geography of the land, together with the archaeological data, makes it now impossible to agree with former scholars who conceived the Conquest to be nothing more than a gradual process of osmosis. On the other hand, it is scarcely surprising to read that up to the time of Israel's first king, Saul, the nation had been able to occupy only the major portion of Palestine's central ridge or hill country, together with a part of Transjordan, areas which had always been difficult for outsiders to control. The invaders were unequipped for siege operations, and they were unable at first to get control of such fortresses as Beth-shan, Taanach, and Megiddo in the great northern plain of Esdraelon, or of Dor and Gezer,

guarding ascents to the hill country along the coast (Judges 1 : 27 ff.). Israelite successes were largely due to surprise attacks. Accustomed to fight on foot, with no weapons but bow, slings, staves, stones, and a few swords and spears, they were weak in pitched battles in the open, where formidable chariots could manoeuvre. Hence the statement that Judah " could not drive out those who lived in the plain because they had chariots of iron " (Judges 1 : 19). This weakness in Israelite tactics was carefully explained to the King of Damascus by his officers at a much later date. The God of the Israelites, they said, " is a god of the hills . . . let us fight them in the plain " (I Kings 20 : 23) !

THE CONQUEST IN ITS HISTORICAL SETTING

Throughout the Near East between 1500 and 1200 B.C. there was a hum of closely interrelated political, religious, and commercial activity. The cities along the Syro-Palestinian coastline must have presented a cosmopolitan appearance. Personal names found in letters and business accounts unearthed in these regions, as well as the variety of scripts and languages employed, inform us that the native Canaanite rubbed shoulders daily with Hittites of Asia Minor, Hurrians (Horites) of the Upper Euphrates, Amorites, close kin of the Israelites, Egyptians, Assyrians, Babylonians, and even Indo-Europeans from the region of Persia. Occasional Greek islanders and Cyprians were to be seen : at least Greek and Cypriot wares arrived by the ship load. Undoubtedly, there were people who were proud of their learning and glad to be alive for such a day.

Thus we must conceive of the movement of Hebrew tribes from their nomadic existence into the settled areas of urban and agrarian activity, as a movement of uncultured " barbarians " into scenes of self-conscious civilization. The people of Israel were never productive in the arts and refinements which make living easier and more luxurious. These they but imperfectly absorbed from their neighbors, while their own contribution to civilization was to be far more permanent and significant. Small wonder, therefore, that the first Israelite towns were so poor and straggly that it is difficult to excavate them !

The first reference to Israel outside the Bible was made by Pharaoh Merneptah about 1220 B.C. In the fifth year of his reign this king set up a monumental stone (Fig. 38) (*stele*) on which was a hymn of victory, relating the great deeds he had accomplished. He wrote (or rather one of his specialists wrote for him) in poetry:

Libya is ruined,	Khatti (Hittite-land) is pacified;
The Canaanite land is despoiled	with every evil.
Ashkelon is carried captive;	Gezer is conquered;
Yanoam is made	as though it did not exist.
The people of Israel is desolate,	it has no offspring;
Palestine has become	a widow for Egypt.[1]

The way " Israel " is written in the Egyptian here indicates that a people was being mentioned who were not yet a settled nation, yet nevertheless sufficiently dangerous to be mentioned as an enemy of Pharaoh. Of course, the latter was indulging in hyperbole for propaganda purposes (like some modern war *communiqués*), for subsequent events proved that Israel was far from desolate and without offspring.

The significance of this mention of Israel is that by 1220 B.C. a group which was to give its name to the nation was already in its later home, though not yet a settled nation. On the other hand, it was pointed out in the last chapter that if Israelites had anything to do with Egyptian royal work projects in the cities Pithom and Raamses (Exod. 1 : 11), some of them must have been still in Egypt at least during the early years of Pharaoh Rameses II (1290–1224). Consequently, the most reasonable hypothesis is that the Exodus under Moses occurred sometime during the first half of the 13th century.

Between the Exodus and the Conquest was the period of the Wandering in the wildernesses of Sinai, Paran, and Zin, a period which was thought to have covered a generation (about 40 years, said the tradition, but that is merely a round number used for a generation). In the last chapter we left the Israelites in the middle of their wandering because we do not know the exact itinerary or the order of events along it. According to the story as it stands, it seems that the Israelites left Sinai and headed straight for Canaan with the avowed purpose of storming it from the south, *via* Beersheba and Hebron (see Fig. 32). Failing in this

38. *Stele* of Merneptah which mentions his defeat of Israel

(Num. 13–14), they fell back on Kadesh-barnea in the wilderness of Zin and spent most of the period of their wandering in that area. There are three main springs which could have served their needs, one of which still preserves the ancient name of " Kadesh ". By far the best, however, is Ain el-Qudeirat which waters a small and fruitful valley (Fig. 39); its ancient name was perhaps Hazar-addar. It was in this general area that Moses had to cope with one rebellion after another, until morale was so low that conquest was impossible.

After considerable time, it was decided, so the story goes, to go through Transjordan and attempt

[1] Translation by W. F. Albright; cf. also J. A. Wilson in *Ancient Near Eastern Texts* (ed. by J. B. Pritchard), p. 378. Ashkelon and Gezer were important cities in southern Palestine, the former on the coast north of Gaza, the latter near the coastal plain as one leaves the hill country on the way from Jerusalem to Joppa. Yanoam was an important Canaanite city in Galilee, north of Lake Huleh in the Jordan valley.

39. Ain el-Qudeirat, near Kadesh-barnea

to storm the land of Canaan from the east instead of from the south. Messengers were sent to the king of Edom (Num. 20 : 14 ff.) asking permission to cross through his territory *via* "the King's Highway". This is a reference to the old highway through Transjordan, used, for example, by the four kings of Gen. 14 in their raid upon the Cities of the Plain. Modern explorers have traced this highway all the way from Aqabah on the eastern arm of the Red Sea, through Edom, Moab, Gilead, Bashan, into Syria. It was paved by the Romans, and is now constructed anew by the Government of Jordan. Israel promised to keep to this highway, turning neither to the right nor to the left, and paying for all food and drink. Permission was refused, and the Israelites made no attempt to force the matter. Their exact itinerary is somewhat obscure, but they seem to have travelled along the western border of Edom in the deep rift of the Arabah, crossing eastward at the northern border at or near the River Zered (modern Wadi el-Hesa).[2] Moab was likewise circumvented, on its eastern or desert border, until the Arnon river

was reached. Standing between them and the Jordan was the kingdom of Sihon, stretching from the Arnon to the Jabbok river ; and Sihon, likewise refusing passage along the King's Highway, was the first victim of the conquest. The battle of Jahaz, the first great Israelite triumph, was celebrated in song and proverb, of which a snatch is preserved in Num. 21 : 27–30. Og, celebrated giant-king of Bashan, whose kingdom north of the Jabbok had capitals at Edrei and Ashtaroth, was next on the list, and was defeated in the Battle of Edrei. Thus the first phase of the Conquest was completed with Israel in possession of Trans-

[2] Two different routes are preserved in the Pentateuch. The Priestly editors of Numbers suggest the route here described. This we know from the presence in their list of Punon (a mining town, modern *Feinan*) on the eastern edge of the northern part of the Arabah (Num. 33 : 43). The Elohist (Num. 21 : 4) and Deuteronomic writers (Deut. 2 : 1–8), however, preserve the tradition of a different route, Israel going southward all the way to Ezion-geber on the Gulf of Aqabah in order to go around Edom on the east by ascending the pass of the *Wadi Yitm*. Of course, both traditions may have had a basis in fact, for not all the people need to have gone the same way. Yet this is something which we have no means of checking.

jordanian territory between the River Arnon and the land of Bashan, the Kingdoms of Moab and Edom, however, having been left intact.

The archaeologist, Nelson Glueck, spent the better part of the decade between 1930 and 1940 in exploring Transjordan, an area which had been inadequately known until that time. By examining hundreds of ancient sites and dating the time of their occupation by means of the broken fragments of pottery still to be found on them he has been able to chart the boundaries of the ancient kingdoms of Ammon, Moab, and Edom. He has also discovered the important fact that they were not founded before the 13th century. For some six hundred years before that time the inhabitants of that territory had apparently lived a roving, nomadic existence, and did not settle in towns. Then quite suddenly, between 1300 and 1100 B.C., towns sprang up all over Southern Transjordan. According to the biblical narrative, the kingdoms of Moab and Edom were already in existence at the time of the Conquest, and thus, it would appear, we have another indication that the date of Moses could not be before the 13th century. It has been argued that the Edomites, Moabites, Ammonites, and Amorites at the time of the Conquest may well have been nomadic and that Glueck's discoveries in no way preclude a date *earlier* than the 13th century since nomadic peoples leave few discoverable remains. Such an assumption, however, is against the implication of the biblical narrative. In addition, some of the towns mentioned in the story of the Conquest were evidently founded in the period in question: for example, *Heshbon*, the capital of Sihon, *Mattanah* (Num. 21:19, probably modern *el-Medeiyineh*), one of the cities through which the Israelites passed, and *Jazer* (Num. 21:32), to which Moses sent spies after the defeat of Sihon.

After the defeat of Og, the book of Numbers continues with the story of the unhappy Balaam (Chaps. 22–4). Balak, king of Moab, apparently became worried over Israelite successes. Being unable to do anything more effective, he called in a specialist to curse Israel, thinking that the latter might be halted by magical means. The name of the specialist was Balaam, and to secure his aid Balak had to send to far-away Pethor, " which is by the River (Euphrates) ", a town which has been identified by inscriptions as lying in the Upper Euphrates region. It has been pointed out that the activities of Balaam are well illustrated by the activities of the Mesopotamian diviner, or *baru*. Babylonians, far more concerned about this life than the Egyptians whose thoughts continually turned to the after-life, developed elaborate methods of divining and predicting by omens of every conceivable kind. During the second millennium this art and the diviners themselves spread everywhere; the personal seal of one of them has been found at Beth-shan in Palestine. A special ritual was developed, and every act of divination had to follow the rules or else results might not come out right. Thus in the morning, we are told, Balaam told Balak to prepare seven altars and seven sacrifices, whereupon both offered a sacrifice on each altar. Then Balak was told to stay by the sacrifices while Balaam determined the omen, that is, the divine word. Each detail of the story follows what we know to have been the diviner's rules, even to the time of day, for best results were thought to be obtained in the morning before the rise of the sun. The first divination did not succeed, or at least the answer came out wrong as far as Balak was concerned. So they went to another place that might provide more favourable results (23:13). The procedure was repeated, but the omen was the same. A third attempt was made. The number three played a very important role in Babylonian magic, and Balak would not give up before a third trial had been made. They went to another place, repeated the performance, but suddenly Balaam gave up the divination (24:1), perhaps for fear he might lose his reputation as a diviner, and he began to utter prophecies. The result of it all was that Balak was much disgusted and refused to pay the promised fee. The story is quite understandable when Balaam is studied as a Babylonian *baru*. Small wonder that he became a classic example of everything a man should not be (cf. II Peter 2:15, Jude vs. 11, and Revelation 2:14); magic could have no effect on the plans of the God of Israel.

The land of Canaan at this time was an Egyptian province organized on the city-state system. The larger cities, each ruled by a native king or " governor ", were able to control a certain amount of the territory around them (Figs. 40–2). The local " governors " were not molested as long as they paid their tribute and contributed their part to royal projects where compulsory labour was required. A type of feudal system was in force. The local princes were supported by chariotry manned by patricians (comparable to medieval knights) and by footmen of the plebeian or serf class. We know from excavations that the center of a typical city was the palace of the local king, while all about were the huts, often little more than hovels, of the serfs or common people. Because the prince had absolute control over his subjects, he was able to form compulsory labor battalions and build around the city tremendous fortifications, so that the cities appeared to Israelites, at least, as " fortified up to heaven " (Deut. I : 28 ; cf. Num. 13 : 28).

Charged with raising the tribute and in general with overseeing the work on Crown projects were the Egyptian commissioners, or " inspectors ", who usually had available contingents of troops, mostly slave or mercenary. Egyptian bureaucracy, however, was notoriously corrupt, and the administration exceedingly bad under the weak Pharaohs, and exceedingly oppressive, in all probability, at any time. At any rate, disturbances were apparently common, and excavations in towns of the period show that conditions must have become steadily worse. Population became thinner ; houses, tombs, fortifications, and standards of art became poorer. This inner weakness and cor-

ruption, then, may furnish a partial explanation of the ability of the Israelites to obtain a foothold in a country controlled by their former masters.

Our most important source of information about Canaan during the era in question is a series of letters, some three hundred and fifty in number, found in the archives of the palace of Pharaoh Amenophis IV (Akhnaton, *ca.* 1377–1360 B.C.) at

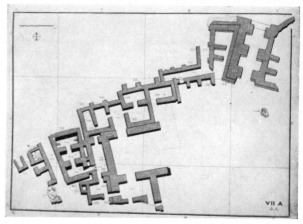

40. City-gate and palace of the Canaanite king of Megiddo about 1200 B.C. (Stratum VIIA)

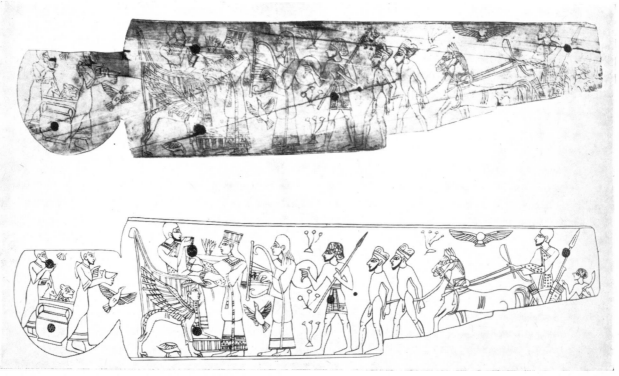

41. One of the ivories from Megiddo, showing a Canaanite king seated on his cherub-throne, his queen, a musician playing a lyre, and captives

42. Foundations of the large temple-fortress at Megiddo, dating from the 16th–13th centuries.　One similar to it, though even more massive, has been found at Shechem

Tell el-Amarna in Egypt.　The original discovery was made by an Egyptian peasant woman in 1887; and since that time many more have been found, including a few from the ruins of Palestinian cities. The letters were written, for the most part, by Asiatic kings and officials to the Egyptian court. Those from Canaan reveal such a chaotic state of plot, counterplot, and contradictory accusation that it is virtually impossible to tell truth from falsehood.　A number of the letters complain about trouble from a people called *Hapiru* (pronounced in Canaan *'Apiru*), a word connected in some way with " Hebrew " (see Chap. III).　Many scholars in the past have interpreted these letters to mean that a great invasion from the desert was taking place, an invasion to be connected in some way with the Hebrew conquest of Palestine.[3]　Recent students of the letters, however, claim that there is within them no evidence whatever of such an invasion.　The *'Apiru* are considered in the letters as " bandits " or lawless gangs, a number of them, at least, ill-paid mercenaries who were joined by an increasing number of people from the oppressed population.　In addition, the term is applied by local kings to neighboring kings and their armies who are seizing land and towns.　The king of Byblos, for example, assumes that anyone who takes his land is an enemy of Pharaoh and calls those who do so *'Apiru*.　Yet those thus named write to Pharaoh, protesting their loyalty.　In this case, the name is used as a base accusation, like the modern tendency to call someone disliked a communist.　It is impossible, therefore, to see any evidence of a great invasion or to connect the disturbances with the Israelite entry into Palestine, because the *'Apiru* were already within the land and were not new invaders.　The letters nowhere contain reference to an invasion; the attackers labelled *'Apiru* were people of other city-states.[4]

[3] H. H. Rowley, *From Joseph to Joshua* (London, 1950), believes that the Patriarchal movement of the Jacob family into Palestine is to be dated this late and to be related with the *'Apiru* of the Amarna period (see especially his Chap. III). On the other hand, T. J. Meek, *Hebrew Origins* (New York and London, 2nd ed., 1950), believes that the letters reflect, in part at least, the invasion of Joshua, though he believes Moses' entry into Palestine was a century and one-half later (see his Chap. I).

[4] This paragraph is based upon an unpublished study of Prof. George E. Mendenhall; see further M. Greenberg, *The Hab/piru* (New Haven, American Oriental Society, 1955); and J. Bottéro, *Le problème des Habiru* (*Cahiers de la Société Asiatique*, XII, 1954).

The studies of W. F. Albright on the political geography of the Amarna period have shown that about 1375 B.C. there were four main city-states in southern Palestine.[5] These were (1) Gezer, (2) Jerusalem, (3) Lachish, and (4) the territory of a king named Shuwardata who ruled the central " Judean " area, presumably from Hebron. In addition, Jarmuth seems just beginning to play a minor independent role, while Eglon was the seat of an Egyptian resident or commissioner with an Egyptian garrison. In the book of Joshua (Chaps. 10–12), however, this area contains no less than *nine* city-states : Gezer, Jerusalem, Lachish, Hebron, Jarmuth, Eglon, Makkedah, Libnah and Debir. The city-wall of the last mentioned site (modern Tell Beit Mirsim) was not erected in this period before the latter part of the fourteenth century. Hence from the standpoint of political geography it is impossible to connect the Book of Joshua with the Amarna period. We must turn instead to the thirteenth century by which time the power of the large, older city-states had been reduced, and the number of such states increased, perhaps with Egyptian aid under a policy of " divide and conquer ".

At this point we may pause to recall the geographical factor in the Conquest. The central portion of Western Palestine is rugged and hilly, rising in some places to a height of 3600 feet above sea-level. This ridge, a continuation of the same one which produces the Lebanon mountains to the north, is composed of soft limestone which is so absorbent as to cause a scarcity of surface water for human consumption. Bordering the ridge to the west is the great Maritime Plain along the shores of the Mediterranean. To the east is the deep cleft of the Jordan Valley, caused by a geological fault which extends from Asia Minor into Africa. To the north the ridge is broken by the broad plain of Esdraelon, connected with the Jordan by the valley of Jezreel. This plain was one of the great wheat fields of ancient times (an Egyptian royal granary at the time of the Conquest), and contained such well known biblical towns as Megiddo, Taanach, Engannim, Shunem, and Jezreel. Eastern Palestine, or Transjordan, is a plateau, some 2000 feet above sea level on the average, sloping off with no distinguishable barrier into the Arabian desert-wilderness.

Israel obtained its foothold in the central ridge or hill country in Western Palestine and in Gilead across the Jordan. Neither of these localities was a center of settled civilization. The cultural center of Palestine from the earliest times lay in the plain along the coast, in Esdraelon, and along the Jordan. As far as we know at the moment, the first major cities in the hill country were Jerusalem and Ai, founded shortly before 3000 B.C.[6] But from this time on until the days of the Judges the hill country was sparsely populated. In all probability, it was thickly wooded with areas where grazing was profitable for cattle, sheep, and goats. The Patriarchs wandered up and down this central ridge with their flocks and herds ; and the men of the Joseph tribes were told to make room for themselves in Mt. Ephraim by clearing the forest (Josh. 17 : 15). During the period of the Judges all this was changed, as we shall have occasion to note again in the next chapter.[7] The Hebrews, then, obtained their " living space " in the civilized world in those areas which were sparsely populated and difficult for others to control.

It was noted above that there were three main phases to the Conquest of Western Palestine as described in Joshua : a foothold gained on the central ridge with the capture of Jericho and Ai, a Judean campaign and a Galilean campaign. *Curiously enough, not a word is said about a conquest of central Palestine.*[8] This was an important region. It was where the Joseph tribes, Ephraim and Manasseh, settled. It was the territory occupied in later times by the Northern Kingdom, and the scene of the prophetic activity of Elijah, Elisha, Amos, and Hosea. The capital of this region in early times was Shechem, situated between Mt. Ebal and Mt. Gerizim, a city which we know from excavations to have been a mighty one indeed (cf. Fig. 43). And while we hear nothing about Joshua conquering this city, yet it was the scene

---

[5] Cf. *Bulletin of the American Schools of Oriental Research*, No. 87 (Oct. 1942), pp. 32–8.

[6] Recent excavations of Tell el-Far'ah, northeast of Shechem (perhaps biblical Tirzah), shows that it, too, was an important city, established probably in the middle or first half of the fourth millennium. Other cities, such as Gezer, Jericho, Megiddo, Beth-shan, and Khirbet Kerak, were founded at the same time or earlier, but none of them are along the central Palestinian ridge.

[7] The intensive settlement of the hill country was made possible, from a technical standpoint, by the invention of slaked-lime plaster for cisterns (see p. 185.)

[8] The only exception is the mention of the defeat of certain kings belonging to the area in Joshua 12 : 17, 18, and 24. The source and nature of the list of kings in Chap. 12 is not entirely clear, though it is easily shown that not all of their towns were captured : e.g. Jerusalem, Gezer, and Megiddo. The list is apparently a summary compilation from different sources of tradition : e.g. it mentions the defeat of the kings of both Ai and Bethel (vss. 9 and 16 ; see below).

43. The plain of Shechem, taken from Mt. Gerizim, showing the enclosure of Jacob's well at the foot of the mountain, the ruins of the ancient city in the valley at the extreme left, and Mt. Ebal rising immediately beyond it with the village of Askar on its lower slopes

of the gathering of all the tribes for the covenant ceremonies described in Josh. 8 : 30–5, after the capture of Ai (cf. Deut. 27), and in Josh. 24, after the Conquest was completed.

What is the explanation of this curious situation? Could it be that the Israelites had friends or relatives in this area who were already in control of it and with whom they were able to make a covenant?

Most scholars believe that this was the case. In control of Shechem at that time, they believe, were Hebrews who had never been in Egypt and, therefore, who did not take part in the Exodus, or else they had been a part of an *earlier* exodus. Perhaps they had been in Egypt with the Hyksos, or were a part of the Hyksos movement, and settled in this area when the foreign rulers were driven out of Egypt about 1550 B.C. Judah and Israel in later times were always very conscious of the differences between them, and it is possible that these differences had their origin at this time.

The actual facts of the situation may never be known, but there are various hints that Shechem may have been held by those who were not a part of the main Exodus under Moses. We know, for example, that a century before Joshua the whole Shechem area was in the control of people who paid no more respect to Pharaoh and their neighbors than was absolutely necessary. This information is furnished us by the Tell el-Amarna letters mentioned above. Shechem's king at the time was a man named Lab'ayu, who controlled a large section of the hill country from his capital city. His communications with the Egyptian king, like those from other kings, were written in Babylonian but were so full of Canaanite words and phrases that they might as well have been written in his native tongue. Protected by the wooded highlands of his area, he was able to adopt a truculent tone which is rather unusual in the letters. He even quoted to the king an old Canaanite proverb about the ant :

77

" If even ants are smitten, they do not accept it (passively) but they bite the hand of the man who smites them " (cf. the proverbs about the same insect in Prov. 6 : 6 and 30 : 25). After he had been murdered by his enemies, his sons were able to carry on in the same manner.

Beginning in 1956 the Drew–McCormick–American Schools of Oriental Research Expedition to Shechem, under the writer's archaeological direction, began the delicate process of dating the ruins exposed by earlier expeditions, which in 1913–14 and between 1926 and 1932 had worked at the site without the benefit of modern archaeological method. We were able to interpret and to date a great double line of fortifications with two city gates as having been erected during the Hyksos period and violently destroyed by the Egyptians *ca.* 1550 B.C., as they took over the Hyksos empire by conquest. From the 17th century, if not earlier, through the Late Bronze Age (1500–1200 B.C.) the city was clearly the strongest and the dominant one of the whole area from the territory of Jerusalem and Gezer on the south to Megiddo in the plain of Jezreel on the north. Furthermore the evidence appears clear that there was no destruction during the 13th century. The greatest break in the city's history after 1550 B.C. appears to have been nearer 1100 B.C. than in the time of Joshua. The great temple of the " Lord of the Covenant " (cf. Fig. 42) was erected about 1650 B.C. and continued in use into the Israelite period before its destruction by Abimelech in the period of the Judges according to the story preserved in Judges 9. If this temple had been considered a purely pagan structure of Israel's enemies, one would have thought that Joshua would have destroyed it, as he had destroyed temples at Lachish and Hazor.

In any event, it has long been realized that Gen. 34 has behind it a tradition of a Hebrew relationship with Shechem which relates to early events not necessarily altered by the Sojourn and Exodus. Even during the Sojourn the city must have been under Hebrew control ; that is, a mixed Canaanite-Hebrew group of clans may have been united by covenant, worshipping a deity called " Baal-berith " (" Lord of the Covenant " ; see Judges 8 : 33 ; cf. 9 : 46), and preserving the memory of a relationship with the Israelite movement. Otherwise we would be at a loss to explain such a tradition as that in Josh. 24. There Joshua seals the covenant with a united Israel, involving the putting away of idols ; and the ceremony took

44. Air view of the mound of Jericho

place in a city which he had not had to conquer. It seems likely that in this ceremony people who had not been involved in the original Sinai covenant there accepted its conditions and its God as their own. Only in some such manner could a united Israel with a common national heritage have come into being.

THE FALL OF JERICHO

Squarely in the path of any invader of the hill country from the southern portion of the Jordan Valley lay the fortress of Jericho (Fig. 44). The account in the Bible tells us that its destruction by the Israelites was an act of God. He it was who caused the city to fall down after seven days of solemn procession around it on the part of his people (Josh. 6). Whatever the physical cause, we now know that the city underwent a terrible destruction or a series of destructions during the second millennium B.C., and remained virtually unoccupied for generations (cf. Joshua's curse, Josh. 6 : 26, and I Kings 16 : 34).

Jericho has been extensively excavated, so extensively in fact that it would be difficult to find a sizable area which is entirely undisturbed. The first excavators there were German scholars, Sellin and Watzinger, who worked at the site between 1908 and 1910. Between 1930 and 1936 an English expedition, under the direction of Professor John Garstang, carried out further excavations with exceedingly important discoveries. It was learned that the town was founded in the latter part of the Stone Age, before the invention of pottery, and is thus the oldest town in Palestine which has thus far been excavated.

For the period in which we are here concerned Garstang believed that he had found ample evidence of Joshua's destruction. He labelled the city of the 15th century "City D". He believed it to have been provided with a strong double wall of brick which encircled the summit of the mound. The inner of the two walls was some twelve feet thick; and was built upon the earlier wall of "City B" (about 2500 B.C.). The outer fortification was six feet thick. And the two together replaced the massive stone bastion with brick rampart which had been erected below against the slopes of the mound for the protection of "City C" of Middle Bronze Age II (17th and 16th centuries).

The excavator described the evidence for a violent destruction of the "City D" walls. The bricks had toppled down the slopes. Layers of burnt brick, gray ash, wall plaster, streaks and pockets of charcoal, were witness to a great conflagration. The tilting of the base of the outer

45. A jar of grain, from *ca.* the 16th century, found at Jericho

wall suggested a disturbance by earthquake, which may have been the act of God referred to in the Book of Joshua. Inside the city burned debris was as much as two feet thick in places, and the remains of foodstuffs, including jars full of grain, suggested that the city had been destroyed shortly after the harvest had been gathered.

On the mound above the spring was found the only evidence for a stratification of the ruins between the Iron and Middle Bronze Ages (that is, from the Israelite period back through the period of Joshua into the 16th and 17th centuries). A very heavily-built, long-roomed building had been found there by the German excavators. It was improperly called a "hilani" building, after a type of architecture designated by that name in Syria. Actually, it is more probably to be interpreted as a granary (Hebrew *miskeneth*, I Kings 9 : 19), judging from several similar structures found elsewhere in Palestine, as W. F. Albright has shown. All of them, including this one at Jericho, date from the tenth or ninth centuries. It was so strongly built, presumably to keep moisture and rodents from the grain, that it preserved some structures below it from erosion. Garstang excavated beneath it a strong structure which he called the "Blockhouse" or "Middle Building", and below that the storage rooms or houses of the 17th–16th centuries.

From the latest pieces of pottery found in the area of the "Middle Building" and in three tombs, Garstang believed that the city was destroyed by Joshua not later than about 1385 B.C. He came to the view that the "Middle Building" represented a reoccupation of the site after that date. W. F. Albright, the present writer, and recently Miss Kathleen Kenyon have independently concluded that the latest pottery of the "Joshua era" is best dated during the second half of the fourteenth century.

From 1952 through 1958 an expedition of the British School of Archaeology worked anew at Jericho, under the direction of Kathleen Kenyon. They found a great deal more evidence for the earliest occupation of the site, including a stone city-wall erected before the invention of pottery, the earliest city fortification known (Fig. 9). Yet a surprising result of the work so far has been the discovery that virtually nothing remains at the site from the period between 1500 and 1200 B.C. The mound has suffered such extensive denudation that almost all remains later than the 3rd millennium B.C. have disappeared from its top. The two walls which surrounded the summit of the old city, which Garstang ascribed to his " City D " and which he believed were destroyed by earthquake and fire in Joshua's time, were discovered to date from the 3rd millennium and to represent only two of some fourteen different walls or wall-components built successively during that age.

These results mean that the many pages written during the last three decades on the date of Jericho's fall to Joshua, and on the question as to whether Joshua could have taken the city at all if it fell in the fourteenth century, are all now outmoded. The work of Miss Kenyon and her associates has shown that the evidence is far too scanty for us to ascertain the nature of the city conquered or the date of its fall. All that remains which can be assigned with any confidence to the period between 1400 and 1200 B.C. are a few pieces of pottery from three tombs and from the area above the spring, and perhaps the " Middle Building ". An inference would be that whatever was there at the time was hardly the imposing city envisaged from the earlier excavations. If the settlement of Joshua's time had a fortification wall at all, it would probably have been a re-use of the 16th-century bastion, though of such re-use there is no evidence. The Jericho of Joshua's day may have been little more than a fort. It was the first victory in Western Palestine for the invaders, however, and the memory of the great city that once stood there undoubtedly influenced the manner in which the event was later related. Yet such remarks are nothing more than suggestions, because at the moment we must confess a complete inability to explain the origin of the Jericho tradition.

THE FALL OF BETHEL-AI

According to the biblical story, the first city to be taken in the hill country proper by Joshua was Ai. This was done by strategy, whereupon it was burned and " made a tell (mound of ruins) forever " (Josh. 8 : 28).

But here we have an account which furnishes further difficulties. Ai has been excavated, and it has been found to have been a small flourishing town, heavily fortified, between the 33rd and 24th centuries B.C. The chief structure within it was a fine temple, beautifully built and the tremendous walls were its protection. So small a site with such a building and such fortifications suggests that here was the religious focus of a league of city states, a Palestinian parallel to the roughly contemporary Sumerian league in lower Mesopotamia whose religious center was Nippur. About 2400 B.C. it was entirely destroyed and was not again inhabited until an Israelite settlement was erected about 1000

46. The modern village on the site of ancient Bethel, looking west

B.C. That means that the city had been in ruins for over a thousand years before the Conquest. In fact, the very name of the site in Hebrew means " The Ruin ", and the real name of the original city is not known for certain, though it is thought by some to have been Beth-aven. How, then, are we to explain the story in the Bible?

Three main theories have been presented. (1) One is that the story was entirely invented at a later date to explain the presence of the ruin. Later Israelites viewing the site might naturally come to the conclusion that Joshua destroyed it because his was the only great conquest about which they knew. (2) The second is that the people of Bethel, a mile and a half away, temporarily occupied Ai in order to check the advance of invaders. The trouble with this theory is that the " king of Ai " is mentioned several times in Josh. 8, and we are expressly told that Joshua hanged him " on a tree until eventide "! (3) By far the most probable theory is that of Professor Albright which is a combination of the other two. This is to the effect that the story of the Conquest of Bethel was transferred at a later time to the old " Ruin " (Ai) near by to explain the latter's existence. We know that Bethel continued as a town while Ai remained in ruins. In support of this view is the fact that the book of Joshua does not contain a story of the capture of Bethel, though the memory of its destruction is preserved in Judges 1 : 22–6 (cf. also Josh. 12 : 16). Certainly we should expect Bethel to fall before the Gibeonites made their league (Josh. 9).

In any event Bethel was standing at that time (Fig. 46), a very prosperous city, as excavations in 1934, directed by Professor Albright, and contiuned by J. L. Kelso between 1955 and 1960, have shown. Sometime during the 13th century the city was destroyed by a tremendous conflagration. It was the privilege of the writer to participate in the first excavation, and even for a beginner in the field of archaeology there was absolutely no mistaking the evidences of by far the worst destruction which the city experienced in all its history. In some places the debris of fallen walls and charred, ash-filled earth was almost five feet thick. The Canaanite city destroyed was a fine one with excellent houses, paved or plastered floors and drains. Compared with them the poor straggly houses of the next town were poverty itself. The break between the two is so complete that there can be no doubt but that this was the Israelite destruction.

THE JUDEAN CAMPAIGN

If Joshua were to lead a campaign against the territory later occupied by Judah, a campaign which avoided and isolated the strong city-states of Jerusalem and Gezer, then we must admit that Josh. 10 describes precisely the way he should have done it. The strength of this territory lay in the fortress cities of the Judean lowlands or Shephelah, between the central ridge and the coastal plain. When Sennacherib and Nebuchadnezzar invaded Judah centuries later, they first reduced these fortress cities, chief among which was Lachish, after which the hill country was comparatively easy to take. At the end of the last century the Joshua account furnished considerable difficulty because of the then current locations of several of the cities mentioned. Today, all of the cities in the chapter can be located with a high degree of probability except one, Makkedah.

According to the story, five Canaanite kings became alarmed at the defection of the four Gibeonite cities to Joshua, " because Gibeon was a great city, as one of the royal cities " (vs. 2). A coalition attacked the town; it was composed of the king of Jerusalem, who was its head and initiator, the king of Hebron, the king of Jarmuth, the king of Lachish and the king of Eglon. (We note, incidentally, that the two kings of the hill country are mentioned first, then three kings of the Lowland in a north-south order.) Considering the importance of the city of Gezer, we are surprised that its king is not a member of the coalition. Evidently, he did not realize the gravity of the situation until it was too late. After the defeat of the coalition, and the fall of two Lowland cities, he made a belated appearance to assist Lachish, too late indeed to be of any help, and his troops, fighting alone, were defeated (vs. 33).[9]

The Gibeonites, relying on their covenant with Joshua, summoned the latter's aid (vs. 6). During the night he and his army ascended to the hill country from the camp at Gilgal in the Jordan Valley and surprised the coalition (vs. 9). The forces of the latter fell back by the only avenue of retreat (the Beth-horon pass, otherwise called the

[9] Special point is made of Gezer here because this verse has often been used to deny the historicity of the chapter. It has frequently been asserted that since we know Gezer was not taken by Joshua, vs. 33 is a complete anachronism (so again most recently H. H. Rowley, *From Joseph to Joshua*, pp. 45 and 100). Yet the writer of this verse does not say that the city itself was taken; he is only recording that a force from that city arrived too late to assist Lachish and was defeated.

47. The mound of Lachish. The projection in the center is the ruins of the ancient Judean palace. At the right below the nob is the city gate. The excavated ring around the edge of the mound shows the line of the lower city wall in Judean times. On the terrace in the left center are the remains of the Canaanite temple, probably destroyed by Israel. The view is looking toward the southeast

Valley of Aijalon). The next verses (16–27) describe how the five kings, their armies in disorganized route, hid themselves in a cave at Makkedah, only to be found and put to death by Joshua. After that, the Israelites stormed and took Libnah at the opening of the Vale of Elah (the valley in which Goliath was later killed by David).

The city which guarded the next important valley which leads up into the hill-country from the plain was Lachish; so, as we should expect, it is next on the list (vss. 31–2). Its ruins have been discovered in the modern Tell ed-Duweir (Figs. 47–8), which was excavated between 1932 and 1938 by a British expedition, under the direction of J. L. Starkey until his murder by Arabs in 1938. Excavations in various parts of the mound have furnished ample witness to the terrific destruction which took place during the 13th century, just as at Bethel. In addition, there was found in the burned debris of the destruction a very ordinary bowl, which turned out to be a remarkable object indeed. After it had been reconstructed from some twenty-five pieces, it was found to have been used as a memorandum, apparently by an Egyptian tax collector. On it he had written in Egyptian a record of wheat deliveries from local harvests. He was thoughtful enough to write down the dates of these deliveries, all of which were in the fourth year of a certain Pharaoh, whose name unfortunately is not given.

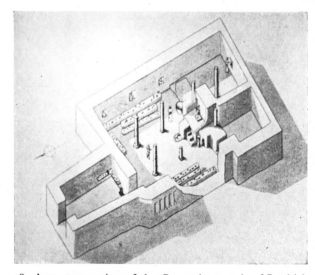

48. A reconstruction of the Canaanite temple of Lachish

Who was this Pharaoh? Specialists in Egyptian say that the writing on the bowl is to be dated about the time of Pharaoh Merneptah (1224–1216 B.C.) and not before. It follows that the "Year 4" which is mentioned must belong to Merneptah or possibly to two of his successors who were able to reign four years or more. The bowl, therefore, is to be dated in the last two decades of the 13th century. Now the importance of this, as Professor Albright has pointed out, is that all the pieces of the bowl were found together in the ruins of the destruction, showing that it had been broken when the city was destroyed. In addition, the bowl was such an unimportant object that it is difficult to imagine anyone holding on to it as a keepsake. It was a very ugly piece of pottery, with some preliminary notes upon it of the sort that the population, long under Egyptian control, must have been very accustomed to. Consequently, the bowl was probably not very old when broken, since the average life of cheap dishes is very short. If the " Year 4 " on the bowl means Merneptah, we are able to say with confidence that Israel smote Lachish " with the edge of the sword " not far from the year 1220 B.C. But in any case Lachish must have fallen to Israel some time between about 1220 and 1200 B.C.[10]

In the history of the Judean campaign under Joshua we are told that after the fall of Lachish, Israel encamped against Eglon, fought against it, took it, and smote it with the edge of the sword. Eglon is now thought to have been situated at the modern Tell el-Hesi, a site on the very edge of a group of foothills jutting out into the plain and one which guards the next valley leading up to the hill country south of Lachish. This is the site where Sir Flinders Petrie, excavating there in 1890, first discovered the value of pottery for purposes of dating. We know from the excavations of Petrie and his successor Bliss between 1890 and 1893 that the city was destroyed about 1200 B.C., but the results are so poorly published that we cannot be precise in the dating.

With the main section of the Lowland now in Israelite hands, Israel would be expected to ascend into the hill country *via* the pass leading up from Beit Jibrin. The next town in the list, therefore, was logically Hebron (vss. 36–7), a town not easily defended. After its capture, Joshua circled south-west and took the last remaining strong fortress, Debir or Kiriath-sepher (vss. 38–9). Professor Albright has located it with a high degree of probability at the modern Tell Beit Mirsim, which

excavations under his directions have unearthed. Between about 1250 and 1200 B.C. it was found to have been completely destroyed, the fortifications demolished and the town burned in a conflagration so intense that the layer of ashes was in some places three feet thick. As was the case at Bethel, the new town founded in the ashes was so different from the preceding that we must think of a new people having built it, a people who must have been Israelites, or closely related to them.

As for the Galilean campaign of Joshua, we are told that the only fortified city that he destroyed was Hazor, which at that time was the chief city of the region (Josh. 11 : 10–13). The location of this city was fixed in 1926 by John Garstang at the magnificent mound of Tell el-Qedah, some ten miles north of the Sea of Galilee near Lake Huleh, on the highway leading from Egypt through Palestine to Syria, Asia Minor and Mesopotamia. The city-mound is one of the largest in Palestine, comprising some 25 acres. Just to the north of it is a huge rectangular plateau, over 3000 feet long by 2000 feet wide, protected where necessary by an earthen wall nearly 50 feet high, outside which on the western side was also a gigantic dry moat. Ever since Garstang's explorations it has been known that this great enclosure was a compound for the horse and chariot army of the Hyksos, a people who created an empire including Syria, Palestine and Egypt about 1700 B.C. by the use of this new weapon of war (see above pp. 56–7 ; and Fig. 29 for a plan).

When did this great city fall to Israel ? Garstang made some soundings at the site and believed that he had found evidence that the Canaanite occupation ended about 1400 B.C. Between 1955 and 1958 a well-staffed Israeli expedition excavated there under the direction of Yigael Yadin. Much to the surprise of the staff they found that the last Canaanite city had occupied not only the mound but had filled the great enclosure also. Hazor, then, with an estimated population of 40,000 people, living within an area of some 175 acres, was indeed one of the great cities of Syria and Palestine, deserving the definition given it in Josh. 11 : 10 : " For Hazor beforetime was the head of all those kingdoms. " Yet it was violently destroyed, not about 1400 B.C. as Garstang had thought, but during the course of the 13th century, as a result of which the enclosure was more or less deserted and the occupation confined to the mound. The heavily fortified gateway of the enclosure or lower city has been partially uncovered. A fine Canaanite temple, with many of

---

[10] Olga Tufnell in *Lachish IV. The Bronze Age* (London, 1958), p. 37, suggests the possibility that the city may have fallen later to the Philistines in the 12th century because in the ruins of the destruction there was found an Egyptian scarab attributed to Rameses III (*ca.* 1180–1149 B.C.). W. F. Albright has observed, however, that the object in question bears a name used by both Rameses II and III, and there is no evidence to attribute it to the latter rather than to the former. Indeed, other than the bowl above mentioned the only really reliable *stratigraphical* evidence for the fall of the Bronze Age city is to be found in the ruins of a small temple erected on the slopes of the mound (*Lachish II. The Fosse Temple*, London, 1940).

its furnishings still in place, a shrine filled with standing stones to honor departed notables, and houses with their many domestic vessels, all testify that the city was destroyed while in full occupation with terrible violence. On the mound proper it is clear that the reoccupation was of a comparatively poor, small and modest type. In other words, the evidence from the great city of Hazor is as vivid for a 13th century destruction as it is in the southern town of Bethel, Lachish and Debir, while Shechem stands apart in striking contrast, as do also Megiddo and Beth-shan (see Chap. VI).

CONCLUSIONS

The manifold evidence for the terrific destruction suffered by the cities of Bethel, Lachish, Eglon Debir (Kiriath-sepher), and Hazor during the 13th century certainly suggests that a planned campaign such as that depicted in Josh. 10–11 was carried out. Its purpose was evidently the destruction of the power of the city-states, though some of these states were carefully avoided, presumably because they were too strong. We may safely conclude that during the 13th century a portion at least of the later nation of Israel gained entrance to Palestine by a carefully planned invasion, the purpose of which was not primarily loot but land. Numerous problems still defy convenient solution, among them Jericho, Ai and Shechem. The last half-century of work, however, has accomplished so much that we are led to hope for far more information in the future.

In conclusion, we must point out that certain figures in the Bible do not harmonize easily with the 13th-century date for the Exodus and Conquest which archaeology has made virtually certain. In I Kings 6 : 1 we read : " And it came to pass in the four hundred and eightieth year after the children of Israel were come out of the land of Egypt, in the fourth year of Solomon's reign . . . that he began to build the House of the Lord." According to the latest studies of the biblical chronology of this age (those of W. F. Albright and M. B. Rowton), the fourth year of Solomon when he began to build the Temple was about 959 B.C. Four hundred and eighty years before that, says our verse, the Exodus occurred : that is, about 1439 B.C. How is this figure to be reconciled with a 13th-century date for the Mosaic Exodus?

It has long been known that the Israelites believed twelve generations to have existed between the Exodus and the time of Solomon. For example, in I Chron. 6 : 1 ff. and again in 6 : 50 ff. we are given the genealogy of the high priests in the Temple of Jerusalem. In these lists since Zadok and Ahimaaz are known from II Samuel to have been priests of David, the first Azariah mentioned must have been priest in the time of Solomon, and from him back to Aaron are twelve generations.

A study of the Old Testament also reveals that Israelites reckoned a generation as forty years (the early Greeks did the same thing); twelve generations of forty years per generation gives the figure 480 years. Supposing, however, that the actual length of a generation was nearer twenty-five years than forty. We know that this was actually the case from the average life-time of kings and nobles in the Ancient East. Then twelve generations (between Solomon and the Exodus) of twenty-five years per generation give us a figure which would place the Exodus during about the third quarter of the 13th century, approximately where it should be according to the weight of archaeological evidence.

In Exod. 12 : 40 we are told that the time spent by the children of Israel in Egypt was *four hundred and thirty years*. Now this figure is not a multiple of forty, and there is no reason to doubt its reliability.[11] If the Exodus occurred early in the 13th century, then this means that Joseph and his family must have been in Egypt about 1700 B.C., that is in the very days when the Hyksos were getting control of the country. That is the time when most scholars believe that the entry into Egypt should have taken place.

That all cannot be completely harmonized as simply as these lines suggest is, however, made evident by such a passage as Judges 11 : 26. There Jephthah tells the Ammonite king that Israel has been in possession of its Transjordanian territory for three hundred years; why then does Ammon conclude at this late date that the territory is actually hers? If Jephthah is dated in the 11th century B.C., the conquest of Transjordan is pushed back into the fourteenth century by this passage. Commentators have long been suspicious of this round number, however, because the addition of the years ruled by the successive judges and the intervening oppressions up to Jephthah's time gives a figure of some 319 years. The coincidence is felt to be so close as to suggest that the 300-year figure was

---

[11] Even this is not absolutely certain, however, because the Greek translation applies the figure not only to the length of time spent in Egypt but also to that of the Patriarchs in Canaan.

artificially derived from the chronology of the Book of Judges, a chronology which is known to be too schematic because some of the judges and the oppressions were contemporary and not successive as the book presents them. If the figure cannot be explained in some such manner as this, then we can only assume that the fact that not all Israel was in Egypt has left its mark on the biblical narrative, and occasional traditions belonging to relatives already in Canaan have been left side by side with the dominant traditions of the Mosaic Exodus and subsequent conquest.

FURTHER READING

An article by the writer entitled " The Literary and Historical Problem of Joshua 10 and Judges 1 ", *Journal of Near Eastern Studies*, Vol. V (1946), pp. 105–14, is documented with references to which the reader is referred. See also John Bright, *A History of Israel* (Philadelphia, 1959), pp. 118–27 : and the writer in *The Bible and the Ancient Near East* (Garden City, N.Y., 1961), pp. 88–94 with reference there cited ; W. F. Albright, *The Archaeology of Palestine* (Pelican Books A199), pp. 96–109. It is to be noted that the recent excavations at Jericho have altered certain phases of the former presentations of the problem. For an excellent summary of the results of these excavations, see Kathleen Kenyon, *Digging up Jericho* (London and New York, 1957) ; and *Archaeology and the Holy Land* (London and New York, 1960), Chap. 8.

Four articles by W. F. Albright in *Bulletin of the American Schools of Oriental Research* are especially recommended:

" Archaeology and the Date of the Hebrew Conquest of Palestine ", No. 58 (April 1935), pp. 10 ff.
" Further Light on the History of Israel from Lachish and Megiddo ", No. 68 (Dec. 1937), pp. 22 ff.
" The Israelite Conquest of Canaan in the Light of Archaeology ", No. 74 (April 1939), pp. 11 ff.
" A Case of Lèse-Majesté in Pre-Israelite Lachish, with Some Remarks on the Israelite Conquest ", No. 87 (Oct. 1942), pp. 32 ff.

While these articles are not available in all libraries, copies of the *Bulletin* may be obtained from the American Schools of Oriental Research, Drawer 93A, Yale Station, New Haven, Conn., or through B. H. Blackwell, Ltd., Oxford, England.

For summaries of the important discoveries at Hazor see Yigael Yadin in *The Biblical Archaeologist*, Vols. XIX–XXII (1956–9). For the fullest statement of the results of the Shechem Expedition in its first three seasons, see L. E. Toombs and the writer in *Bulletin of the Amer. Sch. of Or. Research*, No. 161 (Feb. 1961).

A very valuable summary of the evidence, with full documentation, and with slightly different interpretation of some of the facts is to be found in T. J. Meek, *Hebrew Origins*, Chap. I (" The Origin of the Hebrew People "), New York, Harper & Brothers, 2nd ed., 1950. See also H. H. Rowley, *From Joseph to Joshua* (London, Oxford University Press, 1950).

A. T. Olmstead, *History of Palestine and Syria*, Chaps. XIV, XV, and XVII (Charles Scribner's Sons, 1931), can also be consulted. Professor Meek, followed by the late Professor Olmstead, concludes that the Mosaic Conquest of the 13th century was directly into the south of Palestine from Kadesh, and not around Edom and Moab. In this Conquest there were only the tribes of Levi and Judah with the affiliates of the latter. It does seem improbable that all the tribes in later Israel were involved in the 13th-century phase of the Conquest, but we shall probably never be certain whether Levi and Judah were the only ones or not. In any event it is difficult to give up the biblical tradition of the Mosaic trek through Transjordan, preserved in Num. 20–1, 33, Deut. 2, and Judges 11 : 15 ff., and as well the close association of the Exodus-Sinai tradition with the northern or Joseph tribes. For the important work of a different school of thought, see above the reference at the bottom of p. 52 ; and of particular significance the monograph of Albrecht Alt, " Die Landnahme der Israeliten in Palästina ", *Kleine Schriften zur Geschichte des Volkes Israel*, Bd. I (Munich, 1953), pp. 89–175 ; note also his " Josua ", *ibid.*, pp. 176–92.

For a recent discussion of the Amarna Letters, see Edward F. Campbell, Jr., " The Amarna Letters and the Amarna Period ", *The Biblical Archaeologist*, Vol. XXIII (1960), pp. 2–22.

CHAPTER VI

IN THE DAYS WHEN THE JUDGES JUDGED

" In those days there was no king in Israel ; every man did that which was right in his own eyes " (Judges 21 : 25).

" And the Lord was wroth with Israel . . . , and he sold them into the hand of their enemies round about . . . And the Lord raised up judges who delivered them from the hand of their spoilers. And yet they did not hearken unto their judges, because they went whoring after other gods " (Judges 2 : 14, 16–17).

DURING the 13th and 12th centuries a series of catastrophic events in the ancient Near East brought an end to the " Bronze Age " and ushered in a new age, that of iron. These archaeological terms are based on the fact that, while copper and bronze continue to be used as the most common metals, iron from now on appears by their side in sufficient amount to introduce notable changes in architecture, ship-building, weapons, and especially agriculture (see below). What were the events which brought an end to the old and introduced the new ?

They were a series of invasions and a decline of power in Egypt, Asia Minor and Mesopotamia which left Syria-Palestine largely free of outside domina-

tion for the first time in centuries. Barbarian invasions brought an end to the Hittite empire in Asia Minor. Many Hittites, however, remained in northern Syria where they dominated the cultural life as they had been dominating the political life during the preceding two centuries. By the middle of the 12th century the Egyptian government was unable any longer to control Palestine and southern Syria. Except for a brief period under Tiglath-pileser I (*ca.* 1116–1078 B.C.), Assyria was unable to maintain an extensive empire. Meanwhile, the Canaanites (Fig. 49) in territory under nominal Egyptian control were suffering severe setbacks. During the 13th century invasions into Transjordan

49. Canaanites in Egypt

86

had established the Kingdoms of Edom, Moab, Sidon and Og. The last two were displaced by the Israelite invasion which then crossed the Jordan to seize most of Palestine's central ridge. During the 12th century eastern Syria was inundated by the Aramaeans (the " Syrians " of the English Bible), who were to become well known to Israel because of the rapid expansion of one of their kingdoms which was later established at Damascus. The Ammonites across the Jordan had probably established themselves in the same period, giving their name to their capital city which survives to this day in the form 'Amman as the capital of the Kingdom of the Jordan. Rameses III of Egypt (*ca.* 1175–1144 B.C.)

was attacked by displaced people from the Greek world, the so-called " Sea Peoples ", who in the years before their defeat by this Pharaoh (Figs. 50–1) were evidently responsible for the destruction of a number of cities along the Syrian and Palestinian Coast, including Ugarit (Ras Shamra), Sidon and Tyre. A large group of them, the Pelast (Philistines), seized and settled the Mediterranean coast between Joppa and Gaza and subsequently gave their name to this region (Philistia) and ultimately to the whole land, for the term " Palestine " is our inheritance from them.

The Philistines organized themselves around five principal cities (Gaza, Ashkelon, Ashdod, Ekron,

50. A scene from the sea-battle of the forces of Rameses III (*left*) against the invading Sea Peoples (*right*) among whom were the Philistines

51. Carts of the Sea Peoples being attacked by Egyptian troops

and Gath). Each city with the area it controlled was ruled by a "Lord" or "Tyrant" after the Aegean model, and each was independent of the others, though the five Lords usually acted together on important matters and thus had some kind of centralized control about which we know nothing. Farther to the north in Dor, chief city of the Plain of Sharon, another group of the "Sea Peoples" settled who were called Tjikal (perhaps people from Sicily who in Homer's *Odyssey* are called "Sikel"). We hear about them, not from the Bible but from the Egyptian story of Wenamon, an Egyptian emissary who sailed to Syria for cedar about 1100 B.C. While stopping at Dor, presumably for provisions, one of his crew absconded with valuables brought to pay for the cedar. Wenamon then tried to get the prince of Dor to find the thief, and as a consequence spent some days in the town, though he failed to recover his property.

The Canaanites, after the blows suffered at the hands of this succession of invaders, were left in control of the sea-coast west of the Lebanon mountains and of a number of towns in Palestine, now isolated. The latter were gradually conquered, while a new state with its capital at Tyre emerged to the north, and by the 10th century was sufficiently strong to begin a rapid and remarkable expansion into the Mediterranean by means of trade. Colonies were established on Cyprus; trading expeditions were sent into the western Mediterranean; and during the 9th century at least, one of their mining colonies (probably called *Tarshish*) existed on Sardinia, as we know from Canaanite inscriptions found on the island. The Greeks called the new state Phoenicia, and by 800 B.C. or thereabouts had borrowed its alphabet.

ISRAEL'S PERIOD OF THE JUDGES

During the 12th and most of the 11th centuries Israel was engaged in consolidating her position along Palestine's central ridge and in the constant struggles, most of them local in nature, against invaders and against the remaining city states held by Canaanites. ⌜The excavations suggest that it was a time of anarchy when no strong central government existed to impose peace.⌝ At Bethel, ten miles north of Jerusalem, the excavation of 1934 revealed no fewer than four destructions by fire during these two centuries. A number of Israelite towns were destroyed in the period around 1050 B.C., presumably by the Philistines. The great northern city of Megiddo suffered repeated troubles between the destruction of its great Canaanite fortification and palace (Fig. 40) during the second half of the 12th century and its complete rebuilding as a center of government operations by David and Solomon in the tenth century (Figs. 82–7).

There was a striking difference between the political organization in Israel and that of the surrounding peoples during this time. The nations round about were highly organized. In Transjordan, Edom, Moab, and Ammon were monarchies. The Canaanites remained organized in city-states, each with its own king. Thus Jerusalem, Gezer, Megiddo, Taanach, and Beth-shan kept their independence under their own local monarchies for some time.

In contrast to the strongly organized political groups around her, Israel was only a loose confederation of tribes, held together by no central political figure, but by a religious bond or "covenant". The material symbol of this bond was the Ark of the Covenant in the central sanctuary at Shiloh. With no centralized authority the people were, therefore, in constant danger of attack from raiding parties and "oppressors" on every hand: Moabites, Ammonites, Canaanites, Philistines, Midianites. To defend themselves the Israelites depended upon a spontaneous leadership which would arise when needed. In time, however, pressure, especially from the Philistines, became too strong and a centralized government became a necessity.

⌜Why were the heroes who delivered the people from the "oppressors" called "judges"? The answer seems to lie in their nature. The judges have been called "charismatic" leaders. That is, they were followed because they were believed to possess some special outpouring of divine grace. There was something about them, military prowess or wisdom or honesty or some special gift, which set them apart from ordinary men. Since disputes between individuals and clans were constantly arising, it was only natural that those who were considered to possess divine power would be appealed to for decisions. Consequently, heroes of one sort or another would naturally become judges. The charismatic nature of Israel's leadership during this period is a remarkable feature of the Chosen People to which little among the neighbouring peoples can be compared.⌝

It has been pointed out that there are later parallels from other Mediterranean lands for the tribal organization of Israel and its grouping around a central shrine. The classical writers tell us of a number of them from Greece and Italy, some definitely said to have had twelve tribes. One of their chief characteristics was the central sanctuary, forming a religious bond whereby the political structure was held together. The history of Israel's shrine at Shiloh during the period of the Judges can be reconstructed from the Old Testament records and from excavations of Danish scholars in 1926 and 1929. After the conquest was completed, the tabernacle was moved there from Gilgal, near Jericho (Josh. 18 : 1). During the first half of the 11th century Eli was the priest in charge, and thither went Hannah to sacrifice, and there Samuel was trained for the priesthood (I Sam. 1 ff.). After Israel's great defeat by the Philistines at the battle of Ebenezer (I Sam. 4), we are not told explicitly about what happened to Shiloh, nor about the political consequences for Israel, primarily because the narrator is much more interested in telling us about the fate of the Ark of the Covenant in the land of the Philistines. Jeremiah in his famous Temple Sermon, however, later prophesies that the Temple in Jerusalem is to be destroyed just as was Shiloh (Jer. 7 : 12 ff. ; 26 : 6 ff.). The archaeological discoveries support this information, and we take it that Shiloh was destroyed by the Philistines about 1050 B.C. For the next thirty years Israel had to submit to Philistine domination, while the Ark remained at Kiriath-jearim, feared by the Philistines and the Israelites alike.

HEBREWS AND CANAANITES ARCHAEOLOGICALLY DISTINGUISHED

It was pointed out in the last chapter that the Israelites obtained their foothold in the hill country, whereas all about were great Canaanite fortresses which they were not able at first to subdue. Is it really possible to dig into a town known to have been Canaanite during this period and see any difference between it and one which was Israelite? A prominent historian of the ancient Near East once wrote : " The archaeological discoveries . . . in Palestine have hardly shed as much light as had been hoped upon the ancient culture of Palestine. An important result for the historian is the fact that no difference can be traced in the town-strata between what is Canaanite and what is Hebrew. Their cultures were indistinguishable as, probably, in reality the peoples were also." [1] In part this state-

[1] H. R. Hall, *The Ancient History of the Near East* (New York, Macmillan Co., 1913), pp. 440-1.

ment is correct because Israelites like the Aramaeans (" Syrians " of AV) had no urban culture of their own and consequently adopted that of the country they took over. Yet at the same time we know now that the statement is an exaggeration because differences are indeed clearly apparent.

A careful study of the buildings, metal implements, and various small objects, as dated by the pottery, furnishes a fairly good picture of the period of the Judges and of the early kings of Israel. In the hill country, as distinct from the plains, there are several sites which the Israelites are said to have occupied and which furnish us with an idea of the culture of the invaders. Nomads with little knowledge of the arts of sedentary life, they were ill-acquainted with many of the things which had been well known to their predecessors in this region. The Canaanite royal cities of Bethel, Beth-shemesh, and Kiriath-sepher (Debir), for example, possessed a comparatively high degree of material civilization. A native art had developed and was flourishing. Houses were well built. Floors were paved or plastered. City drainage was in operation. Metal workers, artisans in copper, bronze, lead, and gold, were active. Extensive world trade was carried on with Syria, the Aegean, and Egypt. Wares were even purchased from Egyptian tomb-robbers who were carrying on widespread operations at this time, causing scandals at home but finding a profitable market for their wares in Canaan. It is not unusual, therefore, to find in the ruins of a Canaanite home a beautiful Egyptian stone bowl which had been made some 1500 years before (Fig. 52). Few were the homes, even of the serfs in the employ of resident nobles, which did not possess some appar-

52. A late Pre-Dynastic diorite bowl, dating before 3000 B.C., found in a Canaanite house of the 15th or 14th century at Beth-shemesh in Palestine

ently coveted objects of art from abroad. The feudal system of the Canaanite city-states is well attested by the nature of the towns, in which the royal castle was surrounded by the shacks of the people. Massive city walls and tower gates protected them, built by the labor battalions which were always available at the command of the king.

The contrast between these towns and those built by the early Israelites is very marked indeed. Between 1200 and 1000 B.C. the hill country, for the first time in its history, became dotted with towns, indicating a great increase in the number of people living there (in other words, witnessing to the Israelite settlement). Several of these towns have been excavated: Shiloh, Bethel, Ai, Mizpah (if that village is correctly identified with the modern Tell en-Nasbeh), Gibeah, Beth-zur, and Debir (Kiriath-sepher). The civilization to which their ruins testify is very different from that of the Canaanite cities. Houses, where found, were anything but well built, and they possessed none of the refinements of the Canaanite buildings. Stones had been gathered and built into walls with no attempt to draft them to fit (Fig. 53). Smaller stones were used to fill up the chinks. Little evidence of town planning is observable from the remains. House walls run hither and yon without apparent rhyme or reason. In fact, the average house is much poorer than that of the average Canaanite peasant.

Art in these towns was very crude (Fig. 54), since there was no tradition behind it and apparently little money or inclination to import luxuries from abroad. The technique of firing and fashioning a good pottery vessel was not yet well learned, or at

54. A human head formed on the handle of a storage jar; found at Bethel in ruins of the period of the Judges

least early in this period the Israelites had but few artisans capable of making a good pottery from a clean clay, or of making a kiln fire hot enough to bake the thick clay walls through. City walls, when constructed, were thin, hastily and crudely built, scarcely capable of withstanding any serious attack. Strong city fortifications on a large scale were not built in Israel until the time of David and especially of Solomon, when compulsory labor battalions were introduced under a strong central government. There is not enough evidence to say very much about social organization, though in a later period the town construction is somewhat different from that of the Canaanites, witnessing to a more democratic mode of life. Before about 1050 B.C. there is little evidence in the hill country of any extensive commerce with other peoples, though occasionally a Philistine vase or small Syrian vessel was brought up from the plain. After that time, imported objects, especially from Phoenicia and Cyprus, became increasingly common, and world culture began to affect the hill country.

ARCHAEOLOGICAL EVIDENCE FOR THE PHILISTINES

Around the hill country, bordering Israel to the west and north, were the districts controlled by

53. Ruins of a large house at Bethel, dating from the period of the Judges

55. Philistine vessels from Beth-shemesh

those whom the Israelites were unable to eject. Along the coast to the south of Joppa was the land of the Philistines. Wherever one digs into Philistine cities, he encounters large quantities of their distinctive pottery. As a rule it is very difficult to associate a particular type of pottery with any one racial group. Early Israelite pottery, for example, seems largely to have been modeled after that which the Canaanites around Israel were making, and about the only observable difference is that it is often more crude and lacking the artistic refinement of the latter. At the present moment, therefore, we can scarcely speak of "Israelite" pottery as entirely distinct from "Canaanite" pottery.

When we come to the ceramic culture of the southern coastal plain, however, we have an entirely different situation. Even the beginner in Palestinian archaeology can soon learn to distinguish its fine, well baked clay, its particular shapes, and its decoration, especially its spirals and birds (Fig. 55). This pottery had its center in precisely the region where the Philistines are known to have been, while the farther we move away from that region, the rarer it becomes. In addition, its most characteristic shapes were made, not according to Canaanite models, but according to models well known in the Greek world from which the Philistines are known to have come. Consequently, we are quite safe in calling it Philistine.

Two towns along the border between Philistia and Israel have been sufficiently excavated to in-

dicate the energy and ability of the Philistines. One of these is Gezer (Fig. 22), guarding the Wadi Ali, a pass leading up into the hill country through which the modern road from Jerusalem to Joppa passes. This city may have been able to maintain some semblance of political independence, though of this we have no certain knowledge. In any event the archaeological remains indicate that the city was dominated economically by the Philistines. The other city is Beth-shemesh, guarding the Vale of Sorek, through which the modern railway passes from Tel-Aviv to Jerusalem (Fig. 56). At first this town was a border city of the tribe of Dan. With the rising power of the Philistines, however, this tribe was forced into an area so confined that it decided to migrate and find room for itself north of the Sea of Galilee (Judges 18). From the story of the Ark and the trouble caused after its capture by the Philistines (I Sam. 6) we gain the distinct impression that Beth-shemesh, whither the Ark was borne on its way back to Israel, was in Israelite hands at that time (shortly after 1050 B.C.). Yet the material culture of the city is almost indistinguishable from that of the Philistine Plain. Though occupied by Israelites, Beth-shemesh was undoubtedly under the economic and political control of the Philistines, a state of affairs which was probably typical of most of the border region between the Philistine Plain and the Israelite hill country.

In I Sam. 13:19-22 we have an interesting statement, illustrating the economic stranglehold

56. The biblical Vale of Sorek, looking north. In the center is the mound of Beth-shemesh. On the hill at the top right is the site of Samson's home

which the Philistines had over Israel when Saul came to the throne.

Now there was no smith found throughout all the land of Israel because the Philistines said : " (There must be none) lest the Hebrews make swords or spears." But all the Israelites went down to the Philistines for each man to sharpen his plowpoint, and his axe, and his adze, and his mattock (?). And the price was a pim (2/3 of a shekel) for the plowpoints and for the axes and a third of a shekel for sharpening the adzes and for setting the goads (?—or, fixing the hafts ?). So it came to pass on the day of battle, that neither sword nor spear were to be found in the hand of any of the people which were with Saul and Jonathan. . . .

For many centuries the exact sense of verse 21 remained obscure, especially because the word " pim " was unknown. Little weights with this word inscribed on them, however, have turned up in the excavations, and the general sense is now clear, though some of the names for the agricultural implements are uncertain. Here we are told that the Philistines held such a control over Israel that they would permit no smith in the hill country in order that the Israelites could not stock the supplies of war. Thus the farmers were forced to go down

to Philistia to sharpen their tools (Fig. 57) and there were charged exorbitant prices for the service.

In all probability, however, there is even more to be inferred from the passage. The dominant metal in use for tools and weapons since 4000 B.C. had been copper. It is easy to smelt and easy to work. The coppersmiths had long known how to mix a little tin with the copper to make it harder, thus to make bronze. Iron, on the other hand, was not introduced into common use until after 1200 B.C. Before 1000 B.C. it seems to have been one of the magic products of Western Asia, valued almost as much as were gold and silver, not because of the scarcity of the ore, but because the secrets of the rather complicated smelting process seem to have been jealously guarded by the Hittites. When the king of the Hittites wished to give a present to the famous Pharaoh Tutankhamen (about 1350 B.C.), he sent him a wrought-iron dagger, a rare and novel gift. Throughout the period of the Judges the Israelites, who were always poor in material possessions, were thwarted time and again because of their lack of this important metal for building,

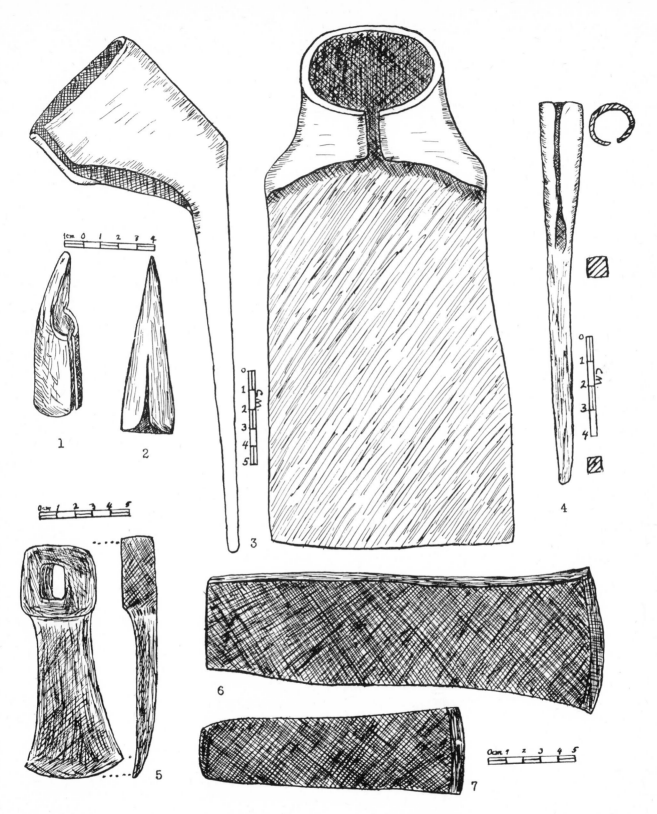

57. Some ancient metal tools found in the excavations. Nos. 1–2 are plowpoints from Gezer. No. 3 is a mattock from Tell Jemmeh, dating about the 10th century B.C.; No. 4 is an ox-goad from Sharuhen, dating about the 11th century B.C.; No. 5 is an adze from Gezer; and Nos. 6 and 7 are axe blades from Gezer, the first dating between the 7th and 1st centuries B.C. and the second about the 10th century. Nos. 3 and 5 are iron; the others are bronze or copper

agriculture, and conquest. They were unable at first to drive out the Canaanites from the plain areas because these people owned " chariots of iron " (Josh. 17 : 16 ; Judges 1 : 19).

Scholars have long inferred from the passage above quoted from I Sam. 13 that the Philistines were the chief cause of the failure of the Israelites to make much use of iron during the period of the Judges. The excavations now inform us that the metal was introduced into Palestine for the making of weapons and jewelry during the 12th century, but it was not used for agricultural tools until the end of the 11th and the beginning of the 10th century. In Philistine tombs iron appears, whereas the first iron implement found in the hill country which we can date is a plowpoint from Saul's fortress at Gibeah (*ca.* 1010 B.C.). It is a safe assumption, therefore, that the metal was introduced into common use in Palestine by the Philistines who had learned about it in the north. Upon reaching the country, however, they held a " corner " on the iron market and closely guarded the trade secrets of its production. It was only after the first kings of Israel, Saul and David, had broken the Philistine power that the metal came into use in Israel, promptly affecting an economic revolution and a higher standard of living for the common man.

CANAANITE CITIES

The Philistines, then, were the most dangerous oppressors of Israel during the period of the Judges, furnishing the occasion for great exploits which were later celebrated in song and story, most notably those of Samson and of David versus Goliath. There were other oppressors, however, some of whom we know very little about. One was the mysterious Cushan-rishathaim, a king from the Upper Euphrates region, whence came the Patriarchs several centuries earlier (Judges 3 : 8). Another was Eglon, king of the Moabites, who lived across the Jordan in the area just opposite the Dead Sea (Judges 3 : 12). The Gileadite tribes across the Jordan experienced some difficulty with the territorial ambitions of their Ammonite neighbors, occasioning the famous vow of Jephthah (Judges 11 : 30) and the interesting " shibboleth " incident related in Judges 12. Apparently a feud had arisen between the Ephraimites west of the Jordan and the Gileadites east of the Jordan over the Ammonite incident. When the Ephraimites tried to get back across the river, they found the men of Gilead in possession of all the fords ; and, when one would say, " ' Let me cross ', the Gileadites would say to him, ' Are you an Ephraimite ? ' If he said, ' No ', they would say to him, ' Then say, Shibboleth.' If he said, Sibboleth, seeing that it is not proper so to pronounce it, they would seize him, and slay him . . ." Most of the Old Testament was written in the dialect spoken in Jerusalem, and this incident indicates the presence of dialectical differences between Israelites even at this early period.

Still another oppressor was a group of Midianites or Arabians who made a raid against northern Palestine up the Jezreel valley and were met and routed by Gideon. This raid is particularly interesting, since it represents the first time, as far as we now know, that camels were extensively used. Ancient reliefs and documents indicate that the camel, so widely used in the Near East today, had not been domesticated on any large scale before this time, probably because it is such a difficult and ill-tempered beast to handle. Ancient nomads, including the Patriarchal Hebrews, were very different from those today, since with their donkeys, sheep, and goats they could never move far from water. The domestication of the camel marked a transition in Arabian life. The nomad was now able to cover great distances on camel back and to live in areas where the shepherd could not exist. The Midianite raid, therefore, must have been a fearful thing to northern Israelites, and it is small wonder that they " made themselves the dens which are in the mountains, and the caves, and strongholds " (Judges 6 : 2).

Not the least among the oppressors, however, were the Canaanites whom the Israelites were only gradually able to subdue. Before 1200 B.C. control of most of the hill country had been wrested from them, but strong cities in the plain areas, where chariots could manoeuvre, held out for some time. Typical of these cities were Megiddo and Bethshan in the north. High on the northwest corner of the mound of Megiddo during the early twelfth century was the palace of the Canaanite king, a strong and elaborate structure built upon the ruins of its predecessors and adjoining the strongly fortified gateway (Fig. 40). This palace was far more elaborate than that of any wealthy Israelite of later times, and in all probability was as large and substantial as that of Solomon. In its basement was the treasure room, looted of all but a number of small objects when the building was destroyed between about 1150 and 1125 B.C. On the floor in a confused mass the excavators found a large number of gold, ivory, and alabaster objects which, while unimportant to the looters, are a great treasure for us, since they so vividly illustrate the comparative wealth and culture of the Canaanite king. The ivories are typical Canaanite workmanship, mostly used for inlay on boxes, furniture, and the cedar walls of " drawing rooms ". Included in the collection are small ivory bowls, figures, combs, and gameboards. On one plaque is a figure of the king himself, or one like him, seated upon his throne, drinking from a small bowl. Before him is his queen and a musician plucking the strings of a lyre, the latter reminding us of David playing the lyre (not the harp) before the moody Saul. The king's throne is interesting, for it is supported by winged sphinxes or lions with human heads, composite beings which are now known to have been called *cherubim* by the Israelites (Fig. 41). We shall see in Chap. VIII that just as this Canaanite king was enthroned upon the cherubim, so the builders of Solomon's Temple thought of God as likewise enthroned, though invisibly, on the cherubim in the Holy of Holies. Among other interesting objects found was a pen case with Egyptian writing on it, telling us that it belonged to the Egyptian " Royal Envoy to all foreign countries ".

The exact cause of the city's terrific destruction during the third quarter of the 12th century is unknown. In any event it was probably during the period when the city lay in ruins and before it was settled again that we are to date the Song of Deborah in Judges 5. This great poem of battle is considered to be one of the oldest extant monuments of Israelite literature, for it was certainly written by an eyewitness of the events described. Its style is spontaneous and vivid, so much so that we can almost hear the noise of the battle and the beating of the hoofs of the horses. Breathing through it is an intense nationalism and a religious enthusiasm centered in the faith that the Lord of Sinai would deliver his people from the hands of their adversaries. The condition to which the central tribes of Israel had been reduced by the Canaanite oppression is colorfully pictured in verses 6–8, and there follows a celebration of a great victory won over the oppressors in the Esdraelon plain (vss. 19 ff.) :

> The kings came ; they fought ;
> Then fought the kings of Canaan ;

> At Taanach, by Megiddo's waters
> No booty of silver did they take !

> From the heavens fought the stars ;
> From their courses they fought with Sisera.

> The torrent of Kishon swept them away . . .

To those who have studied the geography of the plain of Esdraelon the question immediately arises : just where did the battle take place ? We gather that it must have been in that ancient battle area near Megiddo, at the opening of the pass which brings the great international highway from the Plain of Sharon. At that point are the " waters of Megiddo ", the " torrent of the Kishon ". This stream flows around the mound of Megiddo, arising in springs nearby. If this is the case, why is it that the battleground is further identified as being " at Taanach ", a city some four miles to the southeast ? Of course, this is poetry and we cannot be too literal ; nevertheless, it is very strange that the writer did not say that the battle took place at Megiddo, the biggest and strongest city in the whole Esdraelon plain. The explanation of Professor W. F. Albright is that the victory must have occurred at a time when Megiddo was in ruins, unoccupied as a city. Taanach would then have been the nearest town by which to fix the location, though the " waters of Megiddo " could also be used. If so, then Deborah's song is probably to be dated about 1100 B.C., or shortly before or after, for the excavations indicate that Megiddo lay in ruins at that time. We cannot be absolutely certain, since other explanations of the situation are naturally possible ; but this is by far the most plausible and probable.

Beth-shan was another strong fortress-city in the Jordan valley to the east of Megiddo, guarding the Vale of Jezreel which led up from the Jordan into the great plain of Esdraelon (Fig. 58). For three centuries the Egyptians had attempted to control this area, guarding the approaches through Palestine. In fact, Esdraelon had been one of the private granaries of the Pharaoh. During the early 12th century Rameses III, trying desperately to reestablish the Asiatic empire of his forefathers, rebuilt Beth-shan as a frontier post and apparently stationed a garrison of " Sea Peoples " there. His statue was installed in the city and *stelae* or monumental stones set up by two of his predecessors were salvaged from the ruins of the preceding fortress and again erected. His empire scarcely survived

58. The mound of Beth-shan, looking east toward the Jordan and the hills of Transjordan

his death, however, and by the third quarter of the 12th century Egyptian control over Palestine had ceased. This was Israel's golden opportunity, but more blows from oppressors were yet needed to mould her into a political unity.

During the 11th century Beth-shan was rebuilt, probably by the descendants of the old Egyptian garrison of " Sea Peoples " or Philistines. It will be recalled that after the last battle of King Saul, the Philistines cut off his head and placed it in the " house " or temple of Dagon in Beth-shan; his armor was placed in the temple of Ashtaroth (Astarte : Fig. 59); and his body hung on the walls of the city (I Sam. 31 : 10 and I Chron. 10 : 10). These temples evidently have been excavated; in fact, the city's ruins are exceedingly valuable for the light they shed upon Canaanite religion, but we shall reserve a discussion of this subject until the next chapter. Beth-shan finally fell to Israel during the 10th century, as the excavations show, probably in the time of David.

To him who labors and ponders over the reports

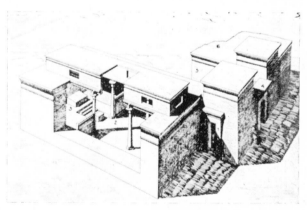

59. Restoration of the northern temple of Stratum V at Beth-shan. This may be the " house of Ashtaroth ", mentioned in I Sam. 31 : 10

of the excavators, the discoveries at Megiddo, Beth-shan, and in the Philistine Plain are extremely revealing, for they vividly illustrate the state of affairs during the period of the Judges. Israel was in her formative stage as a nation, learning from tne people around her, but at the same time in constant conflict with them and oppressed by them. Small wonder that her occasional triumphs were celebrated in poetry and song, like that of Deborah in Judges 5, and like those recorded in the now lost books of Jashar and of the Wars of the Lord.

THE FIRST PROPHETS

According to Israelite tradition, Samuel, who was a priest and judge over all Israel, was evidently the first to take under his patronage those whose inspiration led them to ecstatic utterance. In I Sam. we hear for the first time of an organized group or company of such people, and they are called " prophets ". Formerly, we are told, if a man wished to inquire of God, he customarily went to a " seer ", but now such a person was called a " prophet " (I Sam. 9 : 9). In I Sam. 10 : 5 Samuel tells Saul that as he goes on his way he will " encounter a band of prophets coming down from the high place with harp, tamborine, oboe and lyre before them, and they will be prophesying. Then the spirit of the Lord will rush upon you and you shall prophesy with them and be changed into another person." While this may not have been the first appearance of ecstasy in Israel (cf. Num. 11 : 24–9), it is the first to be recognized officially and organized within the religious institutions by a priestly official.

We are certainly not to think of ecstasy as a specifically Israelite phenomenon ; it has appeared in many different religions in the world. Indeed, its entry into Israel may well have been under foreign inspiration. In the Egyptian story of Wenamon (*ca.* 1100 B.C.) referred to above, the author tells us that while the Prince of the Phoenician city of Byblos " was making offering to his gods, the god seized one of his youths and made him possessed ". We are told that the Egyptian sign for the word " possessed " shows a human figure in violent motion or epileptic convulsion.[2] The Byblian king seems to have interpreted the event as a sign that the Egyptian god, Amon, had actually come to Byblos. The result was that an interview was finally granted Wenamon and after much negotiation and many difficulties the latter was finally able to get the cedar he came for.

In Israel, however, ecstasy did not remain the chief or distinguishing mark of prophecy. The prophet was characteristically God's herald, sent to deliver a message ; hence he customarily began his address : " Thus saith the Lord." By this means he presented his divinely-given commission to deliver orally a word not his own. When attacked, his defense could only be : " The Lord has sent me " (cf. Jer. 26 : 2, 15 ; 28 : 15). Until recently, the prophetic office in this sense had appeared to be unique in Israel. In the archives of the city of Mari on the upper Euphrates (see Chap. II), however, some interesting parallels have been unearthed from *ca.* 1700 B.C. Royal officials in writing to the king of Mari occasionally report to him that a man of such-and-such a god had come with a message for the king. He claimed that the god had sent him and asked that the words of the god be conveyed to the king. Three letters deal with messages from the god Dagan in the city of Tirqa (that is, from the god whose residence or temple was in Tirqa). One reports a dream in which Dagan grants the king victory over the hostile Benjaminites, but requests that the king send him messengers to lay all the royal affairs before him. Another instructs the king to make offerings for the spirit of the previous king. In a third Dagan tells the king through his messenger that these offerings are to be made on the fourteenth day of the following month.

Most interesting is a fourth letter in which the god Adad of the city of Kallassu requires that certain male animals be delivered by the king to him for sacrifice. The god tells the king through his intermediaries that it is he, Adad, Lord of Kallassu, who had raised the king on his own knees, had put him on the throne of his father and had given him a residence. Let the king remember that if he does not make delivery (of the animals), " I am the Lord of the throne, of the soil and of the city, and what I have given I can take away ! If, on the contrary, he accomplishes my desire, I will give him thrones upon thrones, houses upon houses, soil upon soil, towns upon towns ; and the country of the east and the west I will give him."

The royal official who sends this message to the king then adds that this is what certain persons called the *apilu* of the god have told him. He goes on to say that when formerly he lived in Mari he always conveyed to the king the messages of male and female *apilu*, and he is now continuing the same practice. Furthermore, an *apilum* of the god Adad of the city of Khalab had come with a message for

---

[2] J. A. Wilson, *Ancient Near Eastern Texts* (ed. by J. B. Pritchard), p. 26.

the king from the god to the effect that the latter is giving to him " the country from the east to the west ".[3]

The great majority of texts dealing with divine oracles in Mesopotamia belongs in the category of divination. The divine word was obtained by experts from various overt signs procured in various ways : e.g. from the inspection of the liver of a sacrificial animal, from eclipses, astrology, and the like. In fact, the armies of Mari had diviners for each section of troops. The texts mentioned above, however, refer to a different type of functionary. He was one who had received an oral message from a god, and he was sent by the god to deliver it orally. The message came by inspiration, and was delivered when the messenger suddenly appeared, unasked and unbidden. The name *apilum* given to such a messenger was evidently derived from a verb meaning " to reply " or " answer ". This verb, like the corresponding term in the Old Testament, could be used for the revelation given by a deity to one who consulted him (cf. I Sam. 14 : 37 ; 28 : 6, 15). The latter, or *apilum*, is the " respondent " or one who makes answer for the deity.

Inasmuch as ecstasy, though present in Israel's prophetic movement, is not its characteristic feature, the above-mentioned Mari texts appear to depict a phenomenon parallel to prophecy and one from which it undoubtedly sprang. The Old Testament has numerous illustrations of the prophetic mediation of divine oracles : for example, the message to Eli from an unnamed man of God (I Sam. 2 : 27-36) ; to Saul from Samuel ; to David from Nathan (II Sam. 7 and 12) ; to Jeroboam I from Ahijah (I Kings 11 : 29 ff. ; 14 : 1 ff.), etc. Yet one cannot help but see a vast difference between the oracles of the God of Israel, especially as delivered by the great prophets, and those of the various gods to the king of Mari. In the Mari oracles the formal function of the *apilum* was similar to that of the prophet, but the context and range of content in the oracles were more confined. The chief concern of the various gods was to get the king to pay more attention to them, to their temples and to their sacrifices. Threats and promises were made, and all were contingent upon whether the king gave the desired material gifts. Many of the Israelite prophets were undoubtedly concerned in equally detailed and material matters, but the greatest among them were God's charismatic instruments for the interpretation of his intention and action in the history of the time. The essential differences in the two types of office lay not in the form but in the faith which provided their setting. To this difference in the faith we must now turn.

---

[3] See Ad. Lods, " Une Tablette Inédite de Mari, Intéressante pour l'Histoire Ancienne du Prophétisme Sémitique ", *Studies in Old Testament Prophecy* (ed. by H. H. Rowley ; Edinburgh, T. & T. Clark, 1950), pp. 103–10 ; *Archives Royales de Mari* (ed. by A. Parrot et G. Dossin ; Paris, Imprimerie Nationale), II (1950), Letter No. 90 ; III (1948), Letter No. 40 ; and Martin Noth, " History and the Word of God in the Old Testament ", *Bulletin of the John Rylands Library*, Vol. 32 (1950), pp. 194–206.

FURTHER READING

For the most up-to-date general surveys of this period see now W. F. Albright, " The Old Testament World ", *Interpreter's Bible*, Vol. I, pp. 261-4 ; *The Archaeology of Palestine* (Pelican Books, A199), pp. 99–120 ; " The Song of Deborah in the Light of Archaeology ", *Bulletin of the American Schools of Oriental Research*, No. 62 (April 1936). pp. 26–31 ; *From the Old Stone Age to Christianity*, pp. 208–20 ; and *Archaeology and the Religion of Israel*, pp. 95–119, The last two works have full references to the first-hand reports and material. See also now John Bright, *A History of Israel* (Philadelphia, 1959), Chap. 4.

See also G. Ernest Wright, " Archaeological Remarks on the Period of the Judges and Early Monarchy ", *Journal of Biblical Literature*, Vol. LX (1941), pp. 27-42 ; " Iron : the Date of its Introduction into Common Use in Palestine ", *American Journal of Archaeology*, Vol. XLIII (1939), pp. 458-63 ; " The Literary and Historical Problem of Joshua 10 and Judges 1 ", *Journal of Near Eastern Studies*, Vol. V (1946), pp. 105-14.

Three recent articles by Israeli scholars are of especial importance : A. Malamat, " Cushan Rishathaim and the Decline of the Near East around 1200 B.C.", *Journal of Near Eastern Studies*, Vol. XIII (1954), pp. 231-42 ; Trude Dothan, " Philistine Civilization in the Sight of Archaeological Finds in Palestine and Egypt ", *Eretz Israel*, Vol. 5(1958, Mazar Vol.), pp. 55–66 (in Hebrew) ; the author's conclusions are summarized, however, in her article, " Archaeological Reflections on the Philistine Problem ", *Antiquity and Survival*, Vol. II, No. 2/3 (P.O. Box 2030, The Hague, 1957), pp. 151–64. (See also the writer's review based on the work of Mrs. Dothan, " Philistine Coffins and Mercenaries ", *The Biblical Archaeologist*, Vol. XXII, No. 3 [Sept. 1959], pp. 54–66).

For a discussion of the " Sea Peoples " in ancient history, see W. F. Albright, " Some Oriental Glosses on the Homeric Problem ", *American Journal of Archaeology*, Vol. LIV (1950), pp. 162–76.

CHAPTER VII

THE MANNER OF ISRAEL AND THE MANNER OF CANAAN

" For what great people has a god so near unto it as is the Lord our God whenever we call upon him ? "
(Deut. 4 : 7).

BEFORE proceeding further with Israel's history we must pause for a discussion of Israel's faith in relation to the religions of her environment. Only within recent years has the progress of archaeological study reached the point where we can begin to speak with confidence about the theology of the ancient polytheisms around Israel. This means that it is now possible to make certain emphases in describing biblical faith which formerly were not entirely clear ; we can do so because we have more knowledge of the relation and the reaction of the faith to its environment.

In launching our discussion of such a difficult subject, a point of beginning could well be the difference between the Israelite national organization of the period of the Judges and that of the surrounding peoples. This was referred to in the last chapter, and we are indebted to the Alt school of biblical scholarship in Germany for calling it to our attention as a fact of major importance.[1] While the Philistines had their city-states, ruled by lords or " tyrants " who were able to act together on critical occasions, and while other peoples had their kings, Israel persisted in a tribal organization, whose symbol of unity was the Ark at a central sanctuary. The tribes were held together around this sanctuary by a sacred compact or covenant. Decisions were made and justice evidently administered largely by the tribal elders. God was conceived as the direct Ruler of the people, so that no permanent political leadership was believed necessary. When the need arose, God raised up a leader on whom he conferred a special gift of his Spirit which gave to the individual the ability to deal successfully with the crisis. The Greek word for such a gift is *charisma* ; hence the leaders are now being called " charismatic ". They arose spontaneously at critical moments and their function was not passed on to their sons after

their death. Hence no one family was able to secure and perpetuate political power within itself (that is, until kingship was established and David secured the throne).

It is thus clear that Israel was a special religious society which early resisted the typical political organizations of the day, because she had one of her own by sacred compact with her divine Ruler. The charismatic leadership broke down under Philistine pressure and a monarchy was later established " like all the nations " (I Sam. 8 : 5) ; but it was resisted by some because it was a radical departure from traditional ways (cf. Judges 8 : 23 ; I Sam. 8 and 12). What was the nature of the early Israelite sacred compact ?

THE COVENANT

Perhaps the most influential comparative treatment is that of the Danish scholar, Johannes Pedersen, who interpreted the Israelite covenant in terms of modern bedouin covenants in Arabia.[2] The story of Jacob and Laban in Gen. 31 is a biblical reference to this type of pact. Peace was secured and given divine sanction by a covenant between two clans. In nomadic society men lived and moved and had their being in a society stabilized by covenants. The idea of the national covenant between God and Israel represented an adaptation of this type of covenant, it was felt, whereby the human and divine life were brought into relationship by mutual promises and obligations.

It is obvious, however, that such a covenant as that between Jacob and Laban is a parity treaty between equals who incur equal obligations. In Israel, however, the covenant between God and Israel is not one between equals, but it is one between a great Ruler and a people who promise to

---

[1] See Martin Noth, *Das System der zwölf Stämme Israels* (Stuttgart, 1930) ; and Albrecht Alt, *Die Staatenbildung der Israeliten in Palästina* (Leipzig, 1930).

[2] See his *Israel*, I–II (Copenhagen and London, 1926), the Introduction and Part II ; and his *Der Eid bei den Semiten* (*Studien zur Geschichte und Kultur des islam. Orients*, 3. Heft, Strasbourg, 1914).

be his loyal subjects. The Ruler offers it to his people as a gracious act and promises his leadership and protection provided that the nation is loyal to him, follows no other rulers, and obeys his law. Hence if any real parallel exists to the Israelite covenant it ought to be found in compacts of a ruler with a subject, if such exist.

Professor George E. Mendenhall of the University of Michigan has discovered remarkably close and illuminating parallels in the international treaties of Western Asia during the 2nd millennium B.C.[3] These treaties were of two types: the parity treaty between equals and the suzerainty treaty between a great king and a vassal. It is the latter which concerns us here. A suzerain differs from an ordinary king in that he is "the Great King" (II Kings 18:28; Hos. 5:13 [4]), the "King of kings" and "Lord of lords"; that is, he is not a king among other kings and may not even call himself by the term, but he is one who claims authority over other rulers. And this is precisely the role assumed by the God of Israel; he is the Suzerain who has authority over all earthly powers, the "Lord of Hosts" to whom the title "king" was evidently not frequently applied in the early days of the nation's history.

Professor Mendenhall defines covenant as a promise or bond which is made binding by an oath, and which is undertaken between two legal communities when there is no other legal procedure or means of enforcement. In the suzerainty treaties of the 2nd millennium B.C., in which a vassal was bound by an oath, six elements may be distinguished:

(1) The typical treaty begins with the identification of the Great King. He is the one who gives the treaty: "Thus says *X*, the Great King . . ." etc. This immediately recalls the typical early covenant passages of the Old Testament in which God speaks in the first person: "I am the Lord" (Exod. 20:1–2) or "Thus says the Lord, the God of Israel" (Josh. 24:2).

(2) Then follows a detailed presentation of the historical background of the relations between the Great King and the vassal which emphasizes par-

ticularly the benevolent actions of the former. This is never stereotyped but is historical narration, and its purpose is to tie the vassal to the monarch with affection so that he will accept the obligations. So it is also in the Old Testament. Preceding the law in the Old Testament is the historical description of what God has done for his people; their history is narrated in terms of his acts. He is the Lord who brought the people from Egyptian bondage (Exod. 20:2) and gave them a land in which to dwell (see especially the covenant ceremony in Josh. 24:2–13).

(3) The historical proof of the goodness of the monarch toward his vassal having been given, the treaty then presents the stipulations of the covenant, which are a description of the vassal's obligations. Among them there is always the prohibition against the vassal's engaging in foreign relations with foreign powers. The Great King in this was describing his own interests, while leaving the internal relations of a vassal king with his people undisturbed. This reminds us of the First Commandment to Israel which prohibits any relations with other deities (Exod. 20:3; cf. 34:14), and also of the stipulations of Joshua's covenant at Shechem: "Put away the gods which your fathers served beyond the River (Euphrates) and in Egypt, and serve the Lord" (Josh. 24:14). In Israel the Ten Commandments established religious obligation, but they allowed considerable freedom in the conduct of internal civil life. As Professor Mendenhall has further pointed out, the various stipulations for civil law in the "Book of the Covenant" (Exod. 21–3) were not originally intended to be constitutional law, the purpose of which was to enforce morality. They were instead typical examples or descriptions of legal procedure which were written down for the purpose of providing information. Thus the Hebrew word for "law", *torah*, meant "teaching, instruction". Similarly the Babylonian Code of Hammurabi (*ca.* 1700 B.C.) is a collection of common laws and court decisions which contains no reference to obedience to the law; the duties which justice entails are unmentioned. The codification of such laws was a matter of information so that the country could be unified, or (in Israel) that tribal differences in common law could be eliminated so that there could be one "law" and one justice for the whole people. Only later, particularly after the 7th century, was this common law, as written down, used as constitutional law to force and enforce morality. In the earlier period the

[3] See his "Covenant Forms in Israelite Tradition", *The Biblical Archaeologist*, Vol. XVII, No. 3 (Sept. 1954). This is reprinted in his monograph, *Law and Covenant in Israel and the Ancient Near East* (The Biblical Colloquium, Pittsburgh, 1955).
[4] The latter passage contains a reference to the monarch of Assyria which has been rendered "King Jareb" but which is now seen to be *malki rab*, meaning "the great king".

divine Sovereign permitted far more freedom of decision in matters pertaining to daily life.

(4) Next the typical suzerainty treaty stipulated that the document should be deposited in the sanctuary of the vassal and that it should be publicly read at regular intervals, the time not always being specified. In Israel we find similar provisions, as for example in the case of Joshua at Shechem (Josh. 24 : 26) and in Deut. 31 : 9–13 where Moses is said to have written " this law " and to have given it to the priests in charge of the Ark (that is, of the central sanctuary) with the instruction that it should be read " at the end of every seven years " in public assembly. Two strata of Old Testament tradition also affirm that the Decalogue of the original covenant at Sinai was deposited in the Ark (Exod. 25 : 16, 21 ; I Kings 8 : 9) which was housed, when possible, in the central sanctuary.

(5) The fifth section of the typical treaty in question was the invocation of the deities of the respective parties as witnesses to the covenant, concluding with the summarizing statement regarding all the gods : namely, the mountains and the rivers, the heaven and the earth, the winds and the clouds—these are the witnesses " to this treaty and to this oath ". In Israel such witnesses are, of course, lacking. In Josh. 24 God says : " You are witnesses " ; that is, the people themselves, not the gods, are the witnesses. Yet it is interesting to note that the prophets in presenting God's arraignment of Israel for violating her pact with him not infrequently call upon the heavens and the earth as his witnesses (cf. Isa. 1 : 2 ; Hos. 2 : 21–2 ; Micah 6 : 2).

(6) Finally, the treaty concludes with a series of blessings and curses which will come on one who keeps or violates the covenant. These are the sole sanctions of the pact, which thus rests upon a purely religious foundation so that its obligations are not purely legal. Whether the oldest Israelite covenants between God and people contained similar formulas, we do not know. Yet it is important to observe that the " Book of the Covenant ", the " Holiness Code " and the Deuteronomic law all conclude with such hortatory injunctions (Exod. 23 : 20–33 ; Lev. 26 ; Deut. 27 and 28 ; cf. Josh. 8 : 34).

Professor Mendenhall has also noted that the provisions of the vassal treaty are binding only in the lifetime of the participants. When one of them dies, the treaty must be remade. This would suggest an explanation for the ceremonies of covenant-renewal in Israel, and for such a formula as is contained in Deut. 5 : 2–3 to the effect that while the original covenant was made in Horeb (Sinai), the present one is being made " not with our fathers " but with " all of us here alive this day ". Mendenhall further points out that the Hittites and Romans never possessed a word for " covenant ", while the Mesopotamian terms are never found in the treaties. This must warn us that we cannot assume, as has often been done in the past, that the covenant conception is late in Israel just because the term does not happen to occur in all places where we might expect it.

It seems highly probable, therefore, that Israelite faith was given a framework which was borrowed and adapted from international treaties of the 2nd millennium B.C. By its means the people were enabled to interpret their life in terms of loyalty and devotion to the Lord who had done so much for them and who had bound them to himself by solemn pact, and also to view sin as disloyalty and rebellion. It would further suggest the background of so many of the common words in the Israelite religious vocabulary which we know to have been taken over from the realm of law. As far as we know, no other people of the time interpreted their whole national life so completely in terms of a solemn covenant with a single divine Sovereign. One reason for this would certainly be that the focus of religious attention in Israel was single. Only one deity was to be given reverence, worship, and obedience, whereas the national life of other peoples was involved with a plurality of gods, organized (to be sure) in an administrative hierarchy so that the world could be viewed as a cosmic state, but nevertheless providing no such simple and unified conception of life's meaning and vocation as we find in Israel. The covenant framework of the Israelite view of life, however, would not of itself explain all basic differences of religious conception. Israel's ability to interpret her history in terms of the divinely given covenant, after the pattern of the suzerainty treaty, was possible, not only because her worship was single but also because the character of God, his interests and intentions, were conceived very differently from those of the gods of polytheism. To these factors we must now turn.

GOD AND THE GODS

Reference was made above to the witnesses of the international treaties. They were the gods of the respective parties, and at the end of each list it is not unusual to find the summarizing statement that the witnesses were the mountains and the rivers, the heaven and the earth, the winds and the clouds. That is, the gods were actually the elements and powers in the world which were personalized and given names. The primary setting of divine life was thus nature, and the life of nature was the life of the gods. In historical times (that is, after 3000 B.C.), however, the increasing complexity of society and national life meant that the gods of necessity took on an increasing responsibility of a social nature, but their primary relation to nature was seldom, if ever, lost.

How could a doctrine of creation be formulated if there was nothing outside the world to create it? Thought about the world could not reach behind the primordial, static chaos which was conceived as the dark and primeval ocean or " deeps " from which the salt and fresh waters on earth come. In Mesopotamia the " deeps " were personified as Apsu and Tiamat. Creation began by a sexual procreation on the part of this male and female pair, who produced a series of gods, the various elements of the universe as then understood. Order was achieved after a cosmic battle among the gods in which the younger and active forces won the victory over the static chaos, and proceeded to establish world order. One of the younger gods had been made king in order to conduct the battle. Apsu was killed by magic; Tiamat was cut in two, one half becoming heaven and the other earth; and the gods were divided, one half in heaven and the other on earth, charged with their respective duties. Man was created as the slave of the gods to do the menial work of the earth. A divine council for the world state was established for the purposes of making major decisions. A human king was chosen by the council and charged with the social order on earth. Thus Hammurabi in his code of laws is pictured as being commissioned to collect the laws by Sun, Shamash, whose function in the universe was primarily that of Lord Order. But the law was not a revelation; it was claimed by the king as his own and he spoke of it as " my law ", " my words ", and " my justice ". Society was thus neither an order of creation nor of revelation; it was a human contrivance directed by a divinely chosen king. Life was an uncertain thing, and the creation-battle, while it had issued in an initial victory, had to be refought and rewon each year in a ritual New Year's ceremony in which the king took the role of the king of the gods in the ritual drama.

In Egypt the same once-for-all, and yet yearly (and also daily) battle, was waged by Sun (Re) against the dragon of chaos and darkness. Yet in Egypt life was not viewed as so precarious as it was in Mesopotamia. Victory was always assured; society and world order were static and rhythmic, fixed in the order of creation. Hence other approaches to the creation were made which emphasized the fullness and glory of the present order, such as the emergence from the ocean of chaos of the primeval hill on which Sun, the primeval king, began the creation by procreation, which was conceived as an act of masturbation. The security of the social order on earth was assured because the king was not a human being but a divine incarnation, the son of Sun.

In Canaan (Syria-Palestine) the creation doctrine was evidently similar to that in Babylon in its main essentials, though we do not know as much about it. Creation was described as a battle between Baal, the king of the gods, and the primordial dragon of chaos, called Leviathan (Lotan) or Sea (Yam; cf. Fig. 60). This being is described in one

60. A seal showing the seven-headed dragon of chaos being slain

Canaanite religious document with the same adjectives as those employed to describe it in Isa. 27 : 1 : the " swift serpent ", the " twisting serpent ", " the dragon in the sea ". The Old Testament has a number of allusions to this symbol of chaos, using the terms " serpent ", " dragon " or " monster ", and " Rahab ", as well as " Leviathan " and " Sea " (e.g. Psa. 74 : 13–14; 89 : 10; Job 3 : 8 where " day " should be rendered " Sea "; Job 41; Isa. 51 : 9; Amos 9 : 3). And the ultimate background of the " beast " in Revelation is to be found in the same source, including after its destruction the significant words, " the sea was no more " (Rev. 18 : 1). That is, the Bible is able to use the mythological figure to symbolize God's creative power and control over the chaos of the world, though in Isa. 27 : 1 and in Revelation that chaos is not so much an evil in nature as in history. It depicts, not chaos, but sin and the world's alienation from God.

The polytheist thought of creation, then, in terms of a struggle between the various powers of nature, and of world order as an achievement in harmony among many wills. Yet what was it in the world that kept nature orderly and with which the divine wills were themselves in harmony? It was believed that some principle of order had been established at creation, to which even the gods were subject. The Greeks spoke of this principle as *moira*, " fate ", " destiny ", what is fitting and proper. The Egyptians spoke of it as *maat*, usually translated as " truth " or " justice ", but it was " the cosmic force of harmony, order, stability, and security, coming down from the first creation . . . something of the unchanging, eternal, and cosmic " to which everything was subject and which confirmed the *status quo*, particularly the continuing rule of the pharaoh or incarnate king.[5] In Mesopotamia the words *parṣu* and *shimtu* seem to possess a similar significance. *Parṣu* is something mightier than the gods, a world order without which the gods would be nothing. Mankind has its *shimtu* or fate, a destination given it before existence. This conception survives through the Greek philosophers into some forms of modern determinism : that is, there is something fixed in the very constitution of the universe which makes things act the way they do. A popular saying to the effect that " when my time comes, I shall die ", reminds one of the Mesopotamian *shimtu* or fate. According to modern Marxism the world is proceeding inexorably toward the classless society through the conflict of opposing forces ; this movement is taking place because of something fixed in the universe which makes things move this way. In fact, most non-Christian philosophies have believed in some rational principle fixed in the universe that explains its order and movement. One reason why the so-called " mystery " religions of the Graeco-Roman age were so popular was that they promised deliverance from fate. Christianity promised deliverance, too, though it was a deliverance from sin and the powers of darkness, for biblical faith did not believe in any

principle of world order as such nor in anything like the Babylonian *shimtu* or human determinism. To be committed to the God of the Bible meant that a new understanding of the self, its problem and its place in the world must be gained. Furthermore, this world order is not fixed and eternal ; God is engaged in a struggle with an estranged world, so that what we now see is not final.

One of the important things about nature is its orderly movement in the cycle of night and day and in the regular return of the seasons. Thus life and history was believed in the polytheisms to move in a circle with nature. Everything was in rhythm. The chief end of life and society was to be attuned to the gods who were the powers of nature, and thus move with them in their never-ending cycle. This meant that the basic religious literature of the polytheist was not primarily concerned with history or with the life of man on earth. To be sure, human heroes often appear and stories of them are told ; but the basic stories are about the life of the gods which is the life of nature. To us the stories about the loves and wars of the gods seem unreal and irrelevant to our own life. Yet to the polytheist they were reality ; they explained the way the world moves ; and to the universal pattern life must adjust itself. The term " myth " as applied to the polytheist religious literature has been suggestively defined by Professor George E. Mendenhall as " the original divine and timeless cosmic pattern to which life shapes itself ". The Babylonian creation epic, referred to above, in which the king of the gods defeated chaos, set the cosmic pattern to which life was adjusted. The order of affairs in Mesopotamian society was established and defended by it ; the defeat of all forces outside of Mesopotamia was a legitimate aspiration. But when the society fell, then the myth was no longer relevant. The gods and their myths died with the society they buttressed.

Today a number of theologians are using the term " myth " to describe certain characteristics of the Bible : its view of the world as a small space protected by the heavens in the midst of the great " deeps ", its interpretation of history in terms of God's activity, and many of its stories like those of Adam and Eve, the divine covenant, the miracles, the incarnation and resurrection of Jesus, etc. This may be legitimate in the sense that such matters are not the facts of our science but are rather the poetic and pictorial presentations of truth with which science cannot by its limitations deal. That

---

[5] John A. Wilson, *The Burden of Egypt* (Chicago, 1951), p. 48.

is to say, the greatest and deepest truths of life and of God have to be presented by man in his limited language, and to do so he has to use words, expressions and pictures which he knows are not exact blueprints of what he is talking about, but which he nevertheless knows are true, in the sense that they reveal ultimate truth to him. Yet to introduce the term " myth " as a term for the biblical presentation of faith is very confusing, because nothing could be more different than the Bible as a whole from polytheist mythology. The Bible is first of all a historical literature in which the traditions of a people about the past and the historical facts of the present are taken seriously and are used to confess and expound the faith. The literature is not unreal in the sense that it appears removed and separate from ordinary human life. There is no divine cosmic pattern of the polytheistic type to which life is adjusted. Nature is not the focus of attention ; the biblical mind is interested in nature because history takes place in nature, but the life of nature is not necessarily the life of God. The latter has his own independent life, but he has shown his intention and purpose in the life of man by great and continuous acts in history. Hence life and history are not dependent upon nature's rhythm ; they do not move in a cycle as nature does. They move in a direction that God wills ; though deviations caused by man the rebel are frequent, God is not defeated but is Lord even over the world's evil. Man is not adapted to a timeless, cosmic pattern ; integration with the order of nature is not the biblical theme ; history does not go round in a circle according to a heavenly and timeless design. Instead man is God's creature, charged with an earthly vocation, which he is to carry out in obedient love to the Lord who has promised him the good things of earth, including life, blessing and material abundance. Life's pattern is one of obedience in the context of God's promise and fulfilment in history. Thus history is in movement toward a goal ; and human life must adjust itself to God's active, personal will in full knowledge of the promise and the goal in the time which God has created.

In other words, the Bible is not a typical mythology because the God it proclaims is the Lord of history. He is not nature personified or any element in nature ; he is the independent and self-existing source or Creator of nature and all that is. As Creator he is distinct from what he has made and as Ruler he is not what he rules. For this reason Israel could not view the creation as a struggle, but

as an act of the one Deity. Gen. 1, therefore, begins with God who exists before the creation. Yet Hebrew thought started like the polytheists with the watery deep and the primeval darkness. The word for the " deep " is *tehom*, which is from the same original word as the Babylonian Tiamat. But the " deep " is not a dragon or a person. The Hebrews de-mythed the ancient polytheist version of the creation. God said . . . and it came into existence ; and, since God is good, all that he made is good. In the arrangement of his creative work, he established the world's first week ; and he made the heavenly bodies as signs of the seasons. This means that while making the world he created the world's time, which is history's framework. Hence the creation does not suggest to the Hebrew a timeless, cosmic pattern, but instead the beginning of time and history.

How had Israel come to such an understanding of God as would lead them to view the creation in this way ? We do not know of a certainty, but we would suppose that they learned of God in a different way from that of the polytheist. Something must have happened to them in history which someone interpreted in such a way as to lead them to a radically new understanding of the divine. This according to the biblical record was evidently the Exodus from Egypt. A great Power, greater than Pharaoh or anything in the world, delivered the people from Egyptian slavery. In doing so he showed his complete control over the forces of nature, and in the events which followed he further revealed, at least in dim outline, his intentions and purposes. He had saved slaves from bondage and he formed them into a new society which was to worship and serve him alone ; and in the course of the centuries it was seen with increasing clarity that this society was the first-fruits, according to God's intention indeed, the model for the universal kingdom he was establishing on earth. Thus Israel was intensely interested in history and became the first people on earth to preserve and to write a connected account of its own history, because the events of this earth are revelations of God and to tell of them is to confess one's faith. The primary views which the Bible has about God are what was inferred from historical events. These were the focus of attention, not the powers of nature in themselves alone. This was what caused Israel to de-myth the creation myths of antiquity, and to infer that God was the sole Creator because he is Lord of all.

The fact that God has revealed his purpose in

history and has called a new society into being, meant that life and vocation were set before it as a task and a goal. Society was God's special creation and its order of affairs was revealed to it. Man was given great responsibility under God, since the latter had entered into the closest of relations with him and had dignified him with his " Thou shalt ". Hence when Israel recorded its version of creation, its understanding of man was very different from what it was in polytheism. Man possessed a dignity and worth, not because he had within him some portion of divine substance, but because he was given the freedom to be a responsible being, a type of vassal king with power to rule the earth and permission for direct access to, and communication with, his Lord. He was the climax of God's creative work, completely dependent upon his Lord to whom he owes life and all good things, but given a responsible charge and freedom to pursue it. It is thus clear that the dignity of man is something given him by God and is derived from a knowledge of God ; man does not possess a divine " spark " nor the ability to become God or even to " unite " or " fuse " with God in some mystical exercise. God has preserved his independence from what he has created.

Did the Israelite doctrine of divine independence, however, mean that the world of mystery in nature was completely done away ? Did nature become solely an " it " ? A clear answer to this question is not possible. Yet it is doubtful whether Israel rejected entirely the polytheist view of nature as alive and full of power. In Gen. 1 the heavenly bodies are not gods as they were in polytheism ; they are simply God's lights as fixed in heaven's firmament. Yet the words in vs. 26 (" Let us make man ") and those in Gen. 3 : 22 (Man the sinner " has become like one from us ") indicate that God has other supernatural beings associated with him. In Jacob's dream (Gen. 28 : 10–17) a stairway from earth to God's throne in heaven is seen, and on it angels or heavenly messengers are ascending and descending. This depicts a view of God's rule over the earth through his angels who carry out his commission. In Isa. 6 and in many similar passages in prophecy God is represented as sitting on his heavenly throne with his angelic ministers surrounding him. In other words, God was conceived as having a throne and a palace or temple in heaven, and numerous beings were associated with him. In Gen. 6 : 1–4 an old fragment of mythology is preserved to explain the giants who once lived on earth. They are here

said to have been offspring of the union of the " sons of God " with the daughters of men. ✓ The phrase " sons of God " was the usual term for the gods of Canaan in Canaanite polytheism, for they were literally believed to be children of the great gods and goddesses. In Israelite circles the term was taken over as a designation for God's heavenly host. In other words, God was believed to rule over a divine heavenly host, just as the head of a polytheistic pantheon ruled over the gods. This in itself would not be serious unless human curiosity and tendency toward religious borrowing led the people to equate the angels with the heathen nature deities and begin to give them independent worship.

This is precisely what went on in various periods of Israelite history. Except for the time when Jezebel tried to introduce Baal of Tyre into Israel as the national god, we have little evidence that many Israelites thought of giving up the God who had saved them and made them a nation. Instead, they tended to convert their religion into a polytheism by introducing the worship of pagan gods ; and they would have defended their actions by saying that they were not rejecting their great Lord but were simply giving some well-deserved attention to those of his heavenly court who were responsible for making the crops grow, the flocks and herds bear young, etc. In the 7th century it was Judean state policy under King Manasseh to alleviate the tension between him and his Assyrian overlords. One way he did this was to introduce various pagan practices, including altars for the worship of the host of heaven in the very court of the Jerusalem temple (II Kings 21). That such worship was conducted in God's palace (temple) meant, in accordance with ancient ideas, that Manasseh wanted the people to believe that the beings worshipped were God's servants who lived with him in the divine palace. And in the literature of the period we are not left in doubt that the host of heaven worshipped were the sun, moon, planets and stars. The struggle of the leaders of the faith was against the worship of anything in heaven or in earth, except God alone (e.g. Deut. 4 : 19 : Beware " lest you raise your eyes to the heavens and see the sun, the moon and the stars, all the host of heaven, and you thrust yourselves aside and worship them "). Yet the heavenly bodies continued to be identified as members of God's heavenly court, even in pious circles (e.g. Neh. 9 : 6 ; Psa. 148) which did not give them worship. Then again when we hear the prophets calling the whole host of heaven and earth to witness

61. Air view of the excavations of Ras Shamra.   In left center at the edge of the unexcavated section the foundations of the temple of Baal can be seen.   To the right of that was the library where most of the tablets were found

God's indictment of Israel (e.g. Isa. 1 : 2), we know that they do not mean precisely what a polytheist would have meant, but nevertheless we are led to the view that the Israelites did not break so radically with polytheist conceptions that they began to think of an inanimate nature. Like the early Greek philosophers the Israelite continued to think of the elements of nature as possessing a psychic life of their own, and in this respect he is somewhat nearer modern views than the 19th century scientist. When matter is interpreted as energy, it is no longer adequately described as " inanimate ", even though it cannot be said to possess a psyche.

It is now necessary to turn our attention from polytheism in general to the one religion which gave Israel more trouble than any other. This is the religion of Canaan, of Israel's immediate neighbors, whose gods appear frequently in the pages of the Old Testament.   Until recent years our knowledge of Canaanite religion was largely confined to the pages of the Old Testament and to excerpts from Phoenician writings quoted chiefly by later writers.   Now, however, a portion of their long lost religious literature has been recovered.

In 1928 a peasant in cultivating his field accidentally discovered a rich tomb at Minet el-Beida (White Harbor) in northern Syria.   The discovery was communicated to the Syrian Department of Antiquities, and in April 1929 a French expedition began excavations at the site.   The ancient city belonging to the port (Fig. 61) was discovered near by in a great mound known to the Arabs as Ras Shamra (Fennel Head).   Scarcely had a month gone by before one of the most important discoveries of the century was made.   This was the uncovering of a scribal school and library, adjoining a temple. Most of the tablets in the library were written in a strange new script; but they were soon deciphered by Semitic scholars, one of whom had been decorated by the French government for brilliant work on an enemy cipher in the First World War. From this library we have gained more precise information about the Canaanite gods.

THE GODS OF CANAAN

The general Canaanite word for " god " or " divinity " was " el ", and " gods " were either called by the plural of this word or by the phrase " sons of god ", which really means, in Semitic way of speaking: " members of the divine family ". The chief of all the gods, or head of the divine family, was called " El ". While the undoubted controller of the other gods, he is a rather shadowy figure who apparently takes little part in the affairs of men. He lives far away " at the source of the (two) rivers, in the midst of the fountains of the two deeps ". These " deeps " were thought to be below and around the earth, but here and there they break through the earth's crust, giving us the fresh-water springs and rivers, as well as the salt-water oceans. At the source of these " rivers " or " deeps " was apparently the underworld, and there the gods had to go when they wished to consult their father and ruler.

El is called by a number of names: he is " the father of man " as well as of gods; the " father bull "—a characteristic metaphor wherein he is likened to a bull in a herd of cows and calves (!); " the father of years "; and " creator of creatures ". In the Ras Shamra tablets, mentioned above, he seems to have been conceived as one of mild character, good humored, and never refusing something asked of him, though it was always necessary that he be asked (cf. Figs. 62–3). Other sources of information hint, however, that he was not always so, but had obtained his present position by killing his father, Heaven, and emasculating him. Tradition also has it that he killed his favorite son for some reason, cut off his daughter's head, and offered his " only begotten son " as a sacrifice to Heaven. Even in the Ras Shamra literature he has his aberrations; one story tells about his seduction of two women, and after they bear the two children, Dawn and Sunset, he permits them to be driven into the desert (even as was Hagar after bearing Ishmael to Abraham).

62. A bronze statuette, overlaid with gold leaf, of a Canaanite god, presumably El, found at Megiddo and dating from about the 13th century B.C.

El's wife seems to have been Asherah, as her name is spelled in the Old Testament. She is supposed to have borne to El a sizable family, no less than seventy gods and goddesses, some of whom were quite prominent in the divine society. While she was originally the mother-goddess, in practical worship her functions in the world are frequently mixed with those of the goddesses of fertility. In the Old Testament we have a number of allusions to Asherah, though her name is hidden in the Authorized Version by the translation " grove ". Jezebel introduced into Israel four hundred prophets of Asherah (I Kings 18 : 19), and Manasseh had an

63. A plaque showing an attendant before the seated god El, from Ras Shamra

mountain identified by some with one in northern Syria, which was called by the Greeks Mt. Casius. Here perhaps was Tyre's " Holy Mountain ", mentioned in Ezek. 28 : 14, and " Mount Zion in the recesses of the North (Saphon) " in Psa. 48 : 2. The exact identification of the mountain is uncertain, but probably was *originally* thought to be far away at the edge of the world where earth and heaven meet.

Baal is called a number of names. He is " Zabul (the Exalted), Lord of Earth ", whose kingdom was " eternal, to all generations ". He is also called " Lord of Heaven ", and " the Rider of the Clouds ", the latter a title actually given to God in Psa. 68 : 4 (or so it should now be translated, instead of " rideth upon the heavens " with the Authorized Version; see the Revised Standard Version). Zabul as a title for Baal is also preserved in the Old Testament, for poor King Ahaziah, badly injured when he fell out of a second-story window of his palace, and having lost his faith in the God of Israel, sent messengers to the god, Baal-zebul (not " zebub ") in Ekron. It is perhaps appropriate that by New Testament times Baal-zebul had become a title for Satan (e.g. Matt. 12 : 24).

Baal as god of the storm, had a great voice—thunder. He alone reigns over the gods, he says, in order that both the gods and men may become fat, for he alone satisfies the inhabitants of the earth. His great enemy was Mot, " Death ", into whose hands he fell and was slain, whereupon vegetation and conception ceased. In the hand of Mot, we are told, was the staff of childlessness and of widowhood, and the power of halting the productivity of the vine.

Baal, " Lord ", was originally the god's title and not his proper name. The latter was Hadad, though by the 15th–14th centuries B.C. the title was used almost exclusively. The relationship between El and Baal in the divine government was similar to that of the two great gods, Anu and Enlil, in Mesopotamia. Anu was the sky and the source of all authority. Enlil was the Storm, personifying the element of forceful activity in nature. Anu was the passive head of the pantheon of gods, but Enlil was the executive force. El and Baal had the same arrangement, perhaps modelled on the relationship of a king and his prime minister, the latter actually carrying out the administrative activity of government.

In Israel, it is interesting to note, God took over some of the titles and functions of these Canaanite

image of her put in the Temple (II Kings 21 : 7). The symbol of her presence at a place of worship was apparently a sacred tree or pole standing near the altar. One was either set up or planted in Samaria by Ahab (I Kings 16 : 33), and another in Jerusalem by Manasseh (II Kings 21 : 3). Such objects must have been very familiar to the people, for we constantly hear the injunction that they should be cut down, burned, or pulled up because they led Israel astray (Deut. 7 : 5 ; 12 : 3 ; 16 : 21 ; Micah 5 : 14, etc.).

Chief among the offspring of El and Asherah, either as a son or grandson, was Baal, the most colorful and important of all the gods (Figs. 64–5). The Canaanite word *baal* simply meant " lord ", and could be applied to any one of a number of gods, but the Lord or Baal above all others was thought to be the great god who controlled the rain and, therefore, the vegetation. Since the people were entirely dependent on the regularity of the rain and vegetation, it was only natural that they should consider him exceedingly important. His home was on a mountain in the far-away north, a

64. A bronze statue of Baal, found at Ras Shamra

65. A bas-relief showing Baal as God-Storm, discovered at Ras Shamra

gods, particularly those of Baal. *El* and *baal* are both used as names for Yahweh, the God of Israel. We hear of Saul and David naming their children such names as Ishbaal, meaning either " man of Baal " or " Baal exists ", and Beeliada, meaning " May Baal know ". One of David's warriors bore the name Bealiah, meaning " Yahweh is Baal ". This does not mean that the parents of these children worshipped the Canaanite Baal, but that the title was given Yahweh. Yet the danger of confusion and syncretism was so great that in the course of time *baal* was dropped. Hosea, for example, was among those who led the fight against the use of the title. God says through him to the people : " And I shall remove the *baal* names from her (Israel's) mouth, and they shall no longer be remembered in their (Israel's) name(s) " (Hos. 2 : 17). Another Canaanite term for " lord ", *Adon*, did not encounter difficulty and continued in common use as a divine title. *Elyon*, meaning " exalted " or " most high ", was still another Canaanite title frequently used for Yahweh of Israel.

Baal as the active " king " or suzerain of the universe obviously would have been active in many spheres which Yahweh claimed for his own, and forms of thought and expression were borrowed from the former for the latter. Particularly is this true with regard to the storm which Baal personified. Lightning became Yahweh's arrow and thunder his voice (Psa. 18 : 8, 14). God's dramatic appearances on earth could be depicted as a storm, with dark cloud or smoke, thunder or trumpet blast, lightning and the shaking of the earth that accompanies great thunder (Exod. 19 : 16 ff. ; I Kings 19 : 11–12). Psalm 29, dominated by this type of nature imagery, is now believed to have been originally a hymn to

Baal, borrowed and used of Yahweh. It is Yahweh, not Baal, who " maketh the hinds to calve " (Psa. 29 : 9), and gives the blessings of heaven (rain), of the deep (springs and rivers), of breast and womb (Gen. 49 : 25 ; Deut. 33 : 13 ff.). Indeed, Hebrew psalmody is now known to be filled with nature images which were borrowed from Canaan, and along with them certain forms of poetic meter were also taken over.

One of the dangers in polytheism was that rival temples, making rival claims, tended to split up a god's or goddess's personality. Thus in the Old Testament we hear of many baals, though in point of fact Canaanite theologians believed he was one. Probably to counteract this situation the so-called " plural of majesty " came into being. The name for the goddess Ashtoreth frequently appears in the plural (Ashtaroth). An important town in Transjordan was so named (Deut. 1 : 4, etc.), and it is most improbable that a city would be named " Ashtoreths ". The plural must have had another significance. The name for God in the Old Testament which is used more commonly than any other except " Yahweh " is " Elohim ", a plural word also used to mean " gods " though when used of Yahweh it certainly meant the one deity. It is now recognized that this word used to designate one god was thus used in Canaan before it was in Israel. For example, in the Tell el-Amarna letters of about 1375 B.C. Canaanite scribes address the Egyptian Pharaoh as " my gods, my sun-god ", while non-Canaanite scribes use the singular " my god ". Yet the Pharaoh was one, not many. The plural must have come into being to designate the totality of a god's appearances, attributes and personality ; it was a way of emphasizing the one in the many.

Baal's wife was Anath, a goddess of love and war, whom the Egyptians depicted as a naked woman on a galloping horse, brandishing shield and lance. One of her bloody escapades is described in a Ras Shamra poem. For some reason she decided to carry out a massacre, and hewed and smote and slew from the seacoast (west) to the sunrise. Filling her temple with men, she barred the doors and hurled at them chairs, tables, and footstools. Soon she waded in blood up to her knees—nay, up to her neck. " Her liver swelled with laughter ; her heart was full of joy." Satisfied, she then washed her hands in the gore and proceeded to other occupations.

Yet, in spite of her warlike and sadistic nature, she was the goddess of love and fertility. In these functions she was similar to the goddess Astarte, or Ashtoreth as her name is spelled in the Old Testament. These goddesses were responsible for the productivity of animals and man. In an Egyptian text they are called " the great goddesses who conceive but do not bear ". Their role is even clearer when we note that a later Greek writer, Philo of Byblos, quoting from old Phoenician sources, says that Astarte had two sons, named " Sexual Desire " (Pothos) and " Sexual Love " (Eros).

In the Old Testament we hear almost nothing of Anath, but a great deal of Ashtoreth. An altar for her was set up by Solomon in behalf of one of his wives (I Kings 11 : 5), an object which a later writer colorfully labelled " the abomination of the Sidonians " (i.e. Phoenicians) in II Kings 23 : 13. Saul's armor after his death was placed by the Philistines in the Temple of Ashtaroth at Beth-shan (I Sam. 31 : 10), a building destroyed by David when he captured and laid waste the city (Fig. 59).

It is probable that among the Canaanites there was never unanimous agreement as to which of these goddesses was the wife of Baal. At Ras Shamra it was Anath. In the Old Testament, however, Ashtoreth is customarily associated with Baal (cf. Fig. 66), so we may take it that Palestinian Canaanites believed that she was Baal's wife (note Judges 2 : 13 ; 10 : 6 ; I Sam. 7 : 4 ; 12 : 10). Jezebel from Tyre, however, may have had still another idea : namely, that his wife was Asherah ! At least, so we might judge from the association of the two in Jezebel's worship (I Kings 18 : 19).

66. An impression from a cylinder seal found at Bethel, showing Baal and Ashtoreth, the name of the latter being written in Egyptian characters in the center

And so the catalogue of gods might continue. We hear of Dagon, the grain-god, who was an old deity adopted by the Philistines as their chief god, and with whose image they had such difficulty in the presence of the Ark (I Sam. 5). At Ras Shamra he was apparently considered the son of El and the father of Baal, but in Canaanite religion his son seems to have overshadowed him. We hear also of Resheph, the god of pestilence and lord of the underworld ; [6] of Shulman or Shalim, the god responsible for health and well-being, whose name forms the second element in the name of the city, Jerusalem ; of Koshar (or Kathar), the wise inventor and craftsman who makes everything that is beautiful and wonderful, from jewelry, tools, and weapons, to fine buildings fit for the gods. He was also the patron of music, probably both of the poetry and of the instruments, and his favorite abode was in Egypt, a great home of the fine arts. There are many other gods of lesser breed who need not concern us here.

The major gods and goddesses of Canaan were apparently pictured as a rule in the minds of men as having human form, though there were many minor beings who were conceived as birds or animals or hybrids. At least so we might judge from contemporary art. The amazing thing about the gods, however, is that there seems to have been no standard of morality governing their actions. Just as cleanliness and godliness did not necessarily go together, neither did goodness and godliness. The lives of the gods were certainly on a moral level below that of the average of society as a whole, if we can judge from the ancient codes of law. They lived a life of their own, one not to be questioned by man and scarcely providing a model to emulate.

The primary purpose of the stories about the gods was to explain the world and how it works. Basically, the mythology has this in common with some modern theology : namely, that the world was created through conflict and continues its operation in the continual struggle of opposing forces, health, light, and order being perpetually arrayed against the forces of death, darkness, and chaos. Thus we hear of the stories of battle between Death and Life or Vegetation, between Night and Day, between Chaos and the forces of Cosmos.

We shall here mention only that myth which received most attention in Canaan, the essentials of which, however, were present and popular throughout the Near East. To understand it we must know something about the climate of Palestine. From April to the end of October there is no rain, apart from a very occasional and unseasonable shower. Only those vegetables and plants can grow which can secure what water they need from the heavy morning dew. Toward the end of October the rains begin and continue, on and off, throughout the winter to the end of April. The winter, therefore, is one general rainy season, though the Israelites generally divided it into two parts : the early rains (*yoreh*) and the spring rains (*malqosh*). Very early in the spring, about February, the grain is planted, while harvest is in May or June, though the exact time varies with the season and the section of the country. In April, as a result of the rains, the whole countryside is covered with verdure, including beautiful wild flowers of all sorts. By the end of May these have all disappeared, and the landscape is barren except for the trees and the occasional thorny bush which can survive the dry season.

Now the normal mind would ask how and why these things should be so. The Canaanite, personifying the forces of nature, had a reasonable answer. Rain-and-Vegetation (the god Baal) was killed each spring after a great battle with Death (Mot) or with the " Devourers " and " Renderers ", who at Ras Shamra were a group of beings fulfilling the same function. Thus through the summer months Death and the destructive forces reigned supreme. Why do the rains begin again in the fall ? Because Death is vanquished by Baal's ever-loving but warrior wife, and Baal comes back to life. Why does verdure cover the land in the spring ? Because of the mating of Baal and Fertility, his wife (either Anath or Ashtoreth).

Periods of drought and famine were probably explained in the same way. The Ras Shamra story in which Baal was apparently killed by the " Devourers " and " Renderers " may not refer to the yearly cycle at all, but to a drought. In any event we are told that after his death, " El completed seven years, eight yearly cycles, while he (Baal) was clad with the blood of his brethren as a garment, with the blood of his companions as a cloak." During that time " the king ceased to give judgment, women ceased to draw water from the spring, the well of the temple ceased to yield water, and the sound of work ceased in the workshop ". After Death was destroyed, one of the gods had a dream wherein he saw that

> The heavens rained oil ;
>   the valleys ran honey ;
> So I know that triumphant Baal lives,
>   that the prince, lord of earth, exists.

This myth of the dying-rising god was common throughout the Near East. In Babylonia he was called Tammuz, and his wife (Love and Fertility)

---

[6] His name appears in Hab. 3 : 5, though it is hidden in translation by " burning coals " in the A.V. and by " plague " in the R.S.V.

was Ishtar. In Egypt it was Osiris and Isis, and in Greece Adonis and Aphrodite. While the stories in these countries, as in Canaan, were greatly elaborated in numerous ways, the basic plot is as outlined above.

There can be no doubt that the Israelites were well acquainted with this myth, for we find hints of it in several places, though it is difficult to put our fingers on single passages and be sure of their background. It seems probable, for example, that the prophet Hosea (about 740–735 B.C.) makes use of words, phrases, and imagery drawn from the rites of Canaan connected with the worship of Baal. Thus 6 : 1–3 :

Come, and let us return to the Lord,
  For he hath torn and he will heal us ;
    He hath smitten and he will bind us up !
He will bring us to life (again) after two days ;
  On the third day he will raise us up
    That we may live before him.
Let us know ; let us press on
  To know the Lord.
As the dawn is firmly established, (so) is his going forth ;
  And he will come to us like the rain,
    Like the spring rain he will water the earth.

Here the allusions to God's reviving the people on the third day and of his coming to our rescue like the winter rains certainly remind us forcibly of the Canaanite myth about Baal, though of course the theological content of the passage is far different. Well known ways of thinking were being used to convey new truth.[1]

It is possible also that the frequent emphasis in the Old Testament on Yahweh as the " living God " may have been an Israelite reaction to the belief in the dying-rising Baal. Thus Hab. 1 : 12 : " Art thou not from everlasting, O Lord my God, my Holy One ; thou dost not die ! "[1] (contrast the Authorized and Revised English translation).

WORSHIP

While we know a good deal about the mythology of the ancient Near East, we do not know as much as we should like about the practices of the worship and the religious attitudes of the common man. We have noted already his belief that nature is alive and full of strange forces, difficult for him to control. Basically, therefore, his religion was a combination of faith, magic, and superstition. Life was

a desperately serious matter, and it was imperative that he develop ways and means of controlling the forces about him. Otherwise he could not live, let alone prosper. His religion, accordingly, was centered around a variety of acts, controlled and regulated by long lists of rules, and designed to turn the attention of the gods to him that they might prosper his ways. There was little in his religion that might make him a better man. Society had developed its control or laws, and these were given religious sanction, but the *primary* attention was toward those ritualistic, outward acts which would make the gods more favorable to him.

Central to his conception of worship were offerings—the products of his land and of his flocks, even sometimes of his children. These offerings had to be taken to certain specified holy places and given to the gods in certain ways. In the course of centuries the manner of offering became increasingly complicated and it was necessary that there be a group of people who were expert in the law, and who would see to it that the gifts were offered in the proper way, the way most calculated to gain the gods' attention. These were the priests, the mediators between the gods and men who presented the latter's case in the most favorable and proper manner.

The religion of Canaan, as we know it from Ras Shamra and from the Old Testament, undoubtedly involved elaborate systems of ritual, especially of sacrificial ritual. A large variety of animals and birds are known to have been used : cattle, especially bulls and calves, rams, ewes, lambs, kids, deer, stags, wild goats, wild bulls, small birds, especially doves, etc. From numerous biblical and Roman allusions we know also that child sacrifice was occasionally practised, the story of the Moabite king, Mesha (II Kings 3 : 27) immediately coming to mind. The older archaeological literature made much of this custom because so many jars with children's bones were found in the excavations. Infant mortality was exceedingly high, however, and one can be sure that most cases of child-burial which have been found do not represent examples of child-sacrifice. From numerous allusions also we know that various types of divination, ways of peering into the future, were common among the Canaanites (Fig. 67). It was pointed out in connection with the story of Balaam that Mesopotamians were the great experts in this sort of thing, but the Canaanites in course of time could not have been far behind (see, e.g. Deut. 18 : 10).

67. A liver model from Megiddo. It was made of clay in order to preserve an omen which was interpreted from it

68. A plaque showing the Canaanite fertility goddess with a snake draped around her neck

The chief emphasis in Canaanite religion, however, was upon fertility and sex. Worship, therefore, would be concerned first of all with the problem of making land, herds, flocks, and human beings fertile and productive. It is probable that many of the mythological stories were acted out in the religious festivals, and that some of them, at least, would have been every bit as sensuous in the acting as in the telling. This would hold true for the spring festivals especially, when the mating of Rain-and-Vegetation (Baal) with the goddess of Fertility was supposed to have taken place. In any event, we know that sacred prostitution, both male and female, was exceedingly common, practised in the name of religion at the various centers of worship. Fertility as a goddess actually became a sacred prostitute who, curiously enough, was called " the Holy One ". In Egypt she was pictured as a nude woman, standing on a lion, with a lily or lilies in one hand and a serpent or two in the other.

These Egyptian representations are so much like similar representations on clay plaques, found in large numbers in the towns of Late Canaanite Palestine, that there can be little doubt that the plaques also represent the fertility goddess in her role of " the Holy One ", though we are not sure of her personal name (Fig. 68). This type of plaque seems to have originated in Mesopotamia where it represented the mother-goddess, but the Canaanites altered it, emphasizing the sexual features to such an extent as to leave no doubt about the emphasis in Canaanite religion.

Now the fact that these plaques were so common, one or more in every home in all probability, would lead us to suppose that they must have played an important part in the religion of the common people. Perhaps it was thought that by handling such sacred and magical objects, fertility would be imparted to the one in need. The lily probably symbolized the goddess's charm or sex appeal, while the serpent indicated her fecundity.

This sexual emphasis of Canaanite religion was certainly extreme and at its worst could only have appealed to the baser aspects of man. Religion as commonly practised in Canaan, therefore, must have been a rather sordid and degrading business, when judged by our standards. And so, it seems, it appeared to religious circles of Israel. In Deuteronomy there is a direct prohibition of this sort of thing in the name of religion :

There shall be no sacred female prostitute among the daughters of Israel ; neither shall there be a sacred male prostitute among the sons of Israel. Thou shalt not bring the hire of a harlot or the wages of a dog into the house of the Lord thy God for any vow (i.e. to accompany any vow as a gift to God), for both of these are an abomination unto the Lord thy God (23 : 17-18).

Most of the common worship was carried on at the "high places", altars evidently placed at elevated places. People seemed to think that it was easier to attract the gods on hills than in the valleys, and we are reminded of the statement of Jeremiah that idolatrous people were worshipping " upon every high hill and under every green tree " (2 : 20). The best example of a Canaanite altar for burnt offering has been found at Megiddo, dating from about 1900 B.C. (Fig. 24). It is quite large, about six and a half feet high and twenty-nine feet in diameter at the base. Some six steps led to the top and at their foot were found quantities of animal bones, the remains of offerings or sacrifices which had been burned on the top of the altar. The high places at Ramah, where Samuel sacrificed (I Sam. 9) and at Gibeon, where Solomon sacrificed and prayed when he was elevated to the throne (I Kings 3), undoubtedly had altars of this sort. Incidentally, these stories and others in the Old Testament tell us something of the sacrificial practice common to Near Eastern people at that time. The worshipper customarily brought the products of his field, flocks, or herds to the high place. (Hannah brought a three-year-old bull—I Sam. I : 24, Revised Version Margin and Revised Standard Version—and Solomon "a thousand burnt offerings", though the kind of animals is not specified.) Prayers were offered ; vows made ; and there was apparently a sacrificial feast. Only certain choice portions of the animals (especially the fat : Lev. 17 : 6) were burned on the altar. Certain other portions were for the priests, and the rest could be eaten by the worshippers (I Sam. 2 : 12 ff. ; 9 : 22 ff.). In the story of Samuel and Saul chambers for such feasts were built at the high place, and in the feast Saul was served the choicest portions of the sheep : the thigh and the fat tail (the latter to be read instead of the enigmatic " that which was upon it " in I Sam. 9 : 24).

According to the Old Testament, Canaanite high places had other sacred objects present besides the altar. One was the sacred tree, grove, or post, which the prophetic writings exhorted the people to cut down. We have already noticed that these objects were apparently the symbols of the mother-goddess, Asherah. The sacred tree was very common in ancient Near Eastern religion, as we know not only from texts but from ancient art. It even appears in the Garden of Eden (Gen. 2 : 17) ; but we do not yet know as much about it as we should. Also present at most Canaanite high places was the sacred pillar. We have already mentioned these in connection with Patriarchal religion (Chap. III), and quite a number have been found both in Palestine and Transjordan (Fig. 25). Good arguments have been advanced to connect these pillars with ancestor-veneration ; that is, the stones were set up as memorials, and are thus the predecessors of the modern tombstone. It is difficult, however, to explain all of them by this means alone. At the high places, if the sacred tree is the symbol of the mother-goddess, it is also possible, though not certain, that the pillar may have been the symbol of El or Baal. In some late representations of Phoenician temples the pillar occupies the central place in the sanctuary, just where we should expect a statue of the deity (Fig. 69).

After 1100 B.C. a common object at Canaanite sanctuaries was one or more small altars for burning incense (Fig. 70). In some eight Old Testament passages there occurs an obscure expression, " sun-image " as translated in the Revised Version or merely " image " as translated in the Authorized Version, while later Hebrew dictionaries recommend " sun-pillar ", thinking of Egyptian obelisks (see Lev. 26 : 30 ; II Chron. 14 : 3 and 34 : 4, 7 ; Isa. 17 : 8 and 27 : 9 ; and Ezek. 6 : 4, 6). The Hebrew

69. Sketch of a 3rd century A.D. coin minted at Byblos, showing a Phoenician temple with a pillar within it as a symbol for the god there worshipped

70. Objects found in a building of the 10th century at Megiddo, among them two altars of incense

word is *hammanim* always in the plural), and the translators, uncertain as to what it was, derived it from a rare word for " sun ". Such an explanation was only a guess, however, and few were ever satisfied with it.

From various excavations in Palestine have come small limestone altars with " horns " on the corners, the earliest having been found at Megiddo in a shrine of the Israelite period, dating about the time of David or shortly thereafter (early 10th century). These altars are too small for burnt offerings and could only have been used for incense. Recently one such object was found in North Syria at Palmyra, belonging to a much later period, to be sure, but having the word in question inscribed upon it. We are justified, therefore, in crossing out the mistranslation " sun-image " in our Bibles and substituting " altar of incense ". Judging from the passages in which the word occurs, enlightened religious circles in Israel and Judah considered such objects as pagan and condemned them along with the pillars and trees or posts in the severest terms.

High places were only country sanctuaries, however ; there were many more elaborate places of worship situated in Canaanite cities. It was commonly believed that the gods needed houses to live in, just as did men. One of the Ras Shamra myths tells about the erection of a temple for Baal, and this temple and many others have been excavated in Palestine and Syria. A series of them have been found at Beth-shan (Fig. 59), dating from the 14th to the 10th century. One entered the main room of the typical temple through an indirect entrance, for it was not considered proper for the curious to be able to look directly into the interior from the outside. The ceiling of the main room was supported by two columns, the bases and capitals of which were of stone, while the shafts were of wood. Around the room was a low bench where offerings were probably placed. A series of steps led up to a cubicle, the " Holy of Holies ", where the central object of the worship there, probably a statue of the god, was erected on a raised platform (cf. also Fig. 48). Before the steps was an altar for offerings and incense. We may note that both the Israelite Tabernacle and the Temple of Solomon had similar small altars placed before the door of the " Holy of Holies ", the one in the Tabernacle being called an altar of incense (Exod. 30 : 1 and I Kings 6 : 20 ; 7 : 48). The floor of the raised cubicle was found in one case to have been painted a bright blue, and the whole interior must have been highly decorated.

A well-preserved Canaanite temple found at Lachish was destroyed about 1220 B.C. in a terrific destruction by the Hebrews (Fig. 48). Some of the walls were reddened like those of a kiln ; some of the glass objects found had been partially melted ; bits of ivory had been blackened, and some calcined ; charred remnants of the roof beams lay where they had fallen. It is evident from the ruined contents that the building had been destroyed while in full use as a sanctuary. Around the plastered walls were benches for offerings. On one side were niches in the wall for bowls not in use. In front was the raised platform for the idol, three steps leading up to it. Before it was a two-sectioned hearth, perhaps used as a small altar. To the right was a hollow stand, on top of which was a bowl with a hole in the bottom of it, used for sacred libations. Beside it was a niche which held the lamps (pinched saucers holding oil with a wick placed in the pinched part). To the left was a pottery bin for offering or waste material. To the rear were two rooms for storage and for the priests. It is probable that little more than incense was burned in the temple, while burnt offerings were fired on an altar for the purpose outside the building, as was usual in most later temples with which we are familiar.

In the debris around the platform and pottery bin large numbers of animal and bird bones were found. Four types of animals were represented: sheep (or goat), ox, and two wild species such as gazelle or ibex. It is very important to observe that all the animals were young and all identifiable bones were the *upper part of the right foreleg*. This is exactly what we should expect according to the biblical law concerning peace-offerings. Only boneless fat was to be burned upon the altar, and the portion of the priests was the right shoulder (Lev. 3; 7 : 32, Revised Version margin). Presumably the rest could be eaten by the worshippers outside or in some neighboring chamber. Inside the temple, therefore, one would expect to find only the bones of the priests' portion, which is exactly the situation at Lachish. Few of the bones showed evidence of burning, indicating that the meat had been cooked by boiling, presumably outside the temple. Incidentally, it may be recalled that the sin of the sons of Eli was that they were violating this established custom. Instead of waiting until the fat was taken from the cooked meat, and then taking their proper portion, they took what they could get, the choicest portions, before everything else (I Sam. 2 : 12 ff.).

In contrast to the situation in Egypt and Mesopotamia few large idols have been found in Palestine and Syria. If the Beth-shan and Lachish temples had them, as seems probable, they were salvaged from the ruins and the metal in them was re-used for other purposes. Monumental stones with pictures of the gods upon them have been discovered, however, and also large numbers of small metal images, mainly of male deities, most of which are of

Baal. There are several descriptions of these small metal figures in the Old Testament; for example, Hab. 2 : 19:

> Woe unto him that saith to the wood, " Awake ! "
>   to the dumb stone, " Arise; this will teach ! "
> Behold it is overlaid with gold and silver;
>   and there is no breath in its midst !

Well-preserved metal images which have been found are exactly like this description: copper or bronze covered with gold and silver leaf, usually representing the clothes (Fig. 62). None of these have been found in Israelite towns, however, and we shall return to the possible significance of this fact below.

Many objects used in worship at the sanctuaries have been found. Mention has already been made of the cylindrical stand, on which was a bowl with a hole in it. These were used for the pouring out of a holy liquid, a libation. An example from Beth-shan has little doves over the handles and peering through the windows, while snakes twine around them. Snakes and doves appear to have been symbolic of certain aspects of the goddesses of fertility. A number of model shrines (Fig. 71), differing in shape, have been found also, with representations of the serpent, dove, lion, and three gods upon it. While we know these to have been used in temple worship, their exact purpose is not clear, though Mesopotamian pictures show them holding offerings or sometimes sacred plants within.

Canaanites and Semites in general believed that under the earth was the nether world, called in the Old Testament " Sheol ", or simply " the pit ". When a man died, he descended to the Underworld and lived there with the " shades ", those who had gone before him. It was a cheerless, dark place to which one must go regardless of the quality of his life. In other words, the ideas of heaven, resurrection, and rewards in the after-life are not to be found in the religion of Canaan, nor in the religion of Israel (until the last pre-Christian centuries), for the Israelites shared the common Semitic heritage in this regard. Consequently, the burial customs of Canaan and Israel are identical. Graves were usually shared by the members of a family (cf. the Patriarchal Cave of Machpelah). Here the bodies were interred along with objects which had been used in life, and which, it was believed, would be needed in the Underworld. Those things most commonly found are jewelry, weapons, and pottery. Dishes, cups, and jars had been the invariable burial gifts since the invention of pottery; in them food

71. A model shrine from Beth-shan

and drink were placed for the dead to use on his journey to Sheol (Fig. 20).

Such in brief was the manner of Canaan. What was Israel's reaction to it?

ISRAEL AND THE RELIGION OF CANAAN

In the discussion of Canaanite religion thus far a sufficient number of biblical allusions have been given to show something of the influence of the Semitic world in general and of the Canaanite world in particular upon the life of Israel. The Hebrew views of the world order, the sky, the earth, and the underworld were those of the Semitic world. So also was the belief that the proper way to worship was first of all to sacrifice an animal and to bring to the sanctuary gifts from the first fruits of the field, the flock, and the herd. Many of the rules by which sacrifice must be made were common pro-

perty, and it is now evident that much of the sacrificial ritual found in the book of Leviticus was borrowed from Canaan. One hint of this is to be found in the discovery of the right shoulder bones in the Lachish temple. From Canaanite documents, particularly from the Ras Shamra tablets, we learn that at least some of the offerings have the same names in Canaan as in Israel. We are also reminded of the statement of Amos (Chap. 5 : 25) that the elaboration at least of this sacrificial ritual did not go back to Mosaic times, as the priests claimed that it did, and in this contention he was undoubtedly correct:

Sacrifices and meal offerings did ye bring to me
 in the wilderness forty years, O House of Israel?

Even a casual reading of the Old Testament will indicate also that while the enlightened religious leadership of Israel might believe one way, the mass of the people were more tolerant of the ways of the world, adopting many of the practices of their neighbors, until large numbers of them, especially in the early days of the nation, were undoubtedly polytheists or verging thereon. So great was the borrowing of Israel from Canaan that it has been a common view among biblical students that before the prophetic reactionary movement got under way Israelite religion, like her material culture, was so similar to that of Canaan as to make it virtually impossible to distinguish the two in vital matters. Having noted the similarities, the borrowing, and the syncretism, let us now note a few of the differences.

The first remarkable fact about the Israelite conception of God is that he was believed to stand entirely alone, with no other being on his level. He is represented throughout the Old Testament as a "jealous" God: that is, he is concerned that the people do not fall back into polytheism, that they worship and follow none but himself. He has no wife and family. In fact, biblical Hebrew possessed no word for "goddess". Enlightened religious circles apparently did not believe in the female aspect as necessary to explain the working of the world, though to be sure many tolerant Israelites compromised their heritage in worshiping the gods and goddesses of Canaan.

Equally surprising is the prohibition against images. "Thou shalt not make unto thee a graven image" or any "molten gods" (Exod. 20 : 4; 34 : 17). This is a significant commandment since there was nothing like it in the world about. Archaeology offers support for the antiquity of this commandment in Israel in that a figure of Yahweh has yet to be found in debris of an Israelite town. The interesting fact is that Canaanite cities possess quite a series of copper and bronze figurines of male deities, most of which are identified with Baal. But when we come to Israelite towns, the series gives out. Yet Israelites were familiar with such images, as we know from the denunciations in Deuteronomy, Jeremiah, Habbakuk, and Isaiah. In the city of Megiddo, for example, a tremendous amount of debris was moved from the first five town-levels (all Israelite), and not a single example has been discovered.[7]

At the same time, however, large numbers of figurines representing the mother-goddess are found in every excavation into Israelite houses, indicating that many homes had one or more of them. To be sure, they are no longer as sensuous as the Canaanite examples (cf. Fig. 72), but they are nevertheless indisputable evidence of the wide-spread syncretism, verging on polytheism, among the common people. They probably owned them, however, not so much for theological as for magical reasons, using them as " good luck " charms. It would not be surprising to find an occasional image of Yahweh among such unenlightened and tolerant circles in Israel, but the fact remains that the people seemed to understand that God was simply not honored in that way. The antiquity of the Second Commandment thus receives support, and by implication also the First Commandment; and these two prohibitions are certainly among the distinguishing features of Israelite belief.

Reference has already been made to the fact that typical mythology is not characteristic of biblical literature. The Israelite vocabulary of names for God was not drawn from nature, but exclusively from human society. God is lord, king, judge, shepherd, father, husband, and the like. Such terms were also used in polytheism for the gods, but they were superimposed upon more central images from nature, such as sky, storm, the heavenly bodies, fertility, etc. Nature in the Bible, as God's creation, contained no forms on which one could focus his primary religious attention. The biblical representation of deity in human form exclusively

72. A pillar-figurine of the Canaanite mother-goddess, from Beth-shemesh

(anthropomorphism) is a witness to God's personal relation to history and to human society, for the only image possible of him is the mental image of a person with whom man can have personal relations.

Since history is significant as the arena of God's directing activity and the revelation of his activity, there is no timeless, cosmic pattern to which life must adjust. Instead, the personal God is at work, and man must work. God's action in history is a mediate one; that is, he chooses whom he wills and directs them to his purposes, whether they realize it or not. Biblical people believed their society was a new community, specifically formed by God through a series of remarkable acts, and given a revealed order by which to live in the earth. The social order was thus neither to be a human contrivance (Mesopotamia), nor was it an order of creation (Egypt), but a special revelation which explained the meaning of daily life as vocation. Biblical religion is thus the only religion which dignifies work in this manner. Work and all moral activity which it involves, however, do not have the purpose of ushering the Kingdom of God into the earth. God himself is in charge of his Kingdom and will use human works as he sees fit. Faithful work is man's obedient and loving service of his Lord, and man is to fulfill this service because God has

---

[7] An expected exception to these generalizations appeared in the 1958 excavations at Hazor, where a metal figure of a Canaanite god appeared in a jug filled with other metal objects, including an axe (see *The Biblical Archaeologist*, Vol. XXII, 1959, p. 13). Yet since this was a hoard of metal being saved for some other purpose, too much cannot be said about it in this connection because we do not know its source or purpose. The date of the hoard is given as *ca.* 11th century B.C.

commanded him to do so and because God is God. History is the arena of God's great conflict with forces alienated from him, but the future is in his hands when the purposes seen in the present will be fulfilled.

The worship of such a God could make use of many forms used by polytheists, but their inner intent and purpose would be different. In polytheism the individual worshipper stood before his deity with gifts to win the god's favor to his cause and to make atonement for his sins. In Israel the worshipper did the same, but there is much less faith in the power of a rite, no matter how well performed, to reconcile oneself with God unless there was also a real repentance and a real " turning " around in life. The sacrificial system had no magical power over deity; it was a means which God himself gave Israel and which he would accept from the faithful as proper worship. But the " high-handed " sinner, who had little real regard for God and less for the fellowship, could not expect God to receive his acts of worship. Both the law and the prophets lay heavy stress upon proper attitude and a true repentance, else the rites would be of no avail. The whole world of pagan magic was discarded, including spiritualism, astrology and divination; and so also was the world of demons who in polytheism caused so much of life's misery, though in the Intertestamental age a segment of this world was allowed to enter the newly conceived dominion of Satan.

Finally, we may say that whereas Canaan had a profound influence on certain spheres of Israelite life, including forms of worship, psalmody, art, architecture and material culture, there is one very curious religious difference in addition to those already mentioned. That is with regard to the early history of the world as recounted in Gen. 1-11. As has long been known, pagan influence on these traditions came from Mesopotamia and not from Canaan. Indeed, such traditions as those of the Tower of Babel (Gen. 11), Nimrod (Chap. 10), the Flood (Chaps. 6-9), and the numbers seven and ten respectively in the two lists of pre-Flood heroes (Chaps. 4 and 5), are presumably early in Israel and their relation to Mesopotamian sources must be traced back to the Patriarchal period when the Patriarchs were in Mesopotamia. The traditions are too early for us to assume that they were influenced by the Assyrian overlords of Palestine in the 8th and 7th centuries B.C., whereas Canaan, according to our present knowledge, had nothing like them.

Best known, of course, is the story of the great flood which covered the earth and destroyed all life except that preserved by Noah in the Ark. That the Babylonians had a similar story has been known since ancient times from the writings of a Babylonian named Berossus in the 3rd century B.C. In 1872 George Smith announced his discovery of an older version of the story which he had found in the library of Asshurbanapal uncovered at Nineveh in 1853. Since that time, we have learned that this version rests on still older sources which can be traced back to the 3rd millennium B.C.

The Babylonian flood is recounted in the Gilgamesh Epic, a long poem about the ancient king of Uruk in southern Babylonia who, suffering severely from the stark reality of death as he faced it in the death of his friend Enkidu, set out to find everlasting life. After numerous adventures, he gained passage over the waters of death and met Utnapishtim, the only mortal who had gained eternal life. Yet Utnapishtim could not help him because his was a unique gift from the Storm-god Enlil in circumstances that will not recur. In the days of old, when the gods had decided to destroy mankind by a flood, Utnapishtim and his wife had been warned by the god, Ea, had built a ship and had saved himself, his wife and pairs of living things. Afterwards, the Storm, Enlil, repented of the flood as a rash act and rewarded Utnapishtim with eternal life. Gilgamesh, however, is told about a rejuvenating plant at the bottom of the sea. This he obtains, only to have it stolen from him by a snake as he returns home. Thus it comes about that snakes can be reborn but mankind, cheated of the plant, can have no hope of life eternal.

Many of the details of the Babylonian tale of the flood are so close to the biblical story that the ultimate dependence of the latter upon the former seems clear. Not only the general outline of the story, but the building of the ship, the release of birds at the end of the flood, including the dove and raven (the Babylonian story also has a swallow), and the sacrifices of the flood-hero after the boat has landed on some mountains, are common to both accounts.

The differences between the two are, first, that the Babylonian ship landed in the Zagros mountains to the east of Mesopotamia, while the biblical Ark " came to rest upon the mountains of Ararat ", which is Armenia. Thus the Genesis story is probably based upon a northern Mesopotamian version. Secondly, the polytheism of the Babylonian account is a typical feature. After the flood was under way, even the gods feared it, climbed to the highest heaven, and crouched like dogs, cowering at the bulwarks of heaven. After the flood subsided, the gods who had been so long without food are said to have smelled the sweet savor of the hero's sacrifice and " gathered like flies " over it. Thirdly, the whole meaning of the two stories differs in their settings. In the biblical story the flood is no longer a rash and irresponsible act, but the illustration of the righteousness of God, who acts in history to destroy sinners though he preserves his remnant for a new beginning.

Much has been written concerning the historicity of the Flood, particularly since the discovery of a " flood " layer in the excavations of Ur in southern Babylonia by Sir Leonard Woolley in 1929. The confident assurance by this excavator that he had found evidence of the Flood is shown in his book, *Ur of the Chaldees* (1929), and has been enthusiastically shared by many popular handbooks since that time.

Unfortunately, the facts of the situation do not enable the student to become as confident. Woolley seems to have dug some five pits through the early strata of occupation at Ur, but in only two of them did he find deposits of water-borne debris. The logical inference from this is that the flood in question did not cover the whole city of Ur, but only part of it. Furthermore, the site showed no break in occupation, as a result of the flood, which we should expect if there had been a major catastrophe.

Evidence for floods has also been found at Kish, Fara and Nineveh in Mesopotamia, though not at other sites where it might have been expected. Yet no two of these flood layers can be dated to the same period. All of the inundations were of a purely local character. They were the type of thing that still occurs when the Euphrates or Tigris rivers temporarily burst their banks. We must conclude, therefore, that the Flood story is an exaggeration of one such local inundation, or, much more probably, it is an old tradition, going back to the end of the Stone Age before the present bounds of the oceans were fixed. To place the tradition this early would make it possible for us to account for the widespread diffusion over the earth of so many different versions of a catastrophe by flood. Yet for some reason, as far as we now know, the tradition did not take root among Israel's neighbors, the Canaanites. In Western Asia we hear of it only in ancient Babylonia and Israel.

FURTHER READING

H. Frankfort *et al.*, *The Intellectual Adventure of Ancient Man* (Chicago, 1946), an excellent treatment of the theology of polytheism, most of which was subsequently reprinted by Penguin Books under the title, *Before Philosophy*.

W. F. Albright, *Archaeology and the Religion of Israel* (Baltimore, 1942), particularly Chaps. III and IV on the religion of the Canaanites and of early Israel.

M. J. Dahood, " Ancient Semitic Deities in Syria and Palestine ", *Le antiche divinità semitiche*, *Studi Semitici*, Vol. I, ed. by S. Moscati, Rome, 1958.

G. Ernest Wright, *The Old Testament Against its Environment* (London and Chicago, 1950), essentially an elaboration of things summarized briefly in this Chapter. See also John Bright, *A History of Israel* (Philadelphia, 1959), pp. 128–60.

For recent translations of the Mesopotamian creation and flood epics, see the translations of S. N. Kramer and E. A. Speiser in J. B. Pritchard, ed., *Ancient Near Eastern Texts* (Princeton, 1950), pp. 37 ff. and 60 ff. In the same volume (pp. 129 ff.) may be found translations by H. L. Ginsberg of three of the Ugaritic (Ras Shamra) epics. See also A. Heidel, *The Babylonian Genesis* (Chicago, 1942) and *The Gilgamesh Epic and Old Testament Parallels* (Chicago, 1946).

Among numerous other items attention might be called especially to the following : John Bright, " Has Archaeology Found Evidence of the Flood ? " *The Biblical Archaeologist*, Vol. V, No. 4 (Dec. 1942), pp. 55–62 ; William L. Reed, *The Asherah in the Old Testament* (Texas Christian University Press, Fort Worth, 1949—though I do not agree with this author's careful study at one point : namely, that the type of object designated by this name is always a wooden *image*, and not on occasion a wooden symbol) ; Howard Wallace, " Leviathan and the Beast in Revelation ", *The Biblical Archaeologist*, Vol. XI, No. 3 (Sept. 1948), pp. 61–8 ; G. Ernest Wright, " The Terminology of Old Testament Religion and its Significance ", *Journal of Near Eastern Studies*, Vol. I (1942), pp. 304–414 ; and " How Did Early Israel Differ from Her Neighbors ? " *The Biblical Archaeologist*, Vol. VI, No. 1 (Feb. 1943).

CHAPTER VIII

THE GOLDEN AGE

" Then all the elders of Israel gathered themselves together, and came to Samuel unto Ramah. And they said unto him : ' Behold, thou art old and thy sons walk not in thy ways. Now make us a king to judge us like all the nations ' . . . And he said : ' This will be the manner of the king that shall reign over you. He will take your sons and appoint them for himself, for his chariots and his horsemen and to run before his chariots . . . And he will take your daughters to be perfumers, cooks, and bakers. And he will take your fields . . . and give them to his officers, and he will take the tenth of your seed. . . . He will take the tenth of your sheep ; and ye shall be his servants ! ' " (I Sam. 8 : 4–17).

THE greatest and most spectacular age of Israel was just before and after 1000 B.C. These were the days of those colorful and interesting figures, Saul, David, and Solomon, who brought the Israelite state into being and in an incredibly short time made it a nation of no small importance in the contemporary world. In the course of two generations a group of tribes, loosely knit together by a religious covenant and depending upon a spontaneous, charismatic leadership to preserve their independence, became a strong and unified state. This brought material prosperity and a degree of wealth to a people who heretofore had been desperately poor.

Archaeological evidence is plentiful to indicate a " new deal " for the farmer and prosperity for all. After the fall of Shiloh about 1050 B.C., the fortunes of Israel were at their lowest, with Philistine garrisons established in the hill country (e.g. I Sam. 10 : 5 ; 13 : 3) and Hebrews serving in the Philistine army (I Sam. 14 : 21). Saul's greatest service lay in his thrusting the Philistines out of the hills, while it remained for David so to reduce their power and their territory that they were never again a serious enemy. Thereafter the excellent Philistine pottery with its graceful swans and attractive shapes ceased to be made. In fact, the material culture of the plain became increasingly like that of the hills, showing that the center of political and economic gravity had shifted. For the first time in history it was the hill country which determined the cultural " tone " of Palestine, not the contrary as had hitherto been the case. Israel's armies now had the upper hand ; energetic rulers were making brilliant plans for future prosperity ; and extensive commerce with other peoples was begun.

The importance of the Philistine defeat and of the strong central government can scarcely be exaggerated. For one thing, it meant *an industrial revolution*. Philistine power was broken and the secret of the iron smelting process became common property. The first datable iron agricultural implement is a plowpoint found in Saul's capital, Gibeah. After his day, almost every farmer was able to own iron axes, mattocks, plowpoints, pruning hooks, and sickles. Thus methods of agriculture were undoubtedly improved.

Iron pruning hooks and sickles now displaced the crude flint implements (Fig. 73) which had been in use since the Stone Age. Other iron tools were far more serviceable than the soft copper and bronze employed up to this time. Iron nails could now be used in building, whereas copper nails would not have been sufficiently hard. Thus the significance of the statement that " David prepared iron in abundance for the nails for the doors of the gates and for the joiners " is clear (I Chron. 22 : 3). Our evidence indicates also a general increase in the population, an improvement

73. Flint sickles from Tell Jemmeh

74. The ruins of Gibeah

in building techniques, in pottery making, and in the standard of living. All of this is adequately shown in the excavations; Israel's first " boom " age is now at hand.

This great advance in material civilization seems to have been accompanied also by a corresponding progress in other areas of mental life. The age of David and of Solomon during the 10th century was apparently a golden age for Israelite literature. David is credited with being a poet and musician of great ability, and Solomon is said to have been a prolific author of verses and proverbs (I Kings 4 : 32). While little of their work has been preserved as far as we can tell, other writings which have survived indicate that the remarkable Israelite literary genius was already developed. The most extraordinary document of the period is the Court History of David (II Sam. 9–20 ; I Kings 1–2). Here we have an eye-witness account of David as king, picturing him as a real flesh-and-blood man, one of great ability and personal charm, but one who also had many faults. The Ancient East has little to compare with this document, for it is straight, reliable narrative, presenting the facts without bias

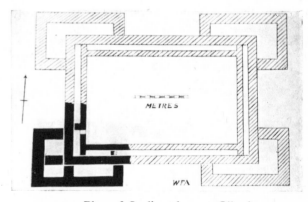

75. Plan of Saul's palace at Gibeah

—a rare thing among the historians of any government, especially in the Near East where the official accounts of a reign were usually sheer braggadocio.

SAUL (about 1020–1000 B.C.)

The only direct light which archaeology has thrown upon the age of Saul comes from the excavation of his capital at Gibeah (Fig. 74). Here were found the remains of his palace—a remarkable and romantic discovery! True, it was in ruins and forts had been built on top of it. True, it was far from being a magnificent affair. Indeed, it was more of a fortress than a palace (Fig. 75), and, while strongly fortified, could scarcely have been considered a comfortable and suitable residence by the monarchs of Egypt, Syria, or Mesopotamia. Nevertheless it was the royal residence of Saul, and its nature was quite in keeping with what we know of him from the stories in I Samuel.

Saul was no wealthy, learned, cosmopolitan statesman. He was a warrior, primarily, who stood head and shoulders above the ordinary Israelite: that is, he was over six feet tall. He was a charismatic hero, just like a number of judges before him, and he owed his position to the fact that people thought he possessed special gifts which had been given him by God, and indeed he did. He differed from judges like Othniel, Barak, and Gideon only by the fact that he was a permanent leader, not a temporary one—chosen as such because of the Philistine crisis. Yet he made few changes in the new state's organization. Like the American colonies the tribes were loosely held together only because of the common peril and common need. No system of regular taxation was imposed. Instead, their simple court was apparently supported by gifts. And when regular taxation was finally imposed by Solomon, it was received with the same grumblings of dissatisfaction as were heard in eighteenth-century America.

We need not be surprised, therefore, to find Saul using as his capital his own home town of Gibeah, located just three miles north of Jerusalem on a hill commanding a fine view of the surrounding country. At its foot there ran and still runs the main highway north to Bethel, Shiloh, and Shechem. On this hill a town had been settled about 1200 B.C., shortly after the main phase of the conquest had been completed. No ready supply of water was available, but people had learned how to slake lime and provide good cisterns for themselves, cut into the soft limestone rock of the hill. A century or more later, however, catastrophe overtook the village. The conifer beams supporting the roofs were burned; the stone side walls of the houses collapsed; and where once had been a town there remained only rubble, covered with the black ashes discovered by the excavator. This seems to have been the destruction of the town about which we are told in Judges 20, the result of an inter-tribal feud.

The palace-fortress built by Saul as his home upon the ruins of the earlier village, like all the better homes of the day, was at least two stories high, the family living on the second floor. A double wall surrounded the fortress, the outer one being very thick, between $6\frac{1}{2}$ and $7\frac{1}{2}$ feet. Roughly shaped stones were used to build it, the chinks being filled with smaller stones and chips. The method of building had been used for centuries, and is still to be seen in Palestine. The weakest part of the enclosure would, of course, be the corners which an attacker might destroy if he attempted to capture the town. These were protected by strong towers, on which the defenders could stand and hurl stones and arrows at the enemy. The exact size of the building is unknown, but it was at least 169 feet long by 114 feet wide and may have been even larger. It was thus quite a sizable affair, much larger than has been commonly realized. Nevertheless its rustic simplicity is just what we should expect of Saul. Any further elaboration at the time would probably have been more than the nation was prepared for.

The contents of the fortress give further evidence of the simplicity of the life. Bronze arrowheads and sling stones, two of the commonest weapons, were found. An iron plowpoint, a whetstone, pottery, spinning whorls, rubbing stones for grinding flour, and large jars for storing grain, wine, and oil are just what we find in every Israelite home of the period. The same is true of the simple pottery, almost entirely utilitarian with little ornamentation. Rough, blackened cooking pots abound. So do small bowls and saucers, often covered with a red slip or coating of clay and smoothed (burnished) with a bone or pebble in parallel and criss-crossed lines which, after baking, shine. The finest wares were the small, black, highly polished, perfume or oil juglets, and also pitchers of pink or buff color which were occasionally decorated with bands of red or brown paint around the body.

Strong as this palace-fort must have been, it was destroyed during Saul's life. We do not know just when the catastrophe fell, but the evidence is clear that it came and that he suffered severe defeat, presumably at the hands of the Philistines. This may have taken place before the great battle of Michmash described in I Sam. 13 and 14. In any event the palace was almost immediately rebuilt along the same lines as the former, though the masonry was less massive and more regularly shaped and laid. What happened to it after Saul's final defeat and death on Mt. Gilboa (I Sam. 31), we do not know. It was either again destroyed, or gradually fell into ruins, out of which Judeans a century or more later built a strong, though small, tower-fort.

DAVID (about 1000–961 B.C.)

There are two traditions as to how David met Saul. The first tells us that he was brought to Saul to soothe the latter's "evil spirit", and that he was "skilful in playing and a mighty man of valor and a man of war and prudent in speech and a handsome person" (I Sam. 16 : 18). It is commonly thought that David's instrument was a harp. In fact, a popular negro spiritual has the refrain, "Little David, play on your harp; hallelu, hallelu." Unfortunately, we now know it was a lyre of the type frequently shown on ancient reliefs (Fig. 76).

The second tradition informs us that David as a boy brought food to his elder brothers in Saul's army while they were fighting the Philistines in the Vale of Elah along the Judean border. David was introduced to Saul after he had volunteered to fight the boastful Philistine giant, Goliath. The young man was the victor in the combat because he made good use of the sling, an instrument which one modern writer has characterized as a truly "frightful weapon" after seeing it used by a

76. A vase from Megiddo, dating about 1000 B.C., showing man with a lyre

skilled hand. The forked stick with a rubber band is a modern invention. The sling used in ancient times consisted of two long cords with a leather or woolen pocket fastened to them. A stone placed in the pocket and whirled around the head, could be shot with terrific force when one of the cords was released. We recall that a short time before David there is said to have been a picked group of seven hundred left-handed Benjaminites in Israel, everyone of whom "could sling stones at a hair-breadth and not miss" (Judges 20 : 16).

77. Ancient slingshots. Those on the left are lead pellets of Roman times. That held on the right is a slingstone from Israelite times; beside it is a water-smoothed stone picked up in the Vale of Elah where the traditional battle between David and Goliath took place

The stones used were quite large, from two to three inches in diameter, made of flint or limestone (Fig. 77). In every excavation in Palestine these stones are found in such quantity that they are often given away as souvenirs. The sling was one of the chief weapons of war, and every city during the course of its existence had many hundreds of slingstones thrown at it.

It is not our purpose here to attempt to settle the problems which the two different stories of David's introduction to Saul bring up, or to decide whether or not David really did fight Goliath in view of the later statement that it was Elhanan who killed him (II Sam. 21 : 19) and of the still later version that the giant Elhanan killed was Lahmi, Goliath's brother (I Chron. 20 : 5)! [1] Both stories are quite in keeping with David's character as we know of it, irrespective of the exact events which took place. Like Saul and the earlier judges David was not chosen as the people's permanent leader because he had any hereditary right to the throne, but because in his person he demonstrated that he possessed special gifts, *charismata*, directly from God. He is thus the last great charismatic hero in Israel, for at the end of his reign the throne in Jerusalem became hereditary. We have previously pointed out that none of the more settled peoples around Israel had anything comparable to the free system of choosing leaders, so characteristic of Israel up to this time. It is another illustration of the religious and social differences existing between Israel and her neighbors.

Israel's growth under Saul and David went hand in hand with the development of military power. David gradually gathered together his own band of professional soldiers whose loyalties were to him alone. Later in his reign this personal army had foreign contingents in it: the Cherethites and the Pelethites, probably Cretans and Philistines, but at any rate Aegean people whose ancestors had settled in Palestine about two centuries earlier. There were also six hundred warriors from the Philistine city of Gath, commanded by one Ittai (II Sam. 15 : 18). This personal army was in part responsible for the success of many of David's wars, since untrained troops from the various tribes could never have won against the powerful forces pitted against them. The eighth chapter of II Samuel especially tells us about David's victories. First of all we know that he consolidated his home front by conquering Canaanite cities like Beth-shan and Jerusalem which hitherto had held out. Then he subdued the Philistines, the Moabites, the Ammonites, and the Edomites, imposing heavy tribute and taskwork upon them. Finally, and most remarkable of all, was his subjugation of the great Aramean (called " Syrian " in the English Bible) state, the main cities of which were Damascus and Zobah. As a result, Israel became the most powerful of all the small states existing between the Euphrates and Egypt.

A close ethnic relationship existed originally between Aramean and Israelite forefathers, as pointed out in Chap. III. These people invaded the northern part of the Fertile Crescent during the 2nd millennium, and during the time when Israel was consolidating its position in Canaan they had spread southward, forming one of their strongest states in the area of Damascus and soon becoming the greatest traveling merchants and traders in Western Asia. Two references from the inscriptions of the kings of Assyria inform us that during the time of David's contemporary, Asshur-rabi II, the Arameans had conquered the territory along the upper Euphrates which had been part of the Assyrian Empire for a century. It follows that this conquest must have taken place before David's defeat and subjugation of Hadadezer, the Aramean king. By the irony of fate, therefore, David's victory may have saved the Assyrian Empire in a period of weakness from being overrun by Aramean hordes. At any rate, this Assyrian information certainly magnifies the importance and greatness of David's army.

How was the new state to be organized ? Was there to be a cabinet, and, if so, what offices were to be included ? Evidence has recently been presented to indicate that David may have used the Egyptian government as a model when setting up his own administration. Two lists of David's officials are preserved, presumably coming from different times in his reign. The earlier is in II Sam. 8 : 16–18, and the later in 20 : 23–5. Chief of the military staff was Joab, while Benaiah was the commander of David's personal army. The rivals, Zadok and Abiathar, were priests, the

---

[1] Many scholars believe that II Sam. 21 : 19 is the true account, that the slaying of Goliath was only later attributed to David, while I Chron. 20 : 5 is an attempt to harmonize the accounts. A recent solution suggests that Elhanan was David's real name, whereas " David " is merely a title. From the Mari letters it was thought that the term " david " was in common use along the Upper Euphrates about 1700 B.C., but only as a title which meant " chieftain ". By 1958, however, B. Landsberger had shown that no such title existed at Mari.

latter being banished by Solomon for suspicious political activity. Of special interest are two other offices. Jehoshaphat was the "recorder"; but what could be the functions of this office? It has been taken generally to be the office of archives and annals. But it is not difficult to show from later passages that the position was too important for that. The interesting thing is that the original Hebrew word has an exact equivalent in the title of the Egyptian Royal Herald. This was the officer in Egypt who regulated the ceremonies in the palace, was the intermediary between the king, other officers, and the people. He also prepared the king's journeys, and was in general the royal officer of public relations.

From the time of David on, another important and powerful official was the Scribe. This office again corresponds to one in Egypt. The man in charge directed both interior and exterior correspondence, functioning as the royal private secretary and as secretary of State. Later copyists were apparently not sure of the exact name of David's scribe, since it was corrupted in transmission, but it seems to have been Shausha or Shisha, or something of the sort. At any rate, it is a perfectly good Egyptian name, and it is quite possible, therefore, that David sent to Egypt for an official to fill the scribal office, one who was dependable, intelligent, and, most important, one who could write. It is interesting to note that the two sons of this man were Solomon's scribes and that one of them is named Elihoreph. The original Hebrew of this name is difficult to reconstruct, but with the help of the versions of the Old Testament we can say that it was probably " Elihaph ", meaning " My God is Haph " (Apis, an Egyptian God). If this is so, then the Egyptian origin of David's scribe is virtually assured.

David had no prime minister, since he apparently governed directly himself. Beginning with Solomon, however, we find an officer in every succeeding court whose title was " the one who is over the house ", that is, over the Royal House (see especially I Kings 4 : 6; 18 : 3; and II Kings 18 : 18). This office corresponds with that of the Egyptian vizier or prime minister. In Egypt we are told in some detail what his duties were. Every morning he presented himself before the king, made his report, and received his instructions. After an audience with the secretary of the treasury, he had the doors of the palace opened (that is, the various governmental offices were thus opened), and the official

day began. Through his hands passed all the affairs of the country. All important documents received his seal. All departments were under his orders : justice, public works, finance, armies, etc. This was the office held by Joseph, to whom Pharaoh said : " thou shalt be *over my house*, and according unto thy word shall all my people be ruled; only in the throne will I be greater than thou " (Gen. 41 : 40). In Israel, as in Egypt, the prime minister had a special robe of office, ruled in place of the king during the latter's absence or sickness, and in one place is even called the " father " of the people (Isa. 22 : 21).

Besides his cabinet David seems to have had an honorary organization known as " The Thirty " (II Sam. 23 : 13, 24, etc.). In the course of time this no longer referred to any fixed number but was an honorary military body, a legion of honour, to which belonged those " mighty men " who had distinguished themselves by feats of exceptional bravery. One of them had slain eight hundred at one time; another three hundred. Still another fought a " goodly " Egyptian who " had a spear in his hand; but he went down to him with a staff and plucked the spear out of the Egyptian's hand, and slew him with his own spear " (II Sam. 23 : 21). It has been pointed out recently that a similar organization existed in Egypt, and David may have received the idea for it from that source.

THE " CITY OF DAVID "

When David was made king over both North Israel and Judah, he was faced with the problem of establishing a neutral capital. If he stayed in Hebron, he would have been accused by the Israelites of favoritism to Judah. If he chose an Israelite city in the north, the opposite would have been the case. To obviate both possibilities he decided to seize a neutral city on the border between the north and south which was still in the hand of a group of Canaanites known as Jebusites. Thus Jerusalem became the new royal city. Since it had been seized by David's personal troops, it became his personal holding, and was renamed " City of David " (II Sam. 5 : 9). We are told that he strengthened its fortifications, with the aid of Phoenician artisans built himself a palace there, reconstructed the Tabernacle and moved the Ark of the Covenant to it so that from that time on Jerusalem was the religious center of the realm.

The city is located on Palestine's central, limestone ridge at a point some 2500 feet above the level of the sea where the ridge has broadened into a small plateau. Extending south from this plateau are two promontories, separated by a valley which in Roman times was called the Tyropoeon (cf. Fig. 162). The name of the eastern promontory was Ophel, first mentioned in Micah (4 : 8, Revised Version margin), while the name of the western was in later times known as Zion. To the west and south ran the Valley of Hinnom, apparently used largely as a dump and place of refuse which in New Testament times became a synonym for Hell (Gehenna), perhaps because of the fires constantly burning there. To the east, separating Ophel from the Mount of Olives, was the Kidron Valley, in which was Jerusalem's main supply of water, the Gihon or Virgin's Fountain. This spring issues from a great crack in the rock, some sixteen feet long. At the western end of the crack is a cave into which the water runs. Normally all the water would discharge through the eastern end of the crack into the valley, but in ancient times a wall was built there, confining the water and compelling it to run into the cave. The name Gihon means " Gusher ", for the spring does not produce a steady flow, but the waters apparently collect in some underground reservoir and occasionally break forth, the frequency depending on the season. To the south below the meeting of the Kidron and Hinnom valleys is a second spring, En-Rogel, where the great feast was held preparatory to installing Adonijah on the throne near the close of David's life (I Kings I). This spring is out in the open valley and could not be protected like the Gihon.

Since 1867 numerous excavations have been undertaken in Jerusalem and a large number of remains from the ancient city have been recovered. We know that the site was occupied as early as 3000 B.C. when the earliest remains are to be dated, and the actual name " Jerusalem " occurs in Egyptian texts as early as 1900 B.C. Yet the peculiar thing about the site is that there is no sign of a " tell " formation : that is, a mound made up of the superimposed remains of one city upon another. The excavations have shown that the city of Old Testament times was situated on Ophel, where most of the excavations have been made. There the remains of the most ancient fortifications have been found but inside these fortifications no stratification of ruins has been discovered. There can be only one explanation for this curious situation. This is that the ancient remains were cleared away inside the city and dumped down the slopes, sometime during the second and first centuries before the time of Christ. Thus on the slopes of Ophel today are vast quantities of debris, filled with fragments of pottery and other objects dating from the 3rd millennium to the 3rd and 2nd centuries B.C. This situation reminds us of the interesting statement of the Jewish historian, Josephus, to the effect that a Syrian fortress built there in the early 2nd century was levelled to the ground by the Jewish patriot, Simon, about 140 B.C., and that the very hill on which the fortress stood was removed, the work taking three years. Further evidence that this is what happened has been discovered in one of the excavations along the city fortifications. Great depths of debris were found outside and between the walls. The first 5 feet were filled with pieces of Arab pottery. Below that, between 6 and 8 feet, were remains of the Hellenistic period, from the 3rd–2nd centuries B.C. From that point down to 20 feet below the surface the debris was filled with pottery of all the earlier periods, but at the 20-foot depth pottery of the Hellenistic period again appeared. The only explanation for this would seem to be as follows : if people during the 2nd century B.C. started digging and throwing the debris over the walls, material from their own time would go first. Then would come the ruins of earlier ages. Finally, as they settled down again, they would deposit things of their own time on top of the debris thrown out. This seems to have been what happened.

These remarks are necessary preparation for the disappointing statement that *not a single discovery has been made in Jerusalem which can be dated with any certainty to the time of David and Solomon.* We know where they lived and built, but practically everything other than the city fortifications has been destroyed. And even the complicated maze of fortifications on the hill Ophel can scarcely be disentangled and dated with any degree of certainty. The first great fortification has been traced around a section of the hill. It was a tremendous affair, 27 feet wide at the highest level found while its base may have been as wide as 40 feet. Its two faces were made of hammer-dressed stones, sometimes of considerable size and irregularly fitted together, and smaller stones were used to fill up the chinks. The interior between the faces was filled up with stone blocks. In two places, at least, where the foundation was not considered sufficiently strong to resist siege, large stepped bastions were erected against the exterior (Fig. 78). At the west a massive fortified gate (Fig. 79) has been found, and at various points where additional protection was needed towers were apparently erected.

This strong system of fortification has usually been called " Jebusite ", since it is believed to have been erected by the pre-Israelite inhabitants of Jerusalem. It had been repaired in several places, and later walls built over and beside it. These later repairs have often been called " Davidic " and " Solomonic "; but unfortunately all these ascriptions are almost pure guesses, since there is so little evidence for the dating. At any rate, this tongue-like promontory was capable of being strongly fortified, and the Jebusites felt perfectly safe behind their walls, taunting David by calling out that " the blind and lame " would prevent him from capturing their city.

Throughout the history of the town great care was taken about the water supply in the Gihon spring. An elaborate system of tunnels in this vicinity is eloquent witness to the fact. One of the earliest attempts to bring the water closer to those who lived inside the walls was made by cutting a passage to a room over a deep shaft. From this room a semi-circular passage was cut down toward the spring some 125 feet through the rock. From that point jugs and pitchers could be lowered down a deep shaft to the water.

The next major attempt seems to have had convenience as its major object. A long aqueduct was cut along the rock scarp under the edge of the hill, running from the Gihon to the southern extremity of the city where it emptied into a pool, called the " *old pool* " (Isa. 22 : 11), apparently at the mouth of the Tyropoeon Valley just outside the city walls.

78. Old fortifications on Ophel in Jerusalem. On the right is a stone revetment ; on the left is a tower built of fitted stones like masonry otherwise first known in the Solomonic period. Careful stratigraphical digging of the debris on the inside of these walls was first undertaken by an expedition directed by Kathleen M. Kenyon during the summer of 1961, following trenching by R. A. S. Macalister and J. G. Duncan during their work on Ophel between 1923 and 1925. What is here seen now appears to be comparatively late (Intertestamental), though covering older structures, perhaps late Judean in date

79. Remains of a gateway in the old Canaanite
("Jebusite") wall of Jerusalem

80. The Gezer water tunnel; view looking upward at
an angle of nearly 40 degrees

It was at the beginning of this aqueduct that Isaiah met Ahaz in his famous interview (Isa. 7 : 3), if in this passage the "*upper pool*" is to be identified with the Gihon, as seems probable. In another passage (8 : 6) Isaiah refers to the water in this aqueduct as "the waters of Shiloah that go softly" and uses them as a figure of God's way for Israel which the people have rejected. As a result, says Isaiah, the Lord will bring upon them the waters of the Euphrates, "strong and many, even the king of Assyria and all his glory!" This conduit was partly tunneled and apparently partly open. Consequently, it was no protection for the water supply in time of siege. For this reason Hezekiah stopped it up before 701 B.C. and built his tunnel (Fig. 122), of which more will be said in Chapter X. At that time this first aqueduct was undoubtedly old, but unfortunately we can say no more about its date than we could about that of the fortifications.

The elaborate arrangements in Jerusalem for an adequate water supply in case of siege recall a number of other installations around the country for a similar purpose. Best known are the great Canaanite water tunnels at Gezer, Gibeon and Megiddo. Those at Gezer and Gibeon are similar to that just described in Jerusalem; they permitted people within the cities to go down a steep passage in order to get to a spring, without going outside the walls. At Gezer a spring was reached about 130 feet below the present surface of the mound; the steps of the tunnel led down to it at an angle of 38 or 39 degrees (Fig. 80).

At Megiddo a wide shaft, over 80 feet deep, was sunk within the city in Canaanite times (see Fig. 2) down into the bedrock. The workers then cut through the rock horizontally in the direction of the spring at the mound's edge, while another group began work at the spring, cutting into the mound. The calculations had been made in advance so precisely that when the two groups of workers met, an error of not more than two feet had been made in any direction.[2] The level of the tunnel was then lowered so that the water flowed from the spring to the base of the shaft, a distance of a little over 165 feet. This water

[2] Hezekiah's water tunnel in Jerusalem was dug in similar manner. It was much longer, however, and the margin of error was greater (see pp. 169 ff.).

system was dug at least as early as the 13th or 12th centuries and continued in use throughout most of the city's subsequent history, until the mound was abandoned during the 4th century B.C. (Fig. 81).[3]

In every city after the 14th century nearly every dwelling unit had one or more cisterns dug beneath it to catch and preserve the water from the winter rains. Some of the cisterns are so large that they could have served the needs of several families, or even of the whole community, for a period of time. At the Judean mound of Lachish early in Israelite times a well instead of a water tunnel was dug. When found, its mouth was flush with the masonry of the outer fortification wall. After a great amount of labor it was cleared and found to be 144 feet deep, and it still supplied water at a level of 16 feet from the bottom.

SOLOMON IN ALL HIS GLORY (about 961–922 B.C.)

Whereas it was David who established the kingdom in its extent and power, it was Solomon who added the glamor! David was a man of war, but the ideal of Solomon seems to have been the picture of a wealthy, worldly, cultured gentleman, and as such he busily engaged himself in the attempt to put a " backwoods " nation on the " civilized " map of the world. Unfortunately we do not know as much about his personality as we should like, nor do we know a great deal about the events of his career. But our sources do tell us about his building operations and commercial activities. He refortified Jerusalem, built there his palace, administrative headquarters, and Temple. In addition he built " store-cities ", and " the cities for his chariots and the cities for his horsemen " throughout the land. He was a great merchant, buying and selling horses and chariots to the neighboring peoples. We may now translate I Kings 10 : 28–9 as follows (with W. F. Albright) :

81. The Megiddo water tunnel

And Solomon's horses were exported from Egypt and from Cilicia [in Asia Minor where fine horses were bred]. The merchants of the king procured them from Cilicia at the current price ; and a chariot was exported from Egypt at the rate of six hundred shekels of silver and a horse (from Cilicia) at the rate of a hundred fifty. And thus (at this rate) they delivered them by their agency to all the kings of the Hittites and all the kings of Aram [area of Damascus and northward].

The shekel, like the English pound, was primarily a measure of weight, and it is difficult to translate it into modern currency. We gather, however, that an Egyptian chariot must have cost Solomon a great deal of money and one wonders just how much he resold it for among Aramean kings to the north !

We are further told that to control the Arabian trade Solomon with the aid of the Phoenicians built a fleet of ships to be based at Ezion-geber on the northeastern arm of the Red Sea just south of Edom. This fleet made the trip southward to Ethiopia and the Arabian Yemen once every three years (that is, one entire year and parts of two others), bringing back gold, silver, ivory, and two

---

[3] For descriptions of the water tunnels at Jerusalem, Gezer and Megiddo, see H. Vincent, *Jérusalem sous terre* (London, 1911 ; English translation, *Underground Jerusalem*) ; R. A. S. Macalister, *The Excavation of Gezer*, Vol. I (London, 1912), pp. 256 ff. ; and R. S. Lamon, *The Megiddo Water System* (Chicago, 1935). The precise history of the Gibeon tunnel is difficult. Beside it was a great " pool ", actually a stairwell, some 35 ft. wide and deep, the steps then leading down within the rock where water collected in a cave. A jar of *ca.* the 7th century was found in the water-cave, whereas the whole great stairwell was filled during the 6th–5th century B.C. This installation, then, is presumably later than the tunnel : see J. B. Pritchard, *Biblical Archaeologist*, XIX (1956), pp. 66–75.

kinds of monkeys [4]—(I Kings 9 : 26 and 10 : 22). Doubtless the visit of the Queen of Sheba was not so much to see Solomon's splendor as to conclude certain necessary trading agreements to the mutual benefit of both. Archaeological discoveries of great importance have also demonstrated that Solomon was a copper and iron baron, having built the largest refinery ever found in the Ancient East, but we shall return to this below.

To support his elaborate court and building program the king found it necessary to institute a regular system of taxation over Israel in addition to the tribute received from the subject peoples. To this end he divided North Israel into twelve administrative districts, only roughly based on the old tribal allotments (I Kings 4 : 7 ff.). Over each he placed a district officer, one of whose main duties it was to see to it that his district furnished provisions for the court one month in the twelve. And a severe load on the district it must have been, for, we are told, the food consumed in just one day consisted of 337½ bushels of flour, 675 bushels of meal, ten fattened cattle, twenty pasture-fed cattle, one hundred sheep, besides numerous fowl and animals of the deer family (I Kings 4 : 22–3).

Evidence of district organization has been discovered in a number of places by the archaeologists. At Beth-shemesh (Fig. 56), for example, one of the main cities in the district first occupied by the tribe of Dan, the residency of the district officer, Ben-Deker, has probably been found, though it has never been completely excavated. Near by were the foundations of a large building with three long narrow rooms. The walls were very thick and the floor originally well above the present foundations. At the city of Lachish (Fig. 47) in the district of Judah a similar arrangement of residency and building with thick walls and long narrow rooms has been found. The palace was erected on a platform with earth-filled interior, still standing on the western side to a height of 23 feet. This podium was about 105 feet square, though in the following century it was lengthened to some 256 feet. Such a palace or citadel on a platform is probably an archaeological illustration of the Millo (" Filling " ?) which David built in Jerusalem (II Sam. 5 : 9). The only conceivable purpose for the buildings with long rooms here and elsewhere in Palestine was, as Professor Albright has shown, to store grain and other provisions.

The thick walls and high floors evidently served to keep the grain from spoiling. If so, and it seems probable, then we have here evidence for " store-cities " of the type which Solomon is said to have built. The Beth-shemesh and Lachish buildings, however, are earlier than Solomon's time and were probably erected by David. This conclusion, based on the dating of the pottery found in the ruins, is an important one, for it may solve what to scholars has been a very difficult problem. While Solomon divided northern Israel into administrative districts, according to I Kings 4 : 7 ff., nothing is said about his doing anything of a similar nature in Judah. Does that mean, as has sometimes been supposed, that he was placing Judah in a favored position so that her people did not have to pay the same taxes as did their neighbors in the north ? The answer would now appear to be that Solomon did not reorganize the administration of Judah because David had already done so before him. The only detailed description of administrative districts in Judah is to be found in Joshua 15 : 21–62, though in its present form this list dates from the time of Jehoshaphat in the 9th century.[5]

The great city of Megiddo in the northern plain of Esdraelon furnishes additional information of Solomonic building. The governor of the province of Megiddo lived in a palace fortress, protected by its own wall, through which one entered by a covered gateway (Fig. 82). This was apparently the residency of Baana, son of Ahilud (I Kings 4 : 12). The courtyard was leveled and paved with lime plaster. The wall has a type of construction that from now on is typical of Israel, though it was probably learned from the Phoenicians. Instead of building the whole wall of fine masonry, strong piers of finely cut stone were inserted every three or four feet, while in between was a filling of roughly coursed rubble. The purpose of this structure was probably largely administrative, though a few soldiers may have been quartered there as policemen.

---

[4] Not peacocks as the English versions have it.

[5] The German scholars, Albrecht Alt and Martin Noth, have proved that Joshua 15 certainly does reflect a governmental organization because the cities and towns are listed by administrative districts. These scholars date the list, however, in the time of King Josiah in the seventh century and use it to illumine the history of this king's reign. See Martin Noth, *A History of Israel* (London and New York, 1958), p. 273 with references there cited. The new evidence which suggests its 9th-century date is presented by Frank M. Cross, Jr., and G. Ernest Wright, " The Boundary and Province Lists of the Kingdom of Judah ", *Journal of Biblical Literature*, Vol. LXXV (1956), pp. 202–36.

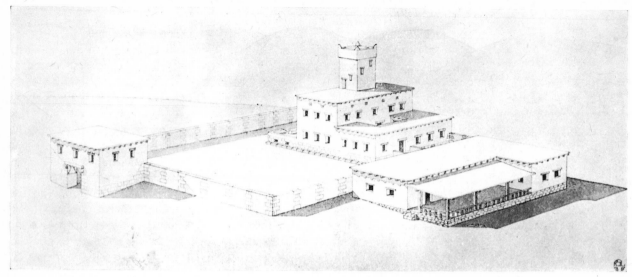

82. Palace at Megiddo as reconstructed; its date is the (Stratum VA–IVB) 10th century B.C.

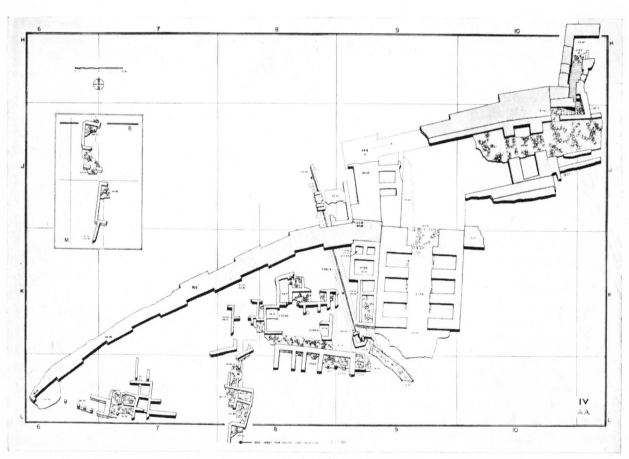

83. Plan of the Solomonic gateway at Megiddo. The city wall connected with it is, however, later, belonging to Stratum IVA of the 9th century B.C.

84. A reconstruction of the Solomonic gateway at Megiddo (though the doorways should have been provided with a lintel, instead of an arch, and wooden doors to close them would have been visible)

The Megiddo excavators picture the 10th-century city of Megiddo as possessing on its eastern and southern sides stables for some four hundred and fifty horses (see Figs. 85, 105). Indeed, according to I Kings 9 : 15–19, one would expect to find them there, for Megiddo was one of Solomon's chariot cities. The eastern group of stables was erected along a paved street leading south from the city gate. In the typical stable there were spaces for a double row of horses which faced a central passageway. These were paved with cobblestones. Hitching posts, which also served as roof supports, separated stone mangers, one for each horse. Along the city wall at the south five of these units were joined together, opening on a large paved courtyard with a drinking trough in the center (Fig. 105). The city wall of the stable period was a solid structure some $11\frac{1}{2}$ feet thick, constructed of " offsets and insets " (Figs. 83–4), as it curved around the edge of the mound.

In the spring of 1960 a small test excavation was conducted at Megiddo by Yigael Yadin of Hebrew University. Below the heavy " offsets and insets " fortification he discovered two lines of walls connected by cross-walls. They formed a type of city fortification known as a " casemate " wall, previously known in 10th-century levels at the Judean provincial centers, Beth-shemesh and Debir. This construction would not have withstood a strong attack of a battering ram, unless the casemates were filled with earth, but it would have formed a basis for a wide wooden platform and barricade to be built

above it for the easy deployment of defensive troops. In addition, strong and well-built towers or forts were evidently erected at the more vulnerable points. One of these forts was found by Yadin to run beneath one of the stable compounds. What this means is that the Solomonic city of Megiddo has never been properly investigated. Called Stratum VA-IVB by W. F. Albright and the writer, it was fortified by a casemate wall which coursed between heavy towers or forts until it reached the gate. What other large structures it included beside the governor's residence (Fig. 82) we are not clear, because Yadin's work has shown that the heavy " offsets-insets " wall and the major stable compounds belong to Stratum IVA of the 9th century. Nevertheless it is highly probable that the stables were an elaboration of an institution begun by Solomon in Stratum VA-IVB.

Perhaps the most spectacular Solomonic fortification at Megiddo is the city gate on the northern edge of the mound (Figs. 83–4). From the plain below one could climb to the gate by a steep stairway, or else he could ascend the ramp up which carts and chariots could also go, then to enter a double outer gateway, undoubtedly covered to ensure easier protection. Passing through it and making a sharp turn to the left, one then came to the main gate, also covered and protected with blanking towers. Great double doors of wood hung from vertical beams which turned in stone sockets. In times of danger these could be closed and barred from within. Four of the entries existed, one behind the other, each with its " guardroom " into which the doors could swing and where troops could stand, partially protected, in any attempt to force the gate. It is interesting that the plan of the Solomonic gate of Megiddo (Stratum VA-IVB), with its four entryways, is precisely that described by Ezekiel as the plan for the gates leading into the court of Solomon's temple (Ezek. 40 : 5–16). On the other hand, the 9th-century gate of Stratum IVA had only three entries, while that of the 8th century (Stratum III) had but two.

Most unusual about the Solomonic gate, and the fort of the same period discovered by Yadin, is the fact that they are made of finely drafted and fitted masonry, here marking its first appearance in Israel, undoubtedly under Phoenician influence. From then on into the 8th century this type of building with tightly fitted stone blocks will characterize special royal architectural work both in Israel and in Judah (cf. Fig. 100).

85. Ruins of one section of the stables at Megiddo

Another provincial center of the Israelite government was Hazor, the administrative center of the province of eastern Galilee (Naphtali; I Kings 4 : 15). Reference to the work at this great site by a Hebrew University expedition under the direction of Yigael Yadin has already been made (Fig. 29 and p. 83). In the city of the Israelite period were large government buildings, including the governor's residence and administrative headquarters of the 9th and 8th centuries (Strata VIII to V; Fig. 107). The area in which they were erected was surrounded by a casemate wall belonging to the 10th-century Stratum X (Fig. 86). The wall was of the same type as those found at Megiddo, Beth-shemesh and Debir, though during the 9th century it had been superceded by a more massive defensive system,

even as had been the case at Megiddo. Within this wall was a four-entryway city gate (Fig. 86). While its masonry is not as fine as that of the Megiddo gateway of the 10th century (Stratum VA-IVB), its dimensions are precisely the same. Yadin has also found in the plans of the Gezer excavation a similar gate hitherto overlooked at that site. Thus I Kings 9 : 15, which speaks of Hazor, Megiddo and Gezer, after Jerusalem, as cities fortified by Solomon, finds an eloquent archaeological commentary.

Here, then, is a considerable body of evidence which is beginning to accumulate for the great changes introduced into Israelite affairs by David and Solomon. ↓The provincial system, administered by officials appointed by the king in Jerusalem, marked the end of the old tribal system for anything

86. The casemate wall and city-gate (*left*) erected by Solomon at Hazor

other than genealogical purposes. The Tribal League was gone and centralized government replaced it.

SOLOMON'S CONTROL OF THE PALESTINIAN METAL INDUSTRY

A wholly unsuspected aspect of Solomon's commercial career has been revealed through the explorations of Nelson Glueck in the great valley of the Arabah, south of the Dead Sea, and at Ezion-geber, Solomon's seaport on the Red Sea. Along the Eastern bank of the Arabah the oldest rock formations in Palestine and Transjordan outcrop. This rock is a soft sandstone which contains many veins of copper and iron ore. The explorations have discovered that this ore was mined during the period of Solomon and the centuries which followed with more intensity than at any other time in history. We are reminded of a description of the Promised Land given in Deuteronomy (8 : 9) as one " whose stones are iron, and out of whose hills thou canst dig copper ".

Near the mines are small furnaces where the ore was given its preliminary smelting (Fig. 88). Around them heaps of slag were thrown out and today furnish a convenient clue to guide the explorer in his search. Walled enclosures were found near some of the slag heaps, within which were the ruins of the miners' huts and smelting furnaces, with heaps of slag between. Such walled encampments were probably necessary to ensure the peaceful progress of the operations, but, as the excavator has pointed out, they probably served another purpose as well. That was to keep the workers from running away. In other words, these are prison camps, for it is highly probable that these mines were manned by slave labor, both when the Israelites and later when the Edomites controlled them. Few places on the earth could be less desirable spots for strenuous work. Water usually had to be carried for miles ; desolation was on every hand ; and the heat so terrific that operations could only have been carried on during the fall, winter, and spring months. No free-born Israelite would have worked there unless he had to and the state slaves were probably forced to do the work. During the early Christian period many

87. A copper furnace at Khirbet Jariyeh on the Edomite edge of the Arabah, south of the Dead Sea

88. The south side of the smelter and refinery at Ezion-geber, showing double rows of flue-holes which pierced each wall

centuries later, writers tell us that the mines at one of these sites were worked by slave labor. The slaves were criminals or Christians, who had been condemned to work there for their crimes or for their convictions.

Even more surprising than these discoveries was Ezion-geber. The excavator began work at the site, thinking he would find the ruins of Solomon's seaport, for it was at this point that Solomon launched his fleet (I Kings 9 : 26). No remains of the port were found, but instead there came to light a great smelting refinery, the largest ever found in the Near East (Figs. 88 and 112). It was first built about the 10th century B.C., almost certainly, therefore, by Solomon. At the northwest corner of the site a large building was unearthed. It was immediately seen to be a novel type of structure because the walls of the rooms had two rows of specially prepared holes in them. Through the middle of the main walls ran a system of air-channels into which the upper row of holes opened. These could only be flues and the structure was obviously a smelter. The ore which had received its preliminary smelting near the mines was brought here and put in crucibles inside the smelter. The rooms were then filled with wood and brush and fired. The draft from the flues made the fire sufficiently hot to refine the metal further so that it could be worked into ingots for shipment. Furnaces found in Palestine remelted the metal and it was then cast or beaten into implements. Green copper stain on the walls of the refinery and of the furnaces just mentioned are the final proof,

if such is needed, of the nature and use of the constructions.

At first glance one of the peculiar features of the Ezion-geber refinery is its situation. There is no water near by and it is one of the most uninviting sites in the area. On the one side are the hills of Edom which continue into Arabia. On the other are those of Palestine which continue into Sinai. Consequently, it is in the center of a wind tunnel, open to the fury of the winds and sandstorms blowing down the Arabah from the north. Yet this must have been precisely the reason why the site was chosen. The flues of the smelter were turned toward the north, and no bellows for forced draft would have been necessary there.

The plan of the refinery was simple. It was in the center of an industrial square, around which on the outside was a row of foundry rooms and living quarters. These rooms were placed against a wall which surrounded the square and which probably acted as fortification. There may have been even stronger walls around the site, walls which were reconstructed in the next century, but all trace of them has disappeared, though the reconstructions, if such they were, are well preserved.

In describing the site the excavator has written : [6]

One can easily visualize the conditions existing about three millennia ago, when the idea of building this place was first conceived and then brilliantly translated into reality. Thousands of laborers had to be assembled, housed, fed, and protected at the chosen building site. As a matter of fact, most of them were probably slaves,

[6] Nelson Glueck, *The Other Side of the Jordan* (New Haven, 1940), pp. 98–9.

who had to be guarded and goaded to work. Skilled technicians of all kinds had to be recruited. Great caravans had to be collected to transport materials and food. An effective business organization had to be called into existence to regulate the profitable flow of raw materials and finished or semi-finished products. There was, so far as we know, only one man who possessed the strength, wealth and wisdom capable of initiating and carrying out such a highly complex and specialized undertaking. He was King Solomon. He alone in his day had the ability, the vision, and the power to establish an important industrial center and sea-port such a comparatively long distance from the capital city of Jerusalem. . . . His far-flung net of activities extended from Egypt to Phoenicia, and from Arabia to Syria. Ezion-geber represents one of his greatest, if indeed up to the present time his least known accomplishments.

SOLOMON'S TEMPLE

Thus far, however, we have not examined the place whereon Solomon expended his greatest architectural energies. That is Jerusalem where he built his palace, Temple, and governmental headquarters. The Jebusite city on Ophel which David had conquered was far too small for Solomon's plans. He leveled a large plot to the north and included it in the city fortifications. There with the aid of Phoenician artists he began his work, and from that day to this it has been the most famous sacred area in world history.

By far the best known of his architectural wonders in Jerusalem was the Temple, undoubtedly a splendid work which reflected his major interest. It was built primarily as a royal chapel with priests made members of the royal court and subject to the king's control. The religious focus of both Israel and Judah was thus united with the king's court and a serious threat to the nation's unity was avoided. No high priest could ever set himself up as head of the state, as happened in Egypt, for example.

Various attempts have been made to reconstruct the Temple, but until recent years sufficient archaeological data have been lacking, and many biblical students have allowed their architectural and artistic imaginations full play. Today, the situation is changed, for there are many new discoveries which bear directly upon our problem.

The first step in reconstructing the Temple is to study the description and dimensions given in I Kings 6 and Ezek. 41. If one is architecturally inclined or interested in puzzles, he can spend an enjoyable evening in attempting to reconstruct the

ground plan from the figures given, perhaps allowing himself the occasional use of a standard Bible dictionary and commentaries. It has long been recognized that Ezekiel's vision in Chap. 41 contains detailed measurements which agree with and supplement the account in I Kings 6 so well that it must preserve in part the data contained in some long-lost description of Solomon's Temple. There are still scholars who are hesitant in placing much confidence in it because of its date and visionary character. The increasing weight of discoveries, however, has led many archaeologists to place more and more reliance upon it.

Yet even after we learn the dimensions of the Temple, something about its ground plan, and the description of the way in which it was built, we still should not know how to visualize it unless we know something about the way in which people built temples in those days. But where are we to look? Shall we examine the great temples of Egypt and reconstruct the Solomonic building after their model? Some have done so, but we now know that they are, for the most part, wrong. Shall we examine the great temples of Mesopotamia? Several scholars have done this also, at least one of whom would see in Solomon's " house " (as the Bible frequently calls it) a typical Assyrian temple. We can now be fairly sure that such a theory is wrong.

The Book of I Kings informs us that Solomon secured the aid of Hiram, king of Tyre, for material and technical advice. Thus while Israel furnished the labor, Hiram furnished the architects and artisans to draw up the plans and direct the work. To learn the character of Solomon's Temple, therefore, we must find out what Phoenician craftsmen were accustomed to build. What was their stock in trade?

Unfortunately, the temple art and architecture of Phoenicia during this period is not well known, since few excavations in contemporary city levels have been made. But from bits of information which can be gathered here and there we are now able to begin piercing the gloom. Various artistic treasures, for example, the collections of ivory panelling and inlay which have been found, enable us to visualize what is meant when we read about " cherubim and palm trees and open flowers " in I Kings 6 : 35 (cf. Fig. 89). Excavations of the Oriental Institute of the University of Chicago at Tell Tainat (ancient Hattina) in Syria have uncovered the small chapel of the 8th-century kings

89. Cherubim guarding a sacred tree

of that city (Fig. 91). This is the only temple contemporary with the kings of Israel ever found in Syria or Palestine, and it is most important to note that its plan is very similar to that of the Temple of Solomon. Of course, various other buildings of this period have been called temples. Especially has this been true in Palestine, where every sizable structure has at one time or another been thought by someone to be a temple unless there was definite proof to the contrary. It can now be categorically stated, however, that not a single temple (differentiating temples from shrines) dating between 1000 and 600 B.C. has been unearthed in Palestine. Consequently, this newly discovered chapel at Tainat is most important. Other discoveries illuminate other details of the Solomonic Temple, some of which will be mentioned below.

Let us imagine for the moment that we are in the position of the Israelite High Priest, and are able to enter the building and look around (Fig. 92). Approaching the entrance from the east, we notice that the whole edifice is set on a platform, about 9 feet high (Ezek. 41 : 8).[7] A flight of ten steps leads up to the entrance, on either side of which are two free-standing columns, known as Jachin and Boaz (I Kings 7 : 21), names which were probably the first words of inscriptions on them. These

90. Palace with chapel at Tell Tainat in Syria, dating from about the 8th century B.C.

columns were made of bronze, and their height, including bases and elaborate capitals, was roughly $37\frac{1}{2}$ feet. The circumference of the shafts is given as 18 feet. While their purpose is obscure, it is suggested that they were gigantic cressets or fire-altars on which sacred incense was burned. Their tremendous size must have been an awe-inspiring spectacle to the Israelites, and casting them would indeed be no minor matter even for us today. But these are only the beginning of the wonders of this Temple, which attracts us not because of its size, but because of its symmetry, delicacy, and good taste.

Ascending the stairs, and stepping through the door, we find ourselves in the vestibule, known

---

[7] The standard Hebrew measure of length was the cubit. The ordinary cubit was just slightly less than $1\frac{1}{2}$ feet, and for purposes of simple computation this is the figure used in the dimensions given here and in what follows. The cubit used in the Temple, however, was probably the sacred or royal cubit which was slightly less than 21 inches. Hence, if we were to be accurate in detail, we would have to add 3 inches to each cubit and the dimensions below would be slightly larger.

91. The Stevens reconstruction of the Solomonic Temple, as drawn from specifications prepared by W. F. Albright and G. Ernest Wright

as the *Ulam*, a room measuring some 15 by 30 feet. In front of us is a double door, about 15 feet in width, decorated with carved palm-trees, flowers, and cherubim. The carved work glitters in the light, because it is inlaid (or " overlaid " as the English has it) with gold leaf " fitted into the graven work " (I Kings 6 : 35). Passing through it, we enter the main room of the sanctuary, the " holy Place ", or *Hekal*. Light streams in from several windows (I Kings 6 : 4) inserted in the walls below the ceiling, and we can get some idea of the interior. The room is about 45 feet high, 30 feet wide and 60 feet long. It is floored with cypress and lined with cedar, so that none of the well-cut stone of the walls and foundations, with which we have been made familiar at Megiddo, can be seen. Its roof is flat, supported by great cedar beams. The walls like the doors are decorated with palm-trees, open flowers, chains (II Chron. 3 : 5), and cherubim, carved in the cedar and inlaid with gold leaf. The walls are divided into panels by the palm-trees. In each panel is a cherub with two faces, a human face looking in one direction, and a lion face looking in the other (Ezek. 41 : 18 ff.). The eerie light coming through the windows above, the delightful odor of the cedar, the delicate decoration on the walls, the great height of the ceiling, the offerings

and furnishings, and above all the knowledge that in the room beyond was the throne of God, lend a sanctity, a pleasant yet fearful mystery, which is indeed awesome.

Around the room had been placed the sacred furniture : the golden candlesticks, the table of shewbread, and a small altar of cedar inlaid (or covered ?) with gold leaf. The last mentioned was placed directly in front of a flight of steps leading into the room beyond. It was square, 3 feet across and $4\frac{1}{2}$ feet high. Had we been living among the Canaanites a few generations earlier we should have been very familiar with this feature, since the Canaanites were accustomed to place such an altar or table in their temples directly in front of the steps leading up to the raised " Holy of Holies " on which was placed the statue of the god. On the small altar were placed offerings of incense with which the deity was thought to be pleased.

Going around the altar and ascending the stairs, we open another door, like the other though smaller, and find ourselves in the " Most Holy Place " or the " Holy of Holies ". Its real name was *Debir*, " Oracle ", for here was the special abode of God. The room is a cube about 30 feet in each of its dimensions, and it contains no windows. No light illumines it except for what comes through the open door from the dim *Hekal*. The pleasant odor of cedar pervades this room also ; so we know that it too is lined with wood from the famous Lebanon forests of Hiram. That which immediately strikes our eye, however, is the dim outlines of two large olivewood cherubim, standing 15 feet high, and " overlaid " with gold leaf. Their faces are towards us, and their wings, each about $7\frac{1}{2}$ feet long, are stretched out as though ready for flight. The two outer wings touch the side walls to the north and south ; the inner wings meet each other in the center of the room. It is difficult to see in the darkness, but in all probability the Ark of the Covenant is to be found on the floor between the cherubim in the center of the room beneath the outstretched wings (I Kings 8 : 6).

Backing reverently out of the *Debir* and closing the double doors quietly behind us, we rapidly leave the interior of the Temple, and walk around the platform on the outside. We have plenty of space in which to wander because there are $7\frac{1}{2}$ feet between the base of the building and the edge of the platform. The north side and the south side each has a door. Entering one of them, we find a stairway leading to two upper stories. In each of the three stories is a whole series of small rooms, the ceilings of which are supported by horizontal ledges in the main wall of the Temple. Each story is $1\frac{1}{2}$ feet wider than the one below. These rooms are apparently vaults used for storing the Temple treasure, the many precious objects used in the Temple worship.

Returning to the front of the Temple and standing by the pillars, Jachin and Boaz, we are in a position to look out over the courtyard. By far the most spectacular objects in front of us are the great altar of burnt offering and the bronze Sea. Both are tremendous affairs. The altar is said to have been 15 feet high and 30 feet square, probably the base measurement (II Chron. 4 : 1). Judging from the description in Ezek. 43 : 13-17, its general appearance was that of a Babylonian temple-tower (ziggurat ; Fig. 92). It was composed of three stages, each of the lower two projecting $1\frac{1}{2}$ feet wider than the one above, so that a ledge was formed around each stage. The topmost stage was the hearth for burnt offerings ; it was about 18 feet square, with " horns " projecting from each corner $1\frac{1}{2}$ feet high. It was called *harel*, meaning probably " mountain of God ", evidently a popular etymology of an Accadian term which could refer either to the underworld or to the cosmic mountain on which the

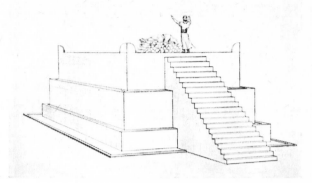

92. The Stevens reconstruction of the altar of burnt offering in Jerusalem, based on Ezek. 43 : 13-17

gods were thought to live. A flight of steps on the east led up to the altar's hearth. The whole structure was set on a foundation-platform, placed in the pavement of the court, and called " bosom ". This peculiar name was again probably borrowed from Babylon where the foundation-platform of the " Tower of Babel " (Etemenanki) was called " bosom of the earth " or " bosom of the underworld ".

The bronze Sea is a great bowl, 15 feet in diameter and $7\frac{1}{2}$ feet high (Fig. 93). It is made of cast bronze, about 3 inches thick, and its brim is " wrought like the brim of a cup, like the flower of a lily " (I Kings 7 : 23 ff.). It rests on the backs of twelve oxen which are arranged in threes, each triad facing one of the points of the compass. Computation has it that such a bronze bowl would weigh between 25 and 30 tons, a tremendous affair, to which one might compare the great bell in St. Paul's in London which weighs but $17\frac{1}{2}$ tons. This Sea and the shafts of the Temple columns must have presented great technical difficulties in casting, and we can but marvel at the genius of the

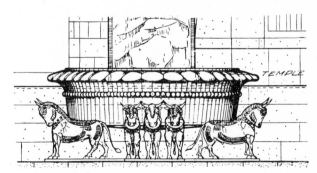

93. A reconstruction of the Bronze Sea by William Morden

artisan Hiram, who "filled with wisdom and understanding and skill, to work all works in bronze", cast them in the clay beds of the Jordan valley, not far from the place where the River Jabbok flows into the Jordan (I Kings 7 : 13 ff. and 46). We are told further that "the weight of the bronze could not be found out", and one would judge that the cost of all that was used in the Solomonic building program would have been prohibitive were it not for the fact that Solomon controlled the Arabah mines whence the ore was taken to be smelted in his great smelter at Ezion-geber.

A later record tells us that the Sea was for the special use of the priests as a place where they could wash (II Chron. 4 : 6). In any event it held some 10,000 gallons of water [8] which was available for ablutions of one sort or another. But why was it named "Sea"? The Jewish historian, Josephus, said it was so named because of its size. In all probability, however, it had a symbolic meaning. The sea played an important part in Canaanite and Babylonian mythology. To the Babylonians it was the ultimate source of all life and fertility, and it was also the abode of the Canaanite Leviathan, the dragon of chaos. Solomon's bronze Sea, therefore, like the cherubim and the columns, was used because it had had a long history in the theology and symbolism of Canaan. Its ultimate fate, however, was assured. There was too much valuable bronze in it. King Ahaz took the oxen from under it to pay tribute to the Assyrian king in 734 B.C., and the Babylonians broke up the bowl and carried the fragments to Babylon after the capture of Jerusalem in 587 B.C. (II Kings 16 : 17 and 25 : 13).

THE ARCHITECTURAL SIGNIFICANCE OF THE TEMPLE

Having thus taken a rapid tour around the Temple, and having examined the two main objects of the courtyard, we may pause to take stock of what we have seen. One feature after another is now known to be perfectly at home in Syria.

(1) The shape of the building with vestibule and free-standing columns is becoming increasingly familiar to us from the evidence available for Syrian architecture. There has been some debate as to whether the two columns should be placed in the door of the vestibule or flanking it on the outside. In the Syrian temple unearthed by the Oriental Institute at Tainat they are in the entrance to the vestibule. A passage in II Chronicles (3 : 15–17) states explicitly, however, that Solomon "made *before the house* two pillars . . . And he set up the pillars before the temple, one on the right hand and one on the left." A number of Near Eastern parallels have been found with which the columns may be compared.

(2) Another connection of the Temple with North Syrian and Phoenician architecture is the cedar lining of the interior. This is practically unknown in Mesopotamia, but several illustrations of it exist in the north. Incidentally, I Kings 6 : 36 tells us that the wall of the Temple courtyard was built "with three courses of hewn stone and a course of cedar beams." This feature seems to be exactly paralleled at Ras Shamra in Syria, and several other sites have a comparable technique in using wood with brick or stone.

(3) Most Phoenician of all is the carved decoration : palm-trees and open flowers (also chains in II Chron. 3 : 5) used for borders and panels with cherubim for filling. Various collections of Phoenician ivory under the strong influence of Egyptian art show us just what this sort of thing was. In the same picture fall the elaborate column capitals "of lily-work", decorated with "nets of checker-work, and wreaths of chain-work" on which were hung large numbers of metal pomegranates (I Kings 7 : 15 ff.).

(4) There is no doubt that the Phoenicians got the idea of lighting a room from windows under the ceiling, above the side rooms around the main room, from the Egyptians. It seems probable also that the clerestory (or clearstory) type of building which the Temple represents is one step in the long history of our modern cathedral which goes back through Greek and Roman architecture into Syria and Egypt.

The Temple of Solomon, therefore, was a typical Phoenician temple. Solomon, engaged as he was in the attempt to place Israel on the cultural map of the world, borrowed the whole religious equipment and paraphernalia of his culturally superior neighbors. Archaeology thus furnishes independent testimony to the fact which has previously been suspected from the Old Testament record that the reign of Solomon marked the greatest

---

[8] The figure given for the Sea's capacity in I Kings 7 : 26 has been considered anachronistic. This problem has been faced by an astronomer with the aid of the latest information on the capacity of the Hebrew measure called the "bath"; see C. C. Wylie, "On King Solomon's Molten Sea", *The Biblical Archaeologist*, Vol. XII, No. 4 (Dec. 1949), pp. 86–90.

period of Israelite religious syncretism. The native religious conceptions of Israel were corrupted by the borrowing of pagan notions, thus ultimately precipitating the great prophetic conflict against such notions. Solomon was a great cosmopolitan; but according to the great prophets from the time of Elijah onwards the destiny of Israel was that she should be a " separate " people, uncorrupted by the paganism around her, in order that the true knowledge of God might be obtained and that " justice might flow down as waters ". Thus they were quite prepared to see the destruction of all that Solomon stood for to the end that the purposes of God might triumph.

THE TEMPLE EQUIPMENT

This conclusion about Solomon and his Temple is further substantiated by the ritual objects made for the Temple service. Let us examine some of them. First of all, what were the cherubim? Why should two such tremendous winged beings be placed in the " Holy of Holies ", and why their prominence on the walls and doors?

Their nature had been forgotten by the 1st century A.D. and the Jewish historian, Josephus, tells us that " no one can tell what they were like ". One thing we can be sure of is that they were not the charming winged boys of Renaissance art, a conception which is traced to little beings in Graeco-Roman art. A number of scholars have thought that they were the great winged bulls which were so popular in Mesopotamia. But a check of the art of Palestine and Syria shows that such monsters are practically non-existent in this area. A process of elimination shows that the cherub can have been only one thing: a winged sphinx, that is, a winged lion with human head. This is the most popular winged being in Phoenician art. It is to be found on artistic objects uncovered in almost every excavation in this area; and it is the only being which could possibly be the cherub.

Why was it used? Among the Megiddo ivories is a plaque which shows a Canaanite king about 1200 B.C. seated on his throne (Fig. 41). This throne is a chair supported by two cherubim. Other Canaanite kings were pictured on similar thrones. Just as these monarchs were enthroned upon the cherubim, so the God of Israel is often designated as " He who thrones (or is enthroned upon) the cherubim ". In official Israelite religion it was against the law to make an image of God;

so in the " Holy of Holies " it was his invisible Presence which was thought to be enthroned upon the two great hybrid beings, just as so many gods and kings of the Near East were often represented.

What was the religious significance of the cherubim? That is something which is rather vague. A fragment of an ancient hymn contained the words: " And He rode upon a cherub and did fly " (II Sam. 22 : 11; Psa. 18 : 10; to which compare Ezek. 10 : 20). Apparently in the religion of Israel as in other Near Eastern religions such winged beings were thought to be assistants who aided a god in getting from place to place. From Gen. 3 : 24 we recall that cherubim were placed at the east of the Garden to guard the Tree of Life. This is exactly the conception which lies behind the cherubim and palm-trees carved on the walls and doors of the Temple. In Phoenician art two cherubim facing a tree is a very common motif. Cherubim as guardians of the tree are a popular subject in the ivory collections, and this fact together with the passage in Genesis gives us another hint as to the religious significance of these strange, divine emissaries.

Besides the great altar and the bronze Sea, Solomon's imported craftsman, Hiram, is said to have made a large number of implements of various sorts for the Temple sacrificial service. Ten lavers of bronze and ten wheel-stands to hold them were cast. According to the Chronicler, they were to hold water in which the instruments used in the burnt offering could be washed. Such lavers have been found in the excavations, both with and without wheels. One unearthed at Ras Shamra in northern Syria has metal pomegranates hanging from the bowl (Fig. 95), which is the sort of thing described as decorating the capitals of Jachin and Boaz (I Kings 7 : 20).

We have found little evidence as to the nature of the golden candlesticks or the table of shewbread. Archaeological discoveries suggest several possibilities, but do not single out any one for either case. But what about the shovels and flesh-hooks (II Chron. 4 : 16), the tongs, cups, snuffers, basins, spoons, and firepans (I Kings 7 : 49 ff.)? If these are common religious instruments, we ought to be able to identify them. This we are able to do for some of them, but not for all.

A shovel from Megiddo, dating about 1300 B.C., is known; and a contemporary example has been found at Beth-shemesh (Fig. 96). The flesh-hooks, according to passages in Exodus and

94. A laver found at Ras Shamra

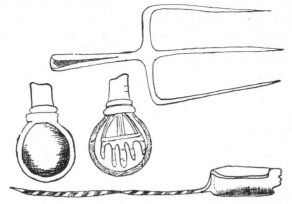

95. Shovel, censer and flesh-hook, drawn from excavated specimens

Numbers, were used in connection with the altar. In the story of Eli (I Sam. 2 : 13 f.) the implement was used to lift meat from cooking pots. Several of these three-tined forks have turned up in the excavations, having been used from very early times. The tongs must have been an enlarged form of the tweezer which is occasionally found in the excavations. The " cups " cannot be identified at present. They must have been used in Canaanite religion, however, since the name for them occurs three times in the well known epic poems of Ras Shamra, but the contexts do not help us to identify them.

The " snuffers " are also rather mysterious. It is not known whether the Hebrew word really means " snuffer ". From its root one would judge that it should be something with which to prune the lamp wicks. " Basin " is another unidentifiable object, but the biblical evidence indicates that it must have been a libation vase. The blood of the sacrifice was probably caught in such vessels and dashed from them upon the horns of the altar, and any other place where it was desirable to have a blood libation (cf. Ezek. 43 : 20). Libation vases are familiar to us on Mesopotamian reliefs, but they have not as yet been identified with certainty in Palestine.

Fortunately, the " spoons " are known. The primary meaning of the Hebrew word for them is " palm ", and numerous bowls with hands carved on their backs (the bowls thus being the palm of the hand) have been found in Palestine and Syria dating between about 1000 and 600 B.C. (Fig. 96). A hollow tube opens into the bowl, which raises the question as to their purpose. The first and best explanation is that they were censers, the hollow tube allowing one to blow on the incense to get it to burn. An Egyptian relief seems to give some support to this theory. The only trouble with it is that little evidence of burning has been found in them. The latest explanation is that they were used for libations of some sort, the stem being connected with a vessel which, when tilted, would allow liquid to flow into the bowl of the " spoon ". This is a very forced explanation, but one must conclude that, given the above evidence, the reader's opinion is as good as any ! The " firepans " have not been identified, but presumably they were used to carry live coals to and from the altar.

The account given of these Temple instruments shows that much work yet remains to be done, but it also illustrates the fact that no accurate translation of the Old Testament can be made without more archaeological work and careful attention to its results.

THE THEOLOGICAL MEANING OF THE TEMPLE

In the ancient polytheistic world kingship and temple were the two institutions which bound the divine and human worlds together. In Egypt the king was the incarnate son of the Sun-god. In Mesopotamia he was the selected representative of the gods to rule the earthly society. His throne thus received divine legitimation and he could be thought of as the gods' adopted " son ". In Israel the king was conceived in a similar way, and could be called in this sense God's " son " (II Sam. 7 : 14 ; Psa. 2 : 7). The purpose of kingship everywhere was to provide internal and external justice and security (I Sam. 8 : 20). From the legends in the literature found at Ras Shamra in northern Syria (see Chap. VII) we learn that the Canaanite ideal was that the good king " judges the cause of the widow, adjudicates the case of the fatherless "— words which are familiar to the student of the Old Testament (cf. Isa. 1 : 17 ; Jer. 22 : 3). It is not improbable that when Israel borrowed the institution of kingship from her neighbors, she took over also the ideals connected with it, ideals which were to form a basis of the conception of the Messiah, the ideal ruler of the time to come.[9]

In Babylon one of the chief religious functions of the king was to preside over the annual New Year's celebration. Central in this celebration was a cult drama in which the creation battle was re-fought and rewon. The king took the part of the king of the gods in the drama, and as a result the order of nature was believed to have been established for the ensuing year. Behind such liturgical dramas in polytheism was the principle of sympathetic magic, of like making like. By imitative action the king could identify himself with a god and thus accomplish what the god had accomplished, for to the polytheistic mind what is like is in some measure identical with what is. In addition to the divine battle-drama of creation, the king also played the crucial role in the other great liturgical festivals which as celebrated in the temple caused nature to act as it had previously acted. Thus the king identified himself in a ceremony also with the god of rain and vegetation, while a priestess became the goddess of fertility. Their union was the union of the creative powers of the spring. " Thus through a willed act of man is achieved a divine union wherein is the all-pervading, life-giving re-creative potency upon which depends, as our texts tell us, ' the life of all lands ' and also the steady flow of days, the renewal of the new moon throughout the new year." [10] In the festival rites in the temple the pagan king created anew the orderly world in the battle against chaos, and

he secured the fertility and the revival of nature in spring and fall.

Some scholars believe that a New Year's festival, comparable to that in Babylon, existed in Israel and was celebrated by the Israelite king in the Solomonic Temple. In the festival as conducted by the Davidic dynasty the enemies of God were not believed to be the dragons of chaos but historical powers who refuse God's rule. In the rites their defeat was celebrated as though it had already taken place or was about to do so. Other scholars feel very strongly that the supposed parallel between the Babylonian and Israelite royal festivals in the Temple does not really exist. While there must have been services in the Temple which employed a number of the Psalms to celebrate God's defeat of earthly enemies and the role of the Davidic king as God's agent in the defeat (e.g. Pss. 2 and 110), the work was or would be God's doing. Sympathetic magic played little part in the ceremonies. The king could not become God by sacramental means.

However this may be, the above remarks suggest the importance of king and temple in pagan life. On what went on in the temple services the whole stability and order of society and nature was believed to be dependent. The temple was indeed " none other than the house of God, . . . the gate of heaven " (Gen. 28 : 17), or " the foundation-platform of heaven and earth " (such being the name given the temple-tower of Babylon). Without doubt there were some in Israel who would like to have conceived a similar role for king and temple in Jerusalem, but they did not succeed in winning over any large segment of the populace to such a view. The Sinai covenant had established a relationship between people and Deity which was prior to kingship and to the Temple, and sacramental rite was never allowed to gain precedence over covenant loyalty and vocational obedience. Indeed, whenever signs of such a reversal appeared, there were those who were ready to speak for the old order and to denounce king, priesthood and Temple.

The term " house of God " was continued in Israel, however, as the Temple's name, as was also the term " palace " (hekal). The ancient Near East seems not to have possessed a special term like our " temple " for a religious edifice. It was simply a house or palace of a god. It was conceived as a manor in which the divine lord resided together with his divine and human servants. The human servants, the priests, had charge of the building

[9] H. L. Ginsberg, " Ugaritic Studies and the Bible ", The Biblical Archaeologist, Vol. VIII, No. 2 (May 1945), p. 50.
[10] Thorkild Jacobsen, The Intellectual Adventure of Ancient Man (Chicago, 1946), p. 199.

and the property belonging to it, for their real task was to make provision for the god's needs. The subjects of the divine lord could visit him and request his aid in solving their problems. When they did so, they would bring the gifts which were the god's due if he owned their land, or they would bring free-will offerings in order that the god might receive them favorably. The daily cult was essentially a provision for the god's daily needs. The sacrifices, offerings and libations were his needed food and drink; and this belief in the deity's physical need seems never to have been spiritualized in the texts we have. One disillusioned Babylonian skeptic could thus infer that because his god so needed his service, that service should be withheld that the god be taught " to run after thee like a dog ".[11] We also recall the statement in the Babylonian flood-story, discussed in Chap. VII, to the effect that after the flood had receded and the flood-hero was able to offer sacrifice, the gods were so hungry that they " crowded like flies about the sacrificer ".

In Israel, however, there were limits to the anthropomorphic conception of deity. Not only did the great Lord transcend the categories of sex, but he certainly had no physical needs which man could supply (cf. Psa. 50 : 12–13). The whole sacrificial system, while in outward form it resembled the systems of polytheism, had a different setting and purpose. It was believed to be God's gift by revelation to Israel. It was a form which he accepted for worship, praise, thanksgiving, communion, and especially for atonement of sin, provided that the sins were not of the presumptuous, high-handed, rebellious type which indicated a hardened, disloyal heart. For such sins sacramentalism was of no avail.

One interesting problem connected with the temple in the ancient world was this: how could a cosmic god, such as the sky, the storm, the sun or the moon, be conceived as living in an earthly house? This is a problem to our logical minds, and it was to some in Israel, as we shall see, but it was not so to the polytheist. The ancient temple was filled with cosmic symbolism so that it was conceived to be a microcosm, a replica in miniature, of the cosmic world in which the deity lived. Since like is like, the temple which is like the universe is in a measure that universe, and the

limitless deity thus could inhabit it. His presence was indicated by his statue placed in the building. To Israel this statue was something lifeless and made with hands, and polytheism was represented as a worship of idols, a fetishism, a devotion to something made. Yet a polytheist could not have understood this criticism. On the principle of like being like, the statue which resembled the deity was that deity. Yet the statue did not confine him; he was numinously present in it, but he still was the cosmic power, to be met in his temple and yet to be met also in the experience of power in nature. The problem of transcendence and immanence was not real to the polytheist because it had been solved by a rich sacramentalism.

The Solomonic Temple was erected in all probability with no more conscious awareness of this problem than existed in polytheism. It was simply the " house of Yahweh ", and his presence was believed to be invisibly enthroned in the darkness over the cherubim in the Holy of Holies, or innermost room. Yet in the course of time the problem was seen and evidently discussed. The most daring and original solution is to be found in the Deuteronomic literature (that is, in Deuteronomy and the Deuteronomic history of Israel in Palestine, from Joshua through II Kings). For example, at the dedication of the Temple, Solomon is represented as giving a very moving prayer in which he says (I Kings 8 : 27–30):

But will God really dwell upon the earth? Behold neither the heaven nor the heaven of heavens can contain thee; how much less this house that I have built! Yet do thou turn unto the prayer of thy servant and to his supplication, O Lord my God . . . that thine eyes may be open toward this house night and day, even toward the place whereof thou hast said, " My name shall be there " . . . And do thou hearken unto the supplication of thy servant and of thy people Israel, when they shall pray toward this place. Yea, hear thou in heaven, thy dwelling place; and when thou hearest, forgive.

Implicit in these words is a denial of the whole polytheistic notion that God can dwell like a human being on earth. His dwelling is in heaven. The Temple is simply the bearer of his Name and a house of prayer, or rather the focus of religious attention to which prayer is directed. The Temple is thus God's gracious accommodation to human need. This is something entirely different from the polytheism which regarded a temple as a god's palace where the human servants supplied his physical needs and sought to please him with gifts.

[11] Thorkild Jacobsen, *The Intellectual Adventure of Ancient Man* (Chicago, 1946), p. 217.

How the priests, who cared for the Temple and its services, interpreted its meaning is not entirely clear. Central to priestly theology was the conception of God's presence in the midst of his people. This presence was the people's blessing and security, and to Ezekiel the vision of God's departure from the Temple was the sign of his determination to destroy it (Ezek. 10–11). Yet that the priests were conscious of the problem is indicated by their terminology. The common term used for human sitting or dwelling on earth was *yashabh*. The priests were careful not to use this term to indicate God's presence in the Temple; the " dwelling " of God was in heaven, not on earth. The term they used for God's earthly presence was *shakan*, an old nomadic word meaning " to tent " or " to tabernacle ". By use of a technical terminology they suggest that while God's " dwelling " is in heaven, the mystery of his presence is nevertheless known on earth, for he " tabernacles " in the midst of his people.[12]

This distinction is recalled in the New Testament. For example, the familiar words of John 1 : 14 are literally rendered : " And the Word became flesh and tented (or tabernacled) among us, full of grace and truth." Yet here the Temple as the sign of God's presence amongst his people has been displaced, for Christ is the presence; he is the new Temple (John 2 : 21 ; cf. Rev. 21 : 22).

---

[12] The significance of this priestly terminology seems first to have been worked out by Frank M. Cross, Jr. ; see provisionally his article, " The Tabernacle ", *The Biblical Archaeologist*, Vol. X, No. 3 (Sept. 1947), pp. 65–8.

FURTHER READING

The most up-to-date sources are those frequently mentioned in preceding bibliographies : W. F. Albright, *From the Old Stone Age to Christianity*, pp. 221–8 ; by the same author, *Archaeology and the Religion of Israel*, pp. 119–55 ; and Millar Burrows, *What Mean These Stones?* (the pertinent subjects must be looked up in the Index of this book for the page reference); John Bright, *A History of Israel* (Philadelphia, 1959), Chap. 5 (see his earlier article also on " The Age of King David ", *Union Seminary Review* [Richmond, Va.], Feb. 1942, pp. 87–109) ; G. Ernest Wright on the stratigraphy of the age in *The Bible and the Ancient Near East* (Garden City, 1961), pp. 94–6 and Chart 8.

For the age of Solomon the reader may also be referred to Nelson Glueck, *The Other Side of the Jordan* (New Haven, American Schools of Oriental Research, 1940), Chaps. III and IV on the copper mines and refinery of Solomon.

Attention may also be called to the following articles among others : G. Ernest Wright, " Solomon's Temple Resurrected ", *The Biblical Archaeologist*, Vol. IV, No. 2 (May 1941) ; Paul L. Garber, " Reconstructing Solomon's Temple ", *ibid.*, Vol. XIV, No. 1 (Feb. 1951) ; a symposium by Harold A. Nelson, A. Leo Oppenheim, G. Ernest Wright and Floyd V. Filson, " The Significance of the Temple in the Ancient Near East ", *ibid.*, Vol. VII, Nos. 3 and 4 (Sept. and Dec. 1944) ; W. F. Albright, " What Were the Cherubim ", *ibid.*, Vol. I, No. 1 (Feb. 1938) ; W. F. Albright, " Two Cressets from Marisa and the Pillars of Jachin and Boaz ", *Bulletin of the American Schools of Oriental Research*, No. 85 (Feb. 1942), pp. 18–27 ; H. G. May, " The Two Pillars Before the Temple of Solomon ", *ibid.*, No. 88 (Dec. 1942), pp. 19–27 ; Carl G. Howie, " The East Gate of Ezekiel's Temple Enclosure and the Solomonic Gateway of Megiddo ", *ibid.*, No. 117 (Feb. 1950), pp. 13–19 ; M. B. Rowton, " The Date of the Founding of Solomon's Temple ", *ibid.*, No. 119 (Oct. 1950), pp. 20–2 ; W. F. Albright, " New Light from Egypt on the Chronology and History of Israel and Judah ", *ibid.*, No. 130 (April 1953), pp. 4–8 ; G. Ernest Wright, " The Discoveries at Megiddo, 1935–39 ", *The Biblical Archaeologist*, Vol. XIII, No. 2 (May 1950), pp. 28–46 ; Yigael Yadin, " New Light on Solomon's Megiddo ", *ibid.*, Vol. XXIII, No. 2 (May 1960), pp. 62–68 ; the preliminary reports on the Hazor excavation by the same author yearly in *ibid.*, Vols. XIX–XXII (1956–9) ; and his " Solomon's City Wall and Gate at Gezer ", *Israel Exploration Journal*, Vol. VIII (1958), pp. 80–6. Note also A. Malamat, " The Kingdom of David and Solomon in its contact with Aram Naharaim ", *The Biblical Archaeologist*, Vol. XXI (1958), pp. 96–102.

CHAPTER IX

DIVISION AND DOWNFALL

" So Israel rebelled against the house of David unto this day. And it came to pass when all Israel heard that Jeroboam was returned that they sent and called him unto the congregation and made him king over all Israel. There was none that followed the house of David but the tribe of Judah only. . . . And there was war between Rehoboam and Jeroboam continually " (I Kings 12 : 19–20 ; 14 : 30).

THE golden age of the great kings did not survive the 10th century. Owing to the policies of Solomon, the kingdom split apart. North Israel retained the name " Israel " for itself and chose as its king Jeroboam, who had once been the Solomonic officer in charge of the northern compulsory labor battalions. The southern kingdom, calling itself " Judah ", retained the Davidic dynasty. The boundary between the two was the northern border of the old tribal area of Benjamin, ten miles north of Jerusalem. The large empire established by David was now no more. The Aramean state centering in Damascus had broken away and was independent. The kingdom of Ammon across the Jordan, with capital at the modern Amman, had either attained its independence, or was shortly to do so, judging from the mention of an independent king of that territory by the Assyrian monarch, Shalmaneser III, in 853 B.C. (cf. also II Chron. 20 : 1). Israel also soon lost its control of Moab to the east of the Dead Sea, and seems not to have reconquered it before 875 B.C., while the land of Bashan, east of the Sea of Galilee, was shortly seized by Damascus. Edom for a time may have gained its independence from Judah (cf. I Kings 11 : 14–22), though later during the first half of the 9th century it was again under the firm control of the Jerusalem court (cf. I Kings 22 : 47).

While Judah adhered firmly to the Dynasty of David, its theology centering in king and Temple, Israel attempted to return to the old charismatic ideal, its kings chosen by God through the mediation of a prophet, as Saul and David had been. Thus Jeroboam received divine sanction through the prophet Ahijah (I Kings 11 : 29–39), though he was soon rejected (13 : 1–10). Baasha was sanctioned, and then similarly rejected (16 : 2–4), as also was Jehu (II Kings 9 : 4–10 ; Hos. 1 : 4). Yet in conflict with the ideal was the desire of each king to found a dynasty, and this led to frequent revolutions. The Omri dynasty, whose most famous figure was Jezebel, was able to hold the throne for at least forty years (ca. 876–842 B.C.),[1] whereas the dynasty of Jehu which followed survived for nearly a century (ca. 842–745 B.C.). The last two decades of Israel's independent history were governed by five kings who had received no divine sanction and could be considered as practically usurpers. Hence Hosea (8 : 4) said of the Israelites in God's name : " They have made kings, but not by me ; they have made princes, but I did not know (them)." [2] This situation meant political instability in the north ; and, to make matters worse, north and south bickered and warred with one another almost constantly, at least when external factors allowed them to do so.

In spite of such troubles, however, there seems to have been a great deal of prosperity among the people of the land. Both Israelites and Judeans were building excellent homes and importing objects from abroad, having learned rapidly about many

---

[1] These dates, and most of those used for the Divided Monarchy, are taken from W. F. Albright, " The Chronology of the Divided Monarchy of Israel ", Bulletin of the American Schools of Oriental Research, No. 100 (Dec. 1945), pp. 16–22. Many of the figures can be considered as only approximate, and variant figures are to be found in the writings of other scholars. Chronology is an exceedingly complex subject ; but the reason Albright is tentatively followed here is because his system is based almost solely upon synchronisms rather than on later scribal computations which are known to contain a number of errors. For example, recent information places the date of the beginning of Solomon's Temple in 959 B.C. with a high degree of probability, and this would mean that Solomon reigned from ca. 961 to 922 B.C. From 922 B.C. to the fall of Israel in 721 B.C. is a period of 201 years, whereas, if we count the length of the reigns of the individual kings of Israel as given us by scribal computation, we obtain a figure of some 241 years for the same period. According to I Kings 16 : 23 Omri became king in the thirty-first year of King Asa of Judah, while Ahab began to reign in Asa's thirty-eighth year (vs. 29). This would mean that Omri reigned for some eight years at most, whereas vs. 23 says that he reigned twelve years. The latter figure is probably a conflation, obtained from adding the years of Tibni, Omri's rival, to those of Omri, whereas the two were not successive but contemporary (Albright, ibid., note 15).

[2] " Know " is here used, as frequently elsewhere (e.g. Amos 3 : 2), in the sense of " choose ".

of civilization's refinements. In certain places, at least, our excavated evidence indicates a gradual increase in the population and a general improvement in the standards of living. The total picture which archaeology presents is not one of great wealth, but nevertheless one of great energy and comparative stability. It is especially interesting to see in those places where blocks of Israelite houses have been well preserved, that on the whole the home of a Hebrew in Canaan was now somewhat better than that of the Canaanite peasant of the 14th and 13th centuries during the period of greatest decadence in Canaanite culture. While conscripted military and laboring groups had to work on governmental projects, the majority of the population in both Israel and Judah evidently had enough time and energy to build good private dwellings and bring the land in the hill country under more intensive cultivation than ever before.

The effect of the Hebrew conquest and settlement is now clear. The material culture of Palestine has become exceedingly uniform, and the remnants of the Canaanite and Philistine cultures in the plain areas have largely disappeared under the economic domination of the people in the hills. In addition, we now enter a period when for over three hundred years the customs of the people are so stable and change so slowly that it is difficult for archaeologists to fix clear cultural phases. This is well illustrated by the pottery which is the main source of dating in all periods of ancient Palestine. Between 900 and 600 B.C. the styles and fashions changed so gradually that it is very difficult to date particular remains within the period. At long last and by dint of much labor we can now date a representative collection of dishes, pots, and jars to the 9th–8th or to the 8th–7th centuries, but that is usually as close as we can come with any degree of certainty. This stability of culture reflects a certain stability in life and thought in spite of the many political upheavals.

ARCHAEOLOGY AND POLITICS

So much for the general situation among the common people. What of the doings of kings and governments?

Jeroboam, we are told, " built " Shechem as his new capital in North Israel (I Kings 12 : 25). This was a natural move, since for a thousand years at least it had been the chief city of the area. Presumably the phrase " built Shechem " refers to the fortification of the city, and some of Jeroboam's

work has probably been discovered. He evidently repaired the older city wall, and at least one fragment of this repair, comparable in type to the Solomonic wall at Megiddo, has been unearthed. At the northwest the old city gate of Canaanite times was re-used—a tremendous affair with three separate entrances, covered over to form a tower (for the type, see Fig. 40). By 800 B.C. or shortly thereafter the great ruins of the old temple of the " Lord of the Covenant ", destroyed by Abimelech (Judges 9), were covered with a six-inch layer of cement on which a large government granary was erected. There taxes in grain, wine and oil from the province of " Mount Ephraim " were evidently paid and stored.

One phase of the activity of Jeroboam has occasioned a number of questions. We are told that since Jerusalem had become the religious capital of all Israel, Jeroboam became worried lest this factor should form a divisive element and endanger his throne. Consequently, he made two golden calves (or rather bulls) and set them up in two cities which had been hallowed by previous tradition, in Dan to the north of the Sea of Galilee and in Bethel, just ten miles north of Jerusalem. At these two places he established the religious services and told his people to worship there instead of in Jerusalem (I Kings 12 : 26 ff.).

The problem now arises : how are these bulls to be interpreted ? Were they supposed to be idols, representing the God of Israel ? Most of the religious leaders of the country seem later to have interpreted them as such, or in any event they were certainly believed to lead the people into idolatry and away from the true traditions of Israel. As a result, the editor of the books of Kings considers Jeroboam as the most wicked king Israel ever had.

It is improbable, however, that Jeroboam really thought that he was turning away from the God of Israel, who through the prophet Ahijah had given him the throne. The question is : did he believe the bulls were actually representations of God, or did he believe that God was invisibly riding upon the back of a bull, just as in Jerusalem he was thought to be invisibly enthroned upon the cherubim ? The archaeological evidence presents a clear answer. Neighboring peoples were accustomed to represent their gods as standing upon the backs of animals or else seated on thrones borne by animals (Fig. 96). The second is the conception borrowed by Solomon for his Temple in Jerusalem. The first was probably in the mind of Jeroboam to whom

96. The Storm-god, Hadad, who in Canaan was called Baal, standing on the back of a bull. From Arslan-Tash in northern Syria, dating from the 8th century B.C.

and so had no chance to misconceive the actual nature of the cherubim. At Bethel and at Dan, on the other hand, the bulls were probably in full sight of all worshippers, and a majority of the unthinking masses would undoubtedly believe that they were worshipping what they could see, the bull itself. This in turn would lead them closer to Canaanite religion, where El and Baal were frequently likened to bulls.

The first great disaster since the reign of Saul descended upon the two kingdoms about 918 B.C. Our books of Kings give us scant information about it:

> And it came to pass in the fifth year of king Rehoboam that Shishak, king of Egypt came up against Jerusalem. And he took away the treasures of the house (Temple) of the Lord, and the treasures of the king's house. . . . And he took away all the shields of gold which Solomon had made (I Kings 14 : 25–6).

This king of Egypt thought more highly of his campaign, however, and on the walls of the great temple of Karnak in Upper Egypt he had his artists carve a picture of himself smiting the Asiatics in the presence of the god Amon, who with a goddess is depicted as presenting to him ten lines of captives. Each captive symbolized a town or locality, the name of which was inscribed below. From these names we can gather the extent of his campaign. The biblical account implies that only Judah was affected, but all of Palestine apparently suffered, for the list includes cities in the Esdraelon, Transjordan, the hill country of both Israel and Judah, and even Edom. There is an interesting reference to the " Field of Abram ", presumably the Hebron area, and this is the first time that a source outside the Bible confirms that Patriarch's connection with a locality in Palestine.[3] Shishak was attempting to restore the great Egyptian empire of bygone days, and since his army was composed of wild African troops from Libya and Nubia, the devastation can readily be imagined (cf. II Chron. 12 : 2 ff.). The king himself was a Libyan whose ancestors had been mercenaries in Egypt, but the hirelings were now strong enough to seize the throne.

The excavations have further supported the extent and severity of the conquest. A fragment of a monumental stone or *stele* set up by the king at Megiddo has been found at the site. A number of

the golden bull may have been the pedestal on which the invisible Lord was thought to stand. At least the archaeological evidence leads us to this conclusion. On the other hand, the later writers certainly speak of the bulls as though they were idols, and they seem to have interpreted Jeroboam's statement literally when he said to the people: " Behold thy God (not 'gods' as the English translations have it), O Israel, which brought thee up out of the land of Egypt! " (I Kings 12 : 28). It may well be that the solution of our problem lies in the difference between the official view and the actual practice among the people. In Jerusalem the worshippers could not enter the Temple

---

[3] The suggestion has recently been made, however, that the list is to be read *boustrophedon* (a method of writing lines alternately from left to right and right to left). If so, then the reading in this case is doubtful.

towns are known or suspected from the archaeological evidence to have been at least partially destroyed, among them Debir, Tell Jemmeh (Jorda?) south of Gaza and even Solomon's great refinery at Ezion-geber. Mammoth fortifications thought to have been built by Shishak have been unearthed at Sharuhen (modern Tell el-Far'ah), southeast of Gaza. A brick wall, 23 feet wide, was constructed around the city and, if correctly ascribed to Shishak, it shows that the king was making no mere raid, but an occupation in force, employing thousands of laborers.

The days of the Egyptian were numbered, however, and he had scarcely time to consolidate his conquest before death occurred. His successors were not as energetic or able. One of them is said to have attempted to repeat his predecessor's exploits, but the Judean narrator claims that king Asa of Judah was able to defeat him (II Chron. 14 : 9 ff.). Thus Judah and Israel were left again to fight with each other without interference from the major powers.

It was probably after Shishak's abortive conquest that Rehoboam began to fortify his kingdom of Judah. He was in danger from all sides, and drastic measures, unnecessary for Solomon, were necessary for him. The cities thus " built " are listed in II Chron. 11 : 5-10, and it is probable that excavations at two of the sites have uncovered some of the work. We shall hear more of Lachish, one of the main frontier fortresses of Judah, in Chap. X, but its great fortifications upon which Judean kings depended so largely for protection were probably built by Rehoboam (Fig. 119). The city was provided with a double wall and a strongly protected gateway. Towers spaced at intervals around the mound gave the defenders opportunity to keep battering rams at a distance. So strong were these fortifications that an Assyrian king who finally conquered the city in 701 B.C. was sufficiently proud of his deed to carve a description of the siege upon the walls of his palace (Figs. 116-18).

Just to the north of Lachish in the Vale of Elah, near the place where David's victory over Goliath was supposed to have taken place, was another main fortress of Judah, Azekah (Fig. 97). This city has been found to have been supplied with a fortified citadel at the highest point on the mound. Its plan

97. The site of Azekah in the Vale of Elah

98. A reconstruction of the fortifications at Tell en-Nasbeh

reminds us of Saul's palace-fortress at Gibeah, for it was built along similar lines, though almost twice as large. It was a defensive enclosure to which the people retreated in time of war, serving the same purpose as the stockades during the Indian wars in America.

Along the highway leading north of Jerusalem into Israel, there were four main towns within the first ten miles: (1) Gibeah, Saul's capital, about three miles from Jerusalem; (2) Ramah, about five miles north; (3) a site which is called today Tell en-Nasbeh, some seven miles north; and (4) Bethel, a royal sanctuary just across the border of Benjamin, the southernmost Israelite town in the hill country and some ten miles from Jerusalem. Three of these cities have been excavated, Gibeah, Tell en-Nasbeh, and Bethel; and all of them show evidence of the rivalry between Israel and Judah. One corner of Saul's ruined palace at Gibeah was rebuilt as a small fortress during the 9th or 8th centuries, presumably to protect Judah's northern border. In the same period Bethel was fortified, though only a few remains of the protective wall have been excavated.

Our clearest evidence is from Tell en-Nasbeh. The fortifications of the ancient city on this site were so strongly rebuilt about 900 B.C. that they were among the most formidable of the Judean Kingdom (Fig. 98). The tremendous wall around the town was originally 20 feet thick, and even wider at the

base. In some places later builders further strengthened it to 26 feet. Towers were built at intervals. A heavy coat of plaster was added to the lower part, making it impossible to scale the wall from the outside. Parts of these fortifications are still standing at a height of 25 feet, and the original height must have been much greater, though it is impossible at present to determine it. At the northeast was the heavily fortified gateway. Long stone seats lined the walls of the tower rooms and the entrance court, for here the elders and deliberative assemblies of the ancient city met, and carried on official business.

Fortifications on a scale such as this could only have been built by conscripted labor, and they remind us immediately of the interesting incident recounted in I Kings 15 : 16-22. We are told that there was war between Asa of Judah (about 913-873 B.C.) and Baasha of Israel (about 900-877 B.C.) all their days. "And Baasha . . . went up against Judah, and built [fortified] Ramah, that he might not suffer any to go out or come in to Asa, king of Judah." Asa gathered together a considerable sum of silver and gold and sent it to Benhadad of Damascus to induce him to attack Israel. Benhadad complied, capturing a few cities in the extreme northern part of the Israelite kingdom. Baasha was forced to break off his work at Ramah, whereupon Asa "made a proclamation throughout all Judah—none were exempted—and they took away the stones of Ramah and the timber thereof wherewith Baasha had builded. And Asa built [fortified] with them Geba [probably Gibeah in this case] of Benjamin and Mizpah."

Most scholars today believe that Tell en-Nasbeh is actually the site of ancient Mizpah, and that the tremendous wall around the site, which the excavations have shown to have been built about this time, is Asa's fortification, largely made of stones carried from Ramah. That the walls are Judean fortifications against Israel, however, is obvious, and they are eloquent testimony to the ill-feeling and civil war between Judah and Israel after the death of Solomon.

THE DYNASTY OF OMRI (about 876–842 B.C.)

Baasha's son and successor in Israel, Elah, reigned two years, when he was slain by one of his army commanders, Zimri. Most of the army, however, refused to support Zimri, but declared Omri, another commander, king. Omri besieged the Israelite capital, Tirzah, and Zimri burnt the royal palace over himself when he saw that his cause was lost. Within a few years Omri had consolidated his position ; and he became the founder of the most notorious dynasty which Israel ever had (I Kings 16 : 8 ff.). His son, Ahab, married Jezebel, the daughter of Itto-baal (Ethbaal), a priest of Astarte in Tyre, who a few years earlier had seized the Phoenician throne by murdering his predecessor, even as had Zimri. Both David and Solomon had likewise married foreign princesses for diplomatic reasons, but none of them, apparently, had the strength of personality, the zeal, and the ruthlessness of Jezebel. Her policy precipitated a bloody revolution, led by the prophetic group under the leadership of Elijah and Elisha, which resulted in the complete extermination of the House of Omri some forty years later.

Seven verses in I Kings 16 give us the sole biblical information about Omri himself, but these verses when combined with archaeological information indicate that he was a king of considerable ability. Even the far-off Assyrians heard of him, so that on many occasions they referred to Israel as " the Land of Omri " or " the House of Omri ", long after the revolution had destroyed all remnants of the dynasty.

Our most direct evidence, however, comes from the excavations of Samaria. Shechem, the natural capital of North Israel, was not a place which could easily be defended. Consequently, Baasha, Elah,

and Zimri had used Tirzah, a city to the northeast of Shechem, as their capital.

In 1930 W. F. Albright suggested that the most probable location of Tirzah is the modern Tell el-Far'ah, a large mound about seven miles northeast of Shechem, on the road leading to Beth-shan and the Jordan Valley. An expedition to the site, directed by Father R. de Vaux, O.P., of the Dominican Biblical School in Jerusalem, began to excavate it in 1947. It was found to have been first established in the 4th millennium, was a great city throughout the Bronze Age, and was destroyed at the end of the 10th or early 9th century B.C. Father de Vaux has discovered a large building erected immediately thereafter, which gives evidence of never having been finished. This he interprets as Omri's palace which he abandoned before completion when he moved his court to Samaria. In the Song of Songs the loved one is said to be " beautiful as Tirzah . . . comely as Jerusalem " (6 : 4). It has been suggested that those words are most naturally dated, in their original edition, during the first half century of Israel's history, when Tirzah was its capital and could be compared with Jerusalem. One would scarcely say this about Tirzah after it had been destroyed and replaced by the remarkable city of Samaria.

Omri, aligning his kingdom with Phoenicia, chose a new capital, the hill of Samaria (Fig. 99), some seven miles northwest of Shechem on the road to Esdraelon, Galilee, and Phoenicia. The first Palestinian archaeologist, Edward Robinson, has written of this site as follows : " The view from the summit of the hill presents a splendid panorama of the fertile basin and the mountains around, teeming with large villages ; and includes also a long extent of the Mediterranean . . . The site of this capital . . . was a chosen one ; and it would be difficult to find, in all Palestine, a situation of equal strength, fertility, and beauty combined. In all these particulars, it has greatly the advantage over Jerusalem. It continued to be the capital of Israel for two centuries . . . During all this time it was the seat of idolatry ; and is often denounced by the prophets, sometimes in connection with Jerusalem. Here too was the scene of many of the acts of the prophets Elijah and Elisha, connected with the various famines in the land, the unexpected plenty in Samaria, and the various deliverances of the city from the Syrians." [4]

---

[4] Edward Robinson, *Biblical Researches in Palestine*, Vol. II (1841), pp. 307, 309.

99. The site of Samaria

The first excavations at Samaria between 1908 and 1910 were directed by two great American archaeologists, George A. Reisner and Clarence S. Fisher, and marked the beginning of a new day in the technique of excavating. Before this time most excavations were treasure hunts, and trenches were dug hither and thither across a mound with little attention paid to city levels or strata. Reisner and Fisher developed the stratigraphical method of digging, which concentrates on the careful excavation of areas, instead of trenches, and on careful surveying and on recording of all objects found. The aim of Reisner and Fisher was to dig by levels, plan every building, and list every object, in such a way as to enable them to reconstruct the whole mound on paper after they had finished, and fit every wall and every object back in place. This scientific method of excavation has been used throughout the Near East since the first World War, and has been responsible for the tremendous progress of archaeology.

The city of Samaria is very difficult to excavate. The reason for this is that it was intensively occupied both before and after the time of Jesus, and builders in Hellenistic and Roman times erected such great structures on bed rock, that the Israelite strata were disturbed and in many places removed entirely.

Actual remains of Israelite days, therefore, are comparatively few and in a chaotic, ruined state. Buildings and walls can be traced to some extent, however, because Omri and his successors hired architects of amazing ability and energy. What remains of their work is the finest construction thus far found in Israelite Palestine. Even where the walls have disappeared, it is possible to trace where they once were because the architects not only laid them on bed rock, but leveled the rock, even cutting trenches in it, before the foundations were laid.

Reisner and Fisher believed they could distinguish three Israelite phases of building. The first they ascribed to Omri, the second to Ahab, and the third to Jeroboam II (about 786–746 B.C.). Between 1931 and 1935 further excavations were carried out at the site under the supervision of the English archaeologist, J. W. Crowfoot. New evidence was discovered which makes it certain that the third phase is not Israelite but is to be dated about 300 B.C. Furthermore, the remaining two Israelite building phases were observed in more detail and broken up into six periods, all dating between about 875 B.C., when the city was first established by Omri, and 721 B.C., when it was destroyed by the Assyrians.

Period I is to be ascribed to both Omri and Ahab; that is, Omri began the construction but, owing to

100. Masonry of the city-wall of Period I at Samaria

101. Proto-Ionic capitals restored in the entrance wall of the Israelite city-gate at Samaria

the short time in which he reigned, we must assume that his work was completed by his son, Ahab.[5] The fortifications consisted of a wall around the summit of the mound which enclosed a large palace and court-yard (Figs. 100 and 103). This was in turn enclosed by two more walls, the first slightly lower on a terrace and the other around the base of the hill. The stone masonry is of such superb workmanship that noth-ing has ever been found in Palestine that surpasses it. The inner wall on the summit was not a par-ticularly large one, being about 5 feet wide, but the stones were so carefully cut and drafted, and the foundations so carefully laid, usually in rock trenches, that it would be difficult to break through. The city-gate on the summit was evidently on the east, probably approached by a monumental fore-court in which there were pilasters with "proto-Ionic" capitals (Figs. 101 and 104). Three complete examples were found, and fragments of three others. They are of a type, known elsewhere at Megiddo and in Transjordan, which was probably introduced into Israel by the Phoenician architects of Solomon. Their attractive shapes, consisting of a central triangle between two volutes, must have been a familiar sight to both Israelites and Judeans; and as developed by the Greeks into the Ionic capital, it has become familiar also to the Western World.

In the ruins of the city were a large number of ivory pieces which had once been used as inlays to decorate boxes and fine furniture (Fig. 102). Most

of these pieces belong to the following century, and they remind us of the words of Amos about those who lie upon beds of ivory (Amos 6 : 4 ; cf. also 3 : 15). The remains of one such bed, decorated with ivory inlay, have actually been found at the site of Arslan Tash in northern Syria, east of Carchemish, and one of the pieces bore the name of Hazael, king of Damascus in the time of Jehu of Israel (about 842–815 B.C.). The earliest of the Samaria ivories, however, belong to the time of the Omri dynasty. From I Kings 22 : 39 we learn that Ahab built an "ivory house", that is a building decorated on the interior with ivory, and it may be that the excavators found the ruins of this building, inasmuch as a large number of the ivory pieces were found in and around the foundations of one build-ing. The workmanship of the ivories was undoubt-edly Phoenician and Damascene, and we would assume that they were imported objects of art, or made by imported artists.

After Ahab's death, we are told that they washed the blood from his chariot " by the pool of Samaria " (I Kings 22 : 38). At the northwest corner of the summit the Harvard Expedition found a large artificial pool which they ascribed to the first period of construction on the site. As originally built, it was some 33 feet long by nearly 17 feet wide. A basin had first been cut in the rock about 3 feet deep. In it heavy stone slabs had been laid in cement to form the floor, and over the bottom and sides was spread a thick layer of cement mixed with wood ashes and as hard as the stone masonry itself. Unfortunately, we cannot now be sure whether the pool belongs to Period I or not, but it is tempting to think of it in relation to the pool mentioned in I Kings 22 : 38.

[5] The dating here is that of the writer, not that of the excavators : see his article, " Israelite Samaria and Iron Age Chronology ", *Bulletin of the Amer. Schools of Or. Research*, 154 (April, 1959), pp. 13–29.

102. Ivories of the Israelite period found at Samaria

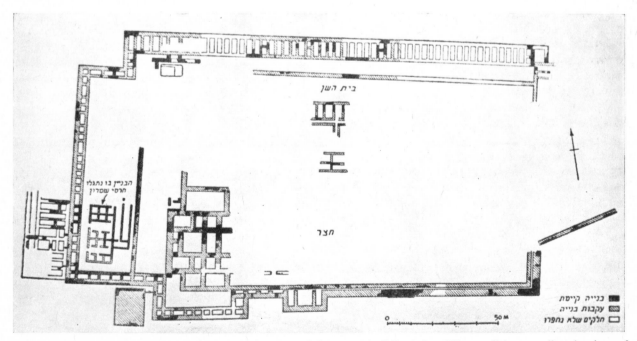

103. Plan of the Israelite constructions on the summit of the mound of Samaria. The small inner wall and palace of the first period were surrounded in the second by the large casemate construction. On the left between the inner and the casemate walls is the building in which the *ostraca* were found

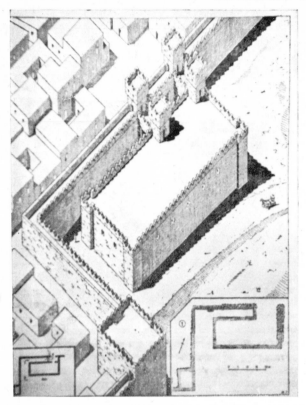

104. A reconstruction of the city-gate on the summit of Samaria, located at the extreme right of the plan in Fig. 103

In external relations the reign of Ahab was marked by intermittent war with the Aramean state of Damascus. A temporary truce must have been made in 854–853, however, for we hear of his joining in a strong coalition with Damascus and a member of other states, including Ammon and perhaps Egypt, against Shalmaneser III of Assyria. The Assyrians were making their first strong attempt to take over all of Syria-Palestine, and the great battle against the coalition took place in 853 B.C. at Qarqar on the River Orontes, north of Damascus. For some reason this battle is unmentioned in the Bible, and we know of it only from the reports of Shalmaneser. The latter tells us that the three main kings of the opposition were: Hadadezer of Damascus with 1200 chariots, 1200 cavalrymen and 20,000 infantry; Irhuleni of Hamath with 700 chariots, 700 cavalrymen and 10,000 infantry; and "Ahab, the Israelite", with 2000 chariots and 10,000 infantry. The horse and chariot as a weapon of war had been introduced into Israel by David and Solomon (II Sam. 8 : 4 ; I Kings 10 : 26), and Ahab

now possessed more of them than his neighbors, though as yet Israel made no use of cavalry. Shalmaneser claimed a great victory at Qarqar. In one inscription he claims to have killed 14,000 soldiers of the combined army, spanning the Orontes on their corpses "before there was a bridge". In another place, he claims the number was 20,500, and in still another the figure is 25,000. Scholars believe that the monarch's claim was exaggerated. Even if he did win the day, he must have suffered very heavy losses himself for he did not follow up the victory. Indeed, time after time in the years which followed he returned to Syria, claimed victory, but did not take Damascus or march into Palestine.[6]

At Megiddo and Hazor government structures erected by the Omri Dynasty as administrative centers for the Esdraelon and Galilee have been uncovered. Stables at Megiddo (Figs. 85 and 105), once attributed to Solomon and capable of housing at least four hundred and fifty of Ahab's chariot horses, are now known to belong to the 9th century (Stratum IVA ; see p. 130 ff.). The magnificent palace of the Israelite governor at Megiddo further indicates the power, prosperity and administrative energy of the Omri Dynasty's government (Fig. 106). Even more massive is the citadel-residency of the governor of Galilee unearthed at Hazor (Fig. 107). Erected evidently by Ahab (Stratum VIII), it continued in use until the city's destruction by Tiglath-pileser III in 733–32 B.C. (Stratum V ; see p. 164). Another remarkable building of the Ahab era is the pillared structure shown to the left of the Solomonic city wall in Fig. 86. Its purpose is unclear though it has been conjectured that it may have been a government storage depot or granary.

Within three years after Qarqar Ahab was again fighting the armies of Damascus in the attempt to win back northern Transjordan, but he lost his life in the battle. After his death and during the reign of his son, Joram (about 849–842 B.C.), King Mesha of Moab successfully rebelled (II Kings 1 : 1 ; 3 : 4 ff.). Mesha commemorated this event by erecting what is now known as the "Moabite Stone". This monument was discovered at the Moabite capital, Dibon, by the young French archaeologist Clermont-Ganneau in 1868 (Fig. 108). It was broken into many pieces by the natives in order to discover the treasure which they believed must be hidden in it, but most of the pieces were

[6] See J. B. Pritchard, ed., *Ancient Near Eastern Texts*, pp. 276–81.

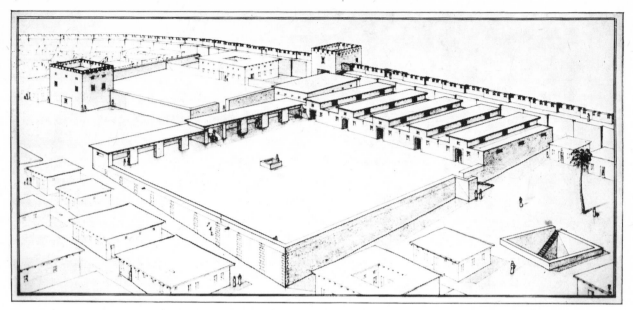

105. A reconstruction of the southern unit of the stables at Megiddo

106. A reconstruction of the palace of the 9th century B.C. at Megiddo

107. Residence and citadel of the Israelite governor at Hazor in Galilee

recovered and sent to the Louvre Museum in Paris. On the monument Mesha tells us that Omri of Israel had humbled Moab for many years because the Moabite god " Chemosh was angry at his land. And his son followed him and he also said, ' I will humble Moab.' In my time he spoke (thus), but I have triumphed over him and over his house, while Israel hath perished for ever ! " [7]

THE DYNASTY OF JEHU (about 842–745 B.C.)

That Jehu was on the throne of Israel by 841 B.C. is indicated by Assyrian records, which claim that he paid tribute to Shalmaneser at that time. The

Assyrian king on his " Black Obelisk " presents the first pictures of Israelites of which we know (Fig. 109). His artist represents Jehu kissing the ground before Shalmaneser. Behind him is a line of Israelites, bearing a variety of tribute. Above the pictures are the following words : " The tribute of Jehu, son of Omri ; I received from him silver, gold, a golden *saplu*-bowl, a golden vase with pointed bottom, golden tumblers, golden buckets, tin, a staff for a king, (and) wooden *purukhtu*." [8] The tribute was evidently received after Shalmaneser's fifth attack on Damascus, following which he had marched his army into Phoenicia. While there he says that he received the tribute of Tyre, Sidon and Jehu, and placed his portrait on the cliff of Ba'lira'si. This portrait, along with those of other kings, including Rameses II of Egypt

---

[7] Translation by W. F. Albright in *ibid.*, p. 320. Mesha further says that Israel had occupied Madeba, north of Dibon, throughout the time of Omri and " half the time of his son, forty years ". " Son " here cannot be interpreted as Ahab since the Bible says that the revolt took place after Ahab's death. If, however, the word be interpreted as " grandson " (as is frequent in the Bible), then the historical problem is solved and the round number " forty years " becomes intelligible : so F. M. Cross, Jr. and D. N. Freedman, *Early Hebrew Orthography* (New Haven, 1952), p. 39 f.

[8] Translation by A. L. Oppenheim in J. B. Pritchard, ed., *Ancient Near Eastern Texts*, p. 281. The last word is the name of some sort of wooden objects, but the meaning is unknown. When Jehu is called " son of Omri ", we infer that the scribe may be using the word " son " in the sense of " successor ", rather than of descent.

108. The victory *stele* of King Mesha of Moab

109. A cast of the Black Obelisk of Shalmaneser III.
In the second register from the top Jehu of Israel is shown
kissing the ground before the king

(13th century), may still be seen on the cliff at the
mouth of the Dog river, north of Beirut (Fig. 110).

The Jehu revolt broke the alliances which the
Omri dynasty had made with Phoenicia and Judah,
so that Israel was left isolated. The kingdom did
not again join with Damascus in attempting to repel
Shalmaneser. After 837 B.C., Damascus was not
troubled again by Assyria until 805 B.C., when her
kingdom was devastated and forced to pay heavy
tribute to Shalmaneser's successor. Meanwhile,
Hazael, king of Damascus, to whom the Assyrians
allude as a "son of nobody" (i.e. a commoner;
cf. II Kings 8 : 7–15), was able to deal blow after
blow to Israel and also to Judah, until by about
810 B.C. Judah had paid heavy tribute to him and
Israel was in such a weakened condition that she

could scarcely defend herself (II Kings 12 : 17–
13 : 23). It was probably in this period that the
city of Megiddo (Stratum IVA) was destroyed.
Considerable rebuilding in Megiddo had been necessary after the Shishak invasion (*ca.* 918 B.C.),
including a new city-gate which employed only three
entrances instead of the Solomonic four. A new
governor's palace and many stables were also erected
(Figs. 105–6). Now, however, they were destroyed,
presumably by Hazael, and the new city of Stratum
III was constructed on an entirely new plan.

At Samaria the remains are more difficult to date.
Period II at the Israelite capital is marked by an
elaborate new fortification which replaced the
Omri-Ahab inner wall around the summit of the

110. Reliefs of Rameses II (*right*) and probably Shalmaneser III (*left*), carved on the clifts of the Dog River in Lebanon

mound. On the north, west, and part of the south sides of the mound a " casemate " wall was built : that is, there were two parallel walls which were joined together by cross-walls. The outer wall was nearly 6 feet thick ; and the inner and connecting walls were slightly less than $3\frac{1}{2}$ feet thick. On the north, the total width of the fortification was nearly 31 feet. The walls were carefully laid in rock trenches, and all stones were bonded together. Here and there the remains of a red line can still be seen, placed there by the masons as vertical and horizontal guides for adjusting the courses. The style of the construction is the same as that of the preceding Omri-Ahab Period I. The work was so beautifully and strongly done that we are not surprised to learn that it was kept in repair and used for centuries, not being replaced until about 150 B.C. by the " Hellenistic Fort Wall " which was erected as a defense against the Maccabees.

Within the city there is evidence for a destruction of this building phase, so that Period III is marked by a great deal of reconstruction, including, it is suggested, the rebuilding of the royal palace. The British excavators of Samaria, J. W. Crowfoot and Kathleen Kenyon, appear to believe that the casemate wall, having been constructed so soon after the original fortifications, may have been the work of Ahab. On the other hand, W. F. Albright has been inclined to date it in the Dynasty of Jehu, perhaps in the first part of the 8th century. If the excavators are correct, however, in seeing evidence of destruction for Period II, it is not unlikely that we should look to Hazael of Damascus for its cause, even as is the case for City IV of Megiddo. If so, then Jehu

himself may have erected the new fortifications as an added protection for his capital, though at the moment we cannot be sure.

In any event, it was during the reigns of Joash and Jeroboam II (between 801 and 746 B.C.) that Israel reached the height of her power and prosperity. Period III at Samaria with its rebuilding of the royal palace is probably to be dated in this time, perhaps in the reign of Joash. The Assyrian kings were occupied at home and left the west virtually undisturbed. This fact, together with royal energy, made it possible for Jeroboam II to conquer Damascus and to restore the old Davidic border on the north in eastern Syria (II Kings 14 : 25, 28). The prophet Jonah, son of Amittai, gave the divine sanction to this enterprise (II Kings 14 : 25), though for Amos it furnished the occasion for a warning that national ruin was soon to follow the triumph (Amos 6 : 13-14 in Revised Version margin, and Revised Standard Version).

It is during the Dynasty of Jehu that the first Israelite inscribed seals which can be dated with certainty are encountered. In Western Asia and in Egypt in ancient times important people had their own personal seals which they used when they wished to sign or seal a document. Judah had to give his to Tamar as a pledge (Gen. 38 : 18) ; apparently he wore it hanging from a cord around his neck. In Israel and Egypt it was also common practice to wear the seal as a ring on the finger. When Jeremiah bought a field from his relative, two copies of the deed were made. One was left open, but the other was signed and sealed (cf. Fig. 152) ; both were put away in a jar for safe-keeping (Jer. 32 : 9-15). In Mesopotamia the most popular seal for millennia was in the form of a small cylinder, beautifully engraved, which was rolled in wet clay to leave its impression. Egypt and Palestine used the small stamp seal, usually in Egypt shaped like a scarab. Syria and Palestine were the meeting place of the two types of sealing, and many examples of both the seals and their impressions have been found. In Palestine during the period of the kings the common personal seal was round or oval with a convex top. On the inscribed face a double line divided the surface ; above it was placed the name of the owner, usually prefixed with the preposition " to " (meaning " belonging to "), and below was the name of the owner's father, often prefixed with the word " son " : e.g. a carnelian seal purchased in Jerusalem in 1885 bears the inscription, beautifully engraved : " To Hananiah son of Azariah " ; an

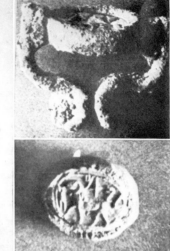

III. Hebrew seals from the 8th century B.C. (*a*) At the left is that of " Shema, servant of Jeroboam ". (*b*) In the center is the seal of "Ushna, servant of Ahaz". (*c*) At the right, above and below, is the seal of Jotham, with an impression made from it, found at Ezion-geber

oval line encloses the letters and outside the line is a connected series of pomegranates.

A special class of the seals once belonged to royal officials. The typical inscription reads : " To *X*, servant of *X* " or " To *X*, servant of the king ". In this connection the word " servant " is the designation of a person in the employ of the royal government. The best known of this class of seal is one found at Megiddo in 1904 (Fig. 111*a*). In the center is a beautifully executed lion in the act of roaring. Above the lion are letters which read, " To Shema ", and below are the words " servant of Jeroboam ". From the shapes of the letters we know that the king in this case is Jeroboam II; Shema was one of his officials, though he is unmentioned in the Bible. Another seal bears the inscription : " To Obadiah, servant of the king." This name brings to mind the Obadiah who was the prime minister of Ahab in the Omri Dynasty, one who risked his position to save the lives of a number of prophets (I Kings 18 : 3–4). The writing, however, is evidently later than the 9th century, and the seal must belong to a royal official of a later date, otherwise unknown. There is only one inscribed Hebrew seal now known which must probably be dated in the 9th century. On it is a bull, and above and below the animal are the words : " To Shemaiah, son of Azariah "—a person unmentioned in the Bible, but his name and that of his father were very common.

In Judah during the early part of the 8th century the great king was Uzziah, also known as Azariah (about 783–742 B.C.). The personal seals of two of his officials, each calling himself " the servant of Uzziyau " (Uzziah), have been found ; one man was named Abiyau (Abijah) and the other Shebanyau (Shebaniah). One of Uzziah's deeds which can be verified archaeologically is the statement that he rebuilt Elath and restored it to Judah (II Kings 14 : 22). The town of Elath is the same as Ezion-geber, which we encountered in the story of Solomon's reign. It was situated south of the Dead Sea, on the northeastern arm of the Red Sea which is called the Gulf of Aqabah. Here Solomon had built his great copper refinery, one which continued in use after his day. During the 10th and 9th centuries the smelter with its accompanying buildings covered only about one and a half acres, but it was surrounded by a double wall, with a three-doored gateway, fortifications strong enough for a large city (Fig. 112). Yet it appears to have been destroyed when Edom gained her independence from Judah during the forties of the 9th century. Uzziah's father had re-subjugated Edom, and now Uzziah himself rebuilt the smelter under a new name, Elath. Not only did the excavator, Nelson Glueck, discover the remains of Uzziah's city, but in it was a beautifully designed seal, in a copper casing, bearing the inscription *lytm* (" Belonging to Jotham ") above the figure of a horned ram (Fig. 111*c*). While we cannot be sure, the seal's owner may well have been Uzziah's son of

112. A reconstruction of the smelter and refinery at Ezion-geber

the same name, who became regent during his father's leprosy before his own reign began. In any event, it is a good Judean name, and the owner did not feel it necessary to give his father's name. Elath and Edom were lost to Judah early in the reign of Jotham's son, Ahaz, that is, about 734 B.C. (II Kings 16 : 6, Revised Standard Version). In the Edomite city which succeeded the Judean the seal of an Edomite royal official was found impressed on a number of jars. This we know because his name, Qausanal, has in its first part the name of an Edomite deity, Qaus.

Beginning in 1956 Professor Y. Aharoni of Hebrew University began work on a high hill called Ramat Rahel, directly south of Jerusalem in Israel. Here he has uncovered a fort which had been erected in the 8th century B.C.; it consists of a small open area surrounded by strong casemate fortifications (double walls connected by cross-walls). In one corner of the area a house or small palace had been erected. Most astonishing about the installation is the manner in which it was built with carefully cut and fitted blocks of masonry like that used earlier at Megiddo and Samaria (cf. Fig. 100). That is, wherever found it appears as royal construction. Yet in this instance the site is too small and too close to Jerusalem to serve either as a major government center or as a vitally needed fortification. Consequently, the excavator has made the interesting suggestion that Ramat Rahel was the separate quarter built for Uzziah during his final years when he was a leper (II Kings 15 : 5). While this view is not susceptible to proof, as a hypothesis it would easily explain the peculiar nature of the ruins.[9]

THE FALL OF ISRAEL

In 745–744 a new Assyrian king came to the throne in Nineveh after a revolt; he was Tiglath-pileser III (*ca.* 745–727 B.C.). Within the first years of his reign he was hard at work in Syria with a great army, beginning the complete subjugation of the whole Syro-Palestinian coastland. Soon northern Syria was firmly in his hands, and the eastern part of it was formed into an Assyrian province, ruled by an Assyrian governor from Arpad (cf. II Kings 18 : 34; 19 : 13).

Jeroboam II of Israel, its last strong king, died just before these events (about 746 B.C.). From then on, evidently because of Assyrian pressure, we hear of civil war and frequent revolts. Uzziah or Azariah of Judah was still king in Jerusalem, though he was a leper and confined to separate quarters. In Syria Tiglath-pileser was confronted with a coalition, headed by one Azriau (that is, Azariah) of Yauda. The last name is the Assyrian spelling of " Judah ". Was Uzziah, then, the head of the opposition to Assyria in the West? This has seemed so improbable, especially since Tiglath-pileser seems to have opposed Azariah's forces, not in Palestine, but in northern Syria, that many scholars have felt that there must have been a northern Judah with a king who bore the name of the Hebrew God, Yahweh (in the abbreviation *Yau* which is customary in proper names). The trouble has been, however, that we have no other information about such a kingdom and little room for it among the known city-states of Syria. In the 19th century many scholars assumed that it was the southern Judah under Uzziah which was involved, and this view has recently been taken up again.[10] At a time when Uzziah was one of the strongest kings with one of the most stable governments in all Syria and Palestine, it seems difficult to suppose that there was another strong state named Judah, with a king of the same name as the Judean monarch. If not, then in the years 744–742 Uzziah or Azariah of Judah was one of the outstanding personalities of Western Asia and the focus for the opposition to Assyria. Even though he was a leper and his son, Jotham, was regent, he must have remained the real power in control of foreign affairs. He died about

[9] See Y. Aharoni, " The Excavation at Ramat Rahel ", *The Biblical Archaeologist*, Vol. XXIV, No. 4 (Dec. 1961); and *Bulletin of the Israel Exploration Society*, Vol. XXIV (1960), pp. 73–116 (in Hebrew).

[10] See especially Edwin R. Thiele, *The Mysterious Numbers of the Hebrew Kings* (Chicago, 1951), Chap. V, and *Journal of Near Eastern Studies*, Vol. III (1944), pp. 155–63; W. F. Albright, *Bulletin of the American Schools of Oriental Research*, No. 100, p. 18, n. 8.

742 B.C., before Assyrian retribution could reach him. At any rate his name suddenly disappeared from the Assyrian records. This reconstruction of events from the documents unearthed in Assyria thus places the history and power of Judah in a fresh perspective, one which we would not have from the Bible itself.

In 738 we hear that Menahem of Israel paid tribute to Tiglath-pileser. II Kings 15 : 19 says that he was forced to pay when " Pul the king of Assyria came up against the land ". " Pul ", we know, was a personal name of Tiglath-pileser. Having received a thousand talents of silver, Pul confirmed Menahem's hold on the royal power. Tiglath-pileser in one of his inscriptions corroborates the biblical statement. He says that he " overwhelmed " Menahem (evidently not by actual fighting but by psychological warfare !) so that the latter " fled like a bird, alone " and bowed at his feet. The Assyrian continued by saying that he returned Menahem to his throne, imposed on him a tribute of " gold, silver, linen garments with multicolored trimmings. . . ."

A group of sixty-three potsherds with ink inscriptions on them was discovered by the Harvard Expedition at Samaria in 1910 when the excavators were uncovering the ruins of a building west of the royal palace. Nearby was the fragment of a jar imported from Egypt with the name of Pharaoh Osorkon II on it. Since this king was a contemporary of the Dynasty of Omri, the pottery fragments were assigned to that time. Subsequent excavation and the type of writing, however, have shown that they belong to the 8th century. The contents of the documents at first sight appear most uninteresting. Typical of them are the following : *Ostracon* No. 1, " In the tenth year. Belonging to Shamaryau from [the town of] Beeryam, a jar of old wine. Pega (son of) Elisha, 2 ; Uzza (son of) . . ., 1 ; Eliba, 1 ; Baala (son of) Elisha, 1 ; Jedaiah, 1 " ; *Ostracon* No. 8, " In the tenth year. From [the town of] Hazeroth, belonging to Gaddiyau, a jar of fine oil." [11] The *ostraca* prove to be administrative dockets which record shipments of wine and oil to Samaria from various towns and districts of the tribal area of Western Manasseh. Whether the shipments were tax payments to the government, or whether they were produce from crown lands, is debated. Nevertheless, it is certain that they belong in some way to the royal fiscal organization.

The dockets were dated by the regnal years of an unnamed king, which was the way people kept track of the time. There was no calendar for the counting of years such as we have. Hence an event would be dated by giving the month, the day of the month, and the year of the reigning king. In Mesopotamia years were named by an event or person, and lists of the years were kept according to their " eponyms ", as they are called, together with the chief events that occurred in them. Such a system, as far as we know, was not used in Palestine.

The dating of the documents within the 8th century has been the subject of some debate, precisely because the king is unnamed. The way the letters were made has been the subject of careful palaeographic study, but at best one could only say that the writing was later than that on the Mesha Stone of the 9th century (Fig. 108) and earlier than that of the Siloam tunnel inscription from a time immediately before 701 B.C. (Fig. 123). The years of the king are indicated by the written words for ninth and tenth, and by number signs generally assumed to indicate the fifteenth and perhaps seventeenth years of the monarch. If so, then only Jeroboam II (about 786–746 B.C.) would be indicated as the king in question because he alone reigned seventeen years or more in the 8th century ; and the *ostraca* would thus come from the 770s B.C. Recently the system used by ancient Israel for writing numbers has been carefully studied by Yigael Yadin from every type of document available.[12] His revised list of numerical signs, almost certainly correct, is as follows :

I	II	III	٦	Λ	(IΛ)	(IIΛ)	T	٦Λ	—	(=)	≡
1	2	3	4	5	(6)	(7)	8	9	10	(20)	30

The signs for 4 and 5 had hitherto been assumed to indicate 5 and 10 respectively, and, when combined, 15. In the new understanding when used together they refer only to the ninth royal year. Thus the documents were all written in the ninth and tenth years of a certain king, provided that the very doubtful group of signs once thought to be " 17 " are now to be understood either as a scribal error or a correction which was illegible when finished.

---

[11] Interpreting the Hebrew of the *ostraca* after Yigael Yadin, " Recipients or Owners ", *Israel Exploration Journal*, Vol. IX (1959), pp. 184–7.

[12] Yadin, " Ancient Judaean Weights and the Date of the Samaria Ostraca ", *Scripta Hierosolymitana*, Vol. III (Jerusalem, Hebrew Univ., 1960), pp. 1–17.

Now the year 738 B.C. when Menahem paid tribute to Tiglath-pileser is the ninth year of that Israelite king. Hence, Professor Yadin suggests, the Samaria documents may well date from that period, and may indeed represent the added taxes Menahem collected to pay his tribute. This last suggestion is not provable, but the possibility of lowering of the date of the *ostraca* to Menahem's reign is generally welcomed by palaeographers, and their purpose, as indicated by the Yadin hypothesis is not improbable.

One of the significant facts about the documents is that they list a number of villages and districts in an area about which we have little information in ancient times. Some of the names still survive in those of modern villages, whereas some of the districts correspond to the names of Manasseh's descendants as preserved in Num. 26 : 29–33 and I Chron. 7 : 14–19 : e.g., Abiezer, Hoglah, Helek, Noah, Shechem, and Shemida. This proves, what scholars have previously suspected, that the sons and daughters of Manasseh in the biblical lists are actually clans, many of which with the aid of the *ostraca* can now be located on the map.

Furthermore, the proper names on the documents are good biblical names, though a surprising number of them contain the element *baal* (" lord "). Indeed, the names with *baal* are at least half as frequent as those with *Yahweh*. In biblical times it was customary for parents to name their children with a little sentence, one that frequently began or ended with the name or title of a god : thus Jonathan means, " Yahweh has given " ; Obadiah, " servant of Yahweh " ; etc. In early Israel *baal* as a title for Yahweh had been borrowed from Canaan along with other divine epithets, but the prophetic reaction against the use of *baal* was very strong because of the danger of confusing the title with that of the great Canaanite storm-god, for whom it was now used almost exclusively as a proper name (cf. Hosea 2 : 16–17). Thus far no instances of baal-names are known from Judah during the 8th and 7th centuries. Yet the fact that they are still so frequent in the Samaria *ostraca* indicates that the revolt of Jehu with its bitter religious rivalry, while reaffirming Yahweh as the God of the nation, had not had a deep theological impact upon a large segment of the population, as far as the use of the term " baal " is concerned.

The crucial years, however, were those between 735 and 732 B.C. Rezin, king of Damascus and Pekah, king of Israel, in forming a coalition against Assyria were provoked by the fact that King Ahaz or Jehoahaz, the grandson of Uzziah in Judah, would not join them. Ahaz or Jehoahaz had just come to the throne (he reigned *ca.* 735–715 B.C.). Rezin and Pekah prepared to attack Jerusalem where the hearts of king and people " shook as the trees of the forest shake before the wind " (Isa. 7 : 2). Ahaz appealed to Tiglath-pileser : " I am your servant and your son. Come up and save me from the hand of the king of Syria and from the hand of the king of Israel, who are attacking me " (II Kings 16 : 7). The biblical narrative continues by saying that Ahaz sent a large " present " to the Assyrian; the latter hearkened, raided Palestine, captured Galilee from Israel, took many into captivity (II Kings 15 : 29), besieged Damascus, killed its king, and carried away captives (II Kings 16 : 9).

Tiglath-pileser confirms this account and adds several details. He began by taking the Philistine plain as far south as Gaza, all of Naphtali (Galilee) and Transjordan from Israel, and finally disposed of Damascus. He further says that the territory taken from Israel was united with Assyria, and " officers of mine I installed as governors upon them ". This means that as a result of his campaign Israel was left as a small territory in the hill country west of the Jordan, while Galilee became an Assyrian province. Furthermore, we know that Tiglath-pileser had introduced a new policy of deporting large numbers of the leading citizens from conquered territories, settling them elsewhere, while importing new groups into the depleted areas. This is the first-known case of large-scale reshuffling of populations in order to keep them passive and submissive.

It was at this time that Hazor (Stratum V) with its great palace-citadel for the administration of eastern Galilee was violently destroyed and never reoccupied except for control forts of the governing powers. Tiglath-pileser also destroyed another great provincial capital of Israel, Megiddo (Stratum III). It was rebuilt by the Assyrian government, however, as the administrative capital of the Assyrian province of Galilee. In the new city of Stratum II the old Solomonic city-wall was no longer used. The site was dominated by a tremendous palace-fort on the eastern side of the mound, part of it resting on the old city-wall. It was some 220 feet long and at least 157½ feet wide, though part of its eastern side may long since have tumbled down the side of the hill. The stone walls of the fort were very thick, varying from 6½ to

113. Sargon II, the con-
queror of Samaria. Relief
in the Turin Museum

114. A reconstruction of the palace of Sargon II at Khorsabad

$8\frac{1}{4}$ feet wide. The plan suggests a large interior courtyard, surrounded on at least three sides by rooms. The entrance was from the top of the mound on the west, as a narrow paved roadway there led into it and then through a threshold some $16\frac{1}{2}$ feet wide into the courtyard. Here, then, was probably the headquarters of the new Assyrian commandant and of the troops stationed there to preserve order.

As an aftermath to the severe setback given Israel in 733 B.C., Pekah was killed in a revolt and Hoshea became king (II Kings 15 : 30). Tiglath-pileser refers to this when he says : " They overthrew their king Pekah and I placed Hoshea as king over them "—thus indicating that in his view vassal kings were enthroned only on his authority. Ahaz in Judah remained a loyal and obedient vassal, and Tiglath-pileser lists his name among the tribute-paying western kings. Ahaz paid his homage to Tiglath-pileser at Damascus in person and came away a thoroughly disillusioned man ; he closed the Jerusalem temple and turned his allegiance from the God who had not supported him to the pagan gods who promised him his desire (cf. II Kings 16 : 10 ff. and II Chron. 28). Isaiah thus had adequate grounds for the warning which he gave in his famous encounter with Ahaz : " If ye will not believe, surely ye shall not be established ! " (Isa. 7 : 9). Ahaz was so weakened in the event that he lost a number of border towns to the Philistine cities (II Chron. 28 : 17–18), while Edom was able to

secure its independence and never again came under Judean control. The great smelter at Ezion-geber-Elath was destroyed by a terrific conflagration at this time, and a new Edomite industrial village was built over the ruins (Ezion-geber Period IV, in the excavator's terminology). The only contemporary occurrence of the king's name, apart from the inscription of Tiglath-pileser, has been found on the seal of one of his officials (Fig. 111b). It belonged " to Ushna, servant of Ahaz ". It is a beautifully wrought carnelian seal in the form of a scarab, now in the collection of Edward T. Newell. The upper half of the inscribed face is given over to a decoration made of Egyptian symbols ; the lower half contains the inscription in two lines.[13]

Hoshea, Israel's last king, evidently found the burden of tribute placed upon him by the Assyrians too heavy to bear. II Kings 17 : 3–4 informs us that he became the vassal of Tiglath-pileser's successor, Shalmaneser V (727–722 B.C.), but relying on Egyptian aid he soon withheld tribute. When Shalmaneser attacked him in 724 B.C., he evidently tried to make his peace with the Assyrian, but the latter " found treachery " in him, took him prisoner and besieged Samaria. In 722 Shalmaneser died and Sargon II (Figs. 113–14), his successor, claimed the honor of victory at the very end of 722 or early

---

[13] C. C. Torrey, " A Hebrew Seal from the Reign of Ahaz ", *Bulletin of the American Schools of Oriental Research*, No. 79 (Oct. 1940), pp. 27–8.

in 721 B.C. Sargon repeatedly boasted of this victory in his inscriptions. In one of them he wrote : "I besieged and conquered Samaria, led away as booty 27,290 inhabitants of it. I formed from among them a contingent of 50 chariots (for the royal corps) and made the remaining (inhabitants) assume their (social) positions. I installed over them an officer of mine and imposed upon them the tribute of the former king." [14]

Thus the curtain was drawn over an independent Israel. Within a short time also part of the Philistine Plain along the coast was reorganized into an Assyrian province, so that Judah alone was left with a semblance of independence.

[14] Translation by A. L. Oppenheim in J. B. Pritchard, ed., *Ancient Near Eastern Texts*, pp. 284-5.

FURTHER READING

For general surveys of the archaeology of this period, see especially W. F. Albright, *The Archaeology of Palestine* (Pelican Books, 1949), pp. 128-42 ; *From the Old Stone Age to Christianity*, pp. 228-40 ; *Archaeology and the Religion of Israel*, pp. 155-64 ; Millar Burrows, *What Mean These Stones ?*, paragraphs 101-2, 112 ff., and the Indices for specific items.

For the comparative stratigraphy of the era, see G. Ernest Wright in *The Bible and the Ancient Near East* (Garden City, 1961), pp. 96-101. For historical survey see John Bright, *A History of Israel* (Philadelphia, 1959), pp. 209-61; Martin Noth, *The History of Israel* (London and New York, 1958), pp. 224-62.

The best source now available for Hebrew and Assyrian historical inscriptions is J. B. Pritchard, ed., *Ancient Near Eastern Texts Relating to the Old Testament* (Princeton, 1950). The chief sources of information otherwise are the excavation reports, of which the following may be listed especially :

W. F. Albright, *The Excavation of Tell Beit Mirsim*, Vol. III, *The Iron Age* (*Annual of the American Schools of Oriental Research*, Vols. XXI-XXII ; New Haven, 1943).

R. S. Lamon and G. M. Shipton, *Megiddo I* (*Oriental Institute Publications*, Vol. XLII ; Chicago, 1939).

G. A. Reisner and C. S. Fisher, *Harvard Excavations at Samaria* (Cambridge, 1924) ; J. W. Crowfoot *et al.*, *The Buildings at Samaria* (London, 1942) ; *Early Ivories from Samaria* (London, 1938); *The Objects from Samaria* (London, 1957).

C. C. McCown, *Tell en-Nasbeh* (Berkeley and New Haven, 1947).

Nelson Glueck, " The Excavations of Solomon's Seaport : Ezion-geber ", *The Smithsonian Report*, 1941, pp. 453-78 (Smithsonian Institution, Washington) ; the articles by the same author on this site in *Bulletin of the American Schools of Oriental Research*, Nos. 71, 75, 79 and 82 ; *The Other Side of the Jordan* (New Haven, 1940), Chap. IV.

Y. Yadin, *et. al. Hazor* I (Jerusalem, Israel, 1958); II (1959); III-IV (1961).

CHAPTER X

THE LAST DAYS OF JUDAH

" The Lord hath purposed to destroy
the wall of the daughter of Zion. . . .
The Lord hath done that which he had devised;
he hath fulfilled his word
that he had commanded in the days of old " (Lam. 2 : 8, 17).

OVER a century and a quarter of semi-independent life remained to Judah after the destruction of Samaria in 721 B.C. Fragmentary remains at Samaria indicate its reoccupation; among them is said to be an alien pottery which may well have been brought to the city by the displaced people from other parts of the Near East whom the Assyrians settled there (II Kings 17 : 24). King Hezekiah (*ca.* 715–687 B.C.) of Judah promptly moved to reunite north and south religiously, as a preparation for political reunion (II Chron. 29–31). He was thus reasserting the claims of the Davidic dynasty for a united Palestine. Failing in his political objective, he became the head of a coalition of small states and with the promise of Egyptian and Babylonian backing, he revolted against Sennacherib (II Kings 18–20). He may have planned the revolt for some time before it actually occurred, but Assyrian annals inform us that though the king of Ashdod had sought Judean aid against Sargon, he did not receive it when the latter attacked him in 711 B.C. (cf. Isa. 20) and reorganized part of the coastal plain into an Assyrian province. Yet when Sargon died in 705 B.C. and the new king, Sennacherib, came to the Assyrian throne, Hezekiah evidently thought the time propitious. He accepted the proposals of Babylonian and Egyptian embassies and withheld tribute. Sennacherib retaliated in 701 B.C., and from him we get a fuller report of the events (Fig. 115).

ARCHAEOLOGICAL INFORMATION RELATING TO SENNACHERIB'S CAMPAIGN IN 701 B.C.

According to Sennacherib's annals, Hezekiah had intervened in Philistine affairs in order to strengthen local rebels, even imprisoning in Jerusalem Padi, king of Ekron, " unlawfully, as though he were an enemy ". Sennacherib further speaks of " the overbearing and proud Hezekiah ", who on becoming afraid called on the Ethiopian king of Egypt for aid. The latter responded with bowmen, chariotry and cavalry, " an army beyond counting ", but was roundly defeated, whereupon Hezekiah released Padi who was put back on the throne of Ekron. Sennacherib continues : [1]

As to Hezekiah, the Jew [rather, Judean], he did not submit to my yoke, I laid siege to 46 of his strong cities, walled forts and to countless small villages in their vicinity, and conquered (them) by means of well-stamped (earth-)ramps, and battering-rams brought near (to the walls), (combined with) the attack of foot soldiers (using) mines, breeches as well as sapper work. I drove out (of them) 200,150 people, young and old, male and female, horses, mules, donkeys, camels, big and small cattle beyond counting, and considered (them) booty. Himself I made a prisoner in Jerusalem, his royal residence, like a bird in a cage. I surrounded him with earthwork in order to molest those who were leaving his city's gate. His towns which I had plundered, I took away from his country and gave them to Mitinti, king of Ashdod, Padi, king of Ekron, and Sillibel, king of Gaza. Thus I reduced his country, but I still increased the tribute and the *katru*-presents (due) to me (as his) overlord which I imposed (later) upon him beyond the former tribute, to be delivered annually. Hezekiah himself, whom the terror-inspiring splendor of my lordship had overwhelmed and those irregular and élite troops which he had brought into Jerusalem, his royal residence, in order to strengthen (it), had deserted, did send me, later, to Nineveh, my lordly city, together with 30 talents of gold, 800 talents of silver, precious stones, antimony, large cuts of red stone, couches (inlaid) with ivory, *nîmedu*-chairs (inlaid) with ivory, elephant-hides, ebony-wood, boxwood (and) all kinds of valuable treasures, his (own) daughters, concubines, male and female musicians. In order to deliver the tribute and to do obeisance as a slave he sent his (personal) messenger.

It will be noted that Sennacherib does not claim to have captured Jerusalem nor to have carried out a wanton destruction of Judean cities. He appears

[1] Translation by A. L. Oppenheim in J. B. Pritchard, ed. *Ancient Near Eastern Texts*, p. 288.

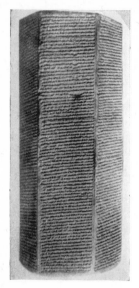

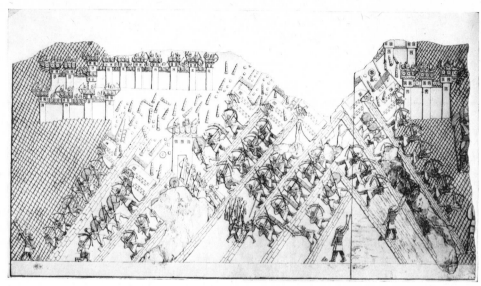

115. A prism of Sennacherib which describes his various military campaigns, including that against Judah in 701 B.C.

116. Sennacherib's siege of Lachish, as portrayed on a relief in his palace at Nineveh

117. Judean captives from Lachish

118. Sennacherib on his throne, receiving the submission of the elders of Lachish

to have laid siege to a large number of fortified towns, including Jerusalem, and to have plundered what he captured, but he left the country together with his army as soon as Hezekiah gave up and accepted the heavy tribute laid upon him. According to II Kings 18 : 14 Hezekiah did this when the Assyrian was encamped at the great Judean fortress of Lachish.

Sennacherib was sufficiently proud of his conquest of Lachish to have a large picture of the event carved in low relief on stone and installed in his palace at Nineveh, where it was found by the early British excavator, A. H. Layard, a century ago (Figs. 116–18). The relief shows the siege in progress and at the same time the fortress in process of surrender. A double wall surrounds the city, and on the frequently spaced towers above revetments the Judean defenders are busy with slings and bows, and evidently also throwing down firebrands upon the wooden siege engines. The Assyrian army is drawn up in orderly array with bowmen, spearmen and slingers supporting the work of the sappers. Earthen ramps have been erected up the slopes against the outer wall. On them large wheeled

vehicles have been pushed up to the wall, and within them, protected from the shower of missiles from above, sappers are at work while men with containers at the end of long handles throw water over the tops of the vehicles, presumably to protect them from the firebrands.

Yet though the siege is in full fury of action Judean men and women are filing out of a small gate, set lower on the side of the mound than the walls as they are shown to the right and left. Nearby Sennacherib is enthroned in splendor, his richly appareled tent and chariot behind him. The elders of the city in their long white robes bow before the king, and behind them is a long line of Judean men and women accompanied by Assyrian soldiers, carts and valuables, evidently prepared for the long journey into exile. In front of the king is an inscription which reads : " Sennacherib, king of the world, king of the land of Asshur, on the *nîmedu*-chair, and the booty of the city of Lachish before him passed."

Lachish was one of the major cities of Palestine at this time, larger even than Jerusalem and Megiddo (Fig. 119). The last two were some $11\frac{1}{2}$ and 13 acres respectively in extent, while the summit of the

119. A reconstruction of Judean Lachish by H. H. McWilliams

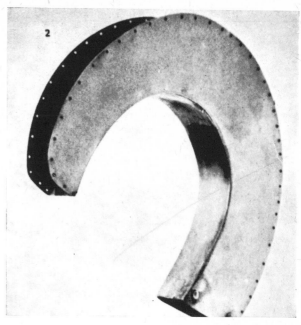

120. A reconstruction of the crest from a helmet worn by an Assyrian soldier, found at Lachish

mound of Lachish contains some 18 acres. The city was situated in the Judean Lowlands (Shephelah) on the edge of the Philistine Plain, protecting the pass leading up to Hebron and supporting the smaller fortresses within the pass. It was the chief fortress in a chain of north-south strongholds in the Lowland which had been fortified by Rehoboam at the end of the 10th century.

The site was excavated between 1932 and 1938 by a British expedition under the leadership of J. L. Starkey. This excavation was one of the most excellent and efficient ever carried on in Palestine. Unfortunately, however, Mr. Starkey was murdered by Arab brigands in 1938 just as he had finished his careful preparatory work and was beginning to work down within the mound's debris near the city-gate and the palace-citadel.

We shall hear more about the important discoveries of the expedition at the end of this chapter when we deal with the final destruction of Judah by the Babylonians. For the period of 701 B.C. three items of information are of special interest. First are the city fortifications. The summit of the mound was surrounded by a brick wall about 19½ feet thick (6 meters). Over 50 feet below it along the slope of the mound was a stone and brick revetment about 13 feet wide (4 meters). The walls had alternating recessed panels and salients, the latter more frequent in the outer wall where a turn was necessary. On the salients were built defensive towers and battlements. The battlements as shown on Sennacherib's Lachish relief were probably built of wood, and the great amount of charcoal mixed in the debris outside the walls probably came from the burning of these wooden structures. Along the

west side of the mound the roadway ascending to the city gate from the valley was discovered, and the gate was found to be protected by a large, free-standing bastion, which a century later was incorporated into the line of the outer revetment. In the Lachish relief the two walls are clearly shown, and the lower gate from which people are filing out may well be intended to represent the bastion. Great ramps of soil, brought up from the valley and piled against the bastion may have been part of the Assyrian siege-ramps, for in the relief the attack seems to be centered around the gateway area. One interesting object found buried in a mass of burnt debris at the base of the outer fortification was a bronze crest mount (Fig. 120), with traces of cloth and leather fastening, once riveted to the top of a helmet. In the Lachish relief such crests are shown on the helmets of the Assyrian spearmen. Whether, however, the object belonged to a member of Sennacherib's army or to a soldier of Nebuchadnezzar over a century later is unknown.

Secondly, within the city was the Palace of the provincial official of the Judean government. It is probable that this building was erected in David's time, during the 10th century. Associated with it was a strong, thick-walled and long-roomed storehouse or royal granary. The same association of palace and granary and dating from the same early period has been found in the Lowland city of Beth-shemesh, some 15 miles north of Lachish. During the next two centuries the palace of Lachish had been doubled in size until it was a formidable structure, as much fort or citadel as palace. Practically nothing of the superstructure remained; only the platform on which it was erected is still to be seen. This platform in Hezekiah's time was about 256 feet long by at least 105 feet wide. On the west side it still stands to a height of 23 feet. It was erected with stone exterior and interior cross walls, and filled with earth. The structure reminds us of the citadel, called the Millo, which David built in Jerusalem (II Sam. 5:9). The term "Millo" means "filling", and it probably refers to a fortified building on an artificial podium, of which the palaces of Lachish and probably Beth-shemesh are examples (see further, p. 131).

Finally at Lachish there was found on the northwest slope of the mound a large pit which had once been a large tomb, associated with five other smaller pits. The astonishing thing about them is their contents: they were filled with a scattered and completely mixed conglomeration of bones. The main tomb held the remains of at least 1500 bodies, but the bones were in such a jumbled mass that no order could be discerned and the skulls, separated from the vertebrae, had rolled to the sides of the chamber from the top of the pile when thrown in. Some of the bones and skulls showed signs of having been burned, and it is clear that the remains had been gathered up from some other area and thrown into this repository after the flesh had decomposed or been burned. Over the solid mass of human bones and spilling over into adjoining pits was a layer of animal bones, most of which were from pigs!

Along with the bones were many pieces of pottery, a large proportion of which were broken fragments. Some of the dishes and bowls, among them fragments of cooking pots, were of the type of vessel which is rarely found in tombs though very common in the ruins of houses. In other words, this deposit was no ordinary cemetery but a place where bones were thrown after having been swept up along with pieces of pottery in some other quarter. First the human bodies were taken care of and then the animal remains. Mr. Starkey, the excavator, originally suggested that the deposit represented the clearance of the city after the siege of Sennacherib, and this explanation has much to commend it. It would explain the conglomerate nature of the deposit, the evidence of burning on some of the bones, and also the fact that few of the people here buried were old. The skeletons were of a group who, in one expert's opinion, were "considerably younger than such as is normally found in ancient or recent cemeteries". Furthermore, "the hypothesis that the bones were cleared from an existing cemetery is . . . unacceptable, both because of the lack of aged people and the high proportion of immature skeletons which are normally too easily damaged to survive more than one removal ".[2]

One further interesting fact is that at least three of the skulls show evidence of the operation known as trepanning (Fig. 121). They are the first specimens found in Western Asia which show this operation. (Since then similar specimens from the 17th century B.C. have been found at Jericho.) On two of the skulls the crude saw marks are still so clear where the piece of bone was removed to relieve the pressure on the brain that we must presume that the patients died almost immediately. Curiously enough, however, the bone of the third skull had begun to grow sufficiently to obliterate the evidence of the saw. This person, then, must have lived for some time after his operation. The evidence of these skulls is a surprising testimony to the advanced state of Judean medicine during the time of the prophet Isaiah.

The presence of so many pig bones in the pits is also surprising and somewhat puzzling in view of the Israelite dietary laws which for good reason forbade the eating of pork. As is well known, pork quickly becomes a dangerous food where good refrigeration is lacking. We know that this prohibition did not extend to Israel's neighbors, however, and it is not impossible that the pigs at Lachish were brought there as a part of the commissariat of the Assyrian army.

Some eight miles southeast of Lachish on the road to Beer-sheba was another fortified Judean city which is known from excavation to have suffered at the hands of Sennacherib in 701 B.C. That is Debir (modern Tell Beit Mirsim), which was explored by an American expedition, headed by W. F. Albright,

---

[2] These are the remarks of D. L. Risdon as quoted by Olga Tufnell, *Lachish III : The Iron Age* (London, 1953), p. 63. It may be added further that the pottery associated with the remains belongs, in this writer's opinion, to the 8th or early 7th century rather than to the period around 600 B.C.—a further support for Mr. Starkey's views. Miss Tufnell, *ibid.*, p. 194, suggests as an alternate view that the tomb " might have been caused by a wholesale clearance of idolatrous burials during the religious reformation of Josiah " (*ca.* 621 B.C.). Yet to me this would necessitate too late a date for the pottery as well as negate the opinion of D. L. Risdon that the bones were scarcely from an existing cemetery.

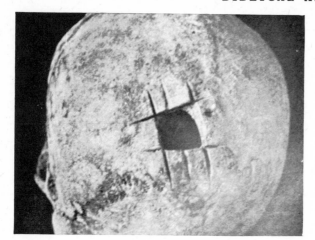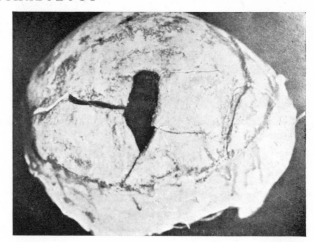

121. Skulls from a cave at Lachish, showing the earliest examples known of an operation on the skull to relieve concussion

in four campaigns between 1926 and 1932. It is a much smaller site than Lachish; the area enclosed by the fortifications is only about 7½ acres. As was the case at Lachish, however, the destruction caused by Sennacherib was by no means complete. The purpose of the Assyrian king was not to destroy the country but simply to force it to submit to his rule and to continue the regular payment of tribute.[3]

In Jerusalem the only evidence which relates directly to Sennacherib's raid has to do with the city's water supply. II Kings 20 : 20 speaks of how Hezekiah " made the pool and the conduit and brought water into the city ". II Chron. 32 : 30 says that he " closed the upper outlet of the waters of Gihon and directed them down to the west side of the city of David ". The verses indicate that in preparation for a siege, presumably that of Senna-cherib, the king arranged for the city to have an interior water supply. The chief source of water for ancient Jerusalem was the Gihon spring in the valley against the eastern side of the Ophel hill. It is a peculiar spring in that by some interior siphon-arrangement of caverns it discharges its water at irregular intervals. In the early days of Canaanite occupation (see above, p. 128) a tunnel had been dug from within the city down to a point where water jugs could be let down to a pool of water formed by the spring; and it is thought by some that Joab opened the city's gates to David by climbing up this tunnel, though this is by no means certain (II Sam. 5 : 8; I Chron. 11 : 6). During early Israelite times the water from the spring was

collected in an open basin called the " Upper Pool ", and an aqueduct, discovered by Shick in 1886, carried the water along the edge of the mound to the " Lower Pool " at the southern end of the city. It was along this open-air aqueduct from the " Upper Pool " that the well-known interview between the prophet Isaiah and King Ahaz took place (Isa. 7 : 3). Here, too, the officers of Sennacherib stationed themselves and tried to persuade the people of Jerusalem to surrender (II Kings 18 : 17). " The waters of Shiloah that go softly " (Isa. 8 : 6) were probably those that flowed in this aqueduct.

Hezekiah, however, prepared a new reservoir and enclosed it within the city fortifications in the south-western quarter of the city; this reservoir is the " Pool of Siloam " (Isa. 22 : 9, 11). He then dug a tunnel (Fig. 122) under the hill to take the water from the Gihon to it, and evidently covered over the Gihon itself so that its presence would not be visible to the attackers. In 1880 some boys dis-covered an inscription (Fig. 123) in the tunnel about 25 feet from the Siloam end. This Siloam inscrip-tion has for many years been the most important monumental piece of writing in Israelite Palestine, and other Hebrew inscriptions have been dated by comparing the shapes of the letters with it. A flat surface had been prepared on the wall of the tunnel for the inscription but only six lines on the lower part remain, the upper half not being preserved. The lines have been translated as follows : [4]

[. . . when] (the tunnel) was driven through. And this is the way in which it was cut through :—While [. . .] (were) still (. . .) axe(s), each man toward his

[3] The widespread but partial destruction is also to be in-ferred from the literary evidence : see R. P. Dougherty, " Sennacherib and the Walled Cities of Palestine ", *Journal of Biblical Literature*, Vol. XLIX (1930), pp. 160–71.

[4] W. F. Albright, *Ancient Near Eastern Texts* (J. B. Pritchard ed.), p. 321.

123. The inscription found in the tunnel of Hezekiah

122. Hezekiah's tunnel in Jerusalem

fellow, and while there were still three cubits to be cut through, [there was heard] the voice of a man calling to his fellow, for there was *an overlap* in the rock on the right (and on the left). And when the tunnel was driven through, the quarrymen hewed (the rock), each man toward his fellow, axe against axe; and the water flowed from the spring toward the reservoir for 1,200 cubits, and the height of the rock above the head(s) of the quarrymen was 100 cubits.

The first people in modern times to discover and explore the tunnel were the American scholar, Edward Robinson, and his friend Eli Smith, a missionary in Syria. Robinson's trip to Palestine in 1838 marks the beginning of modern biblical archaeology, and his description of the land and what he found there is still important and informative reading. In Jerusalem he found it current belief that some sort of passage existed between the Gihon spring and the Pool of Siloam, but no one had explored it. He determined to explore it himself; his description of what he found is as follows: [5]

Repairing one afternoon (April 27th) to Siloam in order to measure the reservoir, we found no person there; and the water in the basin being low, we

[5] E. Robinson and E. Smith, *Biblical Researches in Palestine*, Vol. I (London, 1841), pp. 338–40.

embraced this opportunity for accomplishing our purpose. Stripping off our shoes and stockings and rolling our garments above our knees, we entered with our lights and measuring tapes in our hands. The water was low, nowhere over a foot in depth, and for the most part not more than three or four inches, with hardly a perceptible current. The bottom is everywhere covered with sand, brought in by the waters. The passage is cut wholly through the solid rock, everywhere about two feet wide; somewhat winding, but in a general course N.N.E. For the first hundred feet, it is from fifteen to twenty feet high; for another hundred feet or more, from six to ten feet; and afterwards not more than four feet high; thus gradually becoming lower and lower as we advanced. At the end of 800 feet, it became so low, that we could advance no further without crawling on all fours, and bringing our bodies close to the water. As we were not prepared for this, we thought it better to retreat, and try again another day from the other end. Tracing therefore upon the roof with the smoke of our candles the initials of our names and the figures 800, as a mark of our progress on this side, we returned with our clothes somewhat wet and soiled.

It was not until three days afterwards (April 30th) that we were able to complete our examination and measurement of the passage. We went now to the fountain of the Virgin; and having measured the external distance (1200 feet) down to the point east of Siloam, we concluded, that as we had already entered 800 feet from the lower end, there could now remain not over four or five hundred feet to be explored. We found the end of the passage at the upper fountain rudely built up with small loose stones, in order to retain the water at a greater depth in the excavated basin. Having caused our servants to clear away these stones, and having clothed (or rather unclothed) ourselves simply in a pair of wide Arab drawers, we entered and crawled on, hoping soon to arrive at the point which we had reached from the other fountain. The passage here is in general much lower than at the other end; most of the way we could indeed advance upon our hands and knees; yet in several places we could only get forward by lying at full length and dragging ourselves along on our elbows.

The sand at the bottom has probably a considerable depth, thus filling up the canal in part; for otherwise it is inconceivable, how the passage could ever have been thus cut through the solid rock. At any rate, only a single person could have wrought in it at a time ; and it must have been the labour of many years. There are here many turns and zigzags. In several places the workmen had cut straight forward for some distance, and then leaving this, had begun again further back at a different angle ; so that there is at first the appearance of a passage branching off. We examined all these false cuts very minutely, in the hope of finding some such lateral passage, by which water might come in from another quarter. We found, however, nothing of the kind. The way seemed interminably long ; and we were for a time suspicious, that we had fallen upon a passage different from that which we had before entered. But at length, after having measured 950 feet, we arrived at our former mark of 800 feet traced with smoke upon the ceiling. This makes the whole length of the passage to be 1750 feet ; or several hundred feet greater than the direct distance externally—a result, scarcely conceivable, although the passage is very winding. We came out again at the fountain of Siloam.

In constructing this passage, it is obvious that the workmen commenced at both ends, and met somewhere in the middle. At the upper end, the work was carried along on the level of the upper basin ; and there was a tendency to go too far towards the west under the mountain ; for all the false cuts above mentioned are on the right. At the lower end, the excavation would seem to have been begun on a higher level than at present ; and when on meeting the shaft from the other end, this level was found to be too high, the bottom was lowered until the water flowed through it ; thus leaving the southern end of the passage much loftier than any other part. The bottom has very little descent ; so that the two basins are nearly on the same level. . . . The water flows through the passage gently and with little current.

Robinson's measurement of 1750 feet for the tunnel's length corresponds closely with the figure, 1749 feet, given by Father H. Vincent in his study of Jerusalem's ancient water works. The difference may easily be accounted for either by different points from which the measurements were begun and ended, or by the difficulties encountered by Robinson in his pioneer attempt. In either case, the figures agree with the length of 1200 cubits given by the Siloam inscription, the cubit being a measure of about 17·5 inches.

Across the valley east of the Gihon spring and the mound where the old city of Jerusalem once stood is a rocky slope on which today stands the modern village of Silwan (Siloam). On this slope a number of ancient tombs still exist (cf. Fig. 187). The French archaeologist, Clermont-Ganneau, at the end of the last century discovered one in the village which was different from the others (Fig. 124). It was a rock-cut chamber, about 14½ by 7½ feet in size. In front was a dressed façade and a rectangular door. Over the door on a recessed panel an inscription had been carved, which Clermont-Ganneau cut out and sent to the British Museum in London. It was in such a badly damaged state, however, that no one could read it and its discoverer thought it had been defaced deliberately by a hammer.

Recently, Professor N. Avigad of the Hebrew University in Jerusalem published a very important article on the three-line text.[6] With the aid of photographs and a paper " squeeze " of the original, together with the counsel of a number of different

---

[6] " The Epitaph of a Royal Steward from Siloam Village ", *Israel Exploration Journal*, Vol. 3, No. 3 (1953), pp. 137-52.

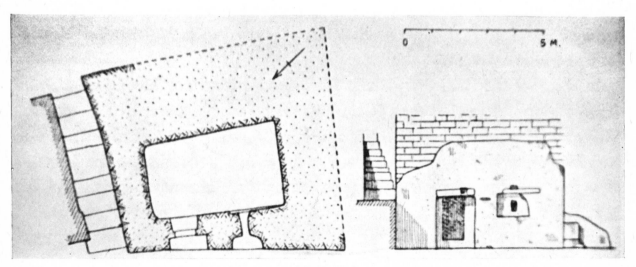

124. The tomb of Shebna (?) in Jerusalem

scholars, he has managed to decipher it. The following is his translation :

1. This is [the sepulcher of . . .] yahu who is over the house.
   There is no silver and no gold here
2. but [his bones] and the bones of his slave-wife with him.
   Cursed be the man
3. who will open this !

The style of the epitaph corresponds closely to that of the Phoenicians (or Canaanites), and the details regarding the contents of the tomb have parallels in Syrian tomb inscriptions. Tomb-robbing was such a common ancient practice that the mere statement of a curse was insufficient; there was also the explicit statement that no valuables were present. Neither the statement nor the curse availed here, however, for the tomb has long since been emptied of its contents.

The date of the epitaph cannot be long before or after about 700 B.C., because the manner in which the letters were formed is so similar to that of the Siloam inscription. Unfortunately, a hole in the panel occurs precisely at the place where the name of the tomb's builder occurs. All that we know is that his name ended in *yahu* (A.V. *iah*), and that he was a high royal official. The words " who is over the house " are actually the title of the Judean Prime Minister (see p. 126).

One cannot but recall the passage in Isa. 22 : 15 ff. where Isaiah excoriates the prime minister of the early part of Hezekiah's reign, " Shebna, who is over the house ", for hewing himself out a tomb in the rock, " on the height ", presumably in plain sight of the city and probably in the very area where the tomb described above exists. This is probably the same official who is mentioned in II Kings 18 : 18 and 19 : 2 at the time of Sennacherib's invasion in 701 B.C. If so, then by that time he had been reduced to the position of royal Scribe or Secretary of State, while Eliakim had been made Prime Minister as Isaiah said he would be (Isa. 22 : 21–3). It has often been observed that Shebna may have been a foreigner because he alone among the officials is listed without the name of his father, that is, without his full name. In any event it has long been known that the name " Shebna " is an abbreviation for *Shebanyahu* (Shebaniah). The tomb discussed here was built during the owner's lifetime, as was that of Shebna ; otherwise the builder would not have said that the bones of his favorite concubine or slave-wife were buried with his own. Thus the combination of date, place and content of the tomb's epitaph suggest that it may indeed have been that of Shebna.

Unfortunately, however, we shall never be entirely certain of the identification, because of that hole in the rock precisely where the name once was. Nevertheless, we can only agree with Professor Avigad when he says that the epitaph is, after the Moabite Stone (Fig. 108) and the Siloam tunnel inscription, " the third longest monumental inscription in Hebrew and the first known text of a Hebrew sepulchral inscription from the pre-Exilic period ".

JUDAH DURING THE 7TH CENTURY

Manasseh, Hezekiah's son and successor (*ca.* 687–642 B.C.), was reckoned by the Deuteronomic historian as being the worst king Judah ever had (II Kings 21). He made the strongest attempt yet tried to turn the religion of Yahwism into another polytheism. Accepting the planet- and star-worship of his Assyrian conquerors, he erected altars for the pagan deities in the very courts of Yahweh's " house ". This means that he encouraged the people to think of the pagan gods as members of Yahweh's heavenly host, associated with him in both the heavenly and earthly temples. This was resisted because Yahweh from earliest times had not permitted the worship of any but himself. Yet the king seems ruthlessly to have stamped out all opposition (II Kings 21 : 16).

The Assyrian emperors during Manasseh's reign were Esarhaddon (681–669 B.C.) and Asshurbanapal (669–*ca.* 633 B.C.). Their great effort during the seventies and sixties of the century was the conquest of Egypt. This they accomplished ; and the fall of Thebes, the great city of Upper Egypt, in 663 B.C. was still remembered by the Judean prophet, Nahum, many years later (No in Nah. 3 : 8 was a name of the city). Both these kings mention Manasseh in their inscriptions. Esarhaddon leaves us a list of twelve kings along the Mediterranean sea-coast whom he forced to supply the wood and stone for his palace at Nineveh. Among them we find the kings of Tyre, Edom, Moab, Ammon and of Gaza, Ashkelon, Ekron and Ashdod, city-states in the Philistine Plain. Manasseh is referred to as *Manasi* king of *Yaudi* (Judah). Asshurbanapal gave a similar list of kings, referring to them as " servants who belong to me ", and saying that he made them accompany his army on its journey through their territory and supply troops and ships to assist him. In each case Manasseh is second in the list, after the king of Tyre; he thus held an important place among the kings of Syria and Palestine.[7]

From the late 8th or early 7th century an undated Assyrian text mentions the tribute sent by the kingdoms of Ammon, Moab, Judah and Edom. Two minas of gold were received from Ammon; one mina of gold from Moab; two minas of silver from Judah, and probably the same amount from Edom.[8] This could not have been a heavy tribute for Judah, though we do not know how often such an amount was required. According to present reckoning a Mesopotamian mina, composed of 60 shekels, as opposed to the Syro-Palestinian mina of 50 shekels, would have weighed approximately 685 grams. Two minas of silver in Mesopotamia would thus be equivalent to the amount of the metal in about 51 silver dollars. The purchasing power of this sum would, of course, have been far greater than it is today. For example, during the final siege of Jerusalem Jeremiah bought a field for 17 shekels of silver (Jer. 32 : 9), which would be equivalent to the weight of the metal in 7 silver dollars. On the other hand, one part only of the tribute imposed on Hezekiah by Sennacherib (see above) was 800 talents of silver, which would be the same as 48,000 minas or the weight of 1,224,000 silver dollars.

Between 652 and 647 B.C. a serious revolt against Assyria occurred, led by Babylon. This would have been the most natural occasion for the revolt of Manasseh as described in II Chron. 33 : 11, though we have no other information about it. It seems probable that the Arab tribes of the Syrian desert took this occasion to press into eastern Syria and Transjordan. Asshurbanapal gives considerable space in his annals to his struggle against the Arabs, having to fight them in Transjordan, especially in the countries of Ammon, Moab and Edom. The remarkable lament over the fall of Moab, preserved in Isa. 15–16, was probably occasioned by the Arabian inundations of Transjordan during the course of this century.

The most remarkable Judean monarch of the century was Manasseh's grandson, Josiah, who reigned from about 640 to 609 B.C. The murder of his father, Amon, probably represented an attempt of extremists to throw off the Assyrian yoke. The more moderate group, " the people of the land ",

regained control, however, and placed Josiah on the throne, though he was but an eight-year-old boy (II Kings 21 : 19–26). His advisors, though proceeding cautiously, laid careful plans, so that by the time Josiah was attaining maturity they were ready to take advantage of the declining power of Assyria.

Recent studies of Assyrian chronology make it possible to correlate Judah's movement toward independence rather precisely with events in Assyria.[9] II Chron. 34 : 3 says that in the eighth year of Josiah's reign (633–632 B.C.) the king " began to seek the God of David his father "; that is, he repudiated the gods of his Assyrian rulers and turned squarely against the syncretistic policies of his grandfather, Manasseh. This action, as now seems probable, followed immediately upon the death of the great emperor in Assyria, Asshurbanapal.

The death of Asshurbanapal's successor, Asshuretelilani, about 629 B.C. was immediately followed by disorders in Assyria and Babylonia. There was a struggle for the succession; no strong king had appeared to strengthen the hold on the empire. This was the obvious occasion for a second, more drastic, move on the part of the vassal state of Judah. II Chron. 34 : 3–7 says that it took place in Josiah's twelfth year (629–628 B.C.) and that it was a thorough-going religious reform in which all idolatrous altars and images were destroyed, not only in Judah, but also throughout the territory of Israel as far as Galilee. Such a purge is unthinkable without military control over the Assyrian provinces of Samaria and Megiddo. In other words, Josiah, probably as a nominal vassal of Assyria, was reasserting the ancient Davidic claim to a united Palestine by annexing the northern Assyrian provinces.

The atmosphere in Judah at this time was probably electric, for a new day seemed to have dawned. In 628–627, during Josiah's thirteenth year, Jeremiah received his call as God's prophet (Jer. 1 : 2). His early prophecies about the northern peril, together with those of his contemporary Zephaniah, have been interpreted by many scholars in the past as occasioned by a great invasion of Scythian hordes from Armenia and southern Russia. This supposition is based solely upon an unverified statement of Herodotus, the 5th-century Greek historian, who claimed that the Scythians invaded Western Asia at this time and ruled over it for " eight-and-twenty

[7] J. B. Pritchard, ed., *Ancient Near Eastern Texts*, pp. 291 and 294.
[8] *Ibid.*, p. 301.

[9] See F. M. Cross, Jr. and D. N. Freedman, " Josiah's Revolt Against Assyria ", *Journal of Near Eastern Studies*, Vol. XII (1953), pp. 56–8.

years, during which time their insolence and oppression spread ruin on every side ".[10]   That the Scythians were a serious trouble to the Assyrians along their northern border seems to have been true, but, as we reconstruct the history of the time from archaeological sources, there is no room or evidence for the Scythian dominion of which Herodotus speaks.   In any event, the decline of Assyria and the rising hope of Judah after Josiah's action would have been sufficient to account for the early proclamations of Jeremiah and Zephaniah, to both of whom the breakdown of world order meant that the Day of the Lord as a day of judgment was at hand.

The finding of the old lawbook in the Temple (some part of Deuteronomy) during the eighteenth year of Josiah's reign (ca. 623–622 B.C.) resulted in a still more thorough-going religious reform, in which all sacrificial worship was confined to the Jerusalem Temple (II Kings 22–3).   This Deuteronomic movement was an earnest attempt to revive the spirit and the legal tradition of the original Mosaic covenant as the ideology of the newly revived state.   On Josiah's part the reform probably signalled the final break with Assyria. We know that by 623 B.C. Assyrian control over Babylonia had ceased entirely and that a Babylonian king, Nabopolassar, had consolidated his position and was preparing to attack Assyria itself.

In 1923 C. J. Gadd of the British Museum published a portion of the Babylonian Chronicle.   This document gives a detailed summary, year by year, of the fall of the Assyrian Empire.   The climax came in 612 B.C. when the capital, Nineveh, fell to the combined forces of the Medes and the Babylonians.   The Assyrian king and his army withdrew into northern Mesopotamia.   In 609 or 608 B.C. they were finally crushed by the Babylonians with the aid of the Medes in the battle of Haran.   According to the Authorized Version of the Bible, Pharaoh Necho of Egypt also " went up against the king of Assyria to the river Euphrates ; and king Josiah went against him and he slew him at Megiddo " (II Kings 23 : 29).   From the Babylonian Chronicle we learn, however, that Necho was going, not against, but to the aid of the king of Assyria at Haran.   For this reason the Revised Standard Version has translated the verse : " Pharaoh Necho king of Egypt went up to the king of Assyria . . ."

Yet why should Josiah of Judah have risked his life and his dream of a united Israel in a futile battle with an Egyptian army he could not hope to defeat ? M. B. Rowton has recently suggested an answer to this puzzling question on the basis of such information as we have from the archaeological and biblical sources.[11]   Necho was interested in regaining Palestine and Syria for Egypt and it would have been to his advantage to have a weak Assyria as a buffer against the Babylonians.   For this reason he went to the Assyrians' aid at Haran.   Josiah was anti-Assyrian, and he must have known that with Necho in control of Syria and Palestine the newly erected state of united Israel could not survive.   His only hope was to so delay the forces of Necho by making them deploy for siege that the latter would not arrive in time at Haran.   This he succeeded in doing, though at the cost of his life.   " Thus it seems very probable that the last of the great Jewish kings laid down his life in a truly heroic and entirely successful bid to avenge the dreadful wrongs his nation had suffered at the hands of Assyria."

The archaeological evidence for the siege of Megiddo, which resulted in Josiah's death, is the destruction of the city of Stratum II at that site. As noted in the preceding chapter the main feature at Megiddo after 733 B.C. was the large palace-fort which was evidently the Assyrian administrative center for the northern part of Israel.   After the battle between Necho and Josiah, Megiddo was never again an important place.   For some two and a half centuries it remained solely a small and perhaps unfortified village, before the mound was abandoned entirely in the 4th century B.C.   With the death of Josiah came the death of Megiddo as one of the great cities of ancient Palestine.

NEBUCHADNEZZAR

Pharaoh Necho was able to control Syria and Palestine until his crushing defeat by Nebuchadnezzar of Babylon at the battle of Carchemish in northern Syria in 605 B.C.   During the following years the armies of Babylon advanced to the border of Egypt, rolling the last vestiges of Necho's power from Asia.   Jehoiakim of Judah promptly submitted and remained loyal for a time before rebelling (II Kings 24 : 1).   A neighboring king did not submit so readily.   This we learn from an Aramaic letter found at Saqqara in Egypt in 1942 and first

<hr />

[10] Herodotus, *History*, Book I, Chaps. 104–6.

[11] " Jeremiah and the Death of Josiah ", *Journal of Near Eastern Studies*, Vol. X (1951), pp. 128–30.

published in 1948. It was written by a Palestinian king to the Pharaoh in an appeal for aid. After the salutation, the letter reads, according to the reconstruction of H. L. Ginsberg : [12]

That [I have written to my lord is to inform thee that the troops] of the king of Babylon have advanced as far as Aphek and have begun to . . . they have taken. . . . For the Lord of Kingdoms, Pharaoh knows that [thy] servant [cannot stand alone against the king of Babylon. May it therefore please him] to send a force to succor m[e for thy servant is loyal to my lord] and thy servant remembers his kindness, and this region [is my lord's possession. But if the king of Babylon takes it, he will set up] a governor in the land and . . .

In other words, Nebuchadnezzar's army has reached Aphek (modern Ras el-'Ain, just northeast of Joppa). Adon, who sends the letter, must be king, therefore, of a city south of there, presumably one of the five great cities of the Philistines (Gaza, Ashkelon, Ashdod, Ekron and Gath). Gaza is out of the question because it had been the residence of the Egyptian governor and had no king of its own. Gath disappeared from history after it was captured and presumably destroyed by Uzziah in the 8th century (II Chron. 26 : 6). Ashdod and Ekron had both been ravaged by the Assyrians and the former, at least, again by the Egyptians, so that Jer. 25 : 20 speaks of the " remnant of Ashdod ". Ashkelon, on the coast some twelve miles north of Gaza, is suggested, therefore, as the best possibility. That Nebuchadnezzar took Ashkelon is confirmed by the judgment against it pronounced by Jeremiah (Chap. 47 : 5 and 7), and also by the fact that Babylonian tablets of a time some ten years later (see below) mention among the captives living in Babylon two royal princes of Ashkelon, being held as hostages, and Ashkelonian foremen and seamen.

The letter is thus an additional note to be added to II Kings 23–4. As John Bright has pointed out : " Had Adon had a Hebrew prophet in his court he would at least have been warned. For always the prophets pointed out the folly of counting on Egypt (cf. Isa. 30 ; 31 ; 36 : 6 ; Jer. 37 : 6 ff.) . . . But poor Adon had no prophet to tell him ; maybe he would not have listened anyhow. The kings of Judah did not . . ." [13]

There is another reason for the importance of the letter. It is one of the oldest Aramaic papyri known

and the first evidence that Aramaic was supplanting Akkadian as the international diplomatic language. We know that Aramaic was the official language of the Persian empire, and that as early as 700 B.C. highly placed persons could converse in the tongue (II Kings 18 : 26) and use it in business. Yet before the discovery of this letter it had not been dreamed that Akkadian was being displaced so early in diplomacy. The Persians, three-quarters of a century later, were not creating a new custom, then, but simply taking over one already in existence.

It was in 599 B.C. that Jehoiakim, king of Judah, rebelled against Nebuchadnezzar, bringing retaliation from the latter in 598 B.C. Less than ten years later Judah again rebelled under Zedekiah, and this time, in 589–587 B.C., Nebuchadnezzar laid the country waste completely, bringing all life and commerce to a virtual standstill. Evidence for the two invasions is to be seen most clearly in the ruins of two Judean fortresses which protected the hill country. These are Debir and Lachish. At Debir in 598 the Babylonian army seems to have destroyed both of the city gates and the fortress in the center of the city, most of the town escaping demolition. Yet in the second invasion the city was completely destroyed, buildings and fortifications pulled down and burned, so that the site was never reoccupied. The excavator has written : " How terrific the conflagration by which it was destroyed may have been can be gauged by the fact that limestone was calcined and slivered, while adobe was burned red ; the ruins were saturated with free lime, which the seepage of water caused to adhere to pottery and other objects until they became coated with a tenacious crust of lime." [14]

Precisely the same situation seems to have been found at Lachish. In 598 B.C. the city-gate, fortifications and palace-citadel appear to have been violently destroyed.[15] The brick superstructure of the palace collapsed or was pulled down and spread over the courtyard. The building was not rebuilt

---

[12] For discussion with bibliography, see John Bright, " A New Letter in Aramaic, Written to a Pharaoh of Egypt ", *The Biblical Archaeologist*, Vol. XII, No. 2 (May 1949), pp. 46–52.
[13] Ibid., pp. 50–1.

[14] W. F. Albright, *The Excavation of Tell Beit Mirsim, Vol. III : The Iron Age* (*Annual of the American Schools of Oriental Research*, Vols. XXI–XXII, New Haven, 1943), p. 68.
[15] Olga Tufnell, *Lachish III : The Iron Age* (London, 1953), Chaps. I and II. The city stratum in question is that of Level III, the destruction of which Miss Tufnell dates in 701 B.C., though Mr. Starkey, the excavator, dated it in 598. After a detailed study of the published material, this writer feels that the evidence does not substantiate Miss Tufnell's conclusion, but rather points to the views of Mr. Starkey. The technical arguments are presented elsewhere. Suffice it to say that this is also the opinion of Professor Albright : see *Bulletin of the American Schools of Oriental Research*, No. 132 (Dec. 1953), p. 46.

until about 500 B.C. when it was made into the residence of an official (see p. 204). The inner wall around the summit of the mound and the city-gate were sufficiently harmed to require rebuilding, and the stone for the purpose was secured from a large quarry dug in the southeastern quarter of the city. The evidence for the city's complete demolition in 589–588 B.C. is as vivid as that at Debir. "Masonry, consolidated into a chalky white mass streaked with red, had flowed in a liquid stream over the burnt road surface and lower wall below which were piled charred heaps of burnt timber. In the angle below the north wall of the Bastion and the west revetment, breaches which had been hurriedly repaired with any material available were forced again; indeed, evidence of destruction by fire was not difficult to find anywhere within the circuit of the walls." [16] As a result, the site was deserted and not reoccupied until nearly a century and a half later.

Nebuchadnezzar himself does not mention these events in any of his surviving inscriptions, probably because it was not Babylonian custom to brag about military exploits in the way the Assyrian emperors had done. Instead, the Babylonian was inclined to tell about the good deeds he had performed for the gods in building and repairing temples, and the like. Apart from the Bible our main source of information about the Neo-Babylonian Empire has been the Babylonian Chronicle, an official document which simply recorded the chief events year by year (see above). In 1956 the discovery of four more tablets of the Chronicle was announced by D. J. Wiseman of the British Museum. They are especially important in that for the first time outside the Bible Nebuchadnezzar's capture of Jerusalem in 598–597 B.C. is described, while itemized information about other events between 626 and 594 B.C. is given, with a break in the text of only six years.

The following information in particular from the newly discovered documents may be mentioned: In 605 B.C. Nebuchadnezzar not only defeated the Egyptian Necho at Carchemish; we are told that he completely annihilated the Egyptian army so that scarcely a man survived. Yet he was prevented from following up his advantage immediately because the death of his father in Babylon made it necessary for him to return home to be crowned. Hitherto unknown is the record of a major battle with the Egyptians in 601 B.C., in which Nebuchadnezzar was defeated. It was probably on the eve of

125. Babylon in the time of Nebuchadnezzar, showing the Tower of Babel and the temple of Marduk

this battle that the king of Ashkelon wrote his Aramaic letter to the Pharaoh for help (p. 178). Furthermore, Nebuchadnezzar's defeat at this time makes it easier to understand why the Judean king Jehoiakim revolted so soon thereafter. In any event, we know that Jehoiakim died or was murdered before the Babylonians arrived, and his young son, Jehoiachin, had to face the consequences (II Kings 24 : 10–12). In the new fragments of the Chronicle we are informed that Nebuchadnezzar in the seventh year of his reign marched his army into the land of Khatti (Syria-Palestine) and besieged Jerusalem. He captured the city on the 2nd day of the 12th month of his seventh year (March 15–16, 597 B.C.) and took the king prisoner. This not only confirms the biblical story; it also places the chronology of the period on a firmer footing. If the twelfth month of Nebuchadnezzar's seventh year fell in March–April 597, this would mean his eighth year together with the first year of the new Judean king, Zedekiah, would have been during the rest of 597, ending in March–April 596 B.C. Jeremiah 52 : 28–9 says that captives were taken from Jerusalem in Nebuchadnezzar's seventh and eighteenth years. The last mentioned, then, would have been the eleventh year of King Zedekiah, which according to II Kings 25 : 1–7 was the year

[16] *Lachish III*, p. 57.

126. Seal of Eliakim, steward of Jehoiachin

127. Seal of " Jaazaniah, servant of the king "

128. Seal of Ahimelech, from Lachish

129. Seal of " Gedaliah, who is over the house "

in which Jerusalem fell for the second and last time. The final siege of Jerusalem, as described in those verses, occurred, therefore, between December–January 589–88 and July–August 587.[17]

In 1939 Dr. Ernst F. Weidner, then of Berlin, published a few of the nearly 300 tablets which had been found years before in the ruins of a vaulted building supposed to have been the substructure of the Hanging Gardens of Babylon (cf. Fig. 125), counted by the Greeks as one of the Seven Wonders of the World. The tablets list payments of rations

in oil and grain from the government to captives and skilled workmen from many nations who were living in Babylon between the years 595 and 570 B.C. Yaukin, king of Judah (as Jehoiachin's name was then pronounced), five royal princes and other Judeans are listed together with the royal princes of Ashkelon and mariners, musicians, shipbuilders, craftsmen, horse-trainers and monkey-trainers from Egypt, Phoenicia, Asia Minor, and Iran. One of the documents mentioning Jehoiachin is dated 592 B.C.

This evidence suggests that Jehoiachin was being held as a hostage for the good behavior of the Judeans and that he was considered the true king. His uncle, Zedekiah, whom Nebuchadnezzar had put on the throne in Jerusalem would then have been a type of regent. Certainly many Judeans considered Jehoiachin the real king, one who might return at any time (Jer. 28–9 ; and note that the framework of the Book of Ezekiel is provided by a series of dates reckoned by the captivity of Jehoi-

[17] The figures here given now seem to be required by the Babylonian chronology. It is to be noted, however, that a source quoted in II Kings 24 : 12 and 25 : 8 date the two captivities in Nebuchadnezzar's eight and nineteenth years. It now seems apparent that either these figures represent a mistaken computation on the part of a Judean scribe, or—and this is more probable—they are figured according to a slightly different computing system than that used by the Babylonian court. For example, if the year of a Judean king were officially computed as beginning in Tishri (Sept.–Oct.) rather than in Nisan (Mar.–April), then the destruction of Jerusalem would have occurred in 586 B.C.

achin). It is no surprise, then, to discover that the line of the Messiah was traced through him (Matt. 1 : 11–12) and not through Zedekiah.[18]

Further confirmation of the status of Jehoiachin in Babylon comes from the discovery in Palestine of three stamped jar-handles which bore the words, "Belonging to Eliakim, steward of Yaukin" (Fig. 126). Two were found at Debir in the southern Judean Shephelah (Lowland) and one at Beth-shemesh in the northern Shephelah. All three were made from the same original stamp-seal. This indicates that between 598 and 587 B.C. a person named "Eliakim" was the steward of the crown property of Jehoiachin when the latter was in captivity, that this property was kept intact and not appropriated by Zedekiah.[19]

Among the other seals and seal impressions from this time two are of special interest. One, bearing an early representation of a rooster, was found at Tell en-Nasbeh (Mizpah?), eight miles north of Jerusalem (Fig. 127). It belonged "To Jaazaniah, servant of the king", a Judean royal official mentioned in II Kings 25 : 23 and Jer. 40 : 8 (cf. also Jer. 42 : 1 and "Azariah" in 43 : 2, all of whom may be the same person). The other was a seal impression found in the ruins of Lachish (Fig. 129 ; cf. also Fig. 128). It bears the inscription, "To Gedaliah who is over the house." This is undoubtedly the same man as the governor whom Nebuchadnezzar appointed "over the people who remained in the land of Judah" after the fall of Jerusalem and who was soon murdered (II Kings 25 : 22–6 ; Jer. 40–1). The seal had been impressed on clay which had been affixed to a papyrus document long since destroyed by the weather. Inasmuch as it was found at Lachish, it probably had been used by Gedaliah before the city fell to Nebuchadnezzar. This would suggest that he was one of the last prime ministers of Judah, since, as we have noted before, the title "who is over the house" was borne by the chief official of the land next to the king. His father, Ahikam, was a high royal official who had saved the life of Jeremiah after the latter's Temple Sermon in 608 B.C. (Jer. 26 : 24) ; and his grandfather, Shaphan, was the

130. Lachish Letter, No. IV

Scribe or Secretary of Josiah (II Kings 22 : 3, 8–12).

The most important single discovery from the last days of Judah is the Lachish Letters. Eighteen broken pieces of pottery on which letters and lists had hastily been written were found by Mr. Starkey in 1935 in the burned debris of a guardroom in the city gate. In 1938 three more were discovered, one on the roadway and two in a room on the mound near the palace. Most of the letters are in a bad state of preservation and only about one-third of them are fairly intelligible. In the words of W. F. Albright : "Since they form the only known corpus of documents in classical Hebrew prose, they have unusual philological significance, quite aside from the light which they shed on the time of Jeremiah."[20]

Most of the documents were notes written by one Hoshaiah to Yaosh, the commander of the Judean forces at Lachish. Hoshaiah appears to have been in charge of an outpost north of Lachish, in a position where he could see the signals of Azekah,

[18] See W. F. Albright, "King Jehoiachin in Exile", *The Biblical Archaeologist*, Vol. V, No. 4 (Dec. 1942), pp. 49–55 ; E. F. Weidner, "Jojachin, König von Juda, in babylonischen Keilschrifttexten", *Mélanges syriens offerts à M. Renè Dussaud*, Vol. II (Paris, 1939), pp. 923–35.
[19] See further W. F. Albright, "The Seal of Eliakim and the Latest Pre-Exilic History of Judah", *Journal of Biblical Literature*, Vol. LI (1932), pp. 77–106.

[20] Quoted from *Ancient Near Eastern Texts* (ed. by J. B. Pritchard), p. 322. The translations given below are those of Albright taken from the same source.

a city guarding the Vale of Elah in the Shephelah to the north. In Letter IV (Fig. 130) he writes, " And let (my lord) know that we are watching for the signals of Lachish, according to all the indications which my lord hath given, for we cannot see Azekah." The situation in the letters may be that depicted in Jer. 34 : 7: " when the army of the king of Babylon was fighting against Jerusalem and against all the cities of Judah that were left, Lachish and Azekah ; for these were the only fortified cities of Judah that remained ". When Hoshaiah says that he " cannot see Azekah ", he may mean that the latter city has already fallen and is no longer sending signals. At any rate, we here learn that Judah had a signal system, presumably by fire or smoke, and the atmosphere of the letters reflects the worry and disorder of a besieged country. A date in the autumn of 589 (or 588) B.C. has been suggested for the bulk of the letters. On Letter XX are the words " the ninth year ", that is, of King Zedekiah. That is the same year in which Nebuchadnezzar arrived to begin the reduction of Judah : " in the ninth year . . . . , in the tenth month " (II Kings 25 : 1; this would be about January 588 B.C., the siege of Jerusalem continuing to July 587 B.C.— II Kings 25 : 2–3 ; but see n. 17 above).

Judah revolted against Nebuchadnezzar because of the usual promise of help from Egypt. It was probably in reference to the matter of Egyptian aid, that Hoshaiah says in Letter III : " And it hath been reported to thy servant, saying, ' The commander of the host, Coniah son of Elnathan, hath come down in order to go into Egypt ; and unto Hodaviah son of Ahijah and his men hath he sent to obtain . . . . from him.' " Hoshaiah continues : " And as for the letter of Tobiah, servant of the king, which came to Shallum son of Jaddua through the prophet, saying, ' Beware ! ' thy servant hath sent it to my lord." Who the prophet was that acted as the bearer of the letter, we, of course, do not know, but the documents do make it clear that important letters were widely circulated, and it is of interest to note Hoshaiah's detailed explanation of the way in which he received the letter which he was about to forward. Letter XVI has another reference to " the prophet " but only the *ahu* (A. V. *iah*) at the end of his name is preserved. He has been identified with Uriah (Jer. 26 : 20) and also with Jeremiah, but again we cannot be sure because there were undoubtedly many prophets whose names ended in this way.

In the sixth letter the princes or royal officials are accused of " weakening " the hands of the army and the people, which is precisely the same thing which the same princes accused Jeremiah of doing (Jer. 38 : 4) :

To my lord Yaosh : May Yahweh cause my lord to see this season in good health. Who is thy servant (but) a dog that my lord hath sent the [let]ter of the king and the letters of the prince[s, say]ing, " Pray, read them ! " And behold the words of the pr[inces] are not good (but) to weaken our hands [and to sla]cken the hands of the m[en] *who are informed about them* [. . . . And now] my lord, wilt thou not write to them, saying, " Why do ye thus [*even*] in Jerusalem ? Behold unto the king and unto [*his house*] are ye doing this thing ! " [And,] as Yahweh thy God liveth, truly since thy servant read the letters there hath been no [*peace*] for [thy ser]vant. . . .

From Jerusalem no archaeological evidence of the Babylonian destruction has been recovered. Yet we can have no doubt but that the devastation was as complete as the Book of Lamentations suggests that it was. The violence visited upon Judah is clear not only from the excavations of such sites as Lachish, Debir and Beth-shemesh, but also from archaeological surveys which show that city after city ceased to be inhabited at this time, many never to be reoccupied. It was two centuries before a numerous population with a degree of prosperity had resettled the land.

Turn thou us unto thee, O Lord, and we shall be turned ; Renew our days as of old. Or hast thou utterly rejected us ? Art thou very wroth against us ? (Lam. 5 : 21–2).

FURTHER READING

For relevant historical texts of this period, see J. B. Pritchard, ed., *Ancient Near Eastern Texts* (Princeton, 1950), especially pp. 284 ff. Jack Finegan, *Light from the Ancient Past* (Princeton, 1946), is very useful for historical background, as is also the *Cambridge Ancient History*. For more detail on the archaeology of Palestine, see W. F. Albright, *The Archaeology of Palestine* (Pelican Books, A 199, 1949), Chaps. 6 and 9. For other sources, the reader could best refer to the footnotes given in this chapter ; to John Bright, *A History of Israel* (Philadelphia, 1959), pp. 261–319 ; Martin Noth, *The History of Israel* (London and New York, 1958), pp. 262–88 ; and for the chronological problem D. N. Freedman in *The Bible and the Ancient Near East* (Garden City, 1961), pp. 211–13—each with references to other literature.

CHAPTER XI

ISRAELITE DAILY LIFE

" For the Lord thy God bringeth thee into a good land, a land of brooks of water, of fountains and springs issuing in valleys and hills ; a land of wheat and barley, and vine and fig and pomegranate ; a land of the oil-olive and honey ; a land wherein thou shalt eat bread without scarceness . . . ; a land whose stones are iron and from whose hills thou mayest dig copper " (Deut. 8 : 7–9).

FARMING

IN 1908 a small plaque of soft limestone, $4\frac{1}{4}$ inches long by approximately half as much in width (Fig. 131), was discovered in the ruins of Gezer, an ancient city midway between Jerusalem and Joppa on the coast. It was evidently used by a schoolboy for his exercises about the time of Solomon during the 10th century, and it shows signs of repeated scraping to clear the surface for new use. The last words scratched on it were unerased ; they appear to be a rhythmic enumeration of the agricultural seasons, used perhaps for purposes of memorization like the modern " Thirty days hath September, April, June and November . . ." A translation of it is as follows : [1]

> The two months of (olive) harvest ;
>   The two months of planting (grain) ;
>   The two months of late planting
> The month of hoeing up of flax ;
>   The month of harvest of barley ;
>   The month of harvest and storage ;
> The two months of vine-tending ;
> The month of summer-fruit.

The document is thus a calendar of the agricultural year and it depicts something of the life of the Israelite farmer. The first three lines, it may be noted, list three two-month periods. They are followed by three one-month designations, while the concluding two lines name the two- and one-month periods successively. The document thus has a carefully worked out structure. It is not a hasty contrivance.

(1) The list begins with the olive harvest in the fall. This is in accordance with the old Hebrew calendar, which still survives as the religious calendar of Judaism, in which the first month of the year begins approximately in the second or third week

of September. The first two months (Sept.–Oct. and Oct.–Nov.) of the typical farmer's year, then, would be occupied largely with olives : that is, picking and pressing them to secure their oil. The principal sources of the natural wealth of ancient Palestine were grain, wine and olive oil (e.g. Deut. 7 : 13 ; Neh. 5 : 11 ; Hos. 2 : 8). The oil was the main source of fat used in cooking (cf. I Kings 17 : 14) ; it was used in lamps, which were saucers with pinched lips, the latter holding the wick ; it was also used for medicinal purposes in mollifying wounds (Isa. 1 : 6), for cleansing the head and body and as a base for various kinds of ointments. To obtain the oil from ripe olives pressure must be used. A basket of olives would be dumped in a prepared vat and part of the oil extracted by pressure from the feet (Micah 6 : 15) or by pounding with a pestle, the latter producing the finer " beaten oil " (cf. Exod. 27 : 20). The pulp might then be placed under weights for a time to extract the oil that remained. Large commercial presses, dating between the 10th and 6th centuries B.C., have been found at Debir and Beth-shemesh in Judah. Large stone vats were filled with the olives and covered with a weight attached to a beam. One end of the beam was inserted in a niche in the stone wall of the building, and at the other end large stones, with holes in them for ropes, were tied. The Feast of Booths or Tabernacles (Deut. 16 : 13–15) was originally the fall harvest festival (cf. Exod. 23 : 16) and associated with the olive industry.

(2) During the next two months on the calendar (Nov.–Dec. and Dec.–Jan.) the farmer planted his grain. After the long summer's drought, the rains had begun to fall again at the end of October or in early November. Then the Israelite, like the modern Arab peasant, began to prepare his soil by plowing. The typical plow was simply a piece of wood with a metal tip, drawn by two oxen (cf. I Kings 19 : 19). Before the 10th century B.C.

---

[1] According to the interpretation of Frank M. Cross, Jr. The difficult world in the sixth line rendered " storage " actually means the " weighing up " of the grain, according to a recently discovered inscription.

131. The Gezer agricultural calendar

plowpoints were made of copper or bronze and those found in the excavations are usually much dented from use. The introduction of iron, however, meant that the plowpoints could be made larger, more efficient and harder so that they were less easily dented. Yet such a plow could not turn a furrow; it could only scratch the surface of the ground to a depth of 3 or 4 inches.

In Mesopotamia we know that a seeder was fixed to the plow (cf. Fig. 132). This was simply a tube, attached to a receptacle, down which the seeds could drop behind the plowpoint. Whether such an instrument was widely used in Israel is doubtful. Most seed was probably scattered over the scratched ground by hand, after which the plow was again used to cover it. The few references to harrowing and leveling the ground (cf. Isa. 28 : 24-5 ; Hos. 10 : 11 ; Job 39 : 10) may refer, not to the use of special tools, but simply to the dragging of branches after the plow to smooth the ground over the seed. The ancient farmer did not have elaborate equipment. His work was laborious and slow, and the size of the fields he could plant was necessarily small.

Between November and January the basic grain crops of wheat and barley were planted. Along with them other seeds, such as flax and spelt, were also sown. Spelt is a poor variety of wheat, though in the Authorized Version it is called " rye ".

(3) " The two months of late planting " refer to the sowing of summer seeds between January and March. Millet, sesame, chick-peas, lentils, melons, cucumbers and the like were planted at this time.

(4) The next three months in the Gezer calendar are those in which the main crops were harvested. The " hoeing up of flax " in March–April refers to the cutting of the plant with the hoe near the ground in order not to waste any of the stalk. The latter was then dried (cf. Josh. 2 : 6) and used to make cord and linen cloth.

The harvest of barley in April or early May, depending upon the locality, and that of wheat and spelt in May–June, was accomplished by the use of small sickles. The reaper grasped the stalks of grain with one hand (cf. Psa. 129 : 7 ; Isa. 17 : 5) and with the other cut them off close to the ear. Before the 10th century the sickle was made of flint chips (Fig. 73) set in a wooden or bone haft. Thereafter it was a small, curved, iron

132. A modern seeder-plow at Aleppo in Syria, similar to a type used in ancient Mesopotamia

blade to which a wooden handle was affixed by rivets.

Threshing was done on a specially prepared floor in the open air outside the village. The grain was spread upon this floor and the kernels separated from the straw by oxen trampling upon it and pulling behind them a threshing-sledge. The latter was of two types: one was probably made of flat boards; the other ran on small wheels or rollers (cf. Isa. 28 : 27-8). After winnowing and perhaps sifting through a sieve, the grain was stored. Large storage jars were often used for this purpose, and a room full of such jars is not infrequently encountered in excavations. Small, plastered silos dug down through the floor of a home were also common. Reference was made in the preceding chapters (pp. 131, 170) to large government granaries erected in various places, and at Megiddo (Fig. 133) and Beth-shemesh huge, stone-lined silos have been excavated. The one at Beth-shemesh, constructed not far from 900 B.C., was 23 feet in diameter at the top and nearly 19 feet deep. It had been dug through the debris of former cities to bedrock.

In connection with the wheat harvest of May-June there is a word on the Gezer calendar which Professor Albright interprets as "festivity". This would refer to the harvest festival which later was to become known as Pentecost. Seven weeks from the beginning of grain harvest (Deut. 16 : 9; cf. Exod. 23 : 16) at approximately the time when

it was completed, a pilgrimage to the central sanctuary with an offering of the " firstfruits " was necessary, and the occasion was celebrated with great joy and feasting.

(5) The two months of vine-tending, June–July and July–August, refer to the pruning and cleaning of the grapevines which took place in the unoccupied time after the harvest. In the area of Gezer the grapes begin to ripen in July and continue through the following months. The vine, of course, was particularly important for wine, which in a country with a scarcity of clean water was the basic drink. One or two baskets of the grapes at a time would be dumped into a small vat, the floor of which sloped toward a small jar or other receptacle (Fig. 134). The juice was then squeezed from the fruit by trampling with the feet. Large numbers of these grape presses have been found in the Judean Shephelah (Lowland), and they may have been used for the production of beaten olive-oil as well.

(6) The final month of the agricultural calendar was the harvest of summer fruit, particularly figs, grapes and pomegranates, during August–September. The fig, like grapes, olives, wheat and barley, was one of the Palestinian staples. It and the date were the main sources of sugar in the ancient diet; it was generally dried and pressed into cakes. Such a cake could even be used for medicinal purposes : Isaiah prescribed it for Hezekiah's boil (II Kings 20 : 7), and in northern Syria

133. A large silo for storing grain, unearthed in Stratum III (8th century) of Megiddo

it is known to have been recommended for use in the treatment of a certain ailment of horses.[2]

A special variety of fig is the sycamore fig. Today it is eaten only by the very poor and is not considered good food. In Bible times, however, people customarily treated it in such a way as to make it larger and more edible. This was done by puncturing each specimen of the fruit while it was still green, after which it rapidly ripened. In David's government there was an official specially charged with the oversight of royal olive and sycamore (meaning sycamore fig) plantations (I Chron. 27 : 28); and when the prophet

Amos identified himself as " a dresser of sycamore trees " (Amos 7 : 14), he was referring to an occupation which was necessary to turn an inedible into an edible fruit.

134. A Judean grape-press, found at Beth-shemesh

[2] The fragmentary texts cannot as yet be translated in their entirety because the meaning of some of the words is unknown. They are published in C. H. Gordon, *Ugaritic Handbook II* (Rome, 1947), texts 55 : 28–30 and 56 : 32–6.

Such a cursory examination of the farmer's year makes vividly clear the simplicity of his diet. Wheat and barley were cooked or parched, or ground into flour by rubbing the grain between two pieces of coarse, black basalt obtained through traders from the Hauran, east of Bashan and the Sea of Galilee. The flour was mixed with olive oil and baked into flat cakes of bread. The common vegetables were lentils, coarse horse-beans, and various kinds of vegetable marrows like the cucumber; squash and pumpkin were as yet unknown. Flavoring was supplied by onions, leeks and garlic. Chick-peas were used instead of the modern popcorn and peanuts. The basic fruits were figs, grapes, pomegranates and sycamore figs; dried figs, raisins and dates, supplemented by wild honey, took the place of sugar cane. The typical daily diet is probably illustrated by the rations brought to David's band by Abigail, the wife of Nabal: bread, wine, parched grain, raisins and figcakes (I Sam. 25 : 18). She also took along with her five sheep, but meat was not eaten as a daily diet. It was reserved for certain festival occasions, even as is the case today among Arab peasants.

The chief domesticated animals were sheep, goats, cattle, donkeys and dogs. Poultry and eggs probably did not become common before the 5th century B.C., though the earliest drawing of a chicken is that of a rooster on a seal found at Tell en-Nasbeh, some 8 miles north of Jerusalem (Fig. 127). Its date is about 600 B.C. Camels were probably owned and used mainly by traders, particularly those engaged in the Arabian trade. Horses were largely confined to the military establishment for chariotry and cavalry. The donkey was the burden-bearer, and oxen pulled the plow or the occasional heavy two-wheeled cart. Sheep were of the fat-tail variety, the tail being considered a very great delicacy.[3] Sheep were a main source of meat for festival meals and of wool for clothing. The " flock ", however, included goats as well as sheep; the two were, and are still, herded together. Goats were also used for meat; their hair was woven into a coarse cloth which was used for tents (cf. the Tabernacle, Exod. 26 : 7) and probably also

for cheaper clothes; their skins were made into the " bottles " (Hebrew *no'd*) in which wine was carried and kept (cf. Josh. 9 : 4); but their chief value then, as among Arabs still, was their function as producers of milk, of which they were a chief source. Until recent years and the introduction of new breeding methods, the Arab cow was a scrawny and unsatisfactory animal which could produce little milk or beef. If we judge by the pictures which survive of ancient cattle, we must conclude that cattle-raising was a far more profitable industry than it had been in modern Arab countries. The cattle were large and healthy creatures, and the variety reared in Palestine seems to have been different from those of today, and an attractive breed indeed.

THE TOWN

The typical Israelite farmer did not live on his small farm, but in the nearest town. Life was somewhat perilous, except in times of exceptionally able government, and the town afforded a measure of protection. Each village lay within the orbit of a strongly fortified city, to which the people could retire in time of war. Both towns and cities were generally erected on hills or knolls which had a spring or springs issuing nearby. The chief problems were those of protection and water supply. Springs and occasional wells served the normal communities satisfactorily, except in times of siege. Extraordinary measures were sometimes taken to protect the spring and make its water accessible inside the city walls. In Jerusalem, Gezer and Megiddo large tunnels were dug from the spring to the city's interior (Figs. 80–1). At Lachish a well, approximately 144 feet deep, had been dug, evidently in early Israelite times. It was at the mound's northeastern corner, and its mouth was flush with the top of the masonry of the outer fortification wall. When cleared of the debris which choked it, the excavators discovered that it still supplied water at a level 16 feet from the bottom.

The Israelite settlement of Palestine, however, was centered in the hill country where occupation hitherto had not been dense. One reason why the Canaanites had not settled in the hills in great numbers was because of the limited water supply. It is probable that the Israelites were able to settle

---

[3] Cf. Exod. 29 : 22. In I Sam. 9 : 24 the words " that which was upon it " in A.V. (or " the upper portion " in R.S.V.) are a mistaken rendering; the Hebrew instead should be translated " the fat tail " (see, e.g., S. R. Driver, *Notes on the Hebrew Text and the Topography of the Books of Samuel*, Oxford, 1913, pp. 75–6). Samuel had reserved for Saul the choice portions, as was customarily done for honored guests.

the area and establish numerous towns within it only because of a new discovery that had been made in the Late Bronze Age, just before the Conquest. That was the process of slaking lime in order to make water-tight cement. During the 14th and 13th centuries B.C. the city of Beth-shemesh in Judah, for example, became a veritable city of cisterns. These were dug out of the solid rock and supplied with narrow necks which were built up with stone masonry through the city debris. There could be no cisterns without cement for the sides in order to prevent the water from seeping away through the porous limestone. We must infer, therefore, that slaked lime had suddenly become cheap enough for common use. In any event the typical Israelite home after the 12th century usually had a cistern beneath it, and water from the winter rains was saved as it flowed from the roof.

We have very little evidence for Israelite city fortification during the period of the Judges (12th–11th centuries). It is clear that there was as yet an insufficiently strong community organization to erect fortresses of exceptional strength. Where possible, as at Shechem and Beth-shemesh, the Canaanite city-walls and gates were repaired and continued in use. The first major Israelite fortifications of which we have knowledge at the moment were erected during the reign of David at Beth-shemesh and Debir (modern Tell Beit Mirsim) in Judah. Not only are the walls contemporary in the two sites, but they are identical in type and in size. Consequently, we must probably conclude that they were erected under a common plan and supervision. They were very unlike the Canaanite city-walls of earlier times. Instead of a single massive structure of unhewn stones, David erected at these two cities, probably as a protection against the Philistines, a type of fortification known as the casemate system. An outer wall about 5 feet thick and a thinner inner wall, about 3½ feet thick, were erected parallel to one another around the mound.[4] The space between them varied between 5 and 7 feet, and in it cross walls were built to join the two together. The rooms (or casemates) thus created were generally filled with rubble to make one massive structure. This principle of construction had been used earlier by Saul in his

fortress at Gibeah (Fig. 75); and it has been found in Solomonic fortification at Hazor, Megiddo and Gezer. It had apparently been developed by the Hittites in Asia Minor between the 14th and 13th centuries and introduced by them into Syria, where Israel learned of it. Its most spectacular application in Palestine was by the Jehu dynasty in the fortification of Samaria (Fig. 103).

The casemate principle, however, was only sporadically used by Israel. Solomon's city-wall at Megiddo and his repair of a Canaanite wall at Gezer illustrate the first use in Palestine of carefully drafted stones. Strength was achieved, not solely by a double wall nor by mere mass, but by the careful fitting and bonding of the masonry on the wall faces, or, where the need was not as critical, solely in the framing of doors and in " posts " set within a wall otherwise poorly made. On the other hand, the main city-wall at Lachish as erected by Rehoboam between about 920 and 915 B.C. was nearly 20 feet thick and made of sun-dried mud-brick. The wall of Tell en-Nasbeh (Mizpah?), some eight miles north of Jerusalem and dating not far from 900 B.C., was of rubble, the exterior of which was plastered (Fig. 98). It originally was 20 feet wide and in some places later strengthened to 26 feet. Both the Lachish and Nasbeh walls were supplied with protective towers at intervals to assist the defenders against attack, and both were in the Canaanite tradition which employed mass for strength.

Entrance into the typical city was through one or more large covered gateways, flanked by protective towers or bastions. The principle of the arch for such an entrance was probably not yet known in Palestine. Instead, heavy beams were laid on the tops of masonry walls, and these in turn supported a roof or second story. The typical gate erected between the 10th and the 7th centuries consisted of two, three or four pairs of piers jutting out from the side-walls and forming deep recesses or side-chambers from which soldiers could defend the gate from attackers (Fig. 83). The main entrance was between the first pair of piers, and this was generally between 13 and 14 feet wide. The opening was closed by two swinging doors of wood. Metal hinges were not yet known. Instead the doors were hung from large vertical timbers which turned in stone sockets on each side. Several of these stone door sockets, smooth and worn from long use, have been found by the excavators. The doors could be locked by a wooden or metal beam which fitted across them. At both Shechem

---

[4] At Beth-shemesh it is possible that the Canaanite wall was re-used along the eastern side, but of this we have no certain knowledge.

and Tell en-Nasbeh a slot in one of the piers was discovered; in it the metal bar which locked the gates could be pushed out of the way when the entry was opened.

Under the paved floor of the gate a drain, made of stone, was nearly always constructed. Water from the city could drain through it without washing over the entryway. The area drained was generally an open space which seems always to have existed just within the entrance. This was the main market and meeting place of the city where much of the public and private business was conducted.

The type of gate described above could vary in detail, but it was typical of the main entrance through which chariots could drive. If there was a second gate, it was usually smaller and for pedestrians and donkeys only. At Debir (Tell Beit Mirsim) in Judah this smaller gate had a substantial building or tower of several rooms and probably a second story built around and over it. This probably served as the public guest house for travelling merchants and public officials. The doors were well built; the floors were plastered; and there were cupboards, a bath, bowls for food, juglets for oil, lamps for lighting, and even three standard weights such as would be used in business establishments.

The greatest density of population in the Israelite town seems to have been reached in the 8th century. At that time people overflowed the narrow confines of the walled city and built houses in any suitable place around it. Not infrequently the debris of occupation had so filled the space between the walls that homes are found built on top of the fortifications. A familiar illustration of this from an earlier day is the house of Rahab, the harlot, in Jericho (Josh. 2 : 15 A.V.). It was built on top of the city wall so that its window opened over it. Professor Albright reckons the number of houses within the $7\frac{1}{2}$ acres of Debir as between 150 and 250. He writes: " Allowing for an unknown number of persons who lived outside the walls, we may estimate the entire population of the town in its flourishing period at between 2000 and 3000." [5] On the basis of this computation we would say that Bethshemesh of comparable size would have had about the same number of people, whereas the 18 acres

of Lachish might have held between 6000 and 7500 and the 13 acres of Megiddo between 3500 and 5000. Such estimates of the population, however, are very tenuous.

Israelite houses within the city had to conform to the available space. There seems to have been no systematic town planning; and when a new house was erected, the builders had to devise its plan to fit between other house walls which often ran at peculiar angles. Hence symmetry in architecture was rare. Between the 10th and 8th centuries it was common practice to erect one or two rows of stone pillars along the axis of the main room of the house. Partition walls of rubble would be filled in around the pillars and used also to make the side-chambers. The pillars served two purposes: both to strengthen the central partition walls and to provide strong support for the ceiling and a second story. From well-preserved stairways, it has been calculated that the ceiling height was normally about 6 feet. In some houses, at least, the main central room was so large that we may guess that it was not completely roofed over and that a portion was left open to the sky. In a city near one of the plains a considerable amount of brick was customarily used, especially for the superstructure. The size of the covered rooms could never be larger than the roofing beams were long. The latter were customarily from local conifer trees which probably did not grow to great height, and the beams were rarely longer than 12 to 15 feet. The roofs which were laid over the beams were of combustible material, the surface evidently made of straw mixed with mud and lime. This was a very serviceable roof except that after each rain it had to be rolled to pack the surface material and prevent it from leaking. Consequently, many homes had their own limestone roof-rollers which, as found by the archaeologists, are rounded stones about 2 feet long.

Quarters for sleeping and relaxation were evidently on the second floor and the roof. Stairways of stone or wood were customary, but where these are not found in well-preserved houses the presumption must be that ladders were used. Around the edge of the roof the law decreed that a parapet should be constructed as a safety precaution (Deut. 22 : 8). On the ground floor, where the household work was done, it is customary to find bins and jars for grain storage, mortars for grinding the grain, basins of hollowed-out stones, a variety of dishes, jugs and cooking pots, one or two

---

[5] *The Excavation of Tell Beit Mirsim, Vol. III (Annual of the American Schools of Oriental Research*, Vols. XXI–XXII, New Haven, 1943), p. 39.

cistern-mouths opening in the floor, and an oven. The ovens were commonly made of four alternating layers of clay and potsherds to form the side walls. They were round and might rise above the floor to a foot or more in height. Cooking pots were set in the fire within the ovens and convex trays for baking flat cakes of unleavened bread were laid over the coals. Where the direct heat of the fire was not desired, flat stones were heated in the ovens, the coals removed or pushed to one side, and the cooking done on the stones (cf. the modern " fireless cooker " in which the same principle is used). Larger ovens for baking leavened bread were undoubtedly communal affairs, as they are today.

Houses of this type in biblical times were frequently burned as a result of enemy attack. That is, the roofs were intentionally set on fire, and, when the beams had burned, the superstructure of the buildings collapsed. This meant that the accumulation of debris within the city walls was inevitably very great over a period of centuries. The comparative stability of Judean life between the 9th and 7th centuries, however, is illustrated at Debir where the street level was inclined to rise through the centuries while the house floors frequently remained at their original level. This suggests that most of the houses were never completely destroyed during this period but simply repaired and kept in use.

From the period of the Judges in the 12th and 11th centuries two very large buildings have been found in the ruins of Bethel (Fig. 53) and Bethshemesh. They were of the courtyard type, consisting of an open court surrounded on two or three sides by at least two stories of rooms. These buildings were probably owned by important elders or chiefs of their respective villages. After the monarchy was established, buildings of this size were probably erected mainly for government officials in the provincial administration. Homes such as these were undoubtedly well furnished, with chairs, tables, and low wooden couches for beds. Canaanite and Egyptian pictures probably suggest what this furniture was like; indeed its appearance is comparatively " modern ". The ordinary home, however, had few such luxuries. There was probably no furniture; beds were usually straw mats on the floor, though occasionally a raised clay bunk has been found on which people may have slept on straw.

DRESS

Most of the clothing worn in biblical Palestine was made of wool and linen, and the making of fine clothes from these materials had become an art. The Assyrian conquerors of Syria and Palestine frequently mentioned garments among the coveted articles taken as booty. During the 8th century, for example, Tiglath-pileser III lists among the precious things captured from the kings of the West, including those of Judah and Samaria, " linen garments with multicolored trimmings, garments of their native (industries) (being made of) dark purple wool ".[6]

This reference emphasizes two characteristics of fine outer clothing worn in Syria and Palestine. The first was the love of decoration in the form of highly colored fringes, borders and tassels (" trimmings ") along the edges of the cloth. The second was the use of a special purple dye for very expensive garments. The word " Canaan " probably originated from this industry and originally meant " Land of the Purple ". From the murex shellfish which was native to the eastern Mediterranean the Canaanites had learned to extract a deep crimson color which became the most coveted dye of the ancient world. It was so expensive that robes dyed in this color were a mark of high rank—hence the familiar sayings still current " born to the purple " and " promoted to the purple ". The Greeks named the Canaanites " Phoenicians ", evidently from their word for " purple ". There were various shades of the colour between blue and red. For example, Solomon requests an artisan from Hiram of Tyre who among other things would be a man skilled in making " purple, crimson and blue fabrics " and could direct the native Israelite artisans in the work (II Chron. 2 : 7). The veil of the Temple was made " of blue and purple and crimson fabrics and fine linen " (II Chron. 3 : 14). These colors were probably all variations made in the same dye.

The city of Debir was discovered by Professor Albright to have been devoted to the weaving and dyeing industry in addition to the ordinary peasant occupations. It was on the edge of the Negeb or Southland where great flocks of sheep undoubtedly pastured. Thus wool was available in quantity. Vast numbers of loom weights were collected in the excavation of the Israelite city, so many that

---

[6] *Ancient Near Eastern Texts* (ed. by J. B. Pritchard), pp. 282–3.

almost every home must have had a loom in it. In addition, there must have been at least twenty or thirty dye-plants in the whole city, judging from the number and distribution of those found in the areas excavated (Fig. 135). In the typical installation there was a room about 20 by 10 feet in size, at one end of which were two massive dye-vats, with shallow basins of cement and a masonry bench adjoining them. In the corners near by were jars containing slaked lime ; and in one room at least there was a jar full of material that looked like gray ashes but was probably decomposed potash. The dye-vats were round blocks of stone, about 3 feet in height and diameter and with flat tops and bottoms. Inside was a spherical basin about 1½ feet across, the opening to which was a narrow mouth about 6 inches across. Around the rim was a circular channel with a hole in its bottom connecting with the vat's interior. The purpose of this channel was to catch the precious dye which splashed over the rim. Nearby were a number of large pierced stones which were probably pressure weights to press the dye out of the material.

The manner in which the dye-plants were used is illustrated by a modern plant in Hebron as observed in 1930. The common dye used today is indigo, introduced from the East and much cheaper than the better dyes of antiquity. Potash and slaked lime were put in the vats and the dye was added after the lime had stood for two days. The first vat received only a little indigo, the second twice as much. On the third day the cloth was put in. For ordinary garments two baths in successive vats were considered sufficient, though the best garments were given as many as ten baths. The purpose of the potash and lime was to fix the dye in the cloth. The Israelite vats are too small to have been used to dye cloth in quantity. The reason is that in the ancient Near East thread was dyed instead of whole cloth, in order to obtain the mixed colors commonly used in weaving.[7]

It is curious that the whole town of Debir was given over to this one industry. The explanation appears to be that the craftsmen and merchants of ancient Palestine were organized into craft-unions or guilds. We know that such unions existed in ancient Babylonia and, according to the Talmud, in Palestine of a later period. Various references in the Old Testament support this supposition, and we hear of a variety of local associ-

135. A dye-plant found at Debir

ations. Thus the phrase " families of scribes who dwelt at Jabez " (I Chron. 2 : 55) must be interpreted as the " guilds of scribes ". Similarly, " the families of the house of them that wrought fine linen " (I Chron. 4 : 21) refers to guilds of weavers ; and a member of a particular guild could be referred to as a " son " of that order (e.g. Neh. 3 : 31 : " Malchiah son of the goldsmith[s] "). At Debir, in all probability, the dye-plants were built and operated by members of an association who, to judge from later parallels, bought and sold together and had a system of mutual aid to insure one another against heavy loss.[8]

It is often supposed that biblical people dressed very much as do the modern Arab bedouins. This would appear to be a mistaken supposition, though to be sure some of the individual garments may have been roughly similar to some of those seen today. The basic garment of the Israelite worker and soldier appears to have been a short wrap-around skirt or waistcloth ('ezor) reaching down to about the middle of the thigh (cf. Figs. 49, 64-5). The finest examples of it were made of linen, the more crude of leather. Elijah and John the Baptist wore skirts of the latter type (II Kings 1 : 8 ; Matt. 3 : 4) ; the " girdle " of Jeremiah's parable or acted sign was of the former type (Jer. 13). The skirt was evidently held in place by a kind of belt or " girdle " (ḥagorah). In the English translations the word " girdle " is often improperly used ; it is employed to translate not only the ḥagorah or belt, but also the skirt ('ezor) and the special sash of the priests ('abnet). Yet the ḥagorah or girdle proper was a kind of waistband which

[7] See W. F. Albright, op. cit., pp. 59–63 ; The Archaeology of Palestine and the Bible (New York, 1932), pp. 119–21.

[8] See especially I. Mendelsohn, " Guilds in Ancient Palestine ", Bulletin of the American Schools of Oriental Research, No. 80 (Dec. 1940), pp. 17–21.

not only held the skirt in place, but also provided a means whereby various articles such as a sword, dagger, weights or valuables could be carried. It appears to have been fastened by tying the ends together, and occasionally a highly decorated end would hang at the side. The better examples were very valuable works of the weaver's art, and were probably made of wool in variegated colors. Joab, David's general, was willing to offer a " girdle " and ten pieces of silver to the man who would kill Absalom (II Sam. 18 : 11), and the worthy woman described in Prov. 31 made them to sell to foreign merchants (vs. 24).

The upper part of the body was bare or covered with a short-sleeved shirt like the modern " T-shirt ". Over this for warmth a man normally wore a *simlah* or cloak, a garment which seems to have existed in a great variety of styles. Elijah and John the Baptist wore an animal skin and a garment of camel's hair respectively (II Kings 1 : 8 ; Matt. 3 : 4) ; that is, the rough apparel of the shepherd, and, indeed, such a hairy mantle may have become a sign of the prophetic office (Zech. 13 : 4). Yet the typical cloak, made of wool or linen, was fairly close fitting, open in front, decorated at the edges and along the bottom, and furnished with sleeves or some sort of draped covering for the arms. If a head-covering was worn, only on rare occasions would it have been a square, flowing scarf like the modern Arab *keffiyeh*. Far more typical was a skull-cap or turban. The latter could have been very elaborate when worn by important people, but the ordinary peasant and soldier seem to have wound a simple strip of cloth around their heads, leaving one fringed end to hang down over the right ear. On the Black Obelisk of Shalmaneser III from the 9th century, Israelite men are shown wearing a kind of stocking cap which may have been fastened in place after the manner of a turban (Fig. 109).

On Sennacherib's Lachish relief of 701 B.C. (see Figs. 116–18) the Israelite soldier is dressed in short skirt, T-shirt, " girdle " or waistband and turban. Either the T-shirt is fairly long, extending over the top of the skirt to the hips, or the waistband has a strip of cloth attached to it which covers the upper part of the hips.[9] The elders and important men of the city, however, are represented

by the Assyrian artist as wearing long, white dresses of a type that fits closely and could be slipped on and off over the head. They reach the lower part of the leg just above the ankle, and their sleeves cover the upper part of the arm to within about 2 inches of the elbow. This dress is the Hebrew *ketonet* or tunic, which the English versions wrongly translate in many instances by " coat ". On the elders of Lachish it is devoid of decoration and worn without a " girdle " or sash. If an Israelite man did not wear the short skirt, he wore the long *ketonet*, for it was a basic garment. From ancient portrayals, however, it is evident that the tunic was often made in much more elaborate fashion than is shown on the Lachish relief. That of the Israelite high priest was probably woven in one piece of fine linen ; it possessed tight sleeves and was girt about the waist with a beautiful sash ('*abnet*; Exod. 28 : 39).[10] Ancient Palestinian and Syrian portrayals indicate that the bottom of the tunic and sometimes the neck band were intricately woven of highly colored materials, and the costume might further be distinguished by the addition of the sash. (For the conical turban of the high priest, cf. Fig. 62.)

The artist of Shalmaneser's Black Obelisk in the 9th century portrayed Israelite men as wearing the same clothing as the men from Syria : long fringed tunics over which are fringed robes or mantles. The latter are probably the Hebrew *me'il*, an outer garment of linen or wool. How this article of clothing differed from the cloak (*simlah*) described above is not clear, unless it was a more elaborate and expensive version which was worn by people of rank. Both at any rate served the same purpose. It is probable that the robe was made in a variety of styles, but basically it appears to have been an open garment, rather close-fitting in comparison with modern bedouin outer garments, with full sleeves extending from the shoulder to the elbow in a draped effect (cf. Fig. 102). None of the upper garments possessed a collar which covered the neck ; instead they fitted around the base of the neck. The *me'il* typically had an elaborately worked border around the top, along the bottom of the sleeves and along the edges which hung open at the front or side. The robe of Israelite times has a very different appearance from that worn by Canaanites in the Late Bronze Age between the 15th and 13th centuries. In the latter period the finer outer

---

[9] Some interpreters have claimed that the soldiers are wearing long tunics which are drawn up above their knees and fastened in place by their " girdles ". Close study of the relief, however, does not appear to me to sustain such a view.

[10] See also Josephus, *Antiquities*, Book III, Chap. VII.

garments give a spiral effect, as though a 12- to 15-inch piece of cloth with an elaborate fringe on the bottom was wound about the body over the tunic (Fig. 49).

The Israelite like all Asiatics of the time had a long black chin beard which extended up the sides of the cheeks, but the upper lip was usually shaved. He could wear his hair long, holding it in place with a band about the forehead, or he could have it fairly close-cropped as is done today. He usually went barefoot, though he also probably possessed a pair of leather sandals which could be held in place by thongs. The Black Obelisk of Shalmaneser III shows Israelites wearing high boots turned up at the toes in Hittite fashion. Such boots were probably a comparatively rare sight in Israel, however, and were foreign importations used only by a few wealthy persons and some royal officials in North Israel during the ninth century.

Neither Israelite men nor women had to concern themselves with buttons. Where a sash or cloak needed fastening, they used the fibula, which was the earliest variety of safety pin. This was introduced into Palestine about the 10th century. Before that time the toggle pin was customarily used for the same purpose (Fig. 136). This was a type of needle with a hole in the middle to which a cord was tied. The pin was inserted in the cloth and held in place by winding the cord over the protruding bottom and top.

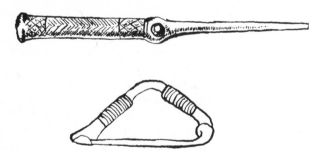

136. An ancient toggle pin and fibula or early safety pin

The clothing worn by women was similar to that of the men, except that they did not wear the short skirt and in all probability they could adorn themselves in a greater variety of garments if they possessed the means to purchase them. The basic garments were the tunic and the cloak or robe (Fig. 137). On the Lachish relief of Sennacherib the tunics of the women are precisely like those of the men (Fig. 117). In addition, they wear a long, comparatively narrow scarf which is draped over

137. A Canaanite maiden, reconstructed from one of the Megiddo ivories

138. The coiffure of a Canaanite lady, as illustrated by a fertility goddess plaque from Debir

the head and extends from the forehead down the back to the hem of the tunic. The most detailed description of the attire of wealthy women is that given by Isaiah in Chap. 3 : 16–23. Some twenty-one different articles of adornment are there mentioned, but, since many of the words are obscure, it is useless to speculate about them without more detailed archaeological information.

The use of jewelry and a variety of cosmetics was very extensive. Anklets, bracelets, rings and beads abound in the ruins of every town. They were made of gold, silver, copper, bone, ivory and a variety of colored stones. Perfumed oils were common, the finest probably imported from South Arabia along with expensive incense. The commonest cosmetic object found in Israelite towns after the 10th century is a small round bowl, about 4 inches in diameter, made of a close-grained hard limestone (Fig. 139a). The type of stone does not seem to occur in southern Palestine at least, and the objects are thought to have been imported from Syria where they were probably made for the peasant trade. The little bowls have a small flat base and in the top a shallow, rounded cavity which is surrounded by a broad flat rim. The latter is generally incised with an elaborate geometric design which once had a dark blue color.

These cosmetic bowls or palettes were used to prepare colors for the face, the mineral substances being powdered in the cavity by means of a spatula. Manganese or antimony (called *puk* or *kuḥl*) gave black which was used to paint the eyebrows and eyelashes. Malachite or turquoise was available to paint the lower eyelids green, and red ochre was used to enhance the color of the lips. Face paints of fine quality were so valuable that in 701 B.C. Hezekiah had to include a quantity of antimony in the tribute he was forced to pay to Sennacherib of Assyria.

The coiffure of women, to judge from such portrayals as we have, was certainly done with far more care than that of men. While most women probably wore their hair long, carefully combed and falling below the shoulders, elaborate styles for putting the hair up, for braiding, trimming and arranging it, were quite fashionable if one chose to follow them. Most of our evidence is derived from the plaques and figurines of the pagan fertility and mother goddesses. All of them illustrate elaborate coiffures which undoubtedly suggest the fashions followed by wealthy women. Before the 10th century the commonest fashion shown on the goddesses can be described as follows: the hair was parted in the middle, drawn down in folds on each side of the head to frame the face, and then curled upward when the folds reached the breast (Fig. 139). The mother-goddess figures after the 10th century, on the other hand, show what appears to be a short "bob" with intricately curled or braided bangs (Fig. 72). Or if the hair were left long in the rear, it was braided and the braids fixed in layers over the bangs on the forehead. All in all, the evidence suggests that the Israelite woman was by no means averse to personal adornment, that there were numerous "high styles" for her to follow, and that undoubtedly she could be as irresponsibly frivolous as Isaiah says that she was (Chap. 3 : 16–23).

ARTS AND CRAFTS

An archaeologist's first impression of Israel's ruins and artifacts is that the people were comparatively poor and uninterested in the arts. This is particularly true if one has come to Palestine from a study of the ruins in Greece, Egypt, Syria or Mesopotamia. For the specialist in Egyptian or Greek antiquity Palestine is the most barren and uninteresting of all the countries of the ancient world, for few objects of artistic beauty or ruins of architectural grandeur are ever unearthed before Roman and Arab times. This impression is a true one, and the interest in ancient Palestine will always remain historical and theological, rather than esthetic.

This does not mean, however, that Israel had no interest in excellent craftsmanship. On the contrary, that craftsmanship is nowhere better seen than in the making of pottery. Yet ceramics as a craft was not followed primarily for artistic purposes in order to produce coveted objects of art. Israelite pottery like that of ancient Egypt had a purely utilitarian purpose. Yet few could deny that the Palestinian's eye for ceramic form was far superior to that of the Egyptian, who for the most part made the most uninteresting pottery of the ancient world. It may be insisted that the Israelite learned his trade and his forms from Syrian teachers. Nevertheless he learned them well, and after the 10th century showed considerable independence. Furthermore, to quote the opinion of a specialist in modern ceramics, " it can be frankly stated that for commercial ware the craftsmanship and the forms are better than for similarly employed wares of today . . . On the whole, we do not produce any better shapes today. The best workmen were already close to ' Greek ' perfection and their work actually had more life and vitality to it than much of the more mathematically perfect Greek shapes . . . Thus the old view that the Israelite had no artistic skill must certainly be revised in the field of ceramics." [11]

By the 9th century a great deal of work seems to have been done in standardizing forms, for very few shapes are found which do not fit into well-known types of pottery (Fig. 139). Furthermore a variety of functional problems were solved and, in general, the simplest good solution to such problems was adopted so that mass production of the wares could be speeded. As a result certain basic shapes and techniques were continued virtually unchanged for over three hundred years, until the fall of Judah in 587 B.C.

The most common material used was a native clay which, when fired, turned to a red or reddish-brown color. It was mixed with water by treading it with the feet, a process alluded to in Isa. 41 : 25. The wares show that while the Israelite potter

---

[11] J. L. Kelso and J. Palin Thorley, " The Potter's Technique at Tell Beit Mirsim, Particularly in Stratum A ", in W. F. Albright, *The Excavation of Tell Beit Mirsim*, Vol. III, p. 100.

knew how to prepare a fine clay when he wished, he ordinarily did not do so for reasons of speed and economy. In common pottery, for example, instead of using a sand, flint or quartz temper to keep the clay from being too sticky, he was likely to use ground limestone because it was available in quantity in the fields next to his workshop.

This meant, as he evidently knew, that he had to fire such pottery with care at a much lower temperature than he would ware from a well-prepared clay, otherwise the limestone would decompose and the gases generated would ruin the pottery.

The potter's wheel had long been known, having been used throughout the Bronze Age with great

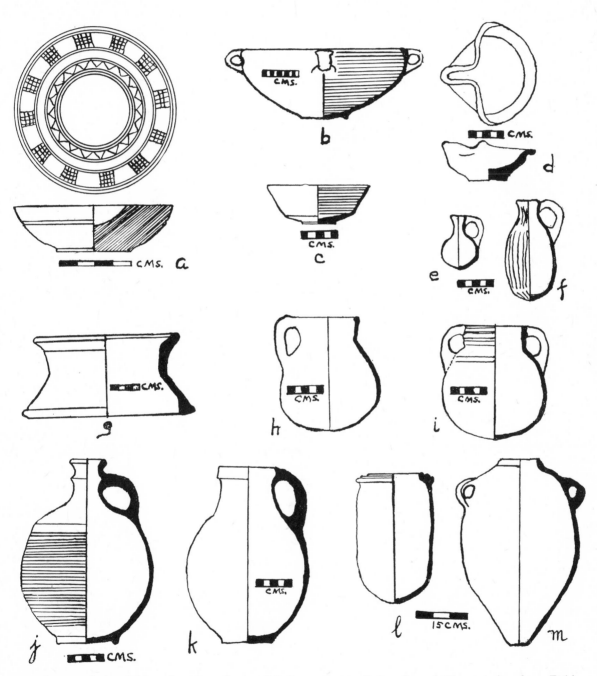

139. A cosmetic bowl (*a*) and various forms of Judean pottery of the 7th and 8th centuries, from Debir

skill. It was of the two-wheeled variety, as we know from the dual form of the Hebrew name for it (*'obnaym*; Jer. 18 : 3). The vessel was thrown on the upper disc while the lower was turned either by hand or foot.[12] While most vessels were fashioned on the wheel individually, at least two special speed-techniques have been noted. In making small juglets for perfumed oil (Fig. 139*e*) a large mass of clay was placed on the wheel and shaped into a tall cone. On the tip of the cone a juglet was formed and then as the wheel continued to turn it was pinched off and another formed, until the cone was used up. A device to cut costs and speed production was used for large bowls. We are told that when such a bowl was done " as a pure throwing job, only an expert could do it so the bowl would hold its correct shape through drying and firing, and he had to use a more refined clay. Commercially, however, this problem was solved by employing less skillful throwers using a cheaper clay and throwing a thicker bowl with a heavy wide foot. Then, when this bowl was leather-hard, it was turned down to the desired shape and thinness, after which it would fire correctly. Other large shapes such as pitchers and crocks were often made by this same short cut. Besides the advantages of cheaper clay and lower wages, this method also speeded production considerably." [13]

Modern pottery looks very different from that made in the ancient biblical world because of the glaze that is put over it before baking. The widespread use of glaze seems to have been introduced into the Western World through the mediation of medieval Arabs, among whom it had been developed, in part perhaps through the influence of Chinese porcelain. In any event, the Israelite potter employed a very different technique in finishing his finer wares. This was the use of a slip, which was simply a thin coating of fine clay wiped or brushed over the parts of a vessel which the potter wished to decorate. The best slips were made out of well levigated clay with a rich iron content, which had been thinned by water to the consistency of thick cream. If a deeper red color were desired, some red ochre was added to make the amount of iron

in it still higher. The Israelite did not paint very much of his ware, other than to draw an occasional line of red or black around the shoulder of a small jar or middle of a small jug or pitcher. His decoration was largely confined to the use of the slip and to burnishing. The latter is the process of sealing the surface pores by rubbing a tool of stone, bone or wood against the clay after it has dried but before it is baked. During the 10th and early 9th centuries this was generally done by hand on juglets, pitchers and bowls. After that time, it was usually done while the vessel turned on the wheel. If the ware is not fired too hot,[14] the burnished areas will shine after baking and give a very pleasing effect. The characteristic Israelite bowl between the 9th and 6th centuries was given a red slip inside and over the rim, and on that a band of burnish was applied beginning in the center and in spiral fashion covering the interior and the rim (Fig. 139*b–c*). This is the familiar " ring-burnished " bowl which is one of the first forms that a beginner in Palestinian ceramics learns. The slip and the burnish reduced the porosity of the ware, though no ancient Syro-Palestinian pottery was completely water-tight, except where solid material in oil, milk or wine filled up the pores.

The most beautiful shape made by the Israelite potter was the ring-burnished " water-decanter ", from the 8th and 7th centuries (Fig. 139*f*). Though at the time it was a strictly utilitarian vessel, considerable care was expended in its manufacture. Even today " its lines would lift it into the truly beautiful and ornamental ",[15] and on the best examples the burnishing is such that they appear at first glance to be glazed. The large storage jars (Fig. 139*l–m*) were made with exceptional skill, and we are told that " probably not over a dozen men in the United States could do this type of work today, since these sizes are no longer thrown ".[16] Beginning in the 8th century Judean kings seem to have made an effort to standardize the volume held by one type of these jars. This we learn from royal stamps which were pressed into the wet clay of many handles before the jar was baked (Fig. 140). On the stamp in the upper register were the letters *lmlk* (*lam-melek*), meaning " Belonging to the king ", while below was the name of one of four cities (Hebron, Ziph, Socoh, and Memshath). The

---

[12] It has been held (*ibid.*, p. 96) that the use of the foot-powered wheel was of Greek origin, Ecclus. 38 : 29–30 (*ca.* 200 B.C.) being the earliest Palestinian description of such a device. It is questionable, however, whether the argument from silence in this case is of sufficient weight to establish the thesis.
[13] *Ibid.*, p. 97.

[14] Cf. *ibid.*, p. 105, where tests are reported to show that a burnished sherd loses its sheen when fired as hot as 970° C.
[15] *Ibid.*, p. 129.
[16] *Ibid.*, p. 136.

140. A storage jar with royal stamps on the handles (*left*). To the right is the impression on the handle of a jar of this type. Above the design is *lmlk* ("Belonging to the king") and below it is the town-name *hbrn* (Hebron)

reds. The black comes from an organic substance which will burn out if the vessels are fired again at a high temperature. The suggestion has been made that the vessels were dipped before firing in milk or oil and then lightly polished. When fired at a low temperature this treatment would produce a beautiful, black satiny finish, which after centuries in the soil has turned into a dead black.

A number of kilns have been found in Palestinian cities, but it is not always easy to tell whether they were used primarily for pottery or for copper. It is not improbable that they were used for both. A cave at Megiddo appears to have been used as a potter's workshop during the 8th and 7th centuries. Just outside of it were the ruins of three U-shaped furnaces. In one of them the ends of the U were still connected with a flue, and in another the interior was full of pottery jar stands, partially fired. Three more kilns of exactly the same type were unearthed at Tell en-Nasbeh (Mizpah ?), eight miles north of Jerusalem. How the pottery was fired in them is not certain. Presumably, however, the vases were stacked in the arms of the U and the fire built at the opening in the U's bottom. When this opening was closed, the flue would draw the flames and heat over the pottery.

At Beth-shemesh during the period of the Judges an earlier type of furnace was found, consisting of just one long, narrow arm. It was enclosed in limestone, the inner surfaces of which had been calcined by the heat. The floor was covered with ashes. While it may have been used for pottery, the evidence shows that it was certainly used for copper smelting on a small scale. The building with which it was associated seems to have been given over to metal-working. Fragments of slag and copper in the ruins were numerous, as also were pottery blow-pipes. An ordinary wood or charcoal fire is not hot enough to melt or smelt copper, unless the blow-pipe or bellows is used. A furnace of the same type just below this and some two centuries earlier had drops of crystallized slag adhering to the side walls and green copper stain around the closed end. More elaborate copper furnaces, dating also from the period of the Judges, have been found at Tell Qasile on the northern outskirts of modern Tell Aviv (Fig. 141), and at Tell Jemmeh, south of Gaza, though the date of those at the latter place is uncertain. These are circular with large brick flues leading air into the fire chamber. Stone tiles were placed on the ashes of the fire within, and on them were set clay

best explanation now appears to be that of Frank M. Cross, Jr.: namely that the four towns refer to royal vineyards from which wine was shipped in the stamped jars. The latter appear to have held two Israelite baths, a bath being a measure equal to about 22 liters or slightly more than 22 liquid quarts. The jars were thus intended to hold about 10 gallons, or slightly less, before the clay lid or stopper was fastened on by cloth bands. At Gibeon, eight miles northwest of Jerusalem, an expedition directed by James B. Pritchard, has uncovered evidence for a privately owned wine industry of great size. Not only have the inscribed handles of many wine bottles been discovered; in addition, 63 bell-shaped wine cellars were found cut into the rock. In some of them the wine was stored in bulk, perhaps during the fermenting stage. After that the wine was placed in two-bath jars, stored in other cellars, a constant temperature of 65° being maintained by the underground rock.[17]

Along with the "ring-burnished" bowls, "water-decanters", and royal-stamped jars, however, there was a very popular and characteristic perfume juglet with one handle (Fig. 139*e*). It is readily recognized, not only by its shape, but also by its black color, a rare feature in the corpus of Palestinian

[17] See Paul W. Lapp, "Late Royal Seals from Judah", *Bulletin of the American Schools of Oriental Research*, No. 158 (April 1960), pp. 11–22; James B. Pritchard, "Industry and Trade at Biblical Gibeon", *The Biblical Archaeologist*, Vol. XXIII (1960), pp. 23–29. Cf. also *ibid.*, vol. XXIV (1961), pp. 19–20.

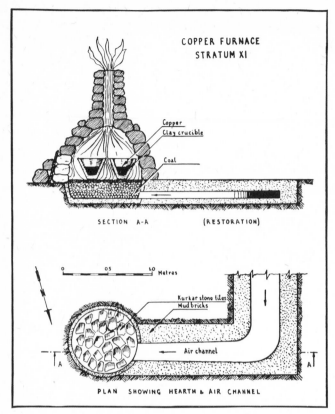

COPPER FURNACE
STRATUM XI

Copper
Clay crucible

Coal

SECTION A-A   (RESTORATION)

0   0.5   1.0 Metres

Kurkar stone tiles
Mud bricks

Air channel

A   A

PLAN SHOWING HEARTH & AIR CHANNEL

141. A copper furnace found at Tell Qasile, near Tell
Aviv

crucibles with copper in them. These furnaces were probably not smelters, but places where the already smelted metal was melted before being poured into molds. It is not unlikely that the same furnaces could also be used as pottery kilns through the regulation of fire and draft.

By Israelite times the technology involved in working gold, copper, iron, lead and silver had long since become quite advanced. Specialists in the metallurgical crafts were to be found in every community large enough to sustain them, and in the Old Testament we learn of one group of wandering smiths, the Kenites, who early attached themselves to Israel (Judges 1 : 16 ; 4 : 11 ; cf. Num. 10 : 29). Gold and silver for millennia had been considered precious metals and media of exchange. The working of copper began as early as 4000 B.C., inaugurating the period which archaeologists call the " Chalcolithic ". The " Bronze " Age, the term which archaeologists use for the period between about 3200 and 1200 B.C., is not a particularly happy name because throughout copper was the dominant metal from which tools and weapons were made. When metallurgists learned how to

make a harder copper, i.e. bronze, by the insertion of tin we do not know. It is not impossible that throughout the Bronze Age many specimens of bronze that have been discovered were made from ore deposits that contained the proper admixture of tin in their natural state. Worked iron objects have been discovered in the Near East from as early a period as the third millennium, though they were made from already " smelted " meteoritic iron. The complex process by which the metal is smelted and worked seems to have been discovered first in Asia Minor, probably during the Late Bronze Age (ca. 1500–1200 B.C.). The Philistines evidently introduced it into Palestine, and the economic revolution caused by its use in Israel, beginning in the time of David, has already been described (see pp. 91–3).

Between the 10th and 8th centuries, at least, one major source of Israelite copper and iron ore was the mines of the Wadi Arabah, south of the Dead Sea. The preliminary " roasting " of the ore was done in small furnaces near the mines (Fig. 87), and the preparation of ingots of metal for export was done in the great smelter built by Solomon at Ezion-geber on the Red Sea (Fig. 112). In Israel, therefore, the furnaces needed only to remelt the metal and forge it into the objects desired. Numerous blocks of stone from various periods have been found in the Near East, with the shapes of a variety of tools and weapons cut into their sides. These are open molds into which metal was poured and left to harden.

The common weapons made of metal were arrowheads, lance and spear tips, swords and daggers, and a variety of battle axes. The larger metal tools in common use were the plowpoint, ox-goat tip, axes, mattocks and adzes (cf. Fig. 57). The ordinary axe was a flat blade with one end sharpened, to which the handle had to be attached by thongs. The double axe was known, as were also the pickaxe, an axe-mattock and an axe-adze. Some of these combined tools look quite modern and have holes in the center for the wooden hafts, just as our own tools do. Other metal objects include the large but ordinary assortment of items that we should expect to find : chisels, large and small, awls, needles, safety pins, tweezers, spatulas, parts for horse-bridles, segments of armor, bracelets, anklets, bowls, small pails and handles for them, etc. Knives cannot, as a rule, be distinguished from short swords, of which a great many are found in each sizable excavation.

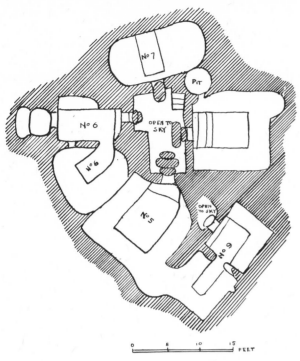

143. A scribe, holding pen-case and bound wooden-tablets, before King Bar-rekub, as discovered in the hall of the king's palace at Senjirli in Turkey

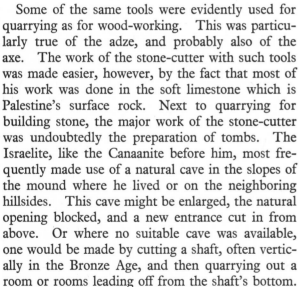

142. Plan of a Judean tomb at Beth-shemesh

Some of the same tools were evidently used for quarrying as for wood-working. This was particularly true of the adze, and probably also of the axe. The work of the stone-cutter with such tools was made easier, however, by the fact that most of his work was done in the soft limestone which is Palestine's surface rock. Next to quarrying for building stone, the major work of the stone-cutter was undoubtedly the preparation of tombs. The Israelite, like the Canaanite before him, most frequently made use of a natural cave in the slopes of the mound where he lived or on the neighboring hillsides. This cave might be enlarged, the natural opening blocked, and a new entrance cut in from above. Or where no suitable cave was available, one would be made by cutting a shaft, often vertically in the Bronze Age, and then quarrying out a room or rooms leading off from the shaft's bottom.

During the 8th and 7th centuries of the Israelite period, however, much more care was taken by the stone-mason than had hitherto been customary. The typical tomb was made somewhat like a house. A horizontal entrance was cut, sometimes with steps leading down into it (cf. Fig. 124). The front was carved from the rock like a doorway, though the opening through this façade was a small square into which a stone, cut away at the edge, was inserted to fit like a stopper. Two or three

steps led down from the opening into a rectangular room, on three sides of which stone benches, like beds, had been left. An elaborate family mausoleum has been found at Beth-shemesh (Fig. 142). This consisted of a small open court cut into the rock, reached by a descending staircase. From this court four of the bench tombs opened. One of them connected with still a fifth which was provided with its own separate entry. The last mentioned tomb was probably an enlargement of the original plan. In all such quarrying operations the regular strokes of the mason's adze are still to be seen on the walls.

The most learned and exacting of the ancient crafts was that of the scribe (Fig. 143). It is here listed among the arts and crafts because writing in ancient times was the business of the specialist. Only the rare person could read and write, and he with few exceptions was one who made these arts his profession. Literacy, as we understand it, was not a quality especially desired for its own sake; it was a way of making a living. The cultural traditions of the people were taught orally and passed from one generation to another orally. To be an educated man, therefore, did not mean that one must necessarily be literate. Why the various types of Old Testament literature came to be written down we do not know with certainty, but we can presume that at least the great collections of historical traditions and of prophetic oracles were reduced to writing only in periods of spiritual crisis, particularly of crisis in confidence when it was feared that the traditions would be lost in social and political changes or upheavals. Most of the scribes found work in business and in government. Correspondence, contracts, receipts, memoranda, and the like took most of the specialists' time. A very few would have had to know engraving techniques so that they could make seals for people who desired to have their names impressed on the documents they " signed " (Figs. 111, 126–9). They would also have been able to incise the names of the various weights on the tops of small stones used for weighing silver and gold in a balance scale. Merchants usually carried a scale and a bag of the proper weight stones (Deut. 25 : 13 ; Prov. 16 : 11). It is improbable that Israel had many experts who were specialists in monumental stone-engraving, though in Egypt and Mesopotamia there was a whole corps of such experts in government work and tomb adornment. The few examples of official display inscriptions recovered in Israelite Palestine (the Siloam inscription, Fig. 123 ; the contemporary tomb inscription of the Judean prime minister, pp. 174–5 ; and an earlier fragment of a monumental stone with one word remaining, which was discovered at Samaria) exhibit a type of lettering which was evidently very close to that used in official documents. It does not appear to be a script especially adapted to stone.

Ezek. 9 : 2 depicts the scribe as a man " clothed with linen, with a writer's inkhorn by his side " (A.V.) : that is, he was dressed in a long white tunic with a pencase (not " inkhorn ") attached to his girdle or waistband. The case held reed pens and had receptacles in which ink could be mixed. Writing in Palestine during Israelite times was done with pen and ink on papyrus-paper, leather, wood and potsherds. Only very rare examples of the Mesopotamian clay tablets with wedge-shaped (cuneiform) signs on them (Fig. 17) appear, and these were undoubtedly the work of foreigners. The Hebrew word for book (*sepher*) generally designated a roll of leather or papyrus-paper, made by sewing or pasting sheets together until the desired length was reached (cf. Fig. 157). The text was written in columns on the rolls (cf. Jer. 36 : 23), and the twenty-two letters used by Israelites to write it were consonants taken from an original consonantal alphabet of some

twenty-seven letters invented by the Canaanites sometime before 1500 B.C.[18]

If we are to judge from what excavators have discovered, we must conclude that Israel had few, if any, artists engaged in the making of beautiful objects for art's sake. Artistic interests were employed in the utilitarian crafts, particularly in the weaving and dyeing, ceramic and perhaps metallurgical industries. Ceramic experiments in modelling a variety of figures are to be found, but they rarely possess artistic merit. That is because no one gave enough time to perfecting them as forms of art. Among surrounding peoples good modelling had been developed as a temple-craft, used especially in the representation of the gods. In Israel nothing material was to be used to depict either God or any subsidiary divine being. Consequently, the making of idols furnished the artist no chance to develop an interest and aptitude in clay, stone or copper figures. To be sure, clay figurines of the Canaanite mother-goddess abounded (Fig. 72), as did ceramic animals and especially horseback riders (the latter in the 8th–7th centuries particularly). Yet these were mass-produced at great speed. The heads of the goddess were made in molds and affixed to a pillar of clay. Occasionally one observes the product of a carefully made mold, but usually the molds were either themselves crude or badly worn from repeated use.

Israelite jewelers produced the usual variety of silver, gold, bone and stone articles for personal adornment. Thus far, however, few items of exceptional merit have been found which illustrate their best work. The finest artistry of Israel during the 9th and 8th centuries may well have been wooden furniture inlaid with ivory panels and insets. The Samaria ivories (see Fig. 102), used for this purpose, must once have been exquisite works of art, delicately carved with a variety of stylized fauna and flora. They were given color by inlays of gold leaf, glass, lapis lazuli and other colored stones. The style and themes are Egyptian, but, as we know from several collections of this type of art, the workmanship is Syrian. Hence the ivories cannot be said to represent Israelite art ; they were either imported by the royal court in Samaria, or they were made by hired foreign artists.

Between 3500 and 1500 B.C. some of the finest

---

[18] The original order and number of the letters has been discovered in two apparently identical lists of the ABCs discovered at Ras Shamra in northern Syria : see W. F. Albright, *Bulletin of the American Schools of Oriental Research*, No. 118 (April 1950), pp. 12–14 ; No. 119 (Oct. 1950), pp. 23–4.

art-work in the Near East was put into seal engraving. After that time workmanship steadily declined. Israelite seals are probably adaptations of Canaanite or Phoenician work. The latter in turn was based upon the Egyptian scarab-seal, and many of the motifs used by the finer lapidary artists were Egyptian (Figs. 111 and 128). Israelite seals show quite a mixture of Egyptian and Syrian elements, the lion, the cherub (a winged lion with human head) and the griffin (a bird-headed, winged animal) being fairly typical.

One reason for the comparative paucity of Israelite works of art may well have been that society in the outlying cities was not stratified to the degree that it was in pagan culture. If great art is to flourish, it generally must have wealthy patrons to encourage and to support it. The Israelite countryside was not wealthy, and the impression one gains from such Israelite towns as Bethel and Tell en-Nasbeh (Mizpah?), north of Jerusalem, and Debir and Beth-shemesh to the west and southwest is that such resources as were available were fairly widely distributed. In areas outside Jerusalem and Samaria there was not a concentration of great wealth and power in the hands of the few. Consequently there exist few great palaces for the archaeologist to dig into, and it is in such places that museum pieces are found. We may say, therefore, that while Israelite culture was far more democratic in the handling of its resources than were other societies of the time, that very fact was at least one of the factors which in a poor country prevented the development of great art. These facts are perhaps disappointing to the archaeologist in search of beautiful objects. In any case, however, Israel would never have been remembered primarily for her art, for her contribution to civilization lay elsewhere.

FURTHER READING

The most informative source material for the subjects treated in this chapter is to be found in the reports of the excavators and in a study of the objects found, particularly W. F. Albright, *Tell Beit Mirsim, Vol. III : The Iron Age* (*Annual of the American Schools of Oriental Research*, Vols. XXI–XXII, New Haven, 1943). Otherwise, there does not exist a detailed and up-to-date summary of the subject. The standard Bible dictionaries, especially Madeleine S. and J. Lane Miller, *Encyclopedia of Bible Life* (New York and London, 1944) and *Harper's Bible Dictionary* (New York, 1952), are useful when employed with care. For a variety of specific topics help can be found in the files of *The Biblical Archaeologist* (see the indices at the end of each fifth volume).

See also : A. Reifenberg, *Ancient Hebrew Arts* (New York, 1950 ; chiefly a book of pictures) ; W. F. Albright, *The Archaeology of Palestine* (Pelican Books, 1949), Chaps. 8 and 9 ; Kurt Galling, *Biblisches Reallexikon* (*Händbuch zum Alten Testament*, I ; Tübingen, 1937) ; A. Lucas, *Ancient Egyptian Materials* (London, 1926) ; R. J. Forbes, *Metallurgy in Antiquity* (Leiden, 1950) ; F. S. Bodenheimer, *Animal Life in Palestine* (Jerusalem, 1935) ; *Everyday Life in Ancient Times* (Washington, National Geographic Society, 1951). G. Contenau, *La Civilisation Phénicienne*, 2nd ed., Paris 1949 ; Pritchard, *Ancient Near East in Pictures Relating to the Old Testament* (Princeton, 1954) ; Eric W. Heaton, *Everyday Life in Old Testament Times* (London and New York, 1956).

Perhaps the greatest work in this area still remains that of Gustaf H. Dalman, *Arbeit und Sitte in Palästina*, 7 vols. Gütersloh, 1928–42).

CHAPTER XII

THE BRAND PLUCKED FROM THE BURNING

"I have overthrown among you, as when God overthrew Sodom and Gomorrah, and ye were as a brand plucked from the burning" (Amos 4 : 11). "The Lord rebuke thee, O Satan; the Lord who has chosen Jerusalem rebuke thee. Is not this a brand plucked from the fire?" (Zech. 3 : 2).

THE title of this chapter, derived from the verses quoted above, is here taken as a symbol of the Jewish community which slowly came into being during the 6th and following centuries. Like the high priest Joshua, to whom the prophet Zechariah is referring, the new community was indeed a brand, badly burned, but plucked from a fire that otherwise would completely have destroyed it. The archaeological evidence which illumines the Post-Exilic and Inter-Testamental Periods is, however, far less extensive than it is for earlier periods. Consequently in this chapter we shall not only survey the main discoveries which bear upon the history of the community between the 6th and 1st centuries B.C., but we shall also be able to review briefly a few items that throw light on the sacred literature of the community, a literature which in this age was attaining its final form.

THE PALESTINIAN COMMUNITY IN THE 6TH, 5TH, AND 4TH CENTURIES

So thorough was Nebuchadnezzar's destruction of Judah that many years pass by before evidence for reoccupation can be detected. In fact, the country's recovery to its former prosperity was very slow and extended over a period of three centuries; and the new Judean community was established, not in the whole of its former territory, but in a comparatively small area around Jerusalem.

North of Jerusalem four towns in particular show evidence of continued occupation during the 6th century. This supports the inference derived from the narrative in II Kings that Nebuchadnezzar confined his attention to Judah and Jerusalem and did not lay waste the areas to the north. These towns are Tell en-Nasbeh (Mizpah?), Bethel, Samaria and Megiddo. None of them yield objects or architecture of especial interest from this time, nor do they show any evidence of economic vigor. Indeed, a portion of the mound at Samaria seems

to have been purposely covered with earth from the surrounding hillsides in order that it could be used as an orchard or vineyard. Bethel was destroyed and abandoned some time before 500 B.C., but we cannot be certain who was responsible for the deed. The town was subsequently resettled and continued to be occupied into the Roman period. Tell en-Nasbeh and Megiddo were not destroyed until sometime in the 4th century when they were abandoned, but again we are not certain about the reason. Of all the excavated cities of Palestine, Samaria alone has revealed a fairly continuous occupation throughout the period from the fall of Jerusalem through Inter-Testamental and New Testament times.[1] It is small wonder, then, that our archaeological knowledge of the Post-Exilic and Inter-Testamental ages is so fragmentary. At the same time this very fact is eloquent testimony to the hardships and privations which the decimated population of the country had to undergo. Only one other period in the country's history can be said to be at all comparable to this, and that was long before in the unsettled time before Abraham (ca. 2400–1900 B.C.).

When a new Judean community was established during the 6th and 5th centuries, it was confined to a small area, extending less than twenty-five miles along the central ridge from a few miles north of Jerusalem to Beth-zur, north of Hebron. Its population by 440 B.C. was reckoned at less than 50,000 (Neh. 7 : 66 ff.), and it was surrounded by hostile and troublesome neighbors. That it was established at all was due to a radically new policy in the treatment of subject peoples which was instituted by the Persian king, Cyrus. In an inscription written for publication in Babylon after its capture in 539 B.C., Cyrus describes how he was able to

---

[1] The great city of Gezer, in the foothills between Jerusalem and Joppa on the Mediterranean, was inhabited through most of this time until its abandonment about 100 B.C. The excavation reports, however, are not of the type which provide us with the detailed information desired.

take the city and what he did after seizing it. He claims that Marduk, the lord of the gods of Babylon, had become angered at the impious acts of the king of the country (Nabonidus).[2] The latter was " a weakling " who interfered improperly with religious affairs, blabbering incorrect prayers, interrupting the regular offerings, and changing the worship of Marduk into an abomination. This god searched through all countries for " a righteous ruler ", chose Cyrus and declared him ruler of the world. As a result Cyrus entered Babylon without a battle, spared the city calamity, and immediately turned his attention to the alleviation of the people's complaints. He then reversed the policy of Assyrian and Babylonian rulers before him of transporting peoples from their homelands and forcing them to live elsewhere. He says that he gathered all the former inhabitants of the various countries, " returned (to them) their habitations ", rebuilt their sanctuaries, and returned the images of their gods which had been taken away.[3]

This information enables us to place the Judean return from Babylonian exile in its proper setting. Ezra 1 : 2-4 and 6 : 3-5 preserve two accounts of the decree of Cyrus permitting the return and the rebuilding of the Temple in Jerusalem. The second is in Aramaic and has generally been considered more reliable than the first, which is in Hebrew, though some scholars have been inclined to doubt the authenticity of them both. Recently, the two documents have received careful study in the light of our present knowledge of royal decrees in the ancient world, particularly in the time of the Persian empire.[4] The result of this study is to the effect that there is no reason to doubt the *substantial* authenticity of either account. The second is explicitly entitled a *dikrona*, an official Aramaic term for a memorandum which recorded an oral decision of the king or other official and which initiated administrative action. It was never intended for publication but solely for the eye of the proper official, following which it was filed away in government archives. According to Ezra 6 it was found in the government archive-building at Ecbatana, where we know that Cyrus stayed during the summer of his first year as king (538 B.C.).

The Hebrew document quoted in Ezra 1 : 2-4, on the other hand, was of a different type and had a different purpose. It was a royal proclamation made throughout the empire to all Judeans. Whereas official letters and documents were generally in Aramaic, verbal proclamation was of necessity in the national language of those addressed. When Ezra 1 : 2 speaks of " a proclamation throughout all his (Cyrus') kingdom ", we are to envisage royal heralds making the announcement both by voice and by poster wherever displaced Judeans were settled, for this was the accustomed manner of publication. In the decree Cyrus simply says that Yahweh, the God of heaven, had given him all the kingdoms of the earth and had given him charge to build the Jerusalem Temple. Hence anyone among Yahweh's people, who desires to do so, may return to Jerusalem, while those who remain where they are should assist those who return with a variety of needed gifts.

One objection which some have had to the decree in this form is to the effect that Cyrus was no convert of the God of Israel and would scarcely be expected to speak as though he were (cf. Isa. 45 : 4). Yet such was precisely his method. We have already noted that in the Babylonian inscription the king says virtually the same thing about Marduk as he here says about Yahweh. In fact, the king, or the bureau which framed the document, may well have had the counsel of a Judean advisor who knew what a great prophet was currently saying back in Judah (cf. Isa. 45 : 1 ff.). In any event, the pagan cast of the royal thinking is revealed in the phrase which identifies Yahweh in the decree : " he is the God who is in Jerusalem " (Ezra 1 : 3) —a manner of speaking common in a polytheistic environment which no good Yahwist of the day would have used. The title " God of heaven " was not employed for Yahweh by Judeans before this time, presumably because for Canaanites and Arameans it commonly designated the great storm-god (Baal or Hadad). Yet during the Persian period it came into common use, perhaps because the Persians had popularized it as one inoffensive and acceptable to most of the subject peoples to whose gods Cyrus was most tactful and receptive.[5]

During the 6th century the political leaders of the new Judah were descendants of the Davidic

---

[2] The Belshazzar of the Book of Daniel (Chap. 5) was the son of this king and virtual ruler in place of his father who gave most of his attention to religious matters. The son was never the real king, as we might otherwise infer from Daniel.

[3] See J. B. Pritchard, ed., *Ancient Near Eastern Texts*, pp. 315-16.

[4] See especially Elias J. Bickerman, " The Edict of Cyrus in Ezra 1 ", *Journal of Biblical Literature*, Vol. LXV (1946), pp. 249-75 ; and Raymond A. Bowman, " Ezra and Nehemiah ", *The Interpreter's Bible*, Vol. III, pp. 570-3, 613-16.

[5] See R. A. Bowman, *ibid.*, p. 572.

144. Tombs of the Persian kings at Naqsh-i-Rustam, Iran. On the right is the tomb of Darius I (522–486 B.C.)

145. Darius I receiving a foreign dignitary. Behind him stands the crown prince Xerxes (biblical Ahasuerus). Relief in the treasury of the Persian government at Persepolis, Iran

house, and this gave many Jews the opportunity to dream again of the re-establishment of a state ruled by the Davidic dynasty. The leader of the first return was one Shesh-bazzar who bore a good Babylonian name (either Sin-ab-uṣur or Shamash-ab-uṣur) and whom the genealogies seem to know as the son of the exiled king Jehoiachin, though the strangeness of the name caused corruption in spelling (I Chron. 3 : 17–18 : " Shenassar "). By 522 B.C., however, he had been replaced by his nephew, Zerubbabel or *Zer-Babil* (" Offspring of Babylon ", a common Babylonian name).

The situation between 520 and 515 B.C., during which time the Jerusalem Temple was rebuilt, is to be understood in the light of the rebellions in every part of the empire following the accession of Darius the Great in 522 B.C. (Figs. 144–5). Professor Albright has reconstructed the situation as follows :

The prophet " Haggai's first oracle, in late August, 520, in which he spurred the men of Judah to take up the long overdue rebuilding of the Temple in earnest, was delivered about two months after the rebellion of Babylonia under a man who called himself Nebuchadnezzar. Less than a month later work actually began. Haggai's second oracle (Hag. 2 : 1 ff.), nearly two months later, exults in the approaching downfall of Persia and the coming of a new Jewish state ; in his fourth oracle (Hag. 2 : 20 ff.), dated in December, while the Babylonian rebellion still appeared to be successful, he explicitly declared that the imperial throne would be overturned and implied that Zerubbabel was the Lord's anointed. Most of Zechariah's prophecies are later, reflecting the situation that followed the complete triumph of Darius over his foes, when the ambiguous stand of the Jews during the previous year naturally became the target of official Persian investigation." [6]

Whether Zerubbabel was removed from office or not, we do not know, but it seems clear that something happened to dash the hopes of Judeans in a restored Davidic state. From that time onwards the new Palestinian province of Judah was largely ruled internally by the high priest, though political affairs were kept in order by a governor appointed by the Persian court. The most famous of these governors was Nehemiah, a Judean layman who had become an official in the court of Artaxerxes I (465–424 B.C.) and who held office in Jerusalem during the third quarter of the 5th century, rebuilding the city wall and initiating a number of

reforms. Beginning in his time and continuing through the 4th century the province was given the status of a semi-autonomous priestly commonwealth, similar to that of the city, Hierapolis, in northern Syria, with the right to levy its own taxes and issue its own coinage.

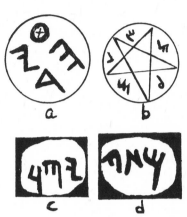

146. Official seals of the province of Judah during the 5th–4th centuries

One source of information which bears on this point has been the discovery of four groups of seal-impressions on jar-handles of the 5th and 4th centuries (Fig. 146). The first group has the three consonants of the word *Yehud* (the official Aramaic spelling of " Judah ") together with a monogram consisting of a cross with a circle around it (Fig. 146*a*). This same monogram appears on contemporary documents in Egypt (see below), but there it follows the words *lam-melek*, " Belonging to the king ", thus indicating that it possesses an official significance. A second group of seals has a circle with a star incised within it. Between the points of the star are the letters of " Jerusalem " (Fig. 146*b*). The writing on both of these groups uses the old Hebrew character. The third class of seals simply bears the letters of the name *Yehud* on a round or oval stamp-seal with no further decoration added (Fig. 146*c*). In this group the writing is no longer in the old style, but is early Palestinian Aramaic This suggests that during the 5th and 4th centuries the older manner of writing was losing out to the newer Aramaic character. In other words, the style of writing changed as did the language commonly spoken. From this time onwards Hebrew was to be spoken only in a few small and conservative groups, while most Jews adopted the tongue used throughout the Persian empire,

[6] W. F. Albright, " The Biblical Period ", *The Jews, Their History, Culture and Religion* (ed. by Louis Finkelstein ; New York, 1949), Vol. I, p. 50 ; issued as a separate monograph by The Biblical Colloquium, 731 Ridge Ave., Pittsburgh 12.

Aramaic. The fourth group of seals consists of twenty-eight specimens found at Tell en-Nasbeh, eight miles north of Jerusalem, and one found at Jericho. The letters of the sealings are now read as *mṣh*, and the writing is in the same style as that of the third group (Fig. 146*d*). What the letters signify, however, is a mystery. One suggestion is that they are an abbreviation for Mizpah, a town which is either Tell en-Nasbeh or another site near by and which, according to Neh. 3 : 7, appears to have had a special status in the Persian administration. Recently, however, a more convincing suggestion interprets the inscription as the town-name, Mosah (Mozah, Josh. 21 : 26), northwest of Jerusalem.[7] The existence of these Judean, Jerusalemite and *mṣh* stamps suggests a flourishing wine industry whence the jars bearing the stamps derive. It is possible that the first group may also have served to guarantee capacity as a standardized measure.

Before the Persian period sums of money in gold and silver were always weighed on scales. In the 5th century stamped coinage made its appearance. The Greeks were the first to simplify the problem of exchange by the invention of coinage, and the Persians soon copied them. In fact, some of the first coins of Asia portray the owl of Athena and were modelled on the Greek daric, thus indicating the source of the borrowing. During the second half of the 5th and during the 4th century coins with Hebrew letters on them appear in Judah (Fig. 147). Several of them bear the letters of the name of the province, *Yehud*.[8] The best known of them, a silver coin in the British Museum, has an inscription which was once mistakenly read *Yahu* (for *Yahweh*) and was thought to have on it a picture of the God of Israel in the form of the Greek god Zeus.[9] The existence of these coins indicates that the province of Judah had been granted considerable local autonomy, with the right to strike its own coinage. Furthermore, when the Biblical Chronicler made several references to the

147. Coins of 4th-century Judah. On the left is an imitation of the Greek tetradrachma, with the Athenian owl and the letters *YHD* (*Yehud*, Judah). On the right is a coin in the British Museum once thought to be the only known representation of the God of Israel, because the three letters were read *yhu* (*Yahu*, a late spelling of the name *Yahweh*). The letters are now read *Yehud*, Judah

daric (I Chron. 29 : 7; Ezra 2 : 69; 8 : 27; Neh. 7 : 70–2), we can understand that he was thinking of a coin which was well known to him. The reference need not be considered anachronistic, as some have inferred, except that in I Chron. 29 : 7 the Chronicler used the term, in writing of a period before it was known, simply in order to suggest the weight or value of gifts made for the Temple.

The Persian empire was organized in a series of large administrative units or satrapies. Judah was a small province in the fifth satrapy, which consisted of Syria-Palestine and was called " Beyond the River " (Transpotamia). Judah's immediate neighbors were the province of Samaria to the north, the province of Ammon east of the Jordan, the province of Ashdod along the southern coast, and the province of Arabia (later known as Idumaea) directly to the south. While the formation of Judah as a new province under the control of returned exiles was made possible by royal decree, it was hindered at every step of its development by its neighbors, and particularly by Samaria which had evidently laid claim to the control of Jerusalem. Even the native Judeans who were not forced into exile opposed the newcomers (Ezra 4 : 4–5). The climax came in the days of Nehemiah (after 445 B.C.), when Sanballat was governor of Samaria, Tobiah of Ammon, and Geshem of Arabia, but Nehemiah describes how their plots were frustrated (Neh. 2 : 19–20; 4; 6). Sanballat's name, of Babylonian origin (originally *Sin-uballit*), appears on contemporary documents found in a Jewish community in Egypt (see below). Geshem is mentioned in a contemporary inscription found at Hegra in Arabia.[10]

[7] H. L. Ginsberg, *Bulletin of the American Schools of Oriental Research*, No. 109, pp. 21–2. The author explains Mizpah's special status as follows : " apparently it was crown land the income from which all went into the 'privy purse' of the satrap of Transpotamia." But see now N. Avigad, *Israel Exploration Journal*, Vol. 8 (1958), pp. 113–19.

[8] See E. J. Sukenik, " Paralipomena Palaestinensia ", *Journal of the Palestine Oriental Society*, Vol. 14, 1934, pp. 178 ff. ; and W. F. Albright, " Light on the Jewish State in Persian Times ", *Bulletin of the American Schools of Oriental Research*, No. 53 (Feb. 1934), pp. 20–2.

[9] See, for example, A. T. Olmstead, *History of Palestine and Syria* (New York and London, 1931), p. 620 and reference.

[10] See R. A. Bowman, *op. cit.*, pp. 681–2, and references there cited.

148. Model of the villa of the Persian period from Lachish

149. A reconstruction of the front of the Tobiah palace in Transjordan

One of his residences may well have been at Lachish, a city near the northwest corner of his province (Fig. 148). By the 5th century we know from excavations in this city that the old Judean walls and gate, destroyed by Nebuchadnezzar, had been rebuilt, and on the ruins of the old Judean governor's palace a fine villa had been erected. New features for Palestinian architecture appear in the building, probably introduced from Mesopotamia. The two main entrances into the inner court were probably quite elaborate, making use of columns; and some of the apartments in the building had doors and ceilings covered by barrel vaults. The vaults were constructed by the same methods which the Romans were later to use so extensively in their architecture throughout the Near East. Not far from the palace was a small temple, which continued in use for some time and was not destroyed until the second century when the Jews regained control of the site.

A small collection of silver vessels was recently acquired by the Brooklyn Museum. The objects are reported to have been found at Tell el-Maskhutah (biblical Succoth) near the Suez Canal in Egypt. Three of the vessels bear Aramaic inscriptions which say that they are offerings to the North-Arabian goddess Han-'Allat. The proper names mentioned, with one exception, are all North Arabic. One is of special interest: " Qainu son

of Geshem (Gusham), King of Kedar." Here, then, is a second reference to Geshem outside the Bible. The evidence is accumulating that the territory ruled by his dynasty was quite extensive, including southern Judah in which Lachish was a chief center, the ancient area of Edom, northern Arabia, Sinai and some portion of the Nile Delta.

Tobiah of Ammon came from a family, which like that of Sanballat, was at least nominally Yahwistic, that is, worshippers of the God of Israel. The history of this family can be traced as far as the early 2nd century when the last of the line died. Its home was at 'Araq el-Emir, north of the River Jabbok in Transjordan. The ruins of a fine palace in Hellenistic style have been found there (Fig. 149); it was evidently built by the last governor in the family between 200 and 175 B.C. Some distance from the palace are a number of rock-cut tombs. On two of them the name " Tobiah ", deeply cut in the rock, still remains. Whether this was the Tobiah of Nehemiah's time or one of his successors is uncertain; scholars are divided in their opinion. We know that in the early third century an Ammonite governor of the family bore the same name because a letter which he wrote has been recovered. It was sent to Zeno, an official in the Egyptian government of Ptolemy Philadelphus (285–246 B.C.), and it states that Tobiah is sending to the king a number of animals, including horses, dogs and camels.

Among the small objects found in Palestinian excavations of this period, the most interesting are the vessels imported from Greece (Fig. 150). Athenian art, whether expressed in architecture, literature or painting and design, reached its zenith during the fifth century; and the painted pottery

150. A Greek amphora found at Samaria

151. A silver bowl of the Persian period like examples found in Palestine; found on Cyprus

produced is some of the most beautiful the human race has ever made. Beginning about 500 B.C. or shortly before, people all along the coastlands of Asia began to buy these coveted objects from Greek traders, and fragments are to be found in the ruins of the homes of almost every well-to-do family (note also the Greek lamp, Fig. 155b).

A flourishing trade with South Arabia existed and found an outlet along the southern coastland of Palestine. This we know from the discovery of small limestone altars of incense. They are square blocks of limestone with four short legs and a shallow trough on top. The sides are elaborately decorated with drawings of desert life, especially palm trees, camels, wild goats, wild donkeys and antelopes. Similar objects have been found in South Arabia, in one of which remnants of a fragrant incense were found. Later altars of the same type bear lists of different kinds of incense on them. South Arabia was the primary source of the best incense, and at this time commerce with Syria-Palestine and Egypt was at its height. Caravan stations dotted the whole long, 1500-mile route from the country of spices to the Mediterranean. The Arab conquests of Edom and southern Palestine had opened the door wider to this trade than ever before.

Finally, we may mention among the objects of art some extraordinarily beautiful and delicate silver vessels of the age which have been discovered at Gezer and Sharuhen (Tell el-Far'ah) in southern Palestine. Typical is a type of fluted silver bowl and dipper, the latter having a handle in the shape of an undraped maiden (cf. Fig. 151). Art of this type seems to have been typical of the whole Persian empire and to have had its center in Syria. In earlier years Canaanites had expended some of their finest artistic energy on ivory-carving. Now ivory had become scarce; herds of elephants no longer ran wild along the upper Euphrates. It is probable, therefore, that these silver objects represent one of the fresh directions to which artists had turned.

EXILES IN MESOPOTAMIA AND EGYPT

The prophet Ezekiel was one of the exiles in Babylonia who lived in or near the town of Tel-abib on the river Chebar. The latter was one of the large irrigation canals; the Babylonians called it Kabar. We do not know precisely where Tel-abib was, but the name is good Babylonian, *til-abubu*, and meant " Mound of the Flood ". During this time towns with names beginning *til* (Heb. *tel*, for " tell " or mound of the debris of previous occupation) were very common, for many old tells, long unoccupied, were being resettled.

The one city in Babylonia which we know from excavation to have had a Jewish colony was Nippur, southeast of Babylon. This city was unearthed by an American expedition from the University of

Pennsylvania between 1889 and 1900, and work there was begun again in 1948 by the Oriental Institute of the University of Chicago and the University Museum of Philadelphia. The most important discovery of the first expedition was the scribal quarter of the city in which most of the 30,000 clay tablets or documents recovered were found. Over 2000 of them, dating between 2500 and 1500 B.C., preserve a part of the literature of the ancient Sumerian culture, which was Babylonia's classic period.[11] In another part of the city over 700 tablets of the 5th century B.C. were discovered; these turned out to be the archives of a great Babylonian firm of bankers and brokers, the firm of Murashu Sons. One of its functions was to serve as the agent of the Persian government in collecting the taxes of the area. In its archives large numbers of personal names appear which reveal the great mixture of peoples that existed in the city and its environs. Of most interest to us here is the large number of Hebrew names in the documents. There thus can be no doubt that a considerable number of the exiles from Judah had been settled in this area and had probably followed the advice of Jeremiah who had told them to seek the welfare of the city where they were sent, to pray for it and to settle quietly there for a long stay (Jer. 29 : 1–14). We may also infer that while the returned exiles were attempting to rebuild Jerusalem, others stayed in Babylonia and prospered. Indeed, many inscribed Hebrew bowls suggest that a colony of Jews lived in Nippur for centuries.[12]

In Egypt the evidence for Jewish settlement comes from the Elephantine Papyri, discovered on an island in the Nile at the first cataract on the country's southern border. The first groups of these papyrus documents were purchased from natives and published by British and German scholars between 1903 and 1911. Another group came to light only recently in the Brooklyn Museum (Fig. 152). It had been purchased by an American, Charles Edwin Wilbour, in 1893 while he was spending the winter on the Nile in a sailing vessel. He died in 1896 without revealing his discovery, and the papyri were found in a trunk when his antiquities were given

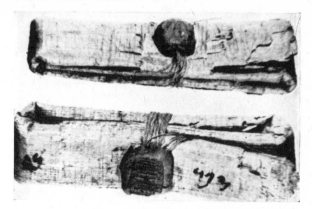

152. Unopened, sealed papyrus documents from Elephantine

to the Brooklyn Museum at the death of his daughter.[13]

During the 5th century Elephantine was a fortress named Yeb which was garrisoned by a colony of Jews who had erected a temple there. The Persian satrap or governor of Egypt during the second half of the century was a man named Arsham (or Arsames). From recently published letters written by him and his officials we learn that he was absent from Egypt in Babylon and Susa between 410 and 408 B.C., and that during his absence there were disturbances in Egypt.[14] In the Elephantine archives of the Jewish colony we have a copy of a letter sent by the priests of the Jewish temple at Yeb to Bagoas, the governor of Judah, telling him that the temple has been destroyed and asking his aid in having it rebuilt. The letter was written in November 407 B.C. and says that in July 410 B.C., when Arsames had left Egypt, the priests of a local Egyptian temple conspired with a " wretch " named Vidaranag to raze and burn the rival Jewish temple. It was an old and honored building, dating " back in the days of the kingdom of Egypt ", before the Persian Cambyses had conquered the country: that is, before 525 B.C. The Jewish priests complain that they had written to Johanan, the high priest of the Jerusalem temple (Neh. 12 : 22–3), but they received no answer. They have also

---

[11] Publication of this important material has only recently been undertaken by S. N. Kramer. See, e.g., his *Sumerian Mythology*, Philadelphia, 1944.
[12] See H. V. Hilprecht, *Explorations in Bible Lands During the 19th Century* (Philadelphia, 1903), pp. 289 ff., especially pp. 408–10.

[13] For this story and for an excellent review of the content and significance of all the documents, see Emil G. Kraeling, " New Light on the Elephantine Colony ", *The Biblical Archaeologist*, Vol. XV, No. 3 (Sept. 1953), pp. 50–67. Basic references for further reading are there listed. See also by the same author, *The Brooklyn Museum Aramaic Papyri*, New Haven, 1953.
[14] See G. R. Driver, *Aramaic Documents of the Fifth Century*, Oxford, 1954.

written to Delaiah and Shelemiah, the sons of Sanballat, governor of Samaria.

An undated memorandum would indicate that answers were received from both Delaiah and Bagoas, who advised that a petition be addressed directly to Arsames about the matter. A copy of this petition has been recovered, signed by five Jews who say they are property-owners in the fortress. It carefully states that no animal sacrifice will be offered, if permission is given for the re-building of the temple, " but (only) incense, meal-offering, [and drink-offering] ".[15] As to why the Jewish community at Elephantine were careful to state that no animals were to be sacrificed there if the temple was erected again, we do not know. One suggestion has been to the effect that Arsames as a Zoroastrian by religion might react more favorably to the request if this promise were made, because his religion disliked the idea of profaning fire by contact with dead bodies. In view of the known Persian tolerance in religious matters, how-ever, this suggestion does not commend itself. It is much more likely that the Jews had been advised to make this compromise in order not to rouse opposition from Jerusalem and from the com-missioner of Jewish affairs in the chancery of Arsames. The " Passover Papyrus " of 419 B.C., some years earlier, was a letter to the community from such a Jewish commissioner, stating that Arsames was ordering the Passover to be celebrated at Yeb according to certain precise regulations. These regulations accord with Pentateuchal law, which suggests that the order of Arsames was an attempt to secure uniformity in Jewish practice under pressure from the priesthood in Jerusalem. At any rate, we know from documents in the Brook-lyn Museum, that the temple was indeed rebuilt; the Elephantine compromise was, therefore, effective.

The very existence of a Jewish temple in Egypt certainly points to a type of Jewish worship which the Jerusalem priests at this time would have con-sidered heterodox. After the reform of King Josiah in 622 B.C., it was considered unlawful for animal sacrifices to be made on any altar except that in Jerusalem. Further indication of heterodoxy is to be found in one of the Elephantine papyri which list the contributors and their contributions to the Egyptian temple. In the final reckoning one portion is set aside for the worship of *Yahu* (the name of the God of Israel as it was spelled by these Jews),

a second portion for a diety named *Ishumbethel*, and a third for *Anathbethel*.[16] The second of these divine names means " Name of the House of God ". The third refers either to the Canaanite fertility goddess, Anath, or else it means " Sign of the House of God ". Another document makes refer-ence to *Anath-Yahu*. This, when taken with *Anathbethel*, seems to suggest that *bethel* (" House of God ") was used as a divine name and a sub-stitute for *Yahu*, just as it was applied to other deities at the time by pagans. Still another docu-ment mentions *Herembethel*, perhaps " Sacredness of the House of God."

The interpretation of these divine names has caused much discussion among scholars. One view is simply that though the Jews at Elephantine worshipped *Yahu* (Yahweh) as the national God, they borrowed other deities from the Canaanite and Aramean environment and worshipped them also. It is more probable, however, that these Jews were somewhat more sophisticated in their religious outlook than this view would suggest. Thus all of the names could be interpreted as a personifying or a giving of separate existence to certain qualities or aspects of Yahweh. A move-ment toward this type of thing had been under way for some time in the pagan religions, and is especi-ally clear in the conception of the Word which issues from a deity's mouth. The manner of speaking, though scarcely the " sophisticated " thought, is illustrated in Isa. 40:8: " the word of our God will stand forever ". In any case, the Jews at Elephantine were developing a somewhat questionable type of Jewish faith under pagan influence.

The documents may also be said to give general indication of the effect which the re-establishment of Judah was having on the Jews of the Persian empire. From the Books of Ezra and Nehemiah we infer that during the second half of the 5th cen-tury certain Jews in Babylon had been able to reach the ear of the Persian king with plans for the reformation of Jewish life. Thus Ezra was ap-pointed as a high commissioner with full power to reform Jewish religious affairs according to " the law of your God, which is in your hand " and to set up an independent judiciary to settle Jewish legal affairs (Ezra 7:11-26). The law in Ezra's hand is taken by scholars to be an edition of the Pentateuchal law, perhaps even the Pentateuch in

[15] See J. B. Pritchard, ed., *Ancient Near Eastern Texts*, p. 492.

[16] *Ibid.*, p. 491.

its final form, which Jewish experts had compiled from old material in Babylon. In any event, with such a movement under way, we can understand the decree to the Elephantine Jews about the keeping of the Passover and also the failure of the Elephantine colony to obtain the right of burnt offerings.

One final observation about the Elephantine papyri is necessary. It was noted above that the high priest in Jerusalem about 410 B.C., when the Egyptian temple was destroyed, was Johanan. He is the one who failed to reply to a letter asking for help in rebuilding the structure. When Nehemiah returned to Jerusalem about 445 B.C., the high priest was Eliashib (Neh. 3 : 1). His successors in order, according to Neh. 12 : 22, were Joiada, Johanan and Jaddua. The third is the last high priest whom the editor of I–II Chronicles, Ezra and Nehemiah knows, and with him the history recorded in the Old Testament ends. When Ezra returned to Jerusalem, one of his first tasks was to secure attendance of all Judeans at a provincial assembly. He went to the chamber of Johanan (or Jehohanan), and the proclamation calling for the assembly was issued from that place (Ezra 10 : 6–8). Many scholars believe that Johanan must have been high priest at the time, because such a directive would only be issued from the office of that official. Yet Johanan was subsequent to Nehemiah's time, as we have seen ; and if in Ezra 10 : 6–8 he was high priest, then Ezra must have followed Nehemiah to Jerusalem instead of preceding him, as the Chronicler assumed. In that case, Ezra 7–10 must be considered out of place and probably to be inserted at the end of Nehemiah. For this and other reasons, perhaps a majority of scholars today believe that Ezra came to Jerusalem either in the seventh year of Artaxerxes II (Ezra 7 : 7 ; 398 B.C.), not of Artaxerxes I (458 B.C.), or sometime after 432 B.C., that is, at the end of the reign of Artaxerxes I.[17]

Among the many other things to be learned from the study of the Elephantine and other documents of the period, there is one technical matter of first importance. That is the increased knowledge of the Aramaic language of the 5th century which this material has made possible. That language was the official tongue of the Persian empire and the one which most people between Babylon and Egypt then spoke. Before these discoveries the Aramaic portions of the Book of Ezra (4 : 8–6 : 18 ; 7 : 12–26) including transcripts of what purport to be official documents of the Persian government, had no contemporary witness by which they could be validated and understood. Now, however, we are able to see that the Aramaic of Ezra is precisely that of its age, while the government documents are of the general type which we have become accustomed to associate with the Persian regime.

PALESTINE IN THE HELLENISTIC AGE

The Persian empire fell to the Greek conqueror, Alexander the Great, in 333–331 B.C., but that ruler's death in 323 B.C. brought an end to his dream of uniting east and west in one great brotherhood, dominated by Greek culture. The empire was divided between his generals, and Palestine became the border country between the Seleucid dynasty of Syria and the Ptolemies of Egypt. Throughout the 3rd century until 198 B.C. it was controlled by Egypt. Then the Seleucids seized the country and attempted to unite it with Syria under a Hellenistic culture, with a mixed Greek and Syrian religion, Greek language, literature, sports and dress. The movement culminated under Antiochus IV or Epiphanes (175–163 B.C.), who attempted to destroy Judaism and convert the Temple into a place where the pagan god, Zeus, was worshipped. This initiated the Jewish Maccabean revolt, and turned the 2nd century B.C. into one of bloody turmoil. The period of Jewish independence ended in 63 B.C. when the Romans took control of the country.

The archaeological discoveries which are to be fitted into this historical framework are by no means comprehensive. Such information as we have comes for the most part from five cities. The first of these is Marisa, the Old Testament Mareshah (Tell Sandaḥannah). The great Judean mound of Lachish, which in the Persian period had been the residence of the governor of Edom or Arabia (Idumea), was now virtually deserted. Its place in control of its area had been taken by Marisa. There about the mid-3rd century a colony of people from Sidon in Phoenicia had settled and buried their dead in a series of remarkable and highly decorated tombs. Elaborate painted de-

---

[17] Artaxerxes I reigned from 464 to 423 B.C. The more important kings who succeeded him were Darius II (423–404 B.C.), and Artaxerxes II (404–358 B.C.). For a review of the difficult problem of the order of Ezra and Nehemiah, see R. A. Bowman, *The Interpreter's Bible*, Vol. III, especially pp. 561 ff. and 624, with references there cited.

153. Niche in the tomb of Apollophanes at Marisa

154. One of the round towers at Samaria erected early in the Hellenistic Period to strengthen the old Israelite fortifications

signs and scenes covered the walls (Fig. 153) together with numerous inscriptions in Greek and Aramaic. The personal names are of Greek, Phoenician and Edomite (Idumean) origin. The plan of the whole city during the 2nd century has been laid bare, and it is one which is most unusual for Asia. It was built like a well-planned Greek town, with streets running at right angles and forming blocks of houses, while the marketplace or agora next to the gate was rectangular, open at one end, with carefully built shops around three sides. Marisa is important, then, because it is a vivid illustration of the process of hellenization which was then going on throughout Syria, Palestine and lower Egypt.

A second town of importance in this period is Beth-zur, north of Hebron, which was a scene of several battles during the Maccabean wars of the 2nd century. As a result of excavation in 1931 we now know that a fortress was built there, probably during the Persian period when the relations between Judah and Idumea were tense. This was rebuilt into a much more elaborate structure by Judas Maccabaeus between 165 and 163 B.C. as an outpost against the Syrians. It was captured, however, and presumably destroyed and rebuilt on a Hellenistic plan by the pagan general, Bacchides, about 161 B.C. Some 250 coins of the age were discovered in the town, but most interesting were the scores of Rhodian jar-handles. The latter were from wine-jars which were used for shipping Aegean wine into Asia. The foreign mercenaries who garrisoned Beth-zur may have been Greek, but whatever their nationality they certainly preferred this imported wine to the native product of local vintage.

At Samaria, our third city, some 2000 Rhodian and other Greek jar-handles have been found, for

this too was a place where mercenary troops under Syrian command were stationed. In fact, from the 3rd century onwards Samaria was a pagan city with a population which was largely foreign. In the Persian period the family of the governor, Sanballat, was at least formally Yahwist in religion, but by the Hellenistic age the former capital of Israel had entered on a career of pagan brilliance. About the time of Alexander the Great the old Israelite fortification walls had been repaired and strengthened with the addition of several, beautifully built, round towers (Fig. 154). About 150 B.C. a new wall around the summit of the mound was erected, evidently as a defence against the Maccabees. Remains of a small temple of about the third century have also been recovered; it was probably destroyed during the Jewish wars between 150 and 100 B.C.

The excavations at the fourth city, Shechem, by the Drew-McCormick Expedition, beginning in 1956, have revealed four strata, extensive occupation and the rebuilding of the old city between ca. 330 and 100 B.C. After centuries had past, the old tell was again inhabited by people as numerous as those who lived there in the city's great age in the past. How and why had this come about? The various accounts in Josephus and other ancient sources are somewhat ambiguous, and scholars have not agreed on how to interpret them. Yet to account for our present knowledge of Shechem, it would appear that the evidence must be interpreted somewhat as follows:

When Alexander the Great appeared in lower Syria and Palestine, laying siege to Tyre in 332 B.C., the Samaritans were particularly anxious to gain his favor and the approval of their newly erected temple on Mt. Gerizim. They even provided a contingent of 8,000 Samaritan soldiers whom Alexander later settled as a garrison in Egypt. Subsequently, for a reason unknown, the Samaritans murdered the governor of eastern Syria and northern Palestine. Alexander responded quickly to this first act of rebellion, laid siege to Samaria, probably early in the year 331 B.C., and turned the city over for settlement to a garrison of his Greek soldiers. The Samaritans, deprived of their capital city, then rebuilt Shechem and for some two hundred years made it the rival of Jerusalem. This situation ended when John Hyrcanus from Jerusalem destroyed the city, probably during his conquest of Samaria in 107 B.C. In any event, the series of coins recovered at the site ends at 110 B.C. A city was never again erected on the old tell, though a small remnant of the Samaritans still exist in nearby Nablus, a city founded by the Roman emperor Vespasian in A.D. 72.

Finally, the great city of Gezer, in the foothills southeast of Joppa, was fortified by the Maccabees about 140 B.C. It apparently had a large Jewish population at this time, and in rocks around the city the legend, " Boundary of Gezer ", had been cut in Hebrew or Aramaic characters, perhaps referring to the limits of a Sabbath day's journey. Both Gezer and Beth-zur were virtually abandoned by about 100 B.C. We are not sure of the reason, unless the expansion of the territory controlled by the Jews had made it unnecessary to maintain garrisons there. On the other hand, the pagan cities of Samaria and Marisa were destroyed by the Jews when John Hyrcanus (135–104 B.C.) seized a large part of the territory that once belonged to David and attempted to Judaize it.

As we draw near to the period of the New Testament, then, the major impression one receives from the excavations in Palestine is this : the cultural changes which have swept across the country have been so extensive and profound since the destruction of Jerusalem that nothing now appears the same. Except for the landscape there are few reminders remaining of the time when Israel controlled the whole country. The things in common use, such as lamps, utensils and jewelry, have all changed radically. The old Canaanite and Israelite saucer lamp (Fig. 139d) gave way in the fourth century to the new and more economical Greek lamp (Fig. 155b), and the local potters during the third and second centuries changed their

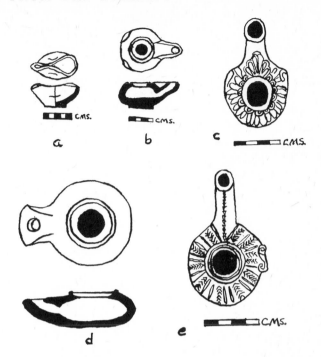

155. Lamps of the Persian, Hellenistic, and Roman periods ; they were made from Greek models, except a which dates from the 2nd and 1st centuries B.C. The earliest of the imitations is b, from the late 5th and 4th century; the latest is d which comes from the period between the 1st century B.C. and the 2nd century A.D. Nos. c and e are typical of the 1st and 2nd centuries B.C.

styles in keeping with the fashions prevailing in Athens and Corinth (Fig. 155c and e). Several pottery shapes survived from the Persian period, but the technique used in making them had changed. Finer prepared clays were used and evidently fired at higher temperatures. The side-walls of the vessels were now thinner, more delicate and brittle. Architecture became increasingly hellenized and the country was filled with foreigners, a few of whom were to become famous as philosophers and scholars. The Jewish community itself was divided in its sympathies and many Jews were by no means sympathetic to the Maccabean revolt. The dispersion of the Jews over the world continued, and the first translation of the Hebrew Bible into Greek took place during the third and second centuries in Alexandria, Egypt, a city which at that time was the intellectual center of the world. Palestine as the bridge between Asia and Egypt was at the crossroads of the world, and the archaeological remains are, at this time especially, an eloquent testimony to the fact.

THE OLD TESTAMENT

During the period under survey in this chapter the literature of the Old Testament was brought virtually into the form in which we now have it. Even the idea of a canon of sacred literature came into being, though its exact limits were not yet precisely defined. Because of the large number of Greek-speaking Jews in Egypt a sacred collection of the writings was translated into Greek in Alexandria during the 3rd and 2nd centuries B.C. In this way what is called the Septuagint came into being. In general its contents are the same as those of the present Hebrew Bibles, except that additional material, composed between the 4th and 2nd centuries B.C., was included. By 100 A.D. what was considered marginal material was omitted from the Palestinian canon, but the Early Christian Church soon came to use the Greek Bible almost exclusively, and to this day the limits of the canon as defined by the Alexandrian rabbis are observed in the Bible used by the Greek Orthodox Churches and with certain exclusions in that of the Roman Catholic Church. Protestants, on the other hand, returned to the Palestinian canon during the Reformation of the 16th century.

Most scholars are of the opinion that when Ezra returned to Judah from Babylon in order to reform the Jewish community " according to the law of your God, which is in your hand " (Ezra 7 : 14), he was taking with him an edition of the Pentateuch which had been prepared by the exiled priests. It is assumed that the Pentateuch, virtually as we now have it, was finished by his time. With the work of the Chronicler in the early 4th century the whole collection of historical material was completed. By the fourth century also it is increasingly apparent that the canon of the prophets and the books of Psalms, Proverbs and Job had reached virtually their final form. This does not mean that the text was completely stabilized by that time, but it does mean that the books were in existence and were probably already considered as belonging to a special canonical collection. By the time of Alexander the Great, then, we have only the books of Ecclesiastes, Esther, Song of Songs and Daniel left to be accounted for.

The service which archaeology is rendering the study of Old Testament literature is three-fold. (1) It has occasionally revealed literary parallels and background to biblical works. (2) It has unearthed ancient inscriptions in such numbers as to enable scholars to trace the history of the Hebrew language and script. (3) It has uncovered ancient biblical manuscripts which have revolutionized our study of the Hebrew text.

Pagan peoples of the day produced no literature which can be compared precisely to the historical and prophetic writings of the Old Testament, including the Book of Daniel. These are unique as literary forms and no background for them can be demonstrated. On the other hand, the study of ancient poetry, particularly that of the Canaanites in the scribal library at Ras Shamra in Syria, has been of invaluable assistance in the study of certain Hebrew poetic forms, vocabulary and allusions. Indeed, an occasional Psalm, like the 29th, was probably an adaptation of a Canaanite original. This study together with other converging lines of evidence has reversed the tendency on the part of earlier generations of scholars to date the composition of most of the Psalms in the post-Exilic period, some of them as late as the Maccabean age of the second century. Present evidence suggests that none of the Psalms are Maccabean and that most of them are pre-Exilic. The collection as we have it, however, is an edition completed by the Judean community of the 5th and 4th centuries.

The one book in the Bible that shows a closer relation to pagan literature than any other is the Book of Proverbs. The type of epigrammatical proverb which it contains was derived from pagan wisemen, and the introduction of the wisdom school of thought into Israel is said to have been the work of Solomon (cf. I Kings 4 : 29–34 ; Prov 1 : 1 ; 10 : 1 ; 25 : 1). In the past the tendency among leading scholars has been to assume that Proverbs was the product of a post-Exilic school of higher Hebrew culture. Today, however, we know that gnomic literature was one of the most international and ancient of the literary forms of the biblical world. In Mesopotamia the earliest proverbs are in Sumerian and undoubtedly come from sources in the 3rd millennium B.C. References to wisdom in Canaanite religious literature and proverbs quoted by Canaanite kings to the Egyptian Pharaoh during the 14th century B.C. reveal the Syro-Palestinian interest in the subject before the time of Israel. One such Canaanite proverb is as follows : " If ants are smitten, they do not receive (the smiting passively) but they bite the hand of the man who smites them " (cf. two ancient Hebrew proverbs about ants in Prov. 6 : 6 and

30 : 25).[18] Egyptian wisdom has long been known; some of it is very close in type to the material in Proverbs. Indeed, it has long been suspected that a relation exists between the Egyptian Wisdom of Amen-em-opet [19] and Prov. 22 : 17–24 : 22, though the precise relationship is difficult to prove. The biblical Proverbs, then, represents a collection of moral insights, for the most part, which had been discovered by pagans and cultivated by a certain school in Israel. The book cannot be said to have been composed at any one time; it probably contains material from many sources and different ages, though the final editing of the book may well have been done as late as the 5th or 4th century B.C.

The Book of Job has no close parallel in form, style or penetration of thought. Yet its theme, the problem of the good man who suffers, is a very old one. That this is so may be seen in the book itself where the personal names used belong, as we now know, to the nomenclature of the 2nd millennium B.C. In addition, there are several Mesopotamian treatments of the problem, the most famous of which is *Ludlul bel Nemeqi* ("I will praise the lord of wisdom").[20] A still earlier Sumerian treatment from the archives at Nippur has recently been discovered, though it is fragmentary and as yet unpublished. Thus the biblical Job belongs to a long sequence of discussions of the problem of evil. When its final form was reached in Israel we do not know. The setting of the great poetry within the framework of a prose prologue and epilogue, however, was probably done in Judah between the 6th and 4th centuries.

The Book of Ecclesiastes is probably to be dated by language and content in the 3rd century B.C., but thus far no real archaeological parallel to it has been discovered. Skeptical poems of an earlier date are known from Egypt and Mesopotamia, but the temper of Ecclesiastes seems more influenced by a Greek atmosphere of thought than by Near Eastern.

The Song of Songs is a collection of love lyrics probably edited in the Persian period, judging from the presence within it of certain Persian words. The songs themselves, however, are much older than this and were probably derived from Egyptian and Canaanite lyrics. The closest parallels are known from Egypt, dating from the period between 1300 and 1000 B.C. There, as in the biblical book, the songs are alternately placed in the mouths of the lover and the beloved who address each other as "brother" and "sister".[21] The geographical allusions in the Song, however, indicate that its authors are Israelite.[22] The archaeological discoveries in Egypt have simply revealed the existence of a type of ancient literature to which the Israelite book is related.

While the purpose and date of Daniel has long been established,[23] the date and original character of Esther remain without archaeological confirmation. In type the book resembles the apocryphal stories of Tobit and Judith from the 3rd and 2nd centuries B.C., though it may belong to a slightly earlier period around 300 B.C.

A discussion of the role of archaeology in illuminating the history of the Hebrew language, and the script with which it was written, would be too technical to include here. Before 1925 the student of Hebrew was generally trained in classical Arabic as the most important cognate language. While Arabic is still very important for vocabulary and verbal system, today the student receives a far more basic training in Northwest Semitic because it is now possible to reconstruct the earlier stages of the Hebrew language from contemporary sources. This is done through the study of Hebrew, Aramaic and Phoenician inscriptions, and particularly Ugaritic, the language of the Canaanite religious documents found at Ras Shamra in northern Syria. The evolution of the Hebrew script can now be traced with considerable accuracy from about 1500 B.C. to modern times. Our knowledge of this subject has accumulated at such a rapid rate that an expert can now give approximate dates to the documents discovered from the way in which the letters were formed. Of special interest for our period is the fact that by the early 2nd century B.C. we now know that a special Hebrew book-hand had already come into existence. This had been developed by Jewish scribes in the careful copying of the sacred texts, and further illustrates the

---

[18] W. F. Albright, "An Archaic Hebrew Proverb in an Amarna Letter from Central Palestine", *Bulletin of the American Schools of Oriental Research*, No. 89 (Feb. 1943), pp. 29–32.

[19] For translation see J. A. Wilson in J. B. Pritchard, ed., *Ancient Near Eastern Texts*, pp. 421–4.

[20] See R. H. Pfeiffer in *ibid.*, pp. 434–7.

[21] See J. A. Wilson in *ibid.*, pp. 467–9.

[22] See above, p. 152, for the reference to Tirzah which suggests that at least one portion of the book was composed as early as about 900 B.C.

[23] The historical allusions from the 3rd and 2nd century are so detailed that the book is dated about 165 B.C., late in the reign of Antiochus Epiphanes (that is, after he had defiled the Temple in 168 or 167 B.C. but before its cleansing by the Jews in Dec. of 164 B.C.). The stories about Daniel in the first part of the book were probably much older than this time, but archaeology has not been able to be of much assistance in fixing them historically.

intensive study of Scripture that had already come into being.[24]

THE DISCOVERY OF OLD TESTAMENT MANUSCRIPTS

The Hebrew manuscript used by most scholars today, when they read the Old Testament in its original language, dates from the 10th century A.D. Two portions of the Hebrew Bible, one in London and the other in Cairo, date from the preceding century. The oldest manuscript in the possession of the Samaritan sect at Nablus in Palestine dates from A.D. 655–6. Before 1947 these were the oldest manuscripts of the Old Testament in Hebrew that were known, except for the Nash Papyrus. The latter is a single leaf found in Egypt, dating from about 100 B.C. It contains the Ten Commandments and the *Shema* (Deut. 6 : 4–5) and was never a part of a longer scroll but was a separate sheet used in teaching or in worship.

Since the medieval Hebrew manuscripts that we have represent one textual tradition for the most part, serious work in the textual criticism of the Old Testament has been difficult and not very productive. In order to get behind the present standardized textual tradition scholars had to make use of the various translations, particularly that in the Greek Bible. The great 4th century A.D. manuscripts of the latter, Codex Vaticanus and Codex Sinaiticus, were for a long time the oldest copies of the Old Testament known. Shortly before the last war, however, the Chester Beatty and the John H. Scheide biblical papyri, found in Egypt, came to the attention of scholars. They contain portions of the Old Testament in Greek from the 2nd or 3rd centuries A.D. Two small fragments of Deuteronomy in Greek from the same period as the Nash Papyrus were published shortly after the war.

While these and other manuscripts of the Old Testament are much older than the great Hebrew documents that we have, it has been difficult to use them extensively in order to correct the Hebrew. There are many variations between the Greek and the Hebrew texts, for example, but how can we be certain of the Greek's reliability? Was the text which the translator followed a good one? How many of the variations really show textual differ-

156. Cave 4 at Qumran, illustrating the difficult access

ences and how many simply exhibit the freedom taken by the translator? The difficulty in deciding such issues had gradually led scholars to more and more dependence on the reliability of the Hebrew text and less and less inclination to make emendations on the basis of the Greek.[25]

Our whole outlook is undergoing change, however, as the result of the phenomenal discovery of the Dead Sea Scrolls, beginning in 1947. In the spring of that year an Arab shepherd, named Mohammad Dib of the Taʿamireh tribe, was looking for a lost sheep in the cliffs at the northwestern edge of the Dead Sea. Idly throwing a rock, he saw it enter a hole and heard it strike against something which shattered. After getting reinforcements from his tribe, he climbed through the hole and found a small cave which contained jars, broken pottery and leather scrolls. During the months which followed, the scrolls came to the attention of

[24] For a recent survey of the study of the Hebrew language in its historical background, see W. J. Moran, S.J., in *The Bible and the Ancient Near East* (G. E. Wright, Editor), pp. 54–72. For the evolution of the manner of writing (paleography), see Frank M. Cross, Jr., *ibid.*, pp. 133–202 ; and for the early period *Bulletin of the American Schools of Oriental Research*, No. 134 (April, 1954), pp. 15–24.

[25] See Harry M. Orlinsky, " The Septuagint—its Use in Textual Criticism ", *The Biblical Archaeologist*, Vol. IX, No. 2 (May 1946), pp. 21–42.

157. The Isaiah manuscript found in Cave I at Qumran, opened at Isa. 39–40. Note the corrections in the text, the manner in which the roll was sewn together from leather sheets, and the darkened exterior caused by ancient usage

scholars in the American School of Oriental Research and the Hebrew University in Jerusalem.

This discovery is that of Cave I in the area of Wadi Qumran, and the manuscripts of that cave and of others subsequently found (Fig. 156) are probably to be reckoned as the most important discovery ever made in the field of biblical archaeology. The first scroll found in 1947 is that of the complete Book of Isaiah in a remarkable state of preservation (Fig. 157). Among the other scrolls there was one containing the last third of the same book and also a commentary on Habakkuk.

Since 1949 scholar and bedouin have been vying with one another in the search for still more manuscripts, with the indefatigable bedouin having by far the greatest success. As a result, several baskets of fragments have been excavated from the fine dust of several caves in the area (Fig. 158).[26] The largest group of manuscript fragments was found by the bedouin in Cave 4 of Qumran (Fig. 156) in 1952 and was supplemented by more fragments from the same cave, found when it was excavated by the Jordan Department of Antiquities during the fall of the same year. In all, some eleven caves of Qumran have yielded important material, while other caves in the Wadi Murabba'at, some twelve miles south of Qumran, have given up manuscripts of a slightly later date, mostly from the time of the Second Jewish Revolt in A.D. 132–5.

The discoveries at Qumran are the fragmentary remains of an extensive library which once belonged to the Essenes, a Jewish sect which lived there during the time of Christ. They retired to this area in order to form a community of the New Covenant, presumably during the 2nd century B.C., but they were forced to leave during the First Jewish Revolt against Rome about A.D. 68, when they were besieged by the Romans and their center

[26] For the story in more detail, see Frank M. Cross, Jr. "The Manuscripts of the Dead Sea Caves", *The Biblical Archaeologist*, Vol. XVII, No. 1 (Feb. 1954), pp. 2–21; John C. Trever, "The Discovery of the Scrolls", *ibid.*, Vol. XI, No. 3 (Sept. 1948), pp. 46–57; and the various articles in *ibid.*, Vol. XII, No. 2 (May 1949); and especially now the eloquent account by one intimately associated with the project, Frank M. Cross, Jr., *The Ancient Library of Qumran*, 1st edn., New York, 1958; revised ed. Doubleday Anchor Books, 1961.

158. Tables of manuscript fragments from Qumran sorted for study in the Palestine Museum in Jerusalem

(Fig. 180) was destroyed. We shall turn to them again in the next chapter when we describe their beliefs and practices, and their probable influence on the New Testament. At this point it is sufficient to note that the fragments of their library which remain must all date before A.D. 68.

A minority of the manuscript fragments which remain are from biblical rolls. Most of them are from a large number of non-biblical works, some already known but most hitherto unknown. Of exceptional interest is the fact that already by the 2nd–1st centuries B.C. commentaries on the Scriptures were being written. These include expositions on Isaiah, the Psalms and some of the minor prophets. The period in question is shown by these discoveries to be one of great literary activity, of intense study of the sacred writings and of composition of a great variety of theological and apocalyptic works under the direct or indirect inspiration of that study.

The biblical manuscripts can be identified quickly by the careful book-hand in which they were written and by the fine quality and color of the leather used. The leather sheets were sewed together to make a roll, the columns for the text planned and measured, and the lines of each column ruled. The letters were then written as though hanging from the line. Occasionally a word or whole phrase was omitted and the same scribe, or a later one, would fill in the missing portion between the lines or sometimes in the margin. So many manuscript fragments have been found that it has become possible to identify different scribal hands and to observe that the same hand had copied several books.

Portions of over one hundred scrolls of Old Testament books have been found. Every book of the Old Testament is represented, except for the Book of Esther. The most popular for study were, as we should expect, Deuteronomy, Isaiah and the Psalms, and evidence for a dozen or so scrolls of each has been discovered. By studying the evolution of the script (that is, by the discipline called " paleography ") it has been possible to arrange the fragments in the approximate order in which they were written. For example, the earliest biblical manuscripts thus far discovered are fragments of a scroll of Samuel (4Q Sam[b]) and one of Jeremiah (4Q Jer[a]), dating not far from 200 B.C. These may have belonged to the original library brought to Qumran by the Essenes and from which later manuscripts were copied. From the middle of the second century there are fragments of Ecclesiastes. The great Isaiah scroll from the first cave (1Q Is[a]) is dated about 100 B.C., whereas the other Isaiah manuscript from the same cave (1Q Is[b]) was copied in the late 1st century B.C. From the same period as the latter is a most important and quite extensive scroll of I–II Samuel (4Q Sam[a]), whereas still another portion of Samuel comes from the first half of the century (4Q Sam[c]). From the 1st century A.D. is a fragment of Daniel (4Q Dan[b]), whereas another portion of Daniel (4Q Dan[a]) was copied toward the end of the 1st century B.C. and still another (from 1Q) is presumably from the early part of the same century.[27] Such a sampling of the material illustrates the chronological spread of the documents, as they now appear to the staff of experts who are studying them.

That the Book of Daniel was found in at least three different copies is very interesting. Indeed, 4Q Dan[a] dates within one and a half centuries of the time when the book was written, while the fragments of a still earlier scroll from the first cave would appear to date within a century of that time. To possess fragments of an Old Testament book which date within 100 years of the time of composition is something that no one had dared to hope for in the field of Old Testament study. The only thing comparable is the Rylands fragment of the Gospel of John, which most scholars date within half a century of the book's composition.

The Book of Ecclesiastes has been dated in the past by most scholars to about 200 B.C. The presence at Qumran of a scroll of that work, dating from the mid-2nd century and written in the book-hand and on the leather used for other biblical books, would suggest that it must have been originally composed much earlier than 200 B.C. Similarly, some scholars have believed that the Book of

Isaiah was not completed in its present form much before 200 B.C. Yet the great Isaiah scroll from the first cave would lead one to conclude that the final arrangement of the chapters had been completed long before the 2nd century. These and similar arguments are leading scholars to earlier dates for the latest material in the Old Testament, except for the Book of Daniel.

The question arises, however, as to the value of these many fragments for the study of the Old Testament. Except for the Book of Isaiah there is no complete scroll of a biblical work in the whole discovery. The surprising thing is, however, that the scraps from Cave 4 will probably prove of more value in the long run than the complete Isaiah from Cave 1. The reason is that they permit a sampling of the text of all the biblical books, sometimes in more than one scroll per book. While most of the fragments show little significant variation from the received Hebrew text, a number of them illustrate variant textual traditions. Most astonishing are texts which are strikingly similar to the Septuagint. This proves that the Greek translation does indeed rest on a real Hebrew text tradition which was actually known and used in Palestine during and before the time of Christ.

159. Fragments of a remarkable manuscript of I–II Samuel, found in Cave 4 at Qumran. Its text is remarkably similar to that behind the Greek translation

---

[27] These dates are those given the writer by Professor Frank M. Cross, Jr., except for the last mentioned fragment of Daniel, for which see B.A., Vol. XII, No. 2 (May 1949), p. 33.

For example, one of the most important scrolls from Cave 4 is a copy of I–II Samuel (Fig. 159), made not far from the time when Jesus was born (4Q Sam[a]). Portions of twenty-four of the thirty-one chapters of I Samuel are preserved, and of twenty-two of the twenty-four chapters of II Samuel. Now it has long been recognized that the Hebrew text of Samuel was taken from a manuscript which was unusually corrupt, while the Greek translation in many places reads much better and makes better sense. The Qumran scroll in question is so close to the Septuagint that line after line of it can be reconstructed from a few words with a high degree of probability. Each column of the scroll was of a certain width which can be closely calculated. In studying the document the scholar first wrote down a portion of the medieval Hebrew text that is in our Hebrew Bibles; under it he then placed the Hebrew which he had translated back from the Greek; and finally the preserved portion of the Qumran scroll was lined up below that. From a comparison of the three texts and a calculation of the amount of space required for the broken portions of the Qumran document, it was immediately seen that the scroll is very close to the Greek, with only occasional variations. And in a number of the variations it represents a better text than the Greek. In fact, if the complete scroll had been preserved, it would probably have been the most reliable copy of Samuel available. As it is, the fragments we have still make it possible to correct the received Hebrew text in a great number of places with far more confidence than ever before.[28]

The combined evidence from Qumran and Murabba'at suggests that the fixing of an authoritative Hebrew text took place in Palestine between the First and Second Revolts (that is, between A.D. 70 and 135). Before that time variant textual traditions were current, at least in Qumran. Not only did the Essenes possess Hebrew books which are very much like the Septuagint in textual readings, but they even had copies of the Greek Bible itself, for one piece of the Septuagint in leather and several in papyrus have actually been found. It is now impossible any longer to say that in every case the Hebrew Bible is superior to the Greek translation. The value of the latter's readings must be considered seriously in each individual case.

The Qumran discoveries, therefore, are of extraordinary importance, for they enable the scholar to get behind the standardized Hebrew text into a period when the transmission of the text was more fluid and when variant traditions had not yet been eliminated.

---

[28] See provisionally Frank M. Cross, Jr., " A New Qumran Biblical Fragment Related to the Original Hebrew Underlying the Septuagint ", *Bulletin of the American Schools of Oriental Research*, No. 132 (Dec. 1953), pp. 15–26 ; and for a brief summary of importance, see the same author, *The Biblical Archaeologist*, Vol. XVII, No. 1 (Feb. 1954), pp. 17–20; and *The Ancient Library of Qumran*, Chap. IV.

FURTHER READING

There is no one book which adequately treats in detail the range of material summarized briefly in this chapter. References to a variety of individual matters have been placed in the footnotes.

For background in the Persian and Hellenistic periods, see especially Jack Finegan, *Light from the Ancient Past* (Princeton, 1946), pp. 192 ff., and A. T. Olmstead, *History of the Persian Empire* (Chicago, 1948).

For the cultural and religious movements in the Hellenistic period, see especially W. F. Albright, *From the Old Stone Age to Christianity* (Baltimore, 1940), pp. 256–92, and references there cited ; and Martin Noth, *History of Israel* (London and New York, 1958), pp. 288–399.

The best review of the archaeology of Palestine during the Persian and Hellenistic periods is Carl Watzinger, *Denkmäler Palästinas*, Vol. II (Leipzig, 1935), Chap. V, though it needs to be supplemented by more recent information which thus far has not been given a detailed analysis.

For the Dead Sea Scrolls, see especially in the very large literature on the subject two volumes of modest size by men who are members of the international team and who control great quantities of material not yet published : Frank M. Cross, Jr., *The Ancient Library of Qumran* (1st ed., 1958 ; revised ed., Doubleday Anchor Books, 1961) ; and J. T. Milik, *Ten Years of Discovery in the Wilderness of Judaea* (London and Naperville, Ill., *Studies in Biblical Theology*, No. 26, 1959). See also Millar Burrows, *The Dead Sea Scrolls* (New York, 1955) and *More Light on the Dead Sea Scrolls* (New York and London, 1959), also H. H. Rowley, *The Zadokite Fragments and the Dead Sea Scrolls* (Oxford, 1952), which contains a very full bibliography up to the time of publication; A. Dupont-Sommer, *The Jewish Sect of Qumran and the Essenes* (tr. by R. D. Barnett, London, 1954); and the successive issues since 1948 of the following journals: *The Biblical Archaeologist; Bulletin of the American Schools of Oriental Research; and Revue Biblique.*

CHAPTER XIII

PALESTINE IN THE TIME OF CHRIST

" Jesus was born in Bethlehem of Judea in the days of Herod the king " (Matt. 2 : 1).

AFTER the Romans took control of Palestine in 63 B.C., the country never again attained independent status in ancient times. When the Parthians of Mesopotamia threatened to take over Jerusalem in 40 B.C., the Romans gave most of the country into the hands of a man named Herod, who held office as a client-king from 37–4 B.C. Herod was of Idumaean (Edomite) ancestry but formally a Jew by religion because his people were forcibly " converted " by John Hyrcanus in 125 B.C. Actually, however, he was a great believer in Greek culture and his reign is marked by the complete victory of Hellenism over the more conservative tendencies of the Maccabees.

160. Altar and steps of the Temple of Augustus at Samaria

PALESTINE AT THE TIME OF JESUS' BIRTH

The greater part of the territory in the former kingdoms of Israel and Judah was placed under Herod's control, and he promptly set about the task of beautifying and strengthening it, until at the time of his death the country was filled with architectural wonders in the western tradition. As the historian Josephus put it a century later, " there was not any place of his kingdom fit for the purpose that was permitted to be without somewhat that was for Caesar's honor ".[1]

Let us examine the ruins of three cities in particular which Herod the Great transformed by his remarkable building campaign.

The first is Samaria which was completely changed and renovated. During the Maccabean wars it had lost its fortification walls. These had been replaced between 57 and 55 B.C., but the city was far from attaining its former glory. In 37 B.C. Herod married his beloved Mariamne there and seven years later the city was formally given him by Caesar Augustus. It was a fine site for him to fortify in order to strengthen his hold upon the country and at the same time to publicize his gratitude and devotion to Augustus. He settled six

thousand of his war veterans there and renamed the site Sebaste (Augusta), which has remained its name to this day.

Herod's new city wall along the lower slopes of the mound enclosed a very large area: a huge, rather irregular, oval, five-eighths of a mile (one kilometer) in width at its greatest extent. Towers were spaced at intervals along it for defensive purposes; and the stone work appears to be that of local masons. It was an adequate fortification, though not exceptional. The major effort was expended upon the erection of a magnificent temple in honor of Augustus (Fig. 160). Samaria was now a pagan city; and the pagan temple adorning it might be said to be a fitting reminder of the work of Jezebel who eight centuries earlier had lived there in a palace, the ruins of which are beneath the temple. On top of the remains of Israelite and later structures and on a platform extending out over the mound's edge, a large forecourt was built. It was over 225 feet long and almost square. A flight of steps led up to the temple from the court, for the structure was erected on a podium so that it could be seen from a long distance. The temple's rectangular plan with vestibule was typical of the

---

[1] *Wars of the Jews*, Book I, Chap. XXI.

temples of the time, as was also the artificial platform for the court. The building is the most imposing ruin still remaining at Samaria and one can imagine that it once would have been an honor to the Roman emperor, even if it had been erected in Rome itself.

East of the temple, on the other side of the city, was the Forum, a large open square surrounded by shops which was a characteristic feature of every Hellenistic city. This was first erected, probably by Herod, in the 1st century B.C. Apart from the temple, however, the finest remaining ruin of the Herodian period is a stadium, built at the edge of the valley north of the mound, but purposely enclosed within the fortification walls. It was a rectangular peristyle in Doric style: that is, it was enclosed with a stone wall and had a series of columns bearing a roof around the inside of the enclosure. While the arena itself was, of course, open, the spectators could sit or stand in the shade. It was approximately 638 feet long by 190 feet wide —a regulation size in antiquity for a track as large as that used in the Olympic games in Greece (600 Olympic feet in length). A stadium at Miletus in Asia Minor is precisely the same length as this at Samaria, though it is only half as wide. The walls of the enclosure were covered with a heavy coat of plaster, painted in a series of panels, red and yellow alternately, with a dado below of yellow marbling. Scratched in the plaster were numerous crude drawings and inscriptions, the typical doodling expected of spectators in any age. The inscriptions are in Greek, though many of the names are Latin, as we should expect in a city of such mixed population.

The introduction of Greek sports, including running and wrestling, was a comparatively recent phenomenon in Palestine. The stadium at Samaria was a fine one. It was used for centuries, indeed completely rebuilt in Corinthian style about the 2nd century A.D. Yet it is not mentioned in ancient literature as the place where any famous contests were held. On the other hand, we know that Herod was a great lover of athletic games, founding them at Caesarea and Jerusalem. At Caesarea, Josephus tells us, Herod arranged for games to be held every fifth year, and himself offered the largest prizes at the 192nd Olympiad, evidently held there in his stadium. Indeed, he is said to have endowed the whole Olympiad institution when it faltered for lack of money, so that the international contests would never fail to be held every five years.

The second city to be mentioned is Caesarea (Fig. 161), mid-way along the coast between Mt. Carmel and Joppa. Before Herod's day it was an unimportant site called " Straton's Tower ". After the king was finished with it, the city was one of the most beautiful and important in Palestine. For most of the time between A.D. 6 and 66 it was the seat of the Roman government in the country. There Paul was tried before Festus and Herod Agrippa before he sailed to Rome (Acts 25 : 23 ff.). The Roman centurion whom Peter converted was stationed there, and as a result of his conversion a church with Gentiles in the membership was established (Acts 10 ; 18 : 22). Beginning in the 2nd century of our era the city became an important center of the Christian Church. One of the church's first great scholars, Origen, taught in a school there for a time, and the historian Eusebius, who later became bishop of Caesarea (A.D. 315-18), was there educated. The area around it was one of the garden spots of Palestine until medieval times, when, after its destruction in the wars of the Crusades, it was allowed to silt up with sand. Even as late as the last century, however, the site was a quarry for good building stone which was shipped as far away as Joppa and Acre.

Caesarea has never been really excavated, but the remains of the Roman city can still be seen. Herod spent twelve years (25-13 B.C.) in building it. A sea mole, 200 feet wide and standing in 120 feet of water (20 fathoms), was built of huge stones to make a harbor the equal, according to Josephus, to that of Athens, if not larger. The remains of this mole are still to be seen as two tongues extending from the land into the sea. A semi-circular wall was erected to enclose the main part of the city with its great public buildings. Within it Herod erected a temple in Caesar's honor, adorned with a colossal statue of him, an amphitheater, a theater, a stadium and a marketplace. The ruins of the theater, amphitheater and stadium are still visible. The amphitheater has only recently been discovered by Israeli archaeologists with the aid of an aerial photograph. This was the place where gladiators fought between themselves and with wild beasts when the town was publicly inaugurated by Herod in 10 B.C., and where hundreds of Jewish prisoners were killed in such combats by Titus in A.D. 70. The arena was oval in shape, slightly more than 300 feet long by 200 feet wide. The building thus enclosed an area which was slightly larger even than that in the great Colosseum in Rome. The latter, inaugurated by Titus in A.D. 80, has an arena

161. Air view of Caesarea, showing : 1. Herod's harbor ; 2. Crusader town ; 3. modern Jewish settlement ; 4. ancient theater ; 5. ancient stadium ; 6. ancient amphitheater ; 7. ancient Roman wall ; 8–9. ancient Roman aqueducts

281 feet long and 177 feet wide. The Roman amphitheater for spectacular combats appears to have been a new phenomenon in Herod's time. The earliest literary reference to this type of structure is about 30 B.C. and the first permanent one to be built in Rome was in 29 B.C. in the Campus Martius.

The importance of Caesarea's stadium for athletic contests has already been mentioned. The theater was for those who were lovers of culture ; there the old Greek plays were undoubtedly enacted, as were also, in all probability, musical concerts. Here, then, was a city where a cosmopolitan population, aping the fashions of Rome, could feel quite at home. On the other hand, it was a city where the pious and conservative Jew would feel himself in the midst of the rankest type of western paganism which had been imported and implanted on the soil of his holy land.

The third city to be described as an example of Herod's transformation of Palestine is Jerusalem. There among other things he repaired the city fortifications, built a new temple for the Jews, rebuilt a citadel at the northwest corner of the temple area and named it " The Tower of Antonia ", and built a magnificent palace for himself.

By the time of Jesus the central part of the city of Jerusalem was no longer on the lower hill (Ophel), south of the Temple area, where it had been in Old Testament times (cf. Fig. 162). It was now to the west and north of the sacred precincts. Furthermore, the Tyropoeon Valley which used to separate the eastern from the western sections of the city was now partially filled up with the debris of the centuries. During the Maccabean age the Jews had erected a strong fortress on the site of the old lower city, which in Herod's day was called the Acra. The Jewish historian Josephus tells us that

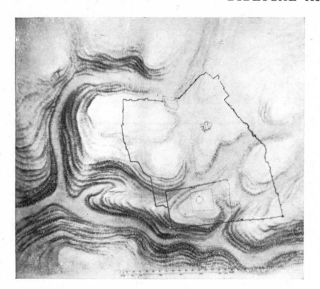

162. Relief map of ancient Jerusalem with the outlines of the present city-wall drawn upon it, together with the Temple area and the Church of the Holy Sepulchre. The City of David was on the hill directly south (*left*) of the Temple area. At the bottom is the Kidron Valley; to the left and top the Valley of Hinnom. Between the City of David (Ophel) and the western hill was the Tyropoeon Valley which today is largely filled with debris

the lower city was once higher than the Temple area, but when the Maccabees built the Acra they cut down the hill's height and filled in the valley intervening between it and the Temple.

The topography of Jerusalem has thus changed through the centuries, but we know enough about it to trace the general outlines of the city's history. The problem of defense in New Testament times was not the same as that in the 10th century B.C. when David first conquered the site. Then the tremendous Canaanite fortifications of the lower hill had simply to be repaired (Figs. 78–9). By New Testament times, however, these old walls were of no further use, except perhaps along the eastern side above the Kidron Valley. The main problem was the protection of both the eastern and the western hills, together with the rapidly expanding suburbs to the north. The southern and eastern boundaries had a natural protection in the deep Hinnom and Kidron valleys respectively, and they could be easily fortified. The northern and northwestern sections were much more difficult. The first northern wall of which Josephus speaks extended westward from about the middle of the Temple enclosure. A second wall began in the region of the northwestern corner of the Temple area and evidently

met the first at or near the present Jaffa gate and the citadel. The exact line of the second wall is uncertain. If the Church of the Holy Sepulchre marks the spot of Jesus' crucifixion and burial, then the line of the second wall must be drawn in such a way as to leave this church outside it. Since this makes a rather unsatisfactory line for a fortification, some scholars believe that the church does not mark the historical place of Jesus' death and that the second wall enclosed a larger area, having been built on higher ground. About A.D. 42 in the reign of Herod Agrippa, a few years after Jesus' death, a third wall was begun still further north of the second to enclose another suburb which Josephus calls Bezetha. It was not completed, however, until the period of the First Jewish Revolt against Rome in A.D. 66.

The first and second walls were already in existence when Herod became king. He strengthened them, especially by erecting three large and magnificent towers at the place where they joined together. These towers were to protect the fortifications at their weakest point, namely the northwest corner (Fig. 163). Directly south of them he erected his sumptuous palace. At the place where the second wall approached the Temple enclosure he rebuilt a Maccabean fortress and named it Antonia in honor of Mark Antony (Fig. 164). Josephus tells us that the castle of Antonia stood on a precipice nearly 75 feet high, and that it had four towers at the four corners. The tower at the southeast corner was some 105 feet high so that all that transpired in the Temple area could be seen from it. A Roman legion was quartered in the Antonia, and Josephus

163. The "Tower of David" at the old Jaffa gate in Jerusalem. The masonry of the lower part preserves the remains of one of Herod's fortification towers

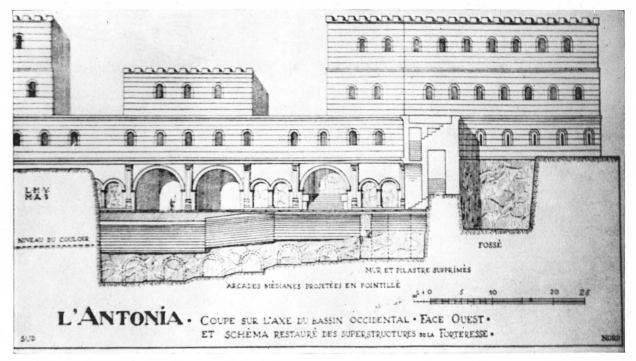

164. A reconstruction of the Tower of Antonia at the northwest corner of the Temple-area in Jerusalem

thinks of the structure as the fortress which guarded the Temple, whereas the Temple was the fortress which guarded the city.[2]

Jerusalem has been carefully studied and repeatedly excavated in modern times. Most of the excavations, however, were conducted before 1930, and careful stratigraphical techniques combined with a detailed study of pottery fragments were seldom used. The result is that while important discoveries have been made, most of them cannot be dated. Among the most important excavations, for example, were those of F. J. Bliss and A. C. Dickie from 1894 to 1897 in the remnants of the city walls along the edge of the Hinnom valley. It is probable that they found the southern wall of Herod around the western hill, but we cannot be sure. Perhaps the finest work, from a scientific viewpoint, has been that of C. N. Johns between 1934 and 1940 in the Citadel at the Jaffa Gate. It is at this spot that the first and second northern walls met and were strengthened by three huge Herodian towers. Mr. Johns found beneath the courtyard of the Citadel a pre-Herodian wall of the 3rd or 2nd centuries B.C., curving southward and strengthened by three towers. The foundations of one of the latter are still used to support the present " Tower of David " (Fig. 163). The stones used in this substructure were very large, having an average weight of 5 tons and a maximum of 10 tons. They are beautifully cut and the jointing is very close. The structure was set into the older wall and is undoubtedly the remnant of one of Herod's three towers. Whether the other two towers found by Johns are Herodian

[2] The whole fortification system of the city, especially after the third wall had been added, was sufficiently imposing to excite the wonder even of the Romans. The Roman historian, Tacitus, wrote in his *History* (Book V, paragraphs 11–12) that in A.D. 70 Titus for a number of reasons wished to conclude the siege of Jerusalem without delay. " But the commanding situation of the city had been strengthened by enormous works which would have been a thorough defense even for level ground. Two hills of great height were fenced in by walls which had been skillfully obliqued or bent inwards, in such a manner that the flank of an assailant was exposed to missiles. The rock terminated in a precipice ; the towers were raised to a height of sixty feet, where the hill lent its aid to the fortifications, and to a height of one hundred and twenty feet where the ground fell away. They had a marvelous appearance, and to a distant spectator seemed to be of uniform elevation. Within were other walls surrounding the palace, and, rising to a conspicuous height, the tower of Antonia, so called by Herod, in honor of Marcus Antonius.

" The temple resembled a citadel, and had its own walls, which were more laboriously constructed than the others. Even the colonnades with which it was surrounded formed an admirable outwork. It contained an inexhaustible spring ; there were subterranean excavations in the hill, and tanks and cisterns for holding rain water " (Tr. by A. J. Church and W. J. Brodribb ; New York, Modern Library, 1942).

166. The pavement of the court in the Tower of Antonia

165. The Ecce-Homo Arch, Jerusalem

is uncertain. Nevertheless the discovery fixes the position of the northwest corner of the Herodian city.

The intensive investigations of the distinguished French archaeologist, Father H. Vincent of the Dominican Biblical School in Jerusalem, have fixed the place and the approximate plan of Herod's Tower of Antonia at the northwestern corner of the Temple area (Fig. 164). This was the place where Paul was imprisoned when a Roman officer rescued him from a mob in the Temple (Acts 21 : 27 ff.). In Father Vincent's view it was also the place where Jesus was tried before Pilate, mocked and scourged (Mark 15). The ancient street level in this area is some 6½ feet below the present surface. Practically the only remnant of ancient construction still existing above ground is the Ecce-Homo Arch (Fig. 165), so called because tradition has claimed it to be the place where Pilate showed Jesus, crowned with thorns, to the mob and said: "Behold the man!" (John 19 : 5). Actually, however, this arch never had a connection with the Tower of Antonia or with the life of Jesus. It was once a triple arch and was erected by the Roman emperor, Hadrian (A.D. 117–38), as the triumphal entry-way into the new city which he had built and from which all Jews were excluded.

The most impressive discovery made by Father

Vincent was the pavement that once covered the court of the Antonia (Fig. 166). It is under the modern convent and school of the Sisters of Zion, and appears to cover an area approximately 165 feet square. The paving stones used are large blocks of hard limestone, approximately 1 foot thick and 3 feet square. This pavement is of special interest because it probably is the one mentioned in John 19 : 13: "When Pilate therefore heard these words, he brought Jesus forth, and sat down in the judgment seat in a place that is called the Pavement (*Lithostroton*), but in Hebrew, Gabbatha." Scratched on the stone slabs was a pattern for a popular Roman game which was evidently enjoyed by the Roman soldiers stationed there.

The finest remains of Herodian construction in Jerusalem are those in the special wall which was built around the great court occupied by the Temple. By this time the Jerusalem sanctuary was a place of pilgrimage for Jews from over the civilized world. Consequently Herod in rebuilding it decided that it needed a much larger courtyard than it had had hitherto in order to accommodate the crowds and to provide it with a proper setting. The present sacred esplanade in Jerusalem is the result of his work, though the outer court did not extend quite as far north as it does today. In order to provide such a large area it was necessary to build a platform, supported by columns and immense vaults over a portion of the southeastern area where the ground fell rapidly away. This extensive system of vaults is still there and is called "Solomon's Stables", because tradition has attributed them to

167. The Jewish Wailing Wall, showing the Herodian masonry along the southwestern side of the Temple enclosure

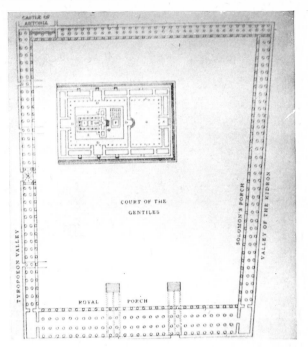

168. Plan of the Temple of Herod with its colonnades

Solomon. Why they are termed "stables" is uncertain, unless the name arose in late medieval times when the Crusaders are said to have stabled horses there.

To support the platform Herod further built a massive retaining wall around it. Portions of this wall are still to be seen along the western, southern and southeastern sides of the enclosure. It was examined to bedrock, in a number of places over 50 feet below the present surface, by Sir Charles Warren between 1867 and 1870. The "Wailing Wall" on the west is the most vivid illustration of typical Herodian construction (Fig. 167). The upper part of the present wall is of later construction, but the lower courses of stone are characteristic of Herod's workmanship. Huge blocks of stone were carefully hewn and fitted, the largest one observed being 16½ feet long by 13 feet wide. Remains of two arches along the western side are probably the places where bridges connected the western hill to the Temple platform, thus spanning the Tyropoeon Valley.

Descriptions of Herod's Temple have been preserved in Josephus and in the Jewish Mishnah (Tractate Middoth). It was evidently a magnificent structure, worthy of comparison with the great temples of the Roman world (Fig. 168). Yet Jesus' prophecy about it was literally fulfilled; he once said to his disciples: "Seest thou these great buildings? There shall not be left one stone upon another, that shall not be thrown down" (Mk. 13 : 2). This literally happened in A.D. 70 when the soldiers of Titus laid waste the whole city and burned and looted the Temple in one of the worst blood-baths in history. Only two pieces of stone have been found which are known to have belonged to it. One was discovered in 1871 in a cemetery (Fig. 169), and a portion of another came to light in 1935 near St. Stephen's Gate. They once were set in the gates leading to the Temple's inner court, and they bear a notice in Greek which reads: "No alien may enter within the barrier and wall around the Temple. Whoever is caught (violating this) is alone responsible for the death (-penalty) which follows."

The general plan of the Temple was fixed by tradition and the existing sanctuary. All Herod could do was to make it higher, affix a magnificent

169. The Herodian inscription forbidding Gentiles to enter the Temple court

170. Masada, overlooking the Dead Sea, with the ruins of the Herodian palace still visible at the top and the Roman siege-wall of A.D. 73 to be seen at the bottom

portico, and adorn it with elaborate decoration, gold plates over the front being an example. Around it were cloistered courts with beautiful colonnades. A defective column which was intended for use in the cloisters, but never moved from the quarry, was discovered years ago in front of the Russian cathedral north of the old city. The cloisters were not completed in Herod's day, however; indeed, they were finally finished only six years before the whole was destroyed in A.D. 70. This Temple was undoubtedly one of the finest structures of the ancient Near East, one which even the Roman Tacitus described as " a temple of immense wealth " and with which Titus was said to be greatly impressed.[3]

The Temple was Herod's device to win the goodwill of the Jews. For the same purpose he erected two great buildings in and near Hebron. Herodian masonry has been studied in the present structure which stands over the traditional site of the Cave of Machpelah where Abraham, Isaac and Jacob were buried. The other building was north of Hebron at the site of Mamre where Abraham's Oak was supposed to have been. Yet these offerings to Jewish piety did not allay suspicion, for all around were reminders of Herod's pagan interests. He is said to have erected a theater and a stadium even in Jerusalem, the center of Jewish life. Where they were located, however, is still a mystery. South of the city, a considerable distance away, a theater was discovered at the end of the last century, but whether it is Herodian is unknown.[4]

Ruins of Herodian public buildings, fortresses, and palaces are still to be seen at a number of other places in Palestine: at Ascalon, Herodium (Frank Mountain south of Bethlehem), Masada on the Dead Sea (Fig. 170), Machaerus on the eastern side of the Sea, Qarn Sartabeh (Alexandrium north of Jericho) and Jericho itself. None of these has been excavated except a portion of the palaces at Jericho and Masada.[5] Enough has been written, however, to suggest the vastly different atmosphere which existed in the Palestine of Jesus' day as compared to that in time of the kings of Israel. Herod the Great had transformed the country. It was again wealthy and prosperous, and from Herod's viewpoint, like that of Solomon's before

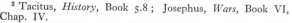

[3] Tacitus, *History*, Book 5.8 ; Josephus, *Wars*, Book VI, Chap. IV.
[4] Conrad Schick, *Quarterly Statement of the Palestine Exploration Fund*, 1887, pp. 161 ff.

[5] See the preliminary reports of J. L. Kelso and J. B. Pritchard in *Bulletin of the American Schools of Oriental Research*, No. 120 (Dec. 1950), pp. 11–22 ; and No. 123 (Oct. 1951), pp. 8–17 ; *The Biblical Archaeologist*, Vol. XIV, No. 2 (May 1951), pp. 34–43. An Israeli expedition began work at Masada in 1955 ; see *Israel Exploration Journal*, Vol. 7 (1957), pp. 1–60 for an archaeological survey of the site.

171. Sela, the natural fortress of the capital of ancient Edom, at Petra

him, it was now a place where a cultured man could live proudly and show its wonders to visiting dignitaries. Yet would the Jews stand for the internationalization of their country under foreign domination? The days of Herodian splendor were not to survive the 1st century of our era.

THE NEIGHBORS OF JUDAEA

One of the most gifted and vigorous peoples in the Near East of Jesus' time were the Nabataeans. The center of their kingdom was in the territory of ancient Edom and their capital was at Petra (the Old Testament Sela, " Rock " ; Fig. 171). Their greatest king was Aretas IV (9 B.C.–A.D. 40), whose realm included southern Palestine (the Negeb), most of Transjordan, northern Arabia, and at the end of his life even included Damascus. At the time of Paul's conversion an official of Aretas tried to apprehend him in Damascus. The apostle wrote about the incident as follows : " In Damascus the governor under Aretas the king guarded the city of Damascus in order to seize me ; but through a window in the wall I was let down in a basket and

escaped his hands " (II Cor. 11 : 32). The son of Herod the Great, Herod Antipas, who reigned in Galilee and Peraea (a territory in Transjordan) from 4 B.C. to A.D. 39 and who was called " that fox " by Jesus (Luke 13 : 32), married the daughter of Aretas. During a visit to Rome, however, he met his sister-in-law, Herodias, over whom he so lost his head that a marriage was arranged with her. For denouncing this marriage John the Baptist was imprisoned and later beheaded (Mark 6 : 17–29). Herod's first wife, the daughter of Aretas, fled to her father and the latter sent an army and soundly defeated his son-in-law in A.D. 36.

The Nabataeans were thus a power with which to be reckoned. They had established themselves across the important trade routes between Arabia and Syria. Caravans with merchandise from Africa, South Arabia, India and even China converged on Petra, there to be re-directed to Syria and Egypt, and to Greece and Italy via Gaza in Palestine. Petra was one of the great merchandise marts of the Near East, but it was more than that. It was a place of great beauty, set in a valley surrounded by red sandstone cliffs. In these cliffs tombs and mausolea of great splendor were cut (Fig. 172), until

172. Tombs cut in the soft, rose-red sandstone of Petra

the city became a kind of wonderland which is still a spectacular sight for the tourist. Aretas played the same role in the adornment of his capital city that Herod the Great had played in Jerusalem.

A number of Nabataean temples and sacred " high places " have been found. One of the temples was excavated by Nelson Glueck in 1937 on the top of a high hill, called Jebel et-Tannur, southeast of the Dead Sea. It was set on a platform, facing east, with a large courtyard in front (Fig. 173). It is a good illustration of the combining of Greek and Semitic architectural traditions, and of the mixing of religious beliefs. The chief Nabataean deity is known to have been a god named Dusares, but at Tannur the Syrian storm-god Hadad (Fig. 174), then identified with the Greek Zeus, was given first place. Next to him was a female deity, named Atargatis, who was identified with the Greek Artemis. She was evidently a personification of the powers of fertility in the world.

Excavation showed three phases in the life of the building, the second and third phases carefully placed over and around the earlier shrine without destroying it. The first building was probably erected in 7 B.C. This we know from a dedicatory inscription which was evidently re-used in the second phase. It says that the monument was erected by one Natayr'el " for the life of Haretat (Aretas), king of the Nabataeans, who loves his people, and for the life of Huldu his wife, in the year II " (that is, of the reign of Aretas).

Most of the Nabataean names seem to be Arabic, but the people spoke Aramaic. The Tannur inscription and others that have been discovered are all in Aramaic, though there are a few which are bilingual, in Greek and in Aramaic. During 1951 and 1952 the first Nabataean business documents on papyrus were discovered in caves in the vicinity of the Wadi Murabba'at along the western shore of the Dead Sea. They date from the 2nd century A.D. and were written in a very cursive script which has been deciphered by Abbé Starcky of the Dominican Biblical School in Jerusalem.[6]

At Petra the finest examples of open-air " high places " yet found in the Near East are preserved. The first was discovered by George L. Robinson in

[6] See *Revue Biblique*, Vol. 61, No. 2 (April 1954), pp. 161–81.

173. Nabataean temple at Khirbet et-Tannur in Transjordan

1900 (Fig. 175). It is on the top of a high ridge above and to the south of the Roman theater, and consists of a sunken, rectangular court, on one side of which are two altars hewn from the rock.[7] In 1934 W. F. Albright excavated another sanctuary on the highest point inside the walled city. It was an open processional way around a sacred rock and one for which a number of parallels exist in Arabia.

The extent and the intensity of the Nabataean occupation have been studied by means of the broken fragments of pottery which remain on sites once inhabited by these remarkable people. Nabataean pottery can never be forgotten after it is once examined. It is unbelievably thin and fragile, so much so that whole pieces of it are very rare (Fig.

176). The best examples of this ware are delicate bowls on which stylized floral and leaf patterns were painted before baking.

Nelson Glueck has fixed the approximate northern boundary of the Nabataean kingdom through most of its history by noting the sudden cessation of the pottery along an east-west line drawn toward the north end of the Dead Sea eastward into the desert. It is also to be found throughout the Negeb (southern Palestine), beginning south of Beersheba. In this area Nabataean villages, cities and fortresses abounded. In Transjordan alone Dr. Glueck has discovered over 500 of them (cf. Fig. 177). The fortresses guarded the kingdom's borders and were strategically spaced along the trade routes. Towns existed in areas where until recent times it was considered virtually impossible for large numbers of people to live. In fact, the most amazing thing about the Nabataeans is that they were able to establish an agricultural economy in what appears to us as bleak and uninhabitable wilderness.

---

[7] This high place is so well-preserved as to surprise all who see it. In December 1934, a party of four men, including Carl H. Kraeling and the writer, followed the remnants of a path and stairs up the hill, not knowing where they led. After an arduous climb, we suddenly came upon the high place, and were filled with the excitement of a fresh discovery, until the writer recognized it from recollections of Dr. Robinson's lectures on Petra.

The chief problem of these southern areas is the lack of water. Springs are few and the rainfall during the winter is very scant. Not many years ago some scholars firmly believed that the climate must have been different in biblical times from what it is today. Otherwise, they said, how are we to explain the existence of these cities in the wilderness? Yet various studies have converged to show that there have been no important changes in climate since the end of the last glacial age, some 10,000 or more years ago. The explorations of Dr. Glueck

174. The god Hadad, found at Khirbet et-Tannur

176. A portion of a painted Nabataean bowl

175. The Robinson High Place at Petra

have provided vivid illustration of the human energy which made urbanism possible even in the Palestinian Negeb. Every bit of water from sky and springs was carefully conserved. Thousands of cisterns, some of them of huge size, were constructed. Water channels and aqueducts were built, as were also numerous dams (cf. Figs. 177–178). The hills were terraced to keep the earth from being swept away. Hence when the rain did fall, the water was not allowed to tear its way down the valleys, soon to disappear. The cisterns were filled ; the dams made reservoirs and small lakes ; and the terraces kept the remainder of the previous liquid from flowing away and caused it to stay on the slopes, sink into the subsoil and there remain through the hot dry summer. To this day trees and vegetation grow even in August in those areas where the Nabataean dams and terraces still function. In the Palestinian Negeb the Israelis are now attempting to imitate their predecessors ; in doing so they are repairing many of the old Nabataean constructions while building others like them.

The Nabataean era extended from the 1st century B.C. to the 2nd century A.D. In A.D. 105–6 the Roman emperor, Trajan, put an end to the country's independence and made it a Roman province called Arabia Petraea (the " Arabia of Petra "). Not long thereafter the beautiful Nabataean pottery came to an end as did also the glory of the desert kingdom. In the words of Nelson Glueck : [8]

In general the Nabataeans may be accounted one of the most remarkable peoples that have ever crossed the stage of history. Sprung swiftly out of the deserts of Arabia to a position of great power and affluence and glory, they were thrust back by the Romans even more swiftly into the limbo of history whence they came. While their turn lasted, the Nabataeans wrought greatly, developing overnight, almost, into builders of magnificent cities, unique in the history of the handiwork of man. They were tradesmen, and farmers, and engineers, and architects of great energy and skill. The ruins which they left behind them testify eloquently to the glory which was theirs.

North of Nabataea in New Testament times there was a group of federated cities, originally ten in number, which was called the Decapolis. In it were the major cities of Transjordan, with one exception which was Scythopolis (Old Testament Beth-shan). The last mentioned was west of the

177. A Nabataean fortress in Transjordan, Qazr el-Feifeh, with remains of an aqueduct

Jordan at the opening of the pass leading to the great northern plain, the Esdraelon (Fig. 58). Among the others the best known are Gerasa (modern Jerash) and Philadelphia (modern 'Amman). These were Hellenistic cities which had been in existence since the 3rd or 2nd centuries B.C. With the coming of the Romans, however, they were banded together and placed under the separate political control of the Roman governor in Syria. The reasons for this were probably the protection of the eastern edge of Roman control and at the same time the preservation of the cause of Hellenistic culture against Semitic and Jewish interests. Historically, the earliest reference to the Decapolis is in the Gospels (Matt. 4 : 25 ; Mark 5 : 20 ; 7 : 31). The teaching ministry of Jesus was confined, however, to the Jews, and we have no record of any preaching which he did in this territory.

The city which most clearly illustrates the nature of the Decapolis is Gerasa, often referred to as " the Pompeii of Palestine " (Fig. 179). It is the site at which some ancient manuscripts locate the scene where Jesus healed the demoniac (Mark 5 : 1 and Luke 8 : 26 in the Revised Standard Version ; cf. Matt. 8 : 28). The city was surrounded by a wall, while a columned and paved street was the main thoroughfare through the center. Great temples to Zeus and Artemis, theaters, baths, a stadium and a marketplace adorned the city, and at

[8] *The Other Side of the Jordan* (New Haven, 1940), p. 200.

178. A Roman dam in the Wadi Dhobai in the desert of Transjordan

179. The ruins of ancient Gerasa

a later time it possessed fine churches. Most of the monumental structures still in existence, however, date from after the creation of the Provincia Arabia by Trajan in A.D. 106. Nevertheless the city was laid out as a typical Roman or Hellenistic city, and it is another indication of the penetrating influence of western culture into even the Palestinian hinterland.

234

THE ESSENES

The chief Jewish sects in Palestine during the time of Jesus were the Sadducees, the Pharisees and the Essenes. The Sadducees were aristocratic and theologically conservative priests who denied any doctrine which they could not find in the Scriptures, particularly the comparatively new doctrines of the resurrection of the dead and of future punishment in Hell. The Pharisees were the theologians and strict legalists of the day, who accepted the developed doctrines of heaven and hell, resurrection and immortality, but who also laid great emphasis upon a large body of oral interpretations of the Law of Moses and considered them of binding authority. One of the basic issues between them and the Sadducees, in other words, was a problem which was to become important in the Christian Church: the relation between Scripture and Tradition and the role which should be accorded the latter. Both of these groups were severely castigated in the New Testament, but no mention is made of the third group, the Essenes. We read about them in Josephus who says that they held their property in common, followed a fairly ascetic discipline, held to a lofty moral code which was " better than that of other men ", and did not offer sacrifices in the Temple " because they have more pure lustrations of their own ".[9] The Roman author, Pliny the elder, mentions them in his *Natural History* (Book V, Chap. 17), a work which was published shortly before his death in A.D. 79. He says they lived on the west side of the Dead Sea, " a solitary race, and strange above all others in the entire world ".

While Josephus says that the Essenes lived in various places throughout the country, the words of Pliny indicate that the main colony lived near the Dead Sea. This is the group which owned the Dead Sea or Qumran scrolls, the discovery of which was described at the end of the last chapter. The reason why far more of their library has not been found is that others probably discovered it before us in ancient times. The Church Father, Origen, in the 3rd century A.D. says that in his critical work on the texts of the Old Testament he used Hebrew and Greek books, among them a Greek translation of the Psalms, which had been found " in a jar near Jericho ". A Nestorian Patriarch, Timothy I, wrote that about A.D. 800 an Arab had found a number of rolls in a cave near the Dead Sea, and that the discovery was reported to the Jews who obtained from the cave a number of Old Testament books and other writings in Hebrew script. During the 8th century A.D. a Jewish sect was founded which called itself the Karaites (" Scripturists "). After A.D. 900 there are references in Karaite and Moslem writers to an ancient group, called the " Cave Folk ", whose writings had been found in a cave. The Karaites were interested in earlier Jewish sects because they wanted to show that orthodox or rabbinic Judaism was not the only type which had existed. In particular they wished to cast doubt on the rabbinic claim that there was an authentic body of oral tradition as old as the written law.

Among the scrolls found in the Qumran caves are documents, particularly a Manual of Discipline, which tell us far more about the sect than we had hitherto known. In addition, the community center at Khirbet Qumran has been excavated by the Jordan Department of Antiquities and the Dominican Biblical School in Jerusalem in a series of campaigns, beginning in 1951 (Fig. 180). A large building had been erected there on the site of a Judean fortress in the time of John Hyrcanus (135–104 B.C.). It suffered badly in an earthquake in 31 B.C., but was repaired and continued to be used until destroyed in A.D. 68 by the Tenth Roman Legion, shortly before the fall of Jerusalem to Titus in A.D. 70. Thereafter only a fort for a military outpost existed at the site until the end of the 1st century A.D. The most interesting discoveries were the large number of cisterns, the cemetery of over 1000 graves, the kitchen, common rooms, and Scriptorium. The last mentioned was the writing room of the Essenes. It contained a large table of plaster (Fig. 181), a plaster bench, a double basin which was probably used for ritual washing before or after a scribe worked on the sacred texts, and two inkpots, one of pottery and the other of bronze. In the community center the Essenes studied the Scripture night and day and worked continuously in copying scrolls for their library. Here, too, they ate their common meals and worshipped together, though their individual living quarters were probably in the caves of the neighboring cliffs.

From the documents found in the caves we gather that the sect was established in Maccabean times by the founder, who is referred to as the " Teacher of Righteousness ". The group separated themselves from other Jews and " the habitation of

---

[9] Josephus, *Antiquities of the Jews*, Book XVIII, Chap. I ; see also his *Wars of the Jews*, Book II, Chap. VIII.

180. Khirbet Qumran, the Essene center, from the cliff looking east over the Dead Sea

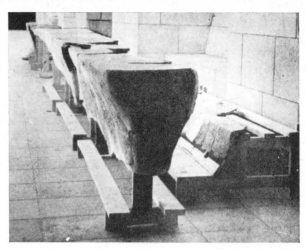

181. The clay table and portions of a bench found at Qumran in a room where manuscripts were copied

perverse men to go into the wilderness to prepare there the way of the Lord ". In saying this the sect quoted Isa. 40 : 3 which they regarded themselves as fulfilling : " In the wilderness prepare the way of the Lord ; level in the desert a highway for our God." In relation to the Jewish nation as a whole the Essenes considered themselves to be a community set apart, " being united (so as to constitute) a holy of holies and a house of community for the Israel(ites) who walk in perfection ".[10]

Like the disciples of John the Baptist and of Jesus this group was an eschatological community ; that is, they accepted a special discipline and task in preparation for the end-time in which God's kingdom would be established under the leadership of the Messiah. They revived the old Israelite conceptions of Holy War, preserved particularly in Deuteronomy, and organized themselves into a little " salvation-army ", giving themselves wholly to a rigorous discipline and organization. Like the New Testament community they appear to have had twelve of their number as their chosen leaders,[11] perhaps as a symbol of the twelve Israelite tribes of old. All property was held in common (cf. Acts

4 : 32–7), and the center of their life was the joint study of the Scripture and the sacrament of a common banquet. In words which remind us of the Lord's Supper an Essene priest initiated the common meal by stretching forth " his hand to invoke a blessing with the first of the bread and the wine ".

The common life of the community was meant to fulfill God's intention in the covenant community of old. The Essenes had instituted the New Covenant and lived within it as a foretaste of life in the Kingdom to come. Entrance into the group meant renouncing one's former ties and undergoing a period of training. On repentance he was baptized with water as a sign of his cleansing, but as in the New Testament the cleansing agent was believed to be God through his Holy Spirit, a " Spirit disposed toward Unity in His truth " which cleansed one of " the spirit of impurity ". Unlike Christian baptism, however, the Essene rite was evidently repeated at intervals as a sign of purification from all evil thoughts and intentions. Great stress was placed, not simply on the quality of one's deeds, but especially on the purity of one's inner thoughts. Repeated examinations before one's elders were held. Lying, slander, an evil temper, the bearing of a grudge or a disposition to take vengeance—all such matters were carefully watched and severely disciplined. According to one passage the procedure of neighborly reproof seems to be precisely the same as that given by Jesus in Matt. 18 : 15–17. The erring brother was first personally reproved. Then the reproof was to be administered before witnesses. Finally, if these steps had no effect, the

[10] *The Dead Sea Manual of Discipline*, tr. by W. H. Brownlee, *Bulletin of the American Schools of Oriental Research, Supplementary Studies*, Nos. 10–12 (New Haven, 1951), Section viii : 13–14 ; ix : 6.

[11] A passage in *ibid.*, viii : 1 speaks of " twelve laymen and three priests ". Professor Frank M. Cross informs me that information now at hand indicates that the twelve laymen represent Israel's twelve tribes of old, while the three priests represent the three clans of the priestly tribe of Levi.

accusation was to be made before the whole community.[12] In all cases the reproof was to be made " in truth and humility and loving devotion to each other. One shall not speak to his brother in anger or in complaint or with . . . a wicked spirit." The Essenes thought of themselves as choosing and following " the Way ", a term which the early Christians also used for their manner of life (e.g. Acts 9 : 2). And one of the names by which the whole community referred to itself was " The Many ". A similar term, if not a direct translation of it, was used for the community of early Christians, though it is obscured in the Authorized Version by the English word " multitude " (Acts 4 : 32 ; 6 : 2, 5 ; 15 : 12, 30).

A surprising discovery emerging from the study of the Dead Sea community of Essenes or Covenanters is, as the above lines imply, the similarity between them and the early Jerusalem church in a number of important respects. In both there was on repentance a baptism by water and the Spirit, as was also the case in the work of John the Baptist. Practising, as they did, the possession of all property in common, the ideal of " holy poverty " was likewise characteristic of all three movements. Leadership by twelve outstanding men, the intense concern for the inner purity of the group, the new life as " the Way ", the new congregation as " the Many ", the reaction against the Sadducees and the Pharisees, the criticism of the existing sacrificial worship of the Temple—all of these seem to have been shared by both the Covenanters and the Jerusalem Christians.[13]

Further similarities are being observed in methods of interpreting Scripture and in language and thought. One of the characteristics of the Early Church was its careful study of the Old Testament and its interpretation of numerous ancient writings as referring to, and being fulfilled in, the recent great events by which the Church had been founded. This study of Scripture with an attitude of expectancy, in the certain knowledge that past events and teaching had a contemporary meaning, was not a dominant characteristic of the rabbinic exposition of the ancient writings. Yet it was precisely the attitude of the Essenes, as we can see from their biblical commentaries. The events of their recent past as well as their " Teacher of Righteousness " were all found foretold in the Old Testament.

They even possessed lists of Old Testament prooftexts, among them Messianic passages and other allusions which they believed to refer to the Messiah. It has long been observed that the author of the Gospel of Matthew must have had some such list because he is very interested in showing how at every point the events of Jesus' life fulfilled Old Testament expectations.

Of even greater interest is the theology of the Qumran sect and its possible relation to the Gospel of John. More than any other Jewish group, the Essenes seem to have been influenced by Iranian or Zoroastrian religious thinking. In the latter the world is the scene of a conflict between two primordial beings who represent good and evil, light and darkness, truth and falsehood. The same is true in Essene theology, except that the two opposing forces were created in the beginning by God.[14] " From the God of knowledge exists all that is and will be . . . He created man for dominion over the world and assigned him two spirits by which to walk until the season of His visitation. They are the spirits of truth and perversion." All men are either the sons of light under the rule of the prince of lights, or they are the sons of darkness and perversity under the control of the angel of darkness. The present life is the battleground between the two spirits, and all the spirits of the angel of darkness, or the spirit of perversion, are at work " to trip the sons of light ". The place of contention between the two spirits is " within man's heart . . . For God has set them in equal parts until the period of the decree and the making of the New ", to the end " that man may know good (and evil) ".

This type of ethical dualism is to be found throughout the New Testament, and particularly in John and Paul. In the letters of Paul we learn of the struggle going on in the world against the principalities and powers of darkness who are the agents of " the prince of the power of the air, the spirit that is now at work in the sons of disobedience " (Eph. 2 : 2 ; 3 : 10). But in Paul the emphasis is a militant one ; the combat is intense, though the victory in Christ is assured. In John and among the Essenes this militant aspect is not so much emphasized. Instead, there is almost a static opposition of the opposing forces.[15] In

---

[12] *Ibid.*, section v : 25–vi : 1 and footnote 3 on p. 23.
[13] For summary see Sherman E. Johnson, " The Dead Sea Manual of Discipline and the Jerusalem Church in Acts ", *Zeitschrift für die Alttestamentliche Wissenschaft*, 66 Band (1954), pp. 106–20.

[14] The Essene creed is summarized in the Manual of Discipline, *op. cit.*, iii : 13–iv : 26.
[15] For summary, see specially W. F. Albright, " Recent Discoveries in Palestine and the Gospel of John ", *Light on the New Testament : Studies in its Background and Eschatology, in honor of C. H. Dodd* (ed. by W. D. Davies and D. Daube), London, 1955.

I John 4 : 6 there appears to be a direct translation into Greek of the Essene spirits in the reference to " the spirit of truth and the spirit of error ". In the Gospel of John the Paraclete or Comforter is " the Spirit of truth " (14 : 17; 15 : 26; 16 : 13) who " will guide you into all the truth ". The characteristic Johannine use of the word " truth " sounds very much like the usage of the Essenes. " Truth ", furthermore, is something to be done : " he who does the truth comes to the light " (John 3 : 21), which is precisely what an Essene would have said.

The contrast between light and darkness plays a particularly striking role in both John and the Qumran literature. On the one side are the " sons of light " (John 12 : 36) who do not walk in darkness but have " the light of life " (John 8 : 12). On the other side are those who " walk in darkness " and reject the light. In saying this John uses almost the precise expressions which the Essenes before him had used.

In the past scholars have sought to explain the Johannine dualism by reference to current and especially later Hellenistic philosophies of varying types. Yet all of them have encountered difficulty of one sort or another, as their critics have not failed to point out. The surprising discoveries of Qumran have raised the whole question again, and it now appears that at least part of the background of John's thinking may be found in the Essene theology of Palestine. At any rate, it is already being claimed that the books of the Essenes provide us with the closest approach that has yet been discovered to the Gospel of John and to Paul, at least in so far as conceptual background and language is concerned, and that the connecting link between the two was the work of John the Baptist. The study of this question is only beginning and will occupy the attention of scholars for many years to come.

In all the similarities that have been observed between the Essene and Christian movements, however, the differences are still more impressive than the similarities. The Qumran Covenanters were conservative legalists who sought salvation in the Mosaic Law, as a preparation for the coming of the Messiah and his kingdom. Yet Christ for the Christian opened a new path to the Father. As Messiah he suffered and died ; he did not come to reign in earthly splendor. And his saving work was for all sinners, not simply for a few elect who saw the light, or simply for the sanctification of his followers. The Essene Gospel of the new righteousness in the New Covenant is far removed from the Christian Gospel of God's love, just as the figure of Christ is very different from the Essene " Teacher of Righteousness ".

ARCHAEOLOGY AND THE GOSPELS

The period covered by New Testament history is so short that archaeology cannot be expected to be as helpful as it has been with the Old Testament, where over fifteen hundred years is surveyed between the time of Abraham and the writing of the latest books. All that we can expect from the explorations for the illumination of the life and work of Jesus and the Palestinian Church are the following : (1) The complex cultural and political situation within which the ministry of Jesus took place ; (2) various details in the Gospel record, including especially the geography of the Gospels ; (3) and information regarding the traditions and text of the Gospels.

In the preceding sections of this chapter a brief summary of the cultural and political situation has been given. Regarding the various details of historical and geographical interest, only a few need be mentioned here as illustrations of the work that has been done.

The Gospel of Luke seeks to set the story of Jesus' birth against the background of current history. Luke writes that Jesus was born in Bethlehem because Joseph and Mary had to go there in order to be enrolled for taxation. This enrollment was ordered by Caesar Augustus (27 B.C.–A.D. 14) when Quirinius was governor of Syria, and it is said to have been the first such taxation-census which had been imposed upon the population (Luke 2 : 1–3). We have a number of witnesses to this type of census for purposes of taxation during the period of Roman domination, and the evidence suggests that the practice began during the reign of Caesar Augustus. Furthermore, an Egyptian papyrus indicates that in A.D. 103–4 at least, there was a census in Egypt which was apparently made on the basis of kinship, and proclamation was then made for all who were residing elsewhere to return to their family homes.[16] This may illuminate the otherwise difficult problem as to why Joseph had to go from Galilee to Bethlehem.

---

[16] F. G. Kenyon and H. I. Bell, *Greek Papyri in the British Museum*, Vol. III (London, 1907), p. 125.

We also have information about Sulpicius Quirinius. He was a Roman senator who was first sent out from Rome to quell a disturbance in Asia Minor in 10–7 B.C. Furthermore, we know that he was Roman governor of Syria in A.D. 6–9, at which time a census was taken, which resulted in a serious Jewish rebellion in Galilee. Yet this census was too late to have occurred at the time of Jesus' birth, since the latter was born before the death of Herod the Great which happened in 4 B.C. (Luke 1 : 5 ; Matt. 2 : 1). This presents a chronological problem which has not been solved. While Quirinius may have been governor in 3–2 B.C., that date, too, is after the death of Herod. One suggestion among others to solve the difficulty has been given by a Roman historian. He believes that Luke 2 : 2 should not be translated as is usually done : " This census was the first during Quirinius' prefectureship of Syria." Instead, he insists, it should be rendered : " This census was the first before that under the prefectureship of Quirinius in Syria."[17] That suggestion would solve the difficulty and it may find support in the Church Father, Tertullian, but it cannot be regarded as more than a suggestion because the Greek text does not lend itself readily to such a translation.

While Jesus was born in the time of Caesar Augustus, his ministry took place during the reign of Tiberius (A.D. 14–37), when Pontius Pilate was the governor or procurator of Judaea (A.D. 26–36), Herod Antipas the tetrarch (ruler) of Galilee and part of Transjordan (4 B.C.–A.D. 39), and his brother Philip the tetrarch of the area north and east of the Sea of Galilee (4 B.C.–A.D. 34). This information is accurately given us by Luke in Chap. 3 : 1. Herod Antipas and Philip were the sons of Herod the Great, but Pontius Pilate was a Roman official. The Romans had taken over the administration of the province of Judaea, but had left other areas in the hands of local rulers. This meant that the areas in which the ministry of Jesus took place were under the control of different rulers. Yet it seems evident that Jesus was able to move freely without passport or challenge, not only in Galilee where most of his ministry took place, but also in the territory of Philip (Mark 8 : 27), the Decapolis, the Palestinian portions of the province of Syria (Mark 7 : 24, 31), and Judaea. By the middle of the 2nd century A.D. the various military camps in these areas were connected with each other and with the outside world by a magnificent series of Roman roads, but in the time of Jesus none of these had as yet been built.

The main cities and towns mentioned in the Gospel narratives have long been known. There are some, however, that have not been discovered, and perhaps never will be because of a confused textual tradition. A few have been located by archaeological exploration, used together with a critical study of ancient sources. For example, in John 4 : 5–7 we are told that before Jesus met the Samaritan woman at Jacob's well he came " to a city of Samaria which is called Sychar " (Fig. 43). This site has usually been identified with the village of 'Askar at the foot of Mt. Ebal, but 'Askar has been shown to be a comparatively recent settlement with a name that means " military camp " in Arabic. Consequently, we must probably take seriously the old Syriac translation at this point and read Sychem (Shechem) instead of Sychar. Shechem was a great city of Old Testament times which guarded the pass between Mounts Ebal and Gerizim, until its destruction by Shalmaneser V of Assyria in 724 or 723. It was rebuilt as the capital city of the Samaritans at the end of the 4th century B.C., when Alexander the Great took Samaria itself for his soldiers, and flourished until destroyed by John Hyrcanus at the end of the 2nd century B.C. In Jesus' time, and from then until today, there was and has been only a small village on the site, built around the copious spring which waters the area. Nearby is the old " Jacob's Well " where the incident in John 4 took place.

When one travels in modern Palestine, guides will show him precisely where every major biblical event took place. For the most part the tourist would be advised to pay little attention to many of the traditional identifications, even though they may go back to early medieval times. One example is Cana of Galilee where Jesus' first miracle, the turning of water into wine, was performed (John 2 : 1–11). This town is traditionally identified with Kefr Kenna, 3¾ miles northeast of Nazareth, on the road to the Sea of Galilee. There one will be shown the place where the miracle took place and the spring from which the water was drawn. Actually, however, the name of the biblical town is preserved in Khirbet Qana, 8 miles directly north of Nazareth. At this site are the ruins of an ancient town ; the surface is strewn with pieces of pottery from the Roman and Byzantine periods. Its location fits the reports of medieval travellers who

---

[17] F. M. Heichelheim in *An Economic Survey of Ancient Rome*, ed. by Tenney Frank, Vol. IV (Baltimore, 1938), p. 161.

182. A reconstruction of the synagogue at Capernaum

183. Theodotos inscription from the Synagogue of the Freedmen

tell us of a monastery and church that once were there, the latter claiming to possess one of the water jars which Jesus used.

Similarly, the location of Capernaum, which was the center of Jesus' ministry in Galilee, was long debated. Most geographers from the seventeenth to the nineteenth century, including the great Edward Robinson in 1838, used to locate the biblical town at a ruin called Khan Minyeh on the north-western shore of the Sea of Galilee. Beginning in 1905, however, excavations were conducted at a site further north, called Tell Ḥum. The remains of a fine synagogue were unearthed and partly restored (cf. Fig. 182), and this site is now generally taken to agree better with ancient testimony regarding Capernaum than Khan Minyeh. The question is not yet definitely decided, however, and probably will not be until further excavations have been conducted. The synagogue at Tell Ḥum is often pointed out as the one in which Jesus worshipped. Unfortunately, archaeologists now believe that it must be dated about A.D. 200, long after the time of Jesus. Earlier ruins of the 1st century A.D. may be beneath it or elsewhere in the site, but further very careful excavation is needed before we can be sure.

Other synagogues in Galilee besides the one at Capernaum were once thought to go back to the time of Christ. Modern study, however, has shown that no surviving ruin of a synagogue is to be dated earlier than the end of the 2nd century A.D. A large number of synagogues have been found at more than forty places in the country, and they are commonly divided into two types. The first type belongs to the 3rd and 4th centuries A.D., of which the synagogues found at Capernaum and Chorazin in Galilee are examples. They were very ornate

structures with a great deal of ornamentation carved in the stone. The second type belongs to the Byzantine period, mostly from the 5th and 6th centuries A.D. These were erected after official permission had been given by Rabbi Abun in the first half of the 4th century for the inclusion of mosaics representing a variety of living creatures in synagogue construction. Consequently, the most notable feature of several of the later synagogues is the presence of elaborate mosaics, depicting animals, people and even the circle of the Zodiac. All of the synagogues are of the formal basilica style, with a main hall and two side aisles separated from each other by rows of columns.

The only certain fragment of a synagogue from before A.D. 70 is an inscription found on Ophel, or the old lower city of Jerusalem, in 1913-14 (Fig. 183). Its text reads: "Theodotus son of Vettenus, priest and synagogue-president, son of a synagogue-president and grandson of a synagogue-president, has built the synagogue for the reading of the Law and the teaching of the Commandments, and (he has built) the hostelry and the chambers and the cisterns of water in order to provide lodgings for those from abroad who need them—(the synagogue) which his fathers and the elders and Simonides had founded." Theodotus' family name is thought to be derived from the Roman family of the Vetteni, which indicates that he or an ancestor was evidently a Jewish freedman from Italy. Consequently, the inscription is believed to refer to the "Synagogue of the Freedmen" which is mentioned in Acts 6 : 9. It was the members of this synagogue who were the strongest opposition to the preaching of Stephen, the first Christian martyr.

The reason that 1st century A.D. synagogues have not been found in Palestine is that they were all destroyed in the Roman conquest of the Jews after their two revolts against Rome in A.D. 66–70 and 132–5. A Jewish tradition credits the Romans with the destruction of 480 synagogues in Jerusalem alone when the city was destroyed in A.D. 70. While the number may be exaggerated, the archaeological discoveries do indicate an almost total disruption in the continuity of life, caused by the First Revolt in A.D. 66–70. Gibeah and Bethel, among other towns, provide in their ruins evidence of disturbance at that time. Roman ruthlessness, when combined with the hostility of the native pagan population then living in Palestine, brought Jewish life virtually to an end. The Christians were caught in the middle, treated as Jews by the pagans and persecuted by the Jews as traitors. The Essene community at Qumran was destroyed, and later tradition says that the surviving Christians from Jerusalem fled to Pella across the Jordan. Earlier persecutions by the Jews had caused many Christians, among them Peter, to go to other parts of the world for their missionary work.

From this situation it is argued that we must assume a complete break in the continuity of tradition about the life of Jesus and the Early Church in Palestine. Any records or memories that were preserved must have been carried, for the most part orally, to other localities outside of Palestine by Christians who left the country before or after the First Revolt. In dealing with the traditions about Christian origins the archaeologist insists that this is a basic point that cannot be ignored.[18] It is no accident, then, that our present Gospels were written outside of Palestine. Mark is generally thought to have been written in Rome, perhaps just before the Revolt began. Matthew and Luke-Acts are dated later, between A.D. 80 and 90, though it is not certain where they were written. John is usually connected with Ephesus in Asia Minor and is dated about A.D. 90 by most scholars. Yet in spite of the fact that the Gospels were composed in places far distant from Palestine, the narrative traditions must be judged historically to have arisen from events in that country before A.D. 70 and to have been transmitted orally for decades before being written down in their final form.

From very early times the Gospel of John has been seen to possess a different character from the other Gospels. It deals more with an interpretation of the person of Christ and with his inner thoughts and teachings. Narratives are recounted, not for their own sake, but for their spiritual, almost allegorical, value. Consequently, in the past the tendency among scholars has been to rely more on Matthew, Mark and Luke than on John, while the long sermons in the latter were interpreted in a variety of ways as being an exposition of the gospel to the Greek mind. Consequently, it has been assumed that there is less in John than in the other Gospels which goes back to an authentic Palestinian tradition. Work on the narrative portions of John in recent years, however, has begun to reverse this judgment. In addition, the new data from the Essene scrolls, described in the preceding section of this chapter, has already given a setting in Palestine for the background of John's thought. For this reason it is becoming clearer that both the narratives and the teaching in the Fourth Gospel must date back to an oral tradition in Palestine before A.D. 70. Its use in the Church undoubtedly occasioned rearrangement and refraction of the material in various ways before it was written down, but there is no longer any reason to suppose that it was a new and artificially constructed document without any solid basis in the Church's Palestinian traditions.

The earliest manuscript of a New Testament book is a fragment of the Gospel of John in the John Rylands Library at Manchester, England, first published in 1935. It was found in Egypt and is dated in the early part of the 2nd century A.D. This proves that the Gospel was being circulated in Egypt less than fifty years after it was written. From approximately the same time there are larger fragments of a papyrus book of an "Unknown Gospel". They contain four different incidents in the life of Jesus, two of which are recorded in the Synoptic Gospels (Matt., Mark, Luke) while the other two are unrecorded in the canonical books that we have. Yet the language of the document is believed to be more like that of John than of the other Gospels. The manuscript would appear to have been written, then, by one who knew John and one or more of the Synoptics, but also had access to material unknown to us. This recalls the statement of Luke that in his time many had undertaken to prepare narratives of Jesus' life and teachings (Luke 1 : 1).

The chief manuscripts of the New Testament are those of the 4th and 5th centuries which had been added to the Septuagint, or the Greek translation

---

[18] See W. F. Albright, *op. cit.*, and *The Archaeology of Palestine*, pp. 240–9.

of the Old Testament, mentioned at the end of the last chapter. These are now supplemented by great numbers of other manuscripts and by 126 imperfect leaves of New Testament books among the Chester Beatty Papyri which are dated in the 3rd century. It can now be said that the text of no other work from antiquity is so well attested by manuscript tradition as that of the New Testament. Neither the classical authors of antiquity nor the sacred literature of any other religion have such a wealth of early manuscripts for the testing and correction of the text.

Perhaps the most unusual manuscript discoveries relating to the New Testament are the fragments of papyrus discovered at Oxyrhynchus in Egypt at the beginning of the present century. They contain a number of reputed sayings of Jesus which were written on these sheets, probably during the 3rd and 4th centuries A.D. Most of the sayings are variants of some in the Gospels, but some are found nowhere else. For example,

" Jesus saith, ' Except ye keep (your life in) the world as a fast, ye shall not find the Kingdom of God ; and except ye keep the (whole) week as a sabbath ye shall not see the Father.'

Jesus saith, ' I stood in the midst of the world and in the flesh was I seen of them, and I found all men drunken, and none found I athirst among them ; and my soul grieveth over the sons of men, because they are blind in their heart, and see not.' "

These and other papyri are fragments of lost gospels and collections of the sayings of Jesus. While they whet our appetites for much more of the same, it is highly probable that the Early Church's special preservation of the four Gospels that we have was not purely accidental but a conscious selection of the most reliable material.

DAILY LIFE IN NEW TESTAMENT TIMES

The first fact to be noted about life in New Testament times is the great increase in the population over what it was in the days of Israel. During the first four or five centuries of our era the population kept increasing in size as a result of the Roman peace. This is evident from an archaeological survey of the country which reveals that there were more than twice as many towns and villages in the Roman period as in the days of Israel. While exact figures are nothing more than rough computations, it is estimated that there may have been at least 2,000,000 inhabitants, if not more, in Palestine and Transjordan during the Christian era as against scarcely 1,000,000 in the time of Isaiah about 700 B.C.

The increase in population meant that the land had to be more intensively cultivated, and undoubtedly new agricultural techniques were introduced to increase the yield. One of the evidences for the increased use of land is the unceasing attention given to the problem of water supply and irrigation throughout the Near East. The plain of Caesarea, for example, was a veritable garden in Roman times, whereas until recently in the modern age it was an unhealthy and unproductive area with undrained swamps. Two great aqueducts were constructed across the plain, one for the city and one largely for irrigation. While both of them were constructed after New Testament times, similar water works must have existed from the time of Herod, who rebuilt the city on such a vast scale. The remains of an aqueduct built by Pontius Pilate to bring water to Jerusalem from pools south of Bethlehem have been discovered. Pilate took funds from the sacred treasury of the Temple for this purpose and caused thereby great dissatisfaction among the Jews. The population of Jerusalem in Jesus' day has been estimated at about 100,000, and the aqueduct was undoubtedly needed. While this structure was erected for the enlarged city, we can be confident that other comparable works were erected with dams throughout the country for purposes of irrigation.

Another indication of improved production techniques is the new types of installations used for the oil, wine and flour industries. The large, rotating stone mill, turned by donkeys, took away a great deal of the drudgery from the task of preparing flour for bread. Great olive and grape mills and presses from the period have been observed throughout the country. The Jewish Talmud forbade the export from Palestine of wine, olive oil and flour in order to prevent scarcity. Palestine had few surpluses for export in the basic foods. Galilee was the district which produced the best oil and wine in the largest quantity, whereas the date-palms of Judaea were famous throughout the ancient world.

New varieties of seed and fruit were introduced, but the basic diet was the same as that in Old Testament times. Rice was being grown where the terrain was wet enough to permit it, but it could not have been a large industry. Perhaps the greatest change in diet was the increased use of chickens and eggs, which had not been common before the 5th century B.C. The probability is, therefore, that the Hellenistic-Roman period initiated few major changes in diet, though there were many advances made in agricultural technology.

As previously indicated, the greatest difference between the periods of the Old and New Testaments lay in the spheres of mind and culture. The influence of Greek philosophical discussion over the centuries had by this time deeply influenced all thinking people in the Roman world. The developing sciences of mathematics, geometry and astronomy had greatly improved the methods of measurement in space and time. Larger mental horizons were made possible through the daily contact with people from all over the Roman empire, and new maps gave a more accurate idea of the known world. Various languages were undoubtedly to be heard on the streets of the major cities. Greek and Aramaic were evidently the common tongues, and most of the urban peoples could probably understand both even in such " modern " or " western " cities as Caesarea and Samaria where Greek was the more common. Roman soldiers and officials might be heard conversing in Latin, while orthodox Jews may well have spoken a late variety of Hebrew with one another, a language that we know to have been neither classical Hebrew nor Aramaic, despite its similarities to both.

The language spoken by Jesus has been much debated. We have no certain way of knowing whether he could speak Greek or Latin, but in his teaching ministry he regularly used either Aramaic or the highly Aramaized popular Hebrew. When Paul addressed the mob in the Temple, it is said that he spoke Hebrew (Acts 21 : 40). Scholars generally have taken this to mean Aramaic, but it is quite possible that a popular Hebrew was then the common tongue among the Jews.[19]

The phenomenal changes in architecture under western influence have already been noted. Huge Roman-type buildings appeared in Palestine, undoubtedly employing the newly invented Roman concrete. How the common man lived, and what his house was like, are, however, still largely unknown. Many wealthy homes were probably built like the typical Roman houses which are so well known from the ruins of Pompeii in Italy. The main part of the building consisted of a square block of rooms around a colonnaded open court. This was entered from the atrium, another open square

which often had a pool in the center to collect rain water from the roof. The atrium was the reception-area, opening on the street. Good furniture was available to make living comfortable : excellent beds for the wealthy or cots for the poor, chairs, stools and tables. Fashionable people had probably adopted the Greek custom of reclining at meals, but we do not know how far this had penetrated among the Jews. At Jesus' Last Supper the Synoptic Gospels say that Jesus " sat " at the table (Matt. 26 : 20 ; Luke 22 : 14), while John appears to suggest that he and the disciples were reclining (John 13 : 23).

A Roman like Pontius Pilate generally began his day early, perhaps with a breakfast of bread and honey or cheese. Lunch was at the sixth hour or noon, and could be an elaborate meal with meat, fish or fowl and vegetables. For some there was " tea " in the afternoon, but the main meal of the day was the *cena*, which usually began at the ninth hour (3 p.m.) if it was a banquet, and could be a long affair. A bath usually preceded this meal, for Romans like the Jews were a clean people. The food was eaten with the fingers, except that a spoon was now available for soup. Wine was the common beverage, never water, coffee or tea. Goatskins were the age-old receptacles for wine, but from Hellenistic times onwards Gentiles, at least, regularly used the large wine-jar or amphora, with narrow mouth and pointed bottom.

The beautiful trays and bowls used to serve the meals were probably of wood, bronze or silver. Pilate probably washed his hands from a metal bowl (Matt. 27 : 24). The common pottery was thin and well-made, but not of great beauty. The styles in which it was locally made were simply continuations of the traditions of the Hellenistic period. The finest pottery was the imported *terra sigillata* ware, as archaeologists call it. It was a sturdy and well-formed red ware, most of which was purchased from Italy. A service of such handsome dishes was probably fairly inexpensive in Rome but a luxury in Palestine where it was expensive to live. In 1867–8 a stamped fragment of this ware was found in Jerusalem ; it bore the name of Camurius, a well-known potter in Arezzo, Italy, about the time of Tiberius and Claudius Caesar (A.D. 14–54). Two more plates by the same man (Fig. 184) and two signed by one Publius Cornelius have been found at Scythopolis, the Old Testament Beth-shan, south of the Sea of Galilee. Many more pieces have been found from about the 1st

---

[19] See Harris Birkeland, *The Language of Jesus*, Oslo, 1954.

184. *Terra sigillata* plate found at Beth-shan ; imported from Arezzo in Italy and signed by Camurius

century A.D., and they are excellent witness to the international trade which connected all parts of the Roman empire. An occasional piece of a slightly later date was imported all the way from Gaul (France).

For the dress of the people in 1st-century Palestine one would need to make a careful study of all monuments of the Graeco-Roman period that have been found in that country and in surrounding territories. This is something which as yet has not been systematically done for this purpose. As is the case with the Israelite period, however, we cannot assume that modern Arab costume would make one look like a biblical person. It may well be that the basic garments of Old Testament times, the short skirt and the tight-fitting dress or tunic which were worn as a rule with a belt or sash (" girdle "), still survived among Jews in the time of Jesus, together with the variety of cloaks or robes used with them. One's impression is, however, that dress had changed considerably under the influence of Greek fashions and that the clothes of the coastal countries of Asia and Africa consisted for the most part of the same type of garments as would be seen in the Aegean and in Rome (cf. Figs. 185–6).

The basic garment for both men and women, as in older times, was the dress or tunic, usually with either short or long sleeves. The major difference between the Greek tunic and the dress of Israelite times, however, was that the former was very full and hung in folds from shoulders and waist. Children or laborers wore either a short skirt or a tunic which reached only to the knees. From ancient sculpture, however, one has the impression that the cord or sash around the waist enabled the wearer to shorten a long tunic at will by pulling its folds

185. Relief from an altar dedicated to the Peace of Augustus by the Roman Senate in 13 B.C. (Ara Pacis). Friends and attendants of the Emperor Augustus are shown in a religious procession. Note the typical flowing garments of the Romans, with loose stoles or togas thrown over them in various ways as a type of cloak

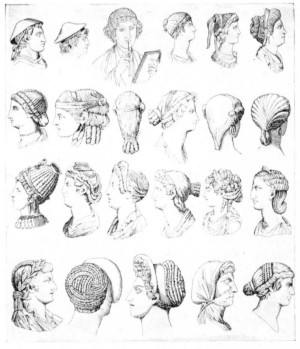

186. The coiffure of Roman women

above the belt and allowing them to fall over it. Some tunics were without sleeves and fastened at one shoulder so that the arms were free for any activity. The most common and indeed the preferred color for the tunic was white. Gone are the intricate weaving of different colored threads, together with the elaborate and multicolored fringes, so characteristic of former days. If the garment were blue or red, it would be a solid color, as though the whole cloth, rather than simply the thread, was now being dyed.

A greater difference still between New and Old Testament times is in the cloaks or robes worn over the tunic. A large variety was, of course, available. Yet the most interesting feature about Graeco-Roman clothing was the manner in which a long piece of cloth could be wound or draped about the body in such a variety of ways. One would imagine that this *chlamys*, as the Greeks called it, or *pallium* in Latin, would be a continual nuisance, falling from the shoulder, loosening and becoming unwound. Evidently the arrangement of this article of apparel was a matter of individual taste and skill, though in certain types of costume it could be fastened in place at the shoulder by a brooch or clasp. When desired, a fold of it could also be drawn over the head, though women evidently also had veils or scarfs for this purpose. When the tunic was white, the *chlamys* or *pallium* was likely to be colored. At times one observes people in the reliefs who seem to be clad solely in some such article wound about the body. It was this type of covering which the young man, presumably Mark, wore when apprehended in the Garden of Gethsemane and which easily came off his body when he fled (Mark 14 : 51 f.).

A special type of *pallium* was the Roman toga. This article would have been seen frequently in Jerusalem because it was the distinctive city dress of the Roman citizen which others were not allowed to wear. Hence it is something which the Apostle Paul must undoubtedly have worn on many occasions, especially during his trials before Roman authorities. It was a large piece of cloth which was draped around the body. One end came forward over the left shoulder; the cloth then fell toward the ground, passed around the back, under or over the right arm, across the front, and the other end was finally thrown over the left shoulder to hang down the back. There were variations, of course, in the manner of wearing and in the shape, depending upon the time and type of costume. Various hats or caps were now used to protect the head, and for the feet there were not only sandals but also shoes and boots. If a man from Mesopotamia arrived in Jerusalem on a trading mission, he probably could have been distinguished by the long pantaloons he wore.

Even more money was being spent by wealthy people of New Testament times on their tombs than was the case in the days of Israel. Around Jerusalem there are a large number of Jewish tombs from this period, some of which are architectural monuments. The best known to the tourist are perhaps those which are called the " Tombs of the Kings ", the " Tomb of the Judges ", and the " Tomb of Absalom " (Fig. 187). None of them, however, date from Old Testament times, but are Herodian or 1st century A.D. The " Tombs of the Kings " is the burial chamber of Queen Helena of Adiabene and her family (Fig. 188); this queen was converted to Judaism and moved to Palestine not long before the First Revolt in A.D. 66–70. Her sarcophagus, recovered when the mausoleum was excavated in 1863, bears a bilingual inscription in Hebrew and Syriac.

It was Jewish practice, when the bodies of the deceased had decomposed and room was needed for new burials, to collect the bones and place them in small stone boxes, now called ossuaries (Fig. 189). A great many of these ossuaries have been found, dating from the 1st centuries B.C. and A.D., and the names of the dead were frequently carved on them in Hebrew or Aramaic, occasionally indeed in Greek. The names are usually the common ones of the period, including those we encounter in the Gospels and Acts. Examples are the following : Jesus, Simon or Simeon, Judas, Ananias, Sapphira, Salome, Lazarus, Elizabeth, Miriam, etc. There is even a " Jeshua (Jesus) son of Joseph "; while not the same as Jesus of Nazareth, the inscription illustrates how common such names were. In 1931 among the old collections in the Russian museum on the Mount of Olives a most unusual inscription was discovered in the script of the ossuaries. It read : " Hither were brought the bones of Uzziah, king of Judah—do not open ! " Sometime during repairs or excavations in Jerusalem during the 1st centuries B.C. or A.D. the tomb of King Uzziah had been encountered and his bones removed to another place (Fig. 190).

The contents of the Jewish tombs of this time lead one to assume that changes had taken place in the attitudes toward death and the hereafter. No longer was it the fashion, as it had been in Israelite times,

187. Ancient tomb monuments in the Kidron Valley, Jerusalem, dating from the Herodian period

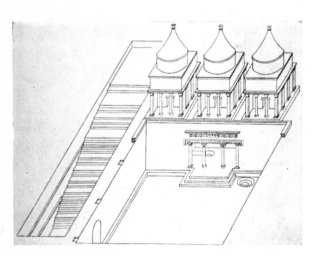

188. A reconstruction of the tomb of Queen Helena of Adiabene

189. Jewish ossuaries in a tomb in Jerusalem

to place large numbers of pottery vessels of many types around the body. Originally, such vessels held food for the deceased to use in the after-life, though in the course of time the pottery may have been continued simply to preserve the ancient custom, but in a largely symbolic fashion. By the

1st century A.D. pottery vessels are still found in the tombs, but not in such numbers. Had that not been the case, we would have a much more detailed knowledge of the pottery chronology of Graeco-Roman times than we now have. The types of vessel which were used in the funerary rites were

246

few; most notable are small bottles and pitchers for unguents and oils, lamps and occasionally also small glass vials. Glass was just coming into common use in New Testament times, because the technique of glass-blowing for mass production had not been introduced until early in the reign of Caesar Augustus (27 B.C.–A.D. 14). During the centuries which followed, there is an increasing concentration upon lamps, which appear in great numbers in every tomb. This evidence may suggest a symbolic connection between light and eternal life, for which the lamp was a sign. In any event, people during the time of Christ no longer appear to have believed in the necessity of placing an adequate supply of food beside the body for future use. Whatever the views a Jew may have held about the after-life—and various opinions on the subject were held—he no longer believed that he by his own efforts could assist in providing for the comfort of the deceased.

190. The gravestone provided for the bones of King Uzziah, after they had been moved from their original tomb

FURTHER READING

For the historical background of this period the most detailed information is to be found in Josephus, *The Antiquities of the Jews* and *The Jewish Wars*, the latest translations of which are by H. St. J. Thackeray and Ralph Marcus (London, 1926–43). For recent summaries with bibliography, see S. Vernon McCasland and Morton S. Enslin in *The Interpreter's Bible*, Vol. VII (New York and Nashville, 1951), pp. 75–113; R. H. Pfeiffer, *History of New Testament Times* (New York, 1949); Martin Noth, *History of Israel* (London and New York, 1958), pp. 400–452.

Detailed information about the archaeology of Palestine in the first century is widely scattered. The best brief reviews are W. F. Albright, *The Archaeology of Palestine* (Pelican Books, 1949), pp. 146–76; C. Watzinger, *Denkmäler Palästinas*, II (Leipzig, 1935), Chap. VI. For material dealing with special sites see especially J. W. Crowfoot, *et al.*, *The Buildings of Samaria* (London, 1942); L. Haefeli, *Caesarea and Meer* (Münster, 1923); A. Reifenberg, " Caesarea : A Study in the Decline of a Town ", *Israel Exploration Quarterly*, Vol. I (1950–1), pp. 20–32; C. H. Kraeling, ed., *Gerasa, City of the Decapolis* (New Haven, 1938); Nelson Glueck, *The Other Side of the Jordan* (New Haven, 1940), Chap. VI, and " Explorations in Western Palestine ", *Bulletin of the American Schools of Oriental Research*, No. 131 (Oct. 1954), pp. 6–15.

The basic studies of the archaeology of ancient Jerusalem are J. Simons, *Jerusalem in the Old Testament* (Leiden, 1952), and L.-H. Vincent, *Jérusalem de l'Ancien Testament*, Paris, 1954.

For ancient synagogues see E. L. Sukenik, *Ancient Synagogues in Palestine and Greece* (London, 1934), and H. G. May, " Synagogues in Palestine ", *The Biblical Archaeologist*, Vol. VII, No. 1 (Feb. 1944).

Information about the Essenes, the Qumran scrolls, and the New Testament is now very scattered, but see particularly the books cited at the end of the last chapter, and Krister Stendahl, ed., *The Scrolls and the New Testament* (New York and London, 1957 and 1958).

For information concerning the bearing of archaeology on the New Testament, see especially Jack Finegan, *Light from the Ancient Past* (Princeton, 1946), pp. 215–51, 305–31. The treatment here of New Testament manuscripts is particularly good. See also A. C. Bouquet, *Everyday Life in New Testament Times* (New York, 1954); F. M. Heichelheim, " Roman Syria ", in Tenney Frank, *An Economic Survey of Ancient Rome*, Vol. IV (Baltimore, 1938), pp. 121–257; *Everyday Life in Ancient Times* (Washington, National Geographic Society, 1951).

CHAPTER XIV

THE CHURCH IN THE WORLD

" And a vision appeared to Paul in the night : a man of Macedonia was standing and summoning him and saying, ' Come over into Macedonia and help us.' And after he had seen the vision, immediately we endeavored to go into Macedonia, assuredly gathering that the Lord had called us to preach the gospel unto them " (Acts 16 : 9–10).

AT the beginning of biblical history we are in the midst of the ancient world, first in Mesopotamia and then in Egypt, the two foci of power in the time of Israel, and there we seek to understand the historical and cultural movements within which the nation of Israel took form. Throughout most of the history, however, our attention is largely confined to Palestine where the events occurred which molded and challenged the biblical community. With the Acts of the Apostles and the Epistles of the New Testament we again move out into the world, a much larger world than that of Abraham or Moses. After A.D. 70, when Jerusalem was destroyed, Palestine is no longer at the center of attention. Christianity obtains its deepest rootage elsewhere, and the Christian historian returns to Palestine only after the passage of many years when Christian churches begin to be established there and the land becomes the traditional " Holy Land ", a place of pilgrimage.

In what direction did Christianity move out from the land of its birth ? Initially, within the period covered by the New Testament it went north and then west, drawn like a magnet to Rome, the hub of the world at that time. The reason for this was the new unity imposed upon the world by Roman power, Roman law and Graeco-Roman culture. The Greek language, learned in Palestine by many of the earliest Christians, made it possible for them to be understood almost anywhere in the empire where they traveled. Jewish communities were to be found in every major city of the empire, and to them the missionaries first preached. Roman provincial administration kept the roads safe and in good condition throughout the controlled areas, so that travel was easy and comparatively free from all hazards except those of the weather. Only after Christianity was firmly intrenched in the Roman provinces of the east, do we begin to encounter signs of its penetration into Mesopotamia and other areas independent of Rome.

ARCHAEOLOGICAL EVIDENCES FOR EARLY CHRISTIAN CHURCHES IN THE EAST

The earliest evidence which the archaeologist has found for Christian communities in the east is in Egypt. The large number of papyrus fragments of the New Testament found in that country show that within one hundred years of Jesus' death thriving Christian groups were in existence as far south as the Egyptian Fayum. The Chester Beatty papyri were probably found in the same area. Among them is a codex of the letters of Paul, dating about A.D. 200, which is earlier by 150 years than the oldest copies of the Pauline letters otherwise known and probably little more than a century from the time when the letters were collected and published together (Fig. 191).

The codex is a book in the modern sense with the leaves laid flat upon one another, in contrast to the scroll or roll. The latter was quite satisfactory for small documents such as letters or for any literary work which is meant to be read through. Yet for a lengthy document to which constant reference needs to be made in order to look up specific passages, it was obviously less convenient than the leaf-book. The evidence now at hand suggests that Christians quickly began to use the codex almost exclusively for their works. During the 3rd century A.D., for example, nearly 85% of all Christian manuscripts discovered are of the codex type, while at the same time nearly 94% of the recovered non-Christian documents of the same period are still of the roll-type.[1]

The earliest remains of church architecture in Egypt, as in most other areas of the Roman empire, are from the 4th century A.D. during and after the time of the emperor Constantine (A.D. 323–37), when Christianity became the official religion sponsored by the Roman government. Many

[1] For a summary of the evidence see C. C. McCown, " The Earliest Christian Books ", *The Biblical Archaeologist*, Vol. VI (1943), pp. 21–31.

191. Chester Beatty Papyrus II, earliest known manuscript of the letters of Paul (*ca.* A.D. 200)

192. A reconstruction of the Dura baptistry in the Yale
Gallery of Fine Arts

churches have been found in Palestine and these,
too, date after the time of Constantine between
the 4th and 6th centuries. At least eleven have
been uncovered in Gerasa alone. The Church of
the Holy Sepulchre in Jerusalem and the Church
of the Nativity in Bethlehem were both built in
Constantine's time, though little remains of the
original structures within the later buildings now
standing.[2]

The oldest known church which archaeologists
have found was excavated in 1931–2 at Dura-
Europos in eastern Syria on the Euphrates. This
town was taken by the Romans and provided with
a garrison in A.D. 167 as an outpost of the empire.
Inside and south of the main city gate was a church
which once had been a private house. In plan it
consisted of a series of rooms around a paved open
court. On a plastered wall was an inscription

[2] See J. W. Crowfoot, *Early Churches in Palestine*, London,
1941.

stating when the house was built, A.D. 232–3 in
our calendar. One of the rooms had been used as a
chapel, which was later enlarged by the opening of
two more rooms so that the whole could seat about
one hundred people. In a small neighboring room
was the baptistry (Fig. 192). At one end of it was
a niche and a receptacle or tub for the water.
Above the latter a scene was painted on the wall,
showing Christ as the Good Shepherd, caring for
his sheep. The figure of the youthful Christ,
carrying a sheep around his shoulders, was a very
popular theme in early Christian art as we know
from painting and sculpture in Italy. Other wall
paintings show Scriptural scenes, such as David
and Goliath, the Samaritan woman, Peter attempting to walk on the water, and the healing of the
paralytic. The meeting places of early Christians
were in private homes, for the most part, and the
Dura building is an excellent example of one such
house-church.

To the north of the main city gate on the same
street as the church was a synagogue, completed
according to an inscription in A.D. 255. This, too,
had been a private home which had been remodelled
for public worship in A.D. 245, before it was replaced by the new synagogue. The walls were
decorated, like those of the church, with pictures
taken from Scripture (Fig. 193): among others
the sacrifice of Isaac, the Return of the Ark from
the Philistines, and scenes from the Exodus, the
life of Moses and the story of Job. Dura was
destroyed when it was recaptured by the Sassanians

193. The Dura synagogue, as reconstructed by H. Pearson in the Museum of Damascus

of Mesopotamia not long before or after A.D. 260. Shortly after that it was abandoned until it was dug out of the desert by the archaeologists of Yale University and the French Academy of Inscriptions and Letters.[3]

Elsewhere in Syria, and for that matter throughout the ancient world, virtually nothing remains of the churches which existed before the time of Constantine, though there are many Christian ruins which date from the 4th, 5th and 6th centuries A.D. The reason probably is that most of the churches were destroyed in the violent persecutions of the emperor Diocletian, which began in A.D. 303. The archaeologist, therefore, cannot hope to find much evidence of specifically Christian ruins which date before that time. Much less can he hope to discover very much that directly illustrates the life of the Church during the second half of the 1st century A.D. when the number of Christians was comparatively small and scattered throughout a vast realm. All that we can do here, therefore, is to follow the Apostle Paul through his missionary journeys in order to see how archaeology has illumined the geographic and cultural background in which the epistles of the New Testament were written.

[3] See M. Rostovtzeff, *Dura-Europos and its Art* (Oxford, 1938), Chap. IV. For details on the Christian Church, see the original report by the excavators, C. Hopkins and P. V. C. Baur, *Christian Church at Dura-Europos* (New Haven, 1934; reprinted from the Preliminary Report of the Fifth Season, Chaps. VII–VIII).

ANTIOCH IN SYRIA

We begin with Antioch in Syria, which, after Rome and Alexandria in Egypt, was the third city of the empire. It was the first major center of Christianity outside of Palestine, and the base from which Paul set out on his missionary journeys. It is situated about 300 miles north of Jerusalem at the point where the Lebanon mountains and the Taurus range from Asia Minor meet. There the River Orontes breaks through the mountains to the Mediterranean (Fig. 194). Antioch was founded about 300 B.C. on the banks of the Orontes some 20 miles from the Sea. Through its seaport, Seleucia, it was in constant communication with the west, while trading caravans from all over the Near East converged upon it. During the 4th century A.D. its male citizens numbered 150,000 to 200,000, and we can assume at least the same number, if not more, in Paul's day. It was the home of great philosophical, medical and rhetorical schools, a famous library, and all the public amusements in full measure: theaters, amphitheaters, stadia and baths. It was as well a center of cattle breeding in the Roman Near East, with rich pasture lands in the neighboring woods. Like other great Hellenistic cities it was bisected from one end to the other by a great colonnaded street, but it is the only one known to us which had a regular system of street lamps.

Nearby at Daphne was a celebrated sanctuary of the god Apollo. There in the pleasure park around the temple vice of various kinds did a flourishing business until Daphnian morals became proverbial far and wide. The citizens of Antioch also enjoyed a reputation for scurrilous wit and the invention of nicknames. Most scholars have interpreted the first use of the name " Christians " in Acts 11 : 26 as another example of Antiochian derisive name-calling. It was in this wildly pagan city that the Christian Church formed its great center outside Palestine. The physician Luke, who was the author of Luke-Acts, has traditionally been thought to be a native of this city, and the Gospel of Matthew may well have been written there. During the 3rd century A.D. a notable Christian scholar, named Lucian, lived in Antioch. He compiled a critical edition of the Septuagint and founded a theological school which opposed the allegorizing tendencies of the School of Alexandria in Egypt. The scholar Theodore and the orator Chrysostom were two of the greatest figures

194. Antioch in Syria

of this school among the early Fathers of the Church.

Excavations were conducted in the city and in its port, Seleucia, between 1931 and 1939 by Princeton University and the Musées Nationaux de France. Perhaps the most important discoveries are hundreds of mosaic pavements which reveal considerable information about the art and even the pagan religious cults of the later Roman and Byzantine periods. Through archaeological and literary remains over a score of ancient churches have been identified in the city and in its suburbs, all of them from the 4th century A.D. or later. One mosaic floor of the 6th century has an inscription which possibly may contain a biblical phrase : " Peace be to your coming in, you who gaze (on this) ; joy and blessing be to those who stay here." Antioch once had a large Jewish colony, and associated with it was a large number of Greek converts or " God-fearers ". It was probably from among these latter that the Christian Church received most of its initial converts. Yet with the possible exception of the mosaic inscription mentioned above, the excavators have found no evidence of the Jewish community other than a marble fragment with a portion of a seven-branched candlestick on it.[4]

The best known object from the area is " The Chalice of Antioch " (Fig. 195). Its discovery was announced in 1916. It is a plain silver cup surrounded by an outer shell decorated with vines and the figures of Christ and the Apostles. The cup was claimed to be the Holy Grail, used by Jesus at the Last Supper, and the figures on the shell were interpreted as 1st-century portraits. These claims were widely publicized and the chalice for a time was the best known object from antiquity. The serious work of a number of scholars, however, has virtually proved that it dates from about the 4th or 5th century A.D. and had nothing to do with the Last Supper in Jerusalem. Nevertheless

---

[4] See Bruce M. Metzger, " Antioch-on-the-Orontes ", *The Biblical Archaeologist*, Vol. XI, No. 4 (Dec. 1948) ; C. R. Morey, *The Mosaics of Antioch* (New York, 1938) ; and the official publications of the expedition which excavated the site, *Antioch-on-the-Orontes*, Vols. I–IV (Princeton, 1934–48).

195. A drawing of the Chalice of Antioch

it still is one of the most important pieces of early Christian silver in existence.[5]

PAUL'S FIRST MISSIONARY JOURNEY

Leaving Antioch by the port-city, Seleucia, Paul in company with Barnabas and John Mark sailed to Cyprus, some sixty miles away (Acts 13). This island was the native country of Barnabas (Acts 4 : 36), and Christian missionaries had gone there during the persecution in Jerusalem that followed the martyrdom of Stephen (Acts 11 : 19), probably because large communities of Jews had established themselves there in preceding centuries.

Cyprus gets its name from the copper mines that were extensively exploited in its mountains during biblical times. In 12 B.C. Caesar Augustus permitted Herod the Great of Palestine to take over half of the output of these mines against a payment of 300 talents. Pottery vessels from the island appear in Palestine as early as 1600 B.C. It was colonized successively by the Myceneans of Greece, by the Phoenicians and then again by the Greeks, until in Paul's day the people and their culture were dominantly Greek, even as they are today.

Paul and his party are said to have spent some time in each of the island's two main cities. These were Salamis, where a famous temple of Zeus was located, and Paphos, where a still more famous temple of the fertility goddess, Aphrodite, existed. These cities were at opposite ends of the island, the second being the capital of the Roman provincial administration. There Paul met Sergius Paulus, "a man of intelligence" who was the Roman proconsul (Acts 13 : 7), or representative of the Roman senate in charge of the territory. An inscription, discovered by the American consul, Louis P. di Cesnola, during his explorations between 1865 and 1877, mentions Paulus as proconsul. It was found at Soli, north of Paphos, is dated about A.D. 55, but describes one incident which took place earlier during Paulus' tenure of office (about A.D. 46–8). It is the one reference we have to this proconsul outside the Bible and it is interesting that Luke gives us correctly his name and title.[6]

From Paphos Paul and Barnabas sailed to the mainland of Asia Minor and promptly ascended into the highlands of the Roman province of Galatia. There they preached and taught in Antioch of Pisidia, Iconium, Lystra and Derbe (Acts 13 : 14–14 : 24). It was probably to the Christian communities there founded that Paul later wrote his Letter to the Galatians.

The name "Galatia" was derived from a group of Gauls from Europe who settled in the northern part of the province during the 3rd century B.C. In the early second century the area became a client-kingdom of Rome, was gradually enlarged and, after the death of its last king in 25 B.C., it became a Roman province. Antioch was the chief city of this province (Fig. 196). It had been founded by Seleucus I of Syria about 300 B.C. as one of some sixteen Antiochs which he established and named after his father. About 189 B.C. it was made a free city by the Romans and by 11 B.C. a Roman colony. As a free city, Antioch had an elective form of self-government, popular assemblies, and a system of education for the young which undoubtedly was Hellenic in spirit. In such a city the political assembly was called by the Greek

---

[5] For a detailed review of this matter, see especially H. Harvard Arnason, "The History of the Chalice of Antioch", *The Biblical Archaeologist*, Vol. IV, No. 4 (Dec. 1941) and Vol. V, No. 1 (Feb. 1942).

[6] The inscription was first accurately published by D. G. Hogarth, *Devia Cypria*, p. 114.

196. Ruins of an aqueduct at Antioch in Pisidia (or Galatia)

197. Monumentum Ancyranum in Ankara, Turkey, on which the description of the reign of Caesar Augustus was inscribed

term *ekklesia*, which was the word the Christians borrowed for the new "Church" established in Christ. As a Roman colony, Antioch was placed in the highest rank of provincial cities with a well-defined social stratification. At the top were the Latin-speaking Roman citizens who had all the privileges in law of a citizen of Rome itself. The bulk of the populace, however, undoubtedly spoke Greek but were ranked only as "residents" or "dwellers" (*incolae*) and lacked the full civil rights of the Roman citizens (*coloni*). Yet these *incolae* undoubtedly lived in hope that because of the favored position of the city they one day would become citizens, for it was Roman policy to hold out the promise of citizenship to all when their education and training was deemed sufficient.

To this city in central Asia Minor Paul and Barnabas went directly from Cyprus. While they at first spoke only to the Jewish community, and evidently in Greek, they soon had achieved an astonishing success among the Gentiles, "and the Word of the Lord spread throughout all the region" (Acts 13 : 49). Asia Minor was filled with a large variety of religious sects. In Antioch the chief god was called "Men", but the cult of the mother-goddess was probably accorded the most attention. Yet the old gods were faced with great difficulty in accommodating themselves to the new age. One of the great documents which circulated in Asia Minor, a partial duplicate of which was found in the excavations at Antioch, was the *Monumentum Ancyranum* (Fig. 197), narrating the "Deeds Accomplished by the Divine Augustus (Caesar)".

Another copy of this document was carved on the walls of the Augusteum, a white marble temple, erected in Ancyra (Ankara) in northern Galatia. The text was probably composed by Augustus himself and completed in A.D. 14. It described the emperor's life and work in the attempt to fulfill the religious, even "messianic", hopes of the time. By Paul's day these hopes had been dashed; the reign of the gods on earth had not come to pass. It is perhaps in this atmosphere that Paul preached in Antioch and encountered so many people who listened to him gladly.

Excavations in Antioch just before and after the First World War uncovered some of the most important ruins of the Roman city of Paul's day. These included the Square of Augustus and the Square of Tiberius, connected by a stairway at the top of which were triumphal archways erected in honor of Caesar Augustus. In the Square of Augustus was a great temple of the god Men, whose symbol was a bull's head. This god, who was thought to bestow upon the people the blessings of nature, was probably identified for a time with Augustus himself, before disillusionment set in. From a later period, the end of the 4th century A.D., came the ruins of a large Christian church, more than 200 feet long. The city that Paul entered was evidently one of great architectural beauty and splendor, combining Greek refinement and simplicity with Roman complexity and massiveness.[7]

The cities of Iconium, Lystra and Derbe were situated southeast of Antioch along the main commercial and military route to the Cilician Gates, or the mountain passes leading into Syria. Iconium, the modern Konya, was some 60 miles from Antioch. Derbe was about 45 miles farther on but to the north of Iconium, with Lystra midway between. Iconium was evidently a far older city than Antioch, judging from the traditions associated with it, and was also thoroughly Hellenized. Lystra and Derbe were much smaller and near the southeastern edge of the Galatian province where the common people evidently spoke a native dialect (Acts 14 : 11). In one of these two cities Paul's best-known convert was Timothy, the son of a Greek father and a Jewish mother (Acts 16 : 1). Absence of archaeological information, however, means that little can be said about these towns from direct evidence.[8]

[7] See David M. Robinson, " A Preliminary Report on the Excavations at Pisidian Antioch and at Sizma ", *American Journal of Archaeology*, Vol. XXVIII (1924), pp. 435–44.

[8] The best survey is still that of W. M. Ramsay, *The Cities of St. Paul* (New York, 1908), Parts III and IV, and *St. Paul The Traveller and the Roman Citizen* (New York, 1896), Chaps. V and VI. Sir William Ramsay has probably done more in recovering the archaeological, historical and cultural background of the Pauline journeys in Asia Minor than any other modern scholar.

THE LYCUS VALLEY

Directly west of the Province of Galatia was the Province of Asia. Along the road from Antioch to Ephesus, one descends from the Phrygian highlands to the valley of the Lycus river and follows it for some twenty-four miles before it joins the Maeander river which leads to Ephesus and the Aegean Sea. In the small Lycus valley in the eastern part of the Asian province there were three main towns in all of which Pauline churches were established. These were Colossae, Laodicea and Hierapolis (Fig. 198), to which two of the letters of Paul were sent. The Epistle to the Colossians was written in Rome when Paul was in prison there sometime after A.D. 60. It was taken to Colossae by one of Paul's disciples, named Tychicus, and was to be read also to the church in Laodicea (Col. 4 : 7–17). Accompanying Tychicus was the runaway slave, Onesimus, whom Paul was sending back to his master Philemon in either Colossae or Laodicea with the beautifully written " Letter to Philemon ". The latter was one of the leaders of the Lycus churches, indeed his home was a meeting place of one of the Christian communities (Phile. 2).

Paul may have passed through the Lycus valley on his way to Ephesus during his third missionary

198. Hierapolis and the Lycus Valley

journey. In both his second and third journeys he had set out from Syrian Antioch to Tarsus, passed through the Cilician Gates and revisited the Galatian churches. On his second journey he had then gone through the northern part of the province of Asia and had crossed into northern Greece. On the third journey he went directly from the Galatian Antioch to Ephesus. While his route may have taken him through the Lycus to the Maeander valley, the churches in the three cities of the Lycus were evidently founded not by Paul himself but by his disciples while he was in Ephesus. One of them was a Colossian named Epaphras (Col. 4 : 12–13), who bore a shortened form of the name Epaphroditus.

While none of the three cities of the Lycus has been excavated, their sites have been located and their surviving ruins explored. Colossae, the oldest of the three, was identified by W. J. Hamilton in 1835 who saw numerous ruins of the ancient city, the surface stones of which have since been removed for modern building elsewhere in the neighborhood. One inscription from the site mentions a T. Asinius Epaphroditus, but it is most doubtful that this is the same as Epaphras. On the other hand, a marble altar from Laodicea is actually thought by some to bear the disciple's name.

Colossae was at the upper or eastern end of the valley, and Laodicea was ten to twelve miles west of it. The latter was founded about 250–240 B.C. as a military stronghold on the western border of the empire of Antiochus II of Syria. The site is on a small hill, about a square mile in area, and on it are still to be seen the ruins of two theaters, a stadium, blocks of stone from the eastern gate, and a gymnasium or bath. In the Book of Revelation the Laodicean church was reproved as being neither hot nor cold, but lukewarm, and as claiming to be rich and in need of nothing when actually it was poor and wretched. Scholars infer from this that reference is being made to the wealthy commercial life of the city and to the actual state of the water supply. The ruins of the old water tower and some terra cotta pipes choked by lime deposits are still there. The water was brought to the city by aqueduct and pipes, probably from hot springs in the neighborhood, and thus was undoubtedly lukewarm.

Hierapolis, mentioned in Colossians 4 : 13, was six miles north of Colossae on the other side of the valley. The ancient town stood on a terrace above the plain which was covered with white travertine deposits. Water from hot springs falls over the cliff, and the sources of this water were undoubtedly sacred to ancient nature deities. The ruins at this site are more extensive than those at Colossae and Laodicea. Two theaters are still to be seen, the smaller one of the Hellenistic period and the larger from Roman times. The ruins of the latter are very impressive ; the seats are still in place and the front width is more than 325 feet. At the edge of the cliff on the western side of the city are the extensive remains of the huge baths, and beside them the gymnasium. Like other Hellenistic cities the town was bisected by a main columned street with covered sidewalks on each side. A number of tombs are still to be seen along this street, and the cemetery has been located outside the north gate. According to tradition Philip the Evangelist, mentioned in Acts 21 : 8, spent the latter part of his life in this city, and one of the four Christian churches which have been located was built in his honor. An inscription refers to it as follows : " Eugenius the least, archdeacon who is in charge of (the church of) the holy and glorious apostle and theologian Philip." Perhaps the best known Christian of the city was a man named Papias, author of the *Exposition of the Oracles of the Lord*, which is known from quotations in later writers. He lived at the end of the first and during the first quarter of the second century, and was especially interested in recording the oral traditions about Jesus which he was able to collect from " the Elders " or Fathers of the Christian community.

The three towns of the Lycus valley contained large and very influential Jewish communities. A number of inscriptions from Hierapolis mention them, but in the course of time they disappeared, probably absorbed for the most part by the Christian Church. For this and other reasons the Christianity of the area contained a number of peculiar features, including a rigid observance of Jewish festivals and a combination of angel-worship and asceticism, against which Paul counseled the Church in his Letter to the Colossians (Col. 2).[9]

EPHESUS

On Paul's third missionary journey more than

[9] For a convenient summary of the history and archaeology of the Lycus valley, see further Sherman E. Johnson, " Laodicea and its Neighbors ", *The Biblical Archaeologist*, Vol. XIII, No. 1 (Feb. 1950).

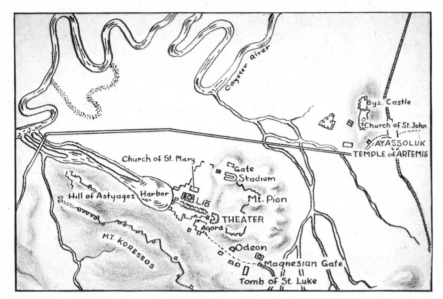

199. A map of Ephesus

200. A reconstruction of the portico of the Temple of Artemis at Ephesus

two years of his work centered in Ephesus. After visiting his churches in Galatia, he " passed through the upper country and came to Ephesus " (Acts 19 : 1). This was the chief city of the Roman province of Asia with a population of at least a quarter of a million (Fig. 199). Three miles to the west was the Aegean Sea, and at that time the Cayster River which emptied into the sea was navigable as far up as the city. Thus Ephesus served as the connecting port for sea trade with the west and the land routes to the east. Ranking in importance with the eastern Mediterranean cities of Antioch in Syria and Alexandria in Egypt, it was an advantageous spot for Paul's preaching.

Literary and inscriptional evidence give eloquent testimony to the enormous wealth of the city. According to the Roman Strabo it was the chief market of Asia Minor. No small part of its money and fame, however, came from the cult of Artemis, the mother goddess, whom the Romans identified with their Diana. Her worship was connected with the fertility of the human family, flocks, and herds. Her background was Asiatic rather than Greek or Roman, and her worship was similar to that of the earlier fertility cults of Canaan which were so seductive an influence upon Israel. The cult was popular, and the evidence supports the statement of Demetrius, the silversmith, that it was she " whom all Asia and the world worshipped " (Acts 19 : 27).

The temple of Artemis at Ephesus was considered one of the Seven Wonders of the ancient world. It was first systematically excavated by the English architect, J. T. Wood. After six years of continuous work, it was found on May 2, 1869, northeast of the city proper at the foot of the Holy Hill of Ayassoluk. Its first primitive structures, dating back to the 8th century B.C., were little more than an enclosure containing a platform, a sacred tree, an altar, and perhaps later a wooden image. About 550 B.C. the temple was constructed on a much larger and grander scale. When completed, it lasted according to tradition until it was burned in 356 B.C. This was succeeded by what is known as the Hellenistic temple, begun in 350 B.C. and completed at the expense of Alexander the Great. This temple stood until A.D. 262 when it was sacked by the Goths.

The platform on which it stood was approximately 239 feet wide and 418 feet long. The temple itself was more than 160 feet wide and 340 feet long and had 100 columns over 55 feet high. At least some of these columns were sculptured to a height of 20 feet (Fig. 200). The foundations of the main altar were 20 feet square. Behind it stood the statue of the goddess which is said to have " fallen from Jupiter " (Acts 19 : 35): that is, it may have been sculptured from a large meteorite. White marble tiles covered the roof, and the building was adorned with sculpture, excellent painting, and gold.

The month of Artemision (March–April) was a time when tourists and religious enthusiasts must have brought great wealth to the temple and the tradesmen. Perhaps it was these crowds that kept Paul in Ephesus until after Pentecost; he says in his first letter to the Corinthians: "But I will tarry at Ephesus until Pentecost, for a wide door for effective work has opened to me, and there are many adversaries" (I Cor. 16 : 8, 9). This was a likely time for the riots, occasioned by the economic effects of his preaching and by jealousy for the gods.

Paul's stay in Ephesus came to an end with the riot stirred up by Demetrius, the silversmith, whose name may possibly have been found on an inscription. The Apostle's persuasion had turned many away from the buying of silver shrines, with the result that Demetrius spoke out against the man who claimed "that there are no gods made with hands" (Acts 19 : 26). The mob gathered against Paul in the great theater on the western slope of Mt. Pion overlooking the city. The theater was approximately 495 feet in diameter and is said to have accommodated 24,550 persons. Its appearance was impressive and many fine statues adorned it.

Tradition has located the "Prison of St. Paul" at a fort on the Hill of Astyages on the western side of the city, though actually this fort belongs to a much later time. Southeast of the theater Wood identified a circular building some 50 feet in diameter as the tomb of St. Luke, but further study has recognized it as a Greek tomb of a family or of a number of soldiers.

The excavations of J. T. Wood were conducted between 1863 and 1874. The entire history of the temple was studied in further excavations by D. G. Hogarth for the British Museum in 1904–5. Perhaps the most important work at the site, however, has been that of the Austrian Archaeological Institute which began its excavations in 1896 and has published its results in four large volumes.[10] Practically all of the main buildings of the ancient city have been unearthed. The marketplace, which the Greeks called the *agora* and the Romans the *forum*, was a large open square, surrounded by colonnades and various important buildings. Most impressive is the city's finest street, the "Arka-

201. A reconstruction of the Arkadiane

diane", which ran from the theater to the harbor, a distance of some 1735 feet (Fig. 201). It was paved in marble, was approximately 36 feet wide, and was lined by a colonnade behind which were shops.

Numerous inscriptions found in the city contain information of importance for the Christian archaeologist. The mention of exorcists in Acts 19 : 13 recalls the popularity of specialists in magical formulas and incantations; Greek and Roman writers refer to the latter as "Ephesian writings". The formula, "I adjure you by . . .", used by paganizing Jewish magicians in the above mentioned passage, appears to have been the regular formula of exorcism. The word in Acts 19 : 18 which the Authorized Version translates "deeds" really means here "magical formulas". The "Asiarchs" of Acts 19 : 31 are frequently mentioned in the Ephesian inscriptions; "Asiarch" was a title for a leader in the rites of the emperor-cult in the province of Asia. Verse 35 mentions the "town clerk" who from the inscriptions was evidently not simply a clerk but the leading public official of the city. The same verse mentions Ephesus as the "temple keeper" of Artemis, and one of the inscriptions says the same thing. This title was used at Ephesus and elsewhere, however, to indicate that the city was also "temple keeper" for the worship of the Roman emperor.

The success of Paul's preaching at this important city must indeed have been great. The Book of Revelation, written toward the end of the first century from the island of Patmos not far from Ephesus, recalls these first days of the Church and

[10] *Forschungen in Ephesos, veröffentlicht von Österreichischen archaeologischen Institute,* 1906–37.

R

exhorts the Christians there to "remember therefore from whence thou art fallen" (Rev. 2 : 5). The New Testament's Letter to the Ephesians is traditionally believed to have been written in Rome about the same time as the Letter to the Colossians and to have been carried to Asia by Tychicus (Ephesians 6 : 21), the disciple of Paul who also took Colossians to the Lycus Valley. The resemblances between the two epistles have generally been felt to be so close that it is difficult to separate them. Yet both the statements of early Church Fathers and the internal contents of the Ephesian letter indicate that in all probability the original manuscript did not bear the title "Ephesians" at all. It is more probable that the letter was a general pastoral epistle to the Christians of Asia. Many scholars have long doubted on internal evidence that it was written by the apostle personally; it may well have been composed by a disciple.

Perhaps the most important event in Christian history associated with Ephesus was the ecumenical Church Council of the year A.D. 431. Its occasion was the split between Nestorius, patriarch of Constantinople together with his followers who included the School of Antioch in Syria, and the bulk of the Church headed by Cyril, bishop of Alexandria. The debate was over the doctrine of the human and divine natures of Christ and over the question as to whether Mary should be called "Mother of God", as Cyril believed, or simply "Mother of Christ", as Nestorius believed. The Council was held in the Ephesian Church of St. Mary. This church, which has been excavated, was erected about A.D. 350 on the ruins of a large pagan school or museum. It had a total length of nearly 481 feet and its plan has the appearance of a double sanctuary with an apse at each end. In the official acts of the Council, written by the faction of Cyril, the church is designated as the "Holy Mary, Mary Mother of God" or simply as "The Great Church".[11]

THE FIRST CHURCHES IN EUROPE

On Paul's second missionary journey he went from Galatian Antioch, through the northern part of the province of Asia, to Troas on the Aegean Sea. This city was about ten miles south of the western end of the Hellespont. Today it is a deserted ruin, but in Roman times it was one of Asia's chief ports. A regular sea route connected it with the end of the great highway, the Via Egnatia, at Neapolis and Philippi. The Egnatian Way was a paved Roman road across Macedonia to Dyrrhachium on the Adriatic Sea. There the Roman traveller took ship again to Brundisium in Italy where the Appian Way began and led him to Rome.

The fact that Paul was in Troas when the vision came which requested his aid in Greece (Acts 16 : 9–10) suggests that the decision to go was not a sudden or unpremeditated departure from previous plans. He was at the port ready to sail, and the vision evidently conveyed to him the certainty that it was God's plan that he should go. From Troas to Neapolis was a journey of two days by sailing vessel (Fig. 202). As was his custom, Paul did not pause at the seaport but made his way inland to the largest city of the area, Philippi. This city is today an uninhabited ruin, about eight miles from Neapolis over a mountain pass. Its chief monuments have been excavated by the French École Française d'Athènes during the period between 1914 and 1938.

The Egnatian Way was once the main thoroughfare of Philippi, and where its pavement was laid bare the ruts worn in the stone by countless wagons and chariots can still be seen. On the western side of the city a great arched gateway was uncovered; through it the road passed and about one mile from the city crossed a small river. This is the only possible place in the neighborhood to which the words in Acts 16 : 13 could refer: "On the sabbath day we went outside the gate to the riverside, where we supposed there was a place of prayer." Evidently there was no synagogue in this city; probably because the Jewish community was small a few of its members met by the river on the sabbath. Inside the gates the Roman Forum has been uncovered (Fig. 203). It was the main center of city life, about 300 feet long and 150 feet wide, with temples overlooking it on each side. While the present remains represent a rebuilding of the 2nd century A.D., they probably illustrate the general plan which existed when Paul was there. On the north side of the Forum was a podium with steps leading up the two sides. This was the tribunal for orators and magistrates, and undoubtedly marks the spot to which Paul and Silas were dragged and

---

[11] For a convenient review of the archaeology of Ephesus see the articles by Merrill M. Parvis and Floyd V. Filson in *The Biblical Archaeologist*, Vol. VIII, No. 3 (Sept. 1945).

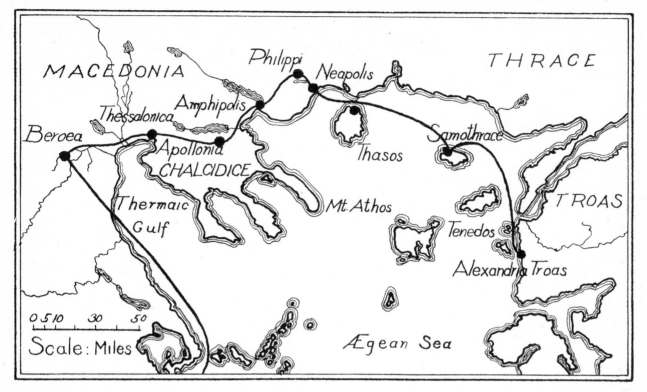

202. Map of Paul's journey into Macedonia

203. Ruins of the market-place and basilica at Philippi

where they were sentenced to prison (Acts 16 : 19 ff.). An ancient writer says that the prison along with other civic buildings bordered the Forum, but its exact location has not been fixed.

The plain of Philippi was the site of the great battle for the control of the Roman empire after the death of Julius Caesar. In 42 B.C. Antony and Octavian there defeated Caesar's murderers, Brutus and Cassius. To celebrate the victory the conquerors made the city a Roman colony, and veterans of the battle were among the first citizens (*coloni*). The arched gateway and the enlargement of the city from a small town around its acropolis probably date from this time.

Except for the remains of Byzantine churches, the most imposing of which are the huge piers of the Derekler basilica, a church almost as large as the Forum, little evidence of Christianity survives. One Greek inscription, dated A.D. 262–3, reads : " Aurelius Capito, junior presbyter of the universal church, set up this monument to his own parents and his own wife, Bebia Paula, and to his dearest son, Elpidus." The church which Paul established there, however, was one to which he was greatly attached. His Letter to the Philippians, unlike his other letters, reveals no serious internal problems within this first Christian community which he established in Europe. He evidently wrote the letter while he was a prisoner in Rome, to acknowledge a gift which his converts had sent him. He wrote as a pastor to a much beloved flock, telling his people about himself and his situation and giving them spiritual advice concerning the Christian life. One of the special problems in the church which he mentions is a dispute between two women, Euodia and Syntyche, who are exhorted " to be of one mind in the Lord " (Phil. 4 : 2).

The next major city along the Via Egnatia in which Paul founded a church was Thessalonica, about 70 miles from Philippi. It is the modern Salonica, the largest city of Greece after Athens. No major excavations have been attempted there because of the modern buildings. The city was founded about 315 B.C. and named after the sister of Alexander the Great. The Egnatian Way is still the main thoroughfare, and at one point it is spanned by a fine triple arch erected by the emperor Galerius (A.D. 305–11). The western entrance to the city was once covered by another Roman arch, called the Varder Gate. This remained standing until 1876, when it was removed for modern construction. An inscription on this gate, now in the British Museum, mentions some city officials called " politarchs ". A number of other inscriptions contain the same word. In Acts 17 : 6 this term is also used as the name of the officials before whom Christians were dragged during the riot caused by Paul's preaching. The word is otherwise unknown in extant Greek literature and the archaeological information is a confirmation of the accuracy of Luke's narrative at this point.

Paul wrote two letters to the church which he established there. They are the earliest of his letters and were evidently written on the same missionary journey after he had arrived in Corinth (A.D. 50–1). They indicate that the converts were largely Gentiles who had been deeply affected by Paul's teaching about the future in contrast to the rather hopeless and dismal lamentations that went on in pagan funerals and are still to be read in pagan tomb inscriptions. Occasionally in such inscriptions there is a hint of immortality, but the prevailing sentiment in the Greek world concerning death was one of utter hopelessness. Yet Paul's new teaching raised several problems. The Thessalonians were living in expectation of Christ's Second Coming in the very near future and were giving up their useful employment in the present world. In addition, they were worried about those who were dying before Christ came again. The letters were written to correct misconceptions and to bring order into a situation that was fast disintegrating into anarchy.[12]

ATHENS

After leaving the Macedonian cities of Thessalonica and Beroea Paul went to Athens and there waited for Silas and Timothy. Athens was now well past the height of its golden age which flowered in the 5th century B.C., but it was still one of the world's leading centers for philosophy, architecture, poetry, and art. In it there still remain today some of the most remarkable and best preserved of the monuments of antiquity (Fig. 204).

One of the finest examples of systematic archaeological study in the world has been done in the Greek *agora* or marketplace by the American School of Classical Studies since 1930. Not only has this ancient center of the city been completely excavated,

[12] See further W. A. McDonald, " Archaeology and St. Paul's Journeys in Greek Lands ", *The Biblical Archaeologist*, Vol. III, No. 2 (May 1940), pp. 18–24 ; Jack Finegan, *Light from the Ancient Past* (Princeton, 1946), pp. 269–71.

but it is being restored at a cost of $1,000,000—perhaps the most important project ever carried out at a classical site. It was in this agora and in the synagogue that Paul argued daily with the Jews, devout persons, and those " that chanced to be there " (Acts 17:17). The agora was the political, commercial and social center of the ancient Greek town and consisted of a large open space bordered by public, religious and political buildings. In ancient Athens the Panathenaean Road crossed the agora diagonally from the northwest to the southeast. Extending into the open space from the south was the Odeion or Music Hall where musical and oratorical contests were held. The first building to be uncovered by the Greek Archaeological Society before the American School of Classical Studies began its work was the long Stoa of Attalos on the east border. On the south two long parallel stoas were found. The various buildings that have been identified on the west side include the circular Tholos where the executive sections of the Athenian Council of Five Hundred were held, the Bouleuterion where the Council met, the Sanctuary of the Mother of Gods, the Temple of Apollo Patroös, and the Stoa of Zeus Eleutherios. A little toward the center of the open space was the Temple of Ares. Archaeological work has been limited on the north because of modern constructions, but it is probably here that one would find the Stoa Poikile where famous historical paintings were on view and where the philosopher Zeno lectured.

Julius Caesar and Augustus probably financed an extension of the Greek marketplace to the east which is known as the Roman Agora. It was a huge undertaking, consisting of shops and arcades along the open rectangular area. Overlooking the Greek Agora to the west is the hill called Kolonos Agoraios on which are the remains of a temple of Hephaistos, the god of fire and metalurgy. The excavation of numerous metal working shops on the slopes around the temple makes its identity certain.

Proceeding south around the base of the Acropolis hill, important identifications have included the Odeion of Pericles, where musical contests were held, and the Theater of Dionysos which was remodeled several times for the production of plays. Farther to the southeast is the magnificent Olympieion, the temple of the Olympian Zeus. This was the largest temple in Greece, measuring 354 by 135 feet at its base and towering to a height of over 90 feet. Begun about 530 B.C. it stood un-finished even in Paul's day, until completed by the Emperor Hadrian (A.D. 117–38). Still standing are fifteen of its massive columns.

The famous and remarkable Acropolis (Fig. 205), a hill 512 feet in height, is usually approached through the ornamental gateway, called the Propylaea, on the west. Most of the majestic architecture of the renowned hill dates to the golden age of Pericles, the 5th century B.C. The little temple of Wingless Victory, recently rebuilt, was slightly to the south, and the beautiful temple known as the Erechtheion was on the northern slope. Crowning the hill is the extraordinary Parthenon, and Phidias, Pericles' sculptor, erected a gold and ivory statue of Athena within it. Pausanias, a traveler who visited Athens between A.D. 143 and 159 and left a remarkable account of his visit, mentions a colossal bronze statue of Athena Promachos, the goddess who leads the fight, as towering above the Acropolis where mariners could see the sunlight flashing on her helmet and spear.[13]

As the New Testament student reads about Paul's short stay in Athens, the incident that most claims his interest is Paul's speech on the Areopagus (Acts 17:19–31). The rocky, bare hill about 377 feet high which is called the Areopagus or Hill of Ares is a little northwest of the Acropolis (Fig. 205). It was the meeting place of the Athenian court for political and religious matters. In the time of Pericles it had been mainly a criminal court, but by Roman times it was again concerned with religion and education. The place of the court's assembly was also referred to as the Acropolis, so that we are uncertain whether Acts is referring to the hill or the court. The latter at times appears to have met in the Royal Stoa which was probably in the agora. Yet in all likelihood the speech was made on the hill since it was the usual place of the court.

The other problem Paul's speech presents is his quotation of the inscription, " To an unknown god ". No such inscriptions have yet been found in Athens. The traveler Pausanias and some later literary works, however, speak of " unknown gods ", and an altar " to unknown gods " was discovered at Pergamum in Asia. Hence there is really nothing strange about the reference which Paul makes.

Paul's visit in this cultural center was short and no letters survive to any Christians there. Yet the city's art and architecture could not have remained

---

[13] Pausanias, *Description of Greece*, I, xxviii, 2.

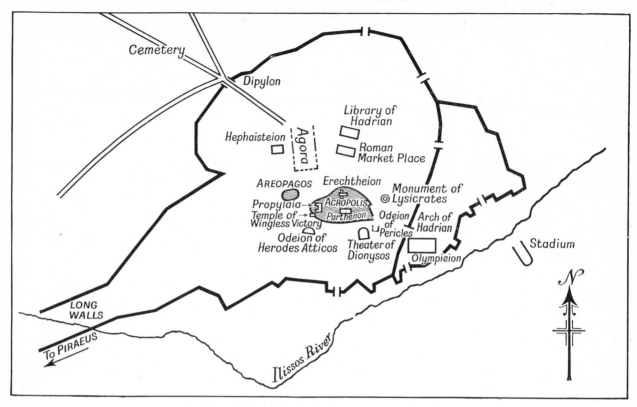

204. The chief archaeological monuments of Athens

205. The Areopagus and the Acropolis in Athens

262

unnoticed. The marvelous temples and the elaborate expressions of religiosity furnish a vivid background for Paul's attempt to use the language of a Greek philosopher in order to proclaim: "God that made the world and all things therein . . . dwelleth not in temples made with hands. Neither is he worshipped with men's hands, as though he needed anything, seeing that he giveth to all life and breath and all things . . . Forasmuch then as we are the offspring of God, we ought not to think that the Godhead is like unto gold, or silver, or stone, graven by art and man's device. And the times of this ignorance God winked at; but now commandeth all men everywhere to repent." [14]

CORINTH

From Athens Paul went to Corinth on his second missionary journey. He was there a year and six months and to the church he founded he later wrote his Letters to the Corinthians. Corinth commanded the land route over the narrow isthmus connecting central Greece and the Peloponnesus; it was thus a natural center for the sea trade of Lechaion on the west and Cenchreae on the east. Small ships were dragged the short distance between the two cities and other cargo was taken overland and reloaded. Otherwise the ships had to make the dangerous 200-mile trip around the peninsula. The Corinth canal that was cut across the narrowest point of the isthmus between 1881 and 1893 is four miles in length and is practically the same route planned and begun by Nero in A.D. 66 (Fig. 206). Located in such a situation Corinth was a great commercial center and Caesar Augustus made it the capital of the Roman province of Achaia and seat of its proconsul.

Excavation has only been possible since 1858 after a terrific earthquake caused old Corinth to be abandoned (Fig. 207). In 1896 the American School of Classical Studies was granted permission to examine it and since that time the work of clearance and excavation has been continued. The earliest occupation of the site goes back to the 4th millennium B.C., and its history shows various invasions, destructions, and subsequent returns to glory. In 146 B.C. it was destroyed by the Romans,

206. The Corinth Canal

but its destruction was probably not as complete as formerly thought. After lying unoccupied for a century, a Roman colony was planted and the city was again on its way to prosperity. In Paul's day it was in the midst of reconstruction and expansion.

In the center of the city was the agora or marketplace where the important civic and religious buildings were situated. The Lechaion Road led into the agora from the north (Fig. 208) and various constructions partially preserved reveal shops opening upon the street or courtyard, doubtless similar to the one in which Paul worked at his trade with Priscilla and Aquila (Acts 18:2, 3). On the right, just before the road entered the agora, there was a large columned hall or basilica. This type of building was used by Romans for civic and judicial purposes, and from it Christians later derived their plan for the nave and aisle type of church. To the left was the Peribolos of Apollo, one of several sanctuaries to this god, and the fountain house of Peirene, Corinth's most important reservoir and still a source of water today. The Propylaea by which one entered the agora consisted of a broad stairway which was once surmounted by a monumental

---

[14] See further W. A. McDonald, " Archaeology and St. Paul's Journeys in Greek Lands. Part II, Athens ", *The Biblical Archaeologist*, Vol. IV, No. 1 (Feb. 1941), pp. 1–10; Jack Finegan, *op. cit.*, pp. 272–8.

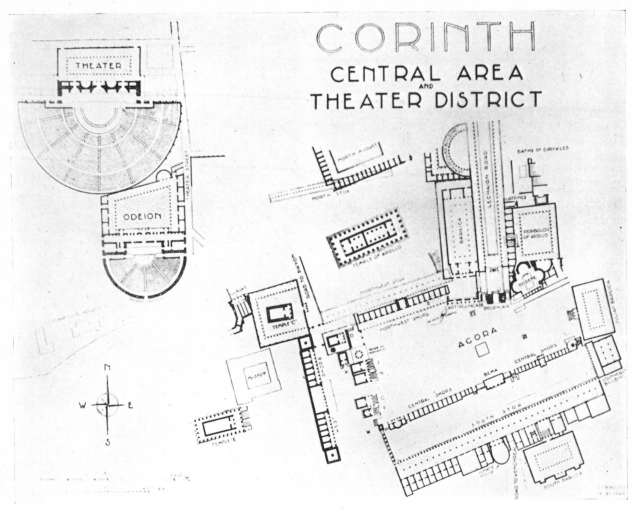

207. A map of ancient Corinth

gateway. At the foot of these stairs an inscription was found, reading " Synagogue of the Jews ". Though later than the time of Paul, it indicates that the synagogue in which Paul preached may not have been far from this area.

In the agora basilicas, temples, and stoas with shops lined the sides. In one of these shops a stone block was found which originally was a doorstep ; it bears an inscription reading " Lucius, the butcher ". This may indicate the section of shops which was the Corinthian Meat Market mentioned by Paul in I Cor. 10 : 25, although other inscriptions, none too certain, have been found among the shop ruins on the Lechaion Road.

The large and unencumbered open space of the agora was divided into two levels, differing by about eight feet in height. The well-built and elaborate Rostra of the higher level protrudes into the lower

at the center of the agora. It is probably this platform to which Paul was taken before Gallio and before which the people rioted (Acts 18 : 12-17). An inscription mentioning Gallio has been found at Delphi on the other side of the gulf of Corinth. It offers one of the few possibilities of dating Paul's work. The inscription can be dated, and Gallio is referred to as proconsul of Achaia. It indicates that Gallio came to Corinth as proconsul in either A.D. 51 or 52 ; and since Acts seems to imply that he had only recently acquired this position when Paul was brought before him, the latter must have arrived there about A.D. 50.

Leaving the agora from the northwest corner to go northward, one passed the Temple of Apollo. Seven massive Doric columns constructed in the 6th century B.C., are still standing and must have been an important landmark in Paul's day. The

208. The Lechaion Road, Corinth

numerous sanctuaries, temples, and fountains testify to the many gods of ancient Corinth and to the cults brought in by the large foreign population. Outstanding among these was the temple of Aphrodite (Venus), a shrine to Athena, the fountain Glauke, and the temple of Asklepios, the god of healing.

Northwest of the city there were two theaters; the smaller was the Odeion or Music Hall, and the larger was a vast affair for plays with a seating capacity of 18,000. A re-used paving block found near the theaters preserves an inscription (Fig. 209) which says that the pavement was the work of Erastus, who was Commissioner of Public Works (*aedilis*). He is generally identified with the Erastus who became a disciple and co-worker of the Apostle Paul (Acts 19 : 22). In Rom. 16 : 23 Paul calls him the *oikonomos* or " chamberlain " of the city. He was thus an important official and an exception to the Apostle's statement to the Corinthians that not many wise or mighty or noble men after the flesh are called (I Cor. 1 : 26).

Many passages in Paul's First Letter to the Corinthians reveal the author's intimate knowledge of the people and their occupations. On this we can do no better than quote the words of the chief excavator of the city, Professor Oscar Broneer :

The Apostle's resolve to lead the life of a wage-earner, mingling freely with citizens and foreigners in every walk of life, was obviously paying dividend. We gather that he had joined the procession to the Isthmia for the celebration of the games (I Cor. 9 : 24-7), where he watched the runners contend for a " corruptible crown " of victory. The term is well chosen for the wreath bestowed upon the winner was made of withered celery. He had seen the boxers engaged in their cruel and often deadly sport, their knuckles strapped with leather thongs to render the blows more effective. Figures of speech borrowed from these engagements came readily to his mind when writing to the Corinthians. He had observed the people crowd to the law courts where strict, though usually fair, justice was administered according to Roman standards, and he exhorted the Christians to arbitrate their differences or even to suffer injustice rather than be judged by unbelievers. He had watched the farmers plow and reap their fields in the fertile plain below the city, and had seen the laborers hoe up the ground around the vines and gather the ripe grapes for which Corinth has for centuries been famous (our word " currant " is a mediaeval corruption for Corinth). He had doubtless many times engaged shepherds in conversation as they drove their flocks to pasture or carried home the milk

265

209. The Erastus inscription, Corinth

at night, so that his words were readily understood by his readers when he wrote : " Who plants a vineyard without eating any of its fruit ? Who tends a flock without getting some of the milk ? . . . the plowman should plow in hope and the thresher thresh in hope of a share in the crop " (I Cor. 9 : 7-10). He felt no scruples about eating of meat that had been sacrificed to the pagan gods and would not have refused an invitation from his non-Christian friends to a feast in a pagan temple (I Cor. 8 : 10), but would rather restrict his freedom than give offence to a fellow-believer of less robust convictions. Though free, he had made himself a " servant unto all, a Jew unto the Jews, to those without the law as without the law ", and could state without boasting : " I have made myself all things unto all men, that I might by all means save some." In the pursuit of his calling Paul had made it his practice to visit every quarter of the city and to be present at every kind of occasion when men gathered for work or play, and he spoke to them not as an outsider but as one of their own people. A perusal of the ruins of ancient Corinth and of the abundant archaeological material gathered in the museum cannot fail to add force and vividness to the homely figures of speech with which the Apostle Paul sought to impress his message upon his hearers.[15]

ROME

Paul's letter to the Romans is the longest and most important of his extant correspondence. It was evidently written from Corinth during his last visit there on his third missionary journey. The

[15] Oscar Broneer, " Corinth : Center of St. Paul's Missionary Work in Greece ", *The Biblical Archaeologist*, Vol. XIV, No. 4 (Dec. 1951), pp. 95-6 ; see also W. A. McDonald, " Archaeology and St. Paul's Journeys in Greek Lands. Part III, Corinth ", *ibid.*, Vol. V, No. 3 (Sept. 1942), pp. 36-48.

fact that the Apostle took such care in writing the letter indicates that already there was an important Christian community in the capital city. He states that he had long wished to visit " God's beloved in Rome ", but had been prevented from doing so. Now, however, as soon as he has taken a collection from his missionary churches to Jerusalem, he plans to go to Spain and to stop off at Rome on the way (Rom. 15 : 23-9). Not long thereafter he did indeed arrive in Rome (probably sometime between A.D. 58 and 60), but he came as a prisoner who had appealed from the Palestinian authorities to the justice of Caesar. He was a Roman citizen and such an appeal was his right according to Roman law.

The antiquities of Italy, together with those of Greece and Palestine, have probably been more carefully and thoroughly explored than those of any other countries in the world. Americans, for example, have for many years maintained three main schools for the archaeology of the ancient world in Rome, Athens and Jerusalem. Scholars from Great Britain, Germany and France have worked more or less constantly in these countries since the second half of the last century. Yet Italy has been in a favored position because of the interest of the Italian government and of the Roman Catholic Church in archaeological work. Rome and Pompeii are two of the most fascinating cities in the world for the archaeological visitor because of the labor and care which have been expended on the ancient monuments.

Paul landed in Italy at Puteoli (Acts 28 : 13) on

the north shore of the Bay of Naples, a larger and more favored harbor for sizable vessels than Ostia, the port of Rome. In Puteoli the Apostle found Christian brethren with whom he stayed for a week before going on to the capital. This was not far from Pompeii, the city which within twenty years was to be covered with volcanic stone and dust from a sudden eruption of Mt. Vesuvius (in A.D. 79). Systematic excavations of Pompeii have been carried on by the Italian government since 1763 and the greater part of the town has been uncovered (Fig. 210). In the ruins of this town we are accorded the most complete view of the life of an ancient people which archaeology has provided. The typical public buildings of the time are all there, but most interesting are the numerous private houses and shops which provide insight into the common life of the population. Among the shops, for example, are those of the silversmiths, grocers, bakers, dyers, a blacksmith, a surgeon, a sculptor, a tanner, and even a purveyor of hot-drinks. Architecture was generally of brick covered with stucco; and the walls of public buildings and private homes were painted, often with elaborate compositions from history and mythology. The presence of Jews in the village is indicated by one such wall-painting which probably depicts the Judgment of Solomon (I Kings 3 : 16–28). There is also a Jewish inscription scratched on a wall which reads " Sodoma, Gomora ".

Readers of Bulwer-Lytton's novel, *The Last Days of Pompeii*, will recall the author's descriptions of Christians in the city before its destruction. Yet until 1936 no evidence of Christians had been provided by the archaeologists. In that year M. Della Corte noticed a peculiar formula on a column recently uncovered and recalled that a portion of the same formula had been found in 1925. It reads :

```
R  O  T  A  S
O  P  E  R  A
T  E  N  E  T
A  R  E  P  O
S  A  T  O  R
```

Four examples of the same combination of letters were found in Dura-Europos on the Euphrates, where the earliest Christian Church so far excavated has been found (see above), and another example has appeared on a Roman structure in Cirencester, England. During medieval times it was still known

210. In the ruins of Pompeii

and used often for magical purposes. The meaning of the formula has been much debated. One view holds that it is Jewish, based on Ezekiel 1 and 10. ROTAS is Latin for " wheels "; OPERA means " works ", TENET " holds ", AREPO perhaps the name of an angel, and SATOR " sower ". A translation, then, might be : " The sower, Arepo, holds as works the wheels." The supposition is that a Jew thought of the angel in Ezek. 10 : 2 as sowing coals of fire taken from between the wheels of God's chariot, and used the formula as a symbol of God's judgment on Rome.

It is possible, however, that a Christian constructed the formula. The letter T was early used as a symbol of the cross, and the vertical and horizontal word TENET combine to make a cross. The twenty-five letters conceal two occurrences each of PATER NOSTER, the first two words of the Lord's Prayer in Latin and also A and O, the Latin representation of Alpha and Omega which is used of God in Rev. 1 : 8 ; 21 : 6 and of Christ in Rev. 22 : 13. It is also possible to conceive of a Jewish Christian as using Ezekiel's visions as a background to express in symbols his new faith.

The probability perhaps leans on the side of the second or third possibilities, which means that the

211. A Roman road near Aleppo, Syria

212. Roman milestones collected near the Arnon River
in Transjordan

formula actually does suggest the presence of Christians in Pompeii, perhaps during and after the persecutions of Nero in A.D. 64. Yet the cryptic nature of such a combination of letters makes it impossible to lay much historical weight upon it.[16] Later, just before the outbreak of the Second World War, the impression of what appeared to be a cross was found in a house, and this is stronger evidence for Christians in Pompeii. Yet, if so, we may safely say that they were few in number ; otherwise more traces of them would have been discovered.

From Puteoli to Rome was a distance of some 150 miles, most of it along the paved highway known as the Via Appia. This road, together with all other important highways of Italy, led into Rome to converge on the Via Sacra which ran through the Roman Forum in the center of the city. These Roman roads are undoubtedly the greatest examples of highway engineering before modern times, and during the first three centuries of our era they were gradually extended throughout the Roman empire for military purposes, until in such faraway provinces as England and Palestine there was a regular network of them. The typical highway was about 14 feet wide (Figs. 211–12). A carefully prepared base was capped with concrete, on which large blocks of hard stone, carefully fitted, were laid. The road was so well built as to be virtually indestructible. It was also notable for preserving a straight course regardless of obstacles ; the final 56 miles of the Appian Way was almost as straight as an arrow as it crossed the marshes and hills on its way to Rome.

The Eternal City in Paul's day is generally reckoned as having a population of over 1,000,000 inhabitants. An inscription found in the city's port, Ostia, in 1941 says that in A.D. 14 the population was 4,100,000, but this figure must surely include all the inhabitants of the surrounding area. The streets of the modern city frequently follow the ancient avenues. For example, the main thoroughfare of present-day Rome is Corso Umberto I. It begins at the edge of the old Capitoline Hill where the vast, white monument to Victor Emmanuel II now stands, crosses the Piazza Venezia where the crowds used to greet Mussolini as he stood on the balcony of the palace, and then goes straight north to the outskirts of the city. Some 15 to 20 feet below it are still to be found the paving blocks of the old Roman Via Flaminia.

Most of the people in ancient Rome lived in large apartment houses, the height of which, on main streets, was limited by a decree of Caesar Augustus to 70 feet. So many people had crowded into the city that the problem of feeding and

[16] For summary see Floyd V. Filson, " Were There Christians in Pompeii ? ", *The Biblical Archaeologist*, Vol. II, No. 2 (May 1939), pp. 13–16.

213. The Roman Forum, looking toward the Arch of Titus and the Colosseum

supporting them was most difficult, particularly when unemployment was so severe. Much of the work was done by slaves, captured in the empire's wars. Elaborate measures were taken to keep the unemployed and the poor who were not slaves fed and contented by a system of food rationing, gifts of grain and elaborate entertainments. As the Via Appia entered the heart of the city, for example, it had to turn northward around the Palatine Hill at the point where it ran into the Circus Maximus. This was the largest of a number of such structures, built for chariot races. It was 1800 feet long and, after the enlargement by Nero (A.D. 54–68), seated some 250,000 spectators. Among the theaters the best preserved is that of Marcellus, erected in 11 B.C. with a capacity of 14,000.

The Roman Forum, the center of the world in Paul's day, lay between the two central hills of the seven on which Rome was built. One entered it on the eastern end at the point where the Arch of Titus now stands (Fig. 213). This was erected in A.D. 81 in honor of the conqueror of Jerusalem, and on its interior shows the booty, taken from the Temple in A.D. 70, being carried in a triumphal procession into Rome (Fig. 214). Directly ahead at the top of the Forum's square was the Capitoline

Hill, with its great temple to Jupiter, the chief of the Roman gods, and the Tabularium, the fireproof building for state records. On the left rose the Palatine Hill where the vast palaces of the emperors were built. In the Forum itself are the remains of a variety of buildings seen by the Apostle (Fig. 215). One of them, on the south side, was

214. The interior of the Arch of Titus, showing booty from the Temple in Jerusalem being brought into Rome in a triumphal procession

215. The Roman Forum, looking toward the Capitoline Hill

the Basilica Julia, dedicated by Julius Caesar in 46 B.C. Since this was the main hall of justice, it is not improbable that Paul was condemned to death within it. Opposite it on the north was a similar building, the Basilica Aemilia. Twenty-four beautiful columns of Phrygian marble (from Galatia in Asia Minor) were taken from the latter and used in the rebuilding of Constantine's church which was erected over the traditional tomb of Paul. This church, *San Paolo fuori le mura* (St. Paul's Outside the Walls), was completed in A.D. 398 and remained standing for over 1400 years until fire destroyed it in 1823. Between the two basilicas at the end of the Forum was the Rostrum from which public addresses and proclamations were made. By it stood the *Miliarium Aureum,* a gilded column erected in 28 B.C., on which were marked the chief cities and distances on the highways from Rome. It was the mile-stone from which the distances on all public thoroughfares were measured. To the north on the edge of the Capitoline Hill was the old state prison, Carcer Mamertinus, the vaults of which are still to be seen beneath the Church of *San Giuseppe de' Falegnami.* Paul, according to an old tradition, was imprisoned here, but, of course,

there is no way of checking the accuracy of that tradition.

Near the eastern end of the Forum is the Colosseum, the greatest building of ancient and modern Rome. It was not standing in Paul's day, but was completed by Titus in A.D. 80 and was originally known as the Flavian Amphitheater. It was erected on the site of an artificial lake which was in the midst of the gardens of Nero's palace where Christians were tortured and burned in A.D. 64. The Colosseum once accommodated 50,000 spectators who viewed a variety of bloody combats which took the lives of many gladiators and Christian martyrs, not to speak of thousands of wild animals.

The earliest evidence for Christians in Rome comes from cemeteries. By Roman law all places of burial had to be outside the city limits. Consequently, many cemeteries have been found along the highways leading into the city. During the 1st century A.D. the Romans customarily cremated their dead and placed the ashes in urns which were deposited in specially prepared vaults or mausoleums. In the 2nd century burial became a regular custom, and wealthy people began to use elaborately decorated sarcophagi (Fig. 219). Jews and Christians did not favor cremation, probably because of their views concerning the resurrection of the dead. Instead they buried in underground chambers, which for convenience were turned into galleries or catacombs. The finest and most elaborate Jewish catacombs ever discovered are at Sheikh Abreiq (Beth She'arim) in northern Palestine. This was evidently a famous Jewish cemetery because pious Jews from far and near were there buried between the 2nd and 5th centuries A.D.[17] Several Jewish catacombs have been found in the environs of Rome. The oldest is near Monteverde, across the Tiber River from the main part of the city, and burials were probably begun there as early as the 1st century A.D. The fact that they were Jewish is most frequently revealed by the symbols on the walls, the most common of which is the menorah or seven-branched candlestick.

The Christian catacombs were far more numerous and elaborate (Fig. 216). Some thirty-five or more have been discovered around the outskirts of the city and the total length of their galleries has been calculated at more than 500 miles. The oldest burials in them were not made much before A.D. 150, some eighty to ninety years after Paul's death. Earlier catacombs may exist, but, if so, they are probably within the present city in areas which were not inhabited before the great suburban extensions of the second and third centuries. The walls of the underground galleries are lined with tombs, one above the other. Horizontal recesses were cut into the soft volcanic tufa, and the bodies, wrapped in Jewish fashion with lengths of cloth, were laid in the recesses, and the openings were closed by bricks or marble slabs. A more elaborate tomb was often made by cutting a semi-circular recess into the wall and then chiseling out a place for the body which was covered with a horizontal slab.

While the catacombs are well known as places where Christians worshiped secretly during times of persecution, they are also important for the study of early Christian art. Indeed, for the 2nd and 3rd centuries A.D. they are the main sources for this study. Many of the designs and motifs were simply borrowed from pagan art, including little winged figures known as Erotes or Amoretti and which by Renaissance times were interpreted

216. A Roman Catacomb

as Cherubs. One of the most common Christian symbols was, of course, the fish. This had been used in pagan art but the Christians made use of it because the five letters of the Greek word for fish were the first letters in the five Greek words which meant " Jesus Christ, Son of God, Savior ". Another common figure in early Christian art was that of the Good Shepherd, by which Christ was shown as a youth carrying a lamb over his shoulders. This figure appears over the baptistry in the early church at Dura on the Euphrates, and its finest example in Rome is a small statue of about the same period (3rd century A.D.; Fig. 217).

The traditional tomb of the Apostle Paul is under the altar of the Church of " St. Paul Outside the Walls ". The first structure erected there was by Constantine, but this was subsequently enlarged into a monumental building which was dedicated by Pope Siricius at the very end of the 4th century. The site was in an ancient Roman cemetery, judging from the tombs unearthed there in 1838.

Perhaps the most interesting search for early Christian remains in Rome has been the excavations under the crypts and altar of the Church of St. Peter. According to tradition both Peter and Paul were martyred in Rome toward the end of Nero's reign, between about A.D. 64 and 68. The traditional tomb of Peter was beneath the altar of St. Peter's, the central and greatest church of Roman Catholicism. In 1941 explorations and excavations were begun under the church when a fitting place was being sought for the tomb of Pope Pius XI. One of the first achievements of the investigation has been the new study of the first church erected on the

---

[17] See Benjamin Maisler, *Beth She'arim : Report on the Excavation during 1936–1940*, Vol. I (Jerusalem, 1950).

217. Statue of Christ as
the Good Shepherd

218. Mausoleums discovered in an ancient Roman cemetery under
the nave of the Church of St. Peter in Rome

219. A pagan Roman sarcophagus found in the cemetery under St. Peter's Church in Rome

site by Constantine in the early 4th century. This was a most unlikely spot in which to build a large church. It was in the middle of a large cemetery stretching from the Vatican hill across the plain to the Tiber River; the most imposing monument still remaining in this cemetery is the tomb of the emperor Hadrian (A.D. 117–38), known today as Castel Sant'Angelo. To build the church Constantine had to pull down part of the Vatican hill, and he used the debris to cover over the cemetery in the valley. To do this it is estimated that he used more than forty thousand cubic meters of earth.

In the debris beneath the floor-level of the Constantinian edifice, and under the present nave of St. Peter's, two rows of mausoleums were found in which wealthy Roman families buried their dead between the 2nd and 4th centuries (Figs. 218–19). Very few Christians were buried here, and those who were date for the most part from the 4th century. One small mausoleum, however, was acquired in the third century by Christians who covered the vault and the walls with a single mosaic plan. These mosaics are the earliest Christian tomb-mosaics yet found. The background is a rich yellow with green leaves and tendrils. On one wall is a fisherman; on another Jonah is being swallowed by a whale; and on a third is a damaged figure, perhaps of the Good Shepherd. Overhead in the vault is a figure of Helios (the Sun), drawn on a chariot pulled by four fiery horses and holding in his left hand an orb, depicting the world. This pagan figure was probably used to represent Christ as " The Sun of Righteousness, the Sun of Salvation ".

Another pagan mausoleum was taken over by a Christian family at the end of the 3rd century. In it by a pagan painting of the god Apollo the Christians have portrayed two heads, one above the other. The lower is traced in red lead and partly re-done in charcoal. It shows an old man with bald head, pointed beard and deeply furrowed brow. The letters PETRUS by the head identify him as Peter, and the name is followed by a prayer to the Apostle, requesting his intercession for all Christians buried near his body. The upper head was probably meant to represent either Paul or Christ, but the identification is uncertain.

Under the present altar and the *Confessio Petri* are the remains of the memorial built by Constantine over the traditional tomb of Peter. Below that is a still earlier memorial, erected about A.D. 160 in

220. Memorial erected to St. Peter about A.D. 160, reconstructed

an open area surrounded by pagan mausoleums (Fig. 220). This was the " trophy " or memorial mentioned by the priest Gaius, who wrote at the end of the second century against the heresy of one Proclus in Asia Minor. The latter was a Montanist who believed that the world was soon coming to an end, and to support the legitimacy of his claim that his beliefs were founded on ancient church tradition he pointed to the tombs of Philip and his four daughters in Hierapolis in Asia. Gaius countered by saying : " But I can show you the trophies of the Apostles. For whether you go to the Vatican, or along the Ostian way, you will find the trophies of those who founded the Church of Rome." [18] In other words, Gaius is able to show in Rome the memorials to Peter and Paul.

Below the site of the monument built about A.D. 160 were still earlier burials, some perhaps as early as A.D. 70, and also a square cavity or hollow. In the latter were some bones which had once belonged to an elderly man of powerful physique,

---

[18] Eusebius, *Church History*, II, 25, 7.

S

but no actual grave appears to have been found. Thus, as Pope Pius XII has stated, it is impossible to identify these bones as those of Peter with any degree of certainty.

The precise significance of these discoveries for the location of Peter's tomb is somewhat debated. While it is now generally agreed that Peter probably did come to Rome late in his life and there suffered martyrdom, some Protestant scholars are not sure that we can be confident that his tomb is under the Church of St. Peter. The persecution of Nero was such that there is always the possibility that Peter's body was not identified or recovered. On the other hand, the place where the Apostle was martyred was doubtless remembered. Hence it is possible to interpret the second century memorial deep under the present altar of St. Peter's as simply a cenotaph which commemorated the place where the martyrdom took place. There is no evidence of a special interest in Christian relics or burial places before the end of the second century, and this being the case it is possible that Peter's grave is and may remain unknown. At any rate the present evidence does not clearly refute such a view, which means that we are left in an uncertain position.[19]

THE CHURCH IN THE WORLD

The Roman world into which Christianity entered was as filled with various religious beliefs as our own. Most of the people were believers in polytheism, that is, in many gods who were conceived as personal beings but who actually were the powers and principles to be observed or experienced in mother nature on earth and in the sky. Educated people, on the other hand, were much more sophisticated in their beliefs. They were monotheists, pantheists, atheists, or any of a number of other things in between. For men like the Roman orator Cicero (106–43 B.C.) or Livy, the historian (59 B.C.–A.D. 17), the old religion was a good and necessary thing for the social order. It was good for the masses and for the state, though, of course, the intelligent man could no longer believe

it unless he radically reinterpreted it in terms of human ideals. Nevertheless, one must be careful not to destroy the faith of the masses; otherwise they may not remain good citizens. Religion has its uses, said one cynical Roman; since that is the case men ought to continue to believe and to sacrifice.

Others, fewer in number, were outright atheists who attacked the old religion as sheer superstition. Many more were highly skeptical about it and spoke of it with indifference or frivolity, and yet when in trouble, returned quickly to it or to some pet superstitions derived from it. Meanwhile the philosophers had for generations been busy, trying to puzzle out systems of belief in which faith and reason could unite. Epicureanism was one of these systems. It taught the existence of countless eternal gods and only denied that they intervened directly in the world. They do not need our worship, but it is natural to us to give it, chiefly by lofty ideas and by following custom. Nevertheless, the real interest of the Epicureans was not in the gods but in man and in the question as to what is the highest human good. That consists in pleasure, while pain is only evil. Pleasure, however, is not for the passing moment but for the whole of life. Hence simplicity and temperance are our guides to it. The Book of Ecclesiastes in the Old Testament shows remarkable resemblances to this point of view.

Stoicism was probably far more influential. For this school God was the reason of the universe, and every person has a spark or fragment of this divine mind or world-soul within him. The gods in whom the people believe are actually intermediary beings, manifestations or "demons" from the great divine unity of all things. The old stories about the loves and wars of the gods should not be taken literally, but are to be interpreted allegorically as pictorial expressions of deep truth. The Stoics were chiefly interested, however, in the problem of human life. Since everyone has within him a portion of the divine reason, he must live by it and not be a slave of his passions. Man must live in accord with nature, that is, in harmony with universal reason. Furthermore, since all men possess this divine spark, they ought to live together as citizens who share a common idealism.

In New Testament times such ideas as the last mentioned formed a powerful background for the ideals of the Roman empire, particularly as established by Caesar Augustus. In the eyes of the poet

---

[19] The best summaries in English of the Vatican excavations are those of the late Father Roger T. O'Callaghan, S.J., " Recent Excavations Underneath the Vatican Crypts ", *The Biblical Archaeologist*, Vol. XII, No. 1 (Feb. 1949); and " Vatican Excavations and the Tomb of Peter ", *ibid.*, Vol. XVI, No. 4 (Dec. 1953). See also Oscar Cullmann, *Peter : Disciple, Apostle, Martyr* (tr. by Floyd V. Filson ; London and Philadelphia, 1953), pp. 132–52.

Virgil (70–19 B.C.), for example, the new era inaugurated by Augustus marked the culmination of efforts since the beginning of time to erect a stable and enduring civilization in which there was a common humanity united by ties of the spirit, a truly universal community based upon the indestructible elements of human personality beyond distinctions of race and color. The power of the state existed for the preservation of order for the common good, which consisted in security, freedom, human dignity and the belief in man's inherent capacity to realize his ideals.

Such lofty ideas, however, had little effect upon the common man's religion. Polytheism with its numerous gods was always tolerant of new and unknown divinities. For centuries in the Roman world a process of amalgamation had been going on, so that the old Greek gods were identified with the Roman, while both were identified with the gods of Asia Minor, Syria and Egypt. The triumph of Hellenic culture meant also a thorough-going syncretism. Meanwhile, numerous cults of Greek, Asian and Egyptian origin arose and were imported into Rome. These were the " mystery " religions, into which the devotees were inducted by special rites of initiation. They then participated in secret ceremonies which customarily conveyed the sense of emotional uplift, purification and salvation. The origin of most of these cults lay in the old nature-religion with its worship of the dying-rising vegetation god, and in the course of time this primitive idea was used as a means of securing renewal of some sort for the individual soul.

In this religious atmosphere the cult of emperor-worship was fostered, beginning in the time of Augustus, and promoted as a means of unifying the empire. In the eastern provinces it had been the custom since the time of Alexander the Great to deify the rulers during and after their life-time. Consequently, the worship of Augustus and the succeeding Caesars was nothing particularly new. In Rome the emperor-cult was an innovation, gradually adopted under the influence of the east but on the basis of the Roman idea of the divine *genius* which resided in and presided over every man. Thus the *genius* or divine double of the emperor was in theory what was worshipped, though in practice the ordinary person probably drew no such subtle distinction between the divine and the human.

Judaism in this world was looked down upon as simply a horrible religion. The Roman historian,

Tacitus, writing during the reign of the emperor Trajan (A.D. 98–117), attempted to describe the origin of the Jewish people and in doing so expressed views which are historically fantastic. He continues : " Things sacred with us, with them have no sanctity, while they allow what with us is forbidden . . . This worship, however introduced, is upheld by its antiquity ; all their other customs, which are at once perverse and disgusting, owe their strength to their very badness . . . Among themselves they are inflexibly honest and ever ready to shew compassion, though they regard the rest of mankind with all the hatred of enemies . . . Those who come over to their religion . . . have this lesson first instilled into them, to despise all gods, to disown their country, and set at nought parents, children, and brethren . . . The Jews have purely mental conceptions of Deity, as one in essence. They call those profane who make representations of God in human shape out of perishable materials . . . The Jewish religion is tasteless and mean." [20]

What to the Roman polytheist was highest and holiest was condemned by the Jew as accursed, so that the Romans regarded him as an enemy of religion. By New Testament times, according to contemporary authorities, a Jewish element was to be found in practically every city, with the result that the Jewish religion was well known. Furthermore the Jews were considered by the Romans as a nation. As such they were accorded certain privileges. Beginning with Julius Caesar in the mid-1st century B.C. it was Roman policy to permit the Jew the free exercise of his religion, a degree of local autonomy in legal matters, exemption from military service and from appearance in a lawcourt on the Sabbath, etc. Hence, though persecution flared up against the Jews on occasion, it was usually localized, while their legal position in the empire was protected by imperial decree.

In addition, in spite of enmity, the Jews gained many friends by their unshakeable piety, the harmony which reigned in their local communities, their diligence, virtue, few wants and contempt of death. All ancient pagan authorities agree that in all lands there were many Gentiles who either obeyed or were influenced by the Mosaic laws. Even in Rome many refrained from business on the Sabbath, for the day of weekly rest was evidently attractive. Yet while the Gentile proselytes and

[20] Tacitus, *History*, Book V, 2–5 (quoted from The Modern Library edition, tr. by A. J. Church and W. J. Brodribb).

" God-fearers " were many, Judaism never proved the threat to paganism that Christianity was to be. As one writer (Gibbon) has put it : Judaism was a religion " admirably fitted for defence, but never designed for conquest ". After the fall of Jerusalem in A.D. 70, an even stricter rabbinic Judaism gradually came into being, with the result that the gulf dividing it from paganism was widened still further and converts became continually fewer.

Christianity from the outset had a far less favored position than Judaism because it was regarded simply as a sect which had broken away from Judaism and was not subject to the legal protection accorded a nation or people. Before the end of the 2nd century A.D. Christians and Christianity were rarely mentioned by classical authors ; and, when they were mentioned, it was with contempt and indifference. While the Jews as a nation were accorded freedom and release from the obligation to worship the gods and the emperor, this freedom was not officially extended to the Christians. Hence the legal position of Christianity was always uncertain, while refusal to worship the emperor and the national deities was regarded as high treason and liable to punishment by criminal law.

The first persecution of Christians for treason against the emperor evidently broke out in Asia Minor in the reign of Domitian (A.D. 81–96) and is reflected in the Book of Revelation. In Asia Minor the emperor-cult was deeply fixed and universally acclaimed ; it was a natural place for persecution to take place on the grounds of loyalty to the empire. For John of Patmos, the author of Revelation, however, the issue was clear : allegiance to Christ and worship of the emperor were absolutely incompatible. He speaks of Pergamos (Pergamum), the center of emperor worship in the province of Asia, as " Satan's seat ", of one Antipas as a " faithful martyr " there (Rev. 2 : 13), and of those " that were beheaded for the witness of Jesus, and for the word of God, and which had not worshipped the beast " (20 : 4).

Tacitus wrote in some detail about the earlier persecution of Nero during which Peter and Paul evidently lost their lives. In A.D. 64 a terrible fire destroyed most of Rome and the people of the city believed that Nero himself had started it in order to have the glory of founding a new city called by his name. Tacitus continues :

Consequently, to get rid of the report, Nero fastened the guilt and inflicted the most exquisite tortures on a class hated for their abominations, called Christians by the populace. Christus, from whom the name had its origin, suffered the extreme penalty during the reign of Tiberius at the hands of one of our procurators, Pontius Pilatus, and a most mischievous superstition, thus checked for the moment, again broke out not only in Judaea, the first source of the evil, but even in Rome, where all things hideous and shameful from every part of the world find their centre and become popular. Accordingly, an arrest was first made of all who pleaded guilty ; then, upon their information, an immense multitude was convicted, not so much of the crime of firing the city, as of hatred against mankind. Mockery of every sort was added to their deaths. Covered with the skins of beasts, they were torn by dogs and perished, or were nailed to crosses, or were doomed to the flames and burnt, to serve as a nightly illumination, when daylight had expired.

Nero offered his gardens for the spectacle, and was exhibiting a show in the circus, while he mingled with the people in the dress of a charioteer or stood aloft on a car. Hence, even for criminals who deserved extreme and exemplary punishment, there arose a feeling of compassion ; for it was not, as it seemed, for the public good, but to glut one man's cruelty, that they were being destroyed.[21]

Christianity, unlike Judaism, however, considered the spread of the Gospel as a sacred duty and it had the strength to break through the barriers which stood in its way. While educated people despised the new religion as superstition and while the masses hated it as " atheism " and were increasingly inclined to claim every reversal in the national fortunes as due to the wrath of the gods against its spread, the movement could not be stopped. In the breakdown of paganism the Gospel offered a new hope and a new security, especially for the poor and depressed. In Asia Minor during the early second century we hear of a general defection from the popular religion which emptied the temples and alarmed the responsible officials. Into this religious decay Christianity stepped with vigor and daring, willing to risk everything, including loss of life, for the cause of Christ. In the long run it was also able to wage a successful battle for the mind of the pagan intellectual. The dreams of the new order of Augustus Caesar, based upon the classical idealism, virtually collapsed during the third century, and the Christian doctrines of man and society gradually became a doctrine of salvation in a dying culture.

---

[21] *Annals*, Book XV, 44.

FURTHER READING

Undoubtedly the best single summary of the material covered in this chapter is to be found in Jack Finegan, *Light from the Ancient Past* (Princeton, 1946), pp. 252–459, where many references are cited. Summaries of the archaeological discoveries in the more important cities as published in *The Biblical Archaeologist* have been referred to at relevant places in the footnotes. The most informative studies of Asia Minor in New Testament times are, of course, those of Sir William M. Ramsay. Two of his books which are of special interest to the New Testament student are listed in footnote 8, and there are others of a more technical nature which can easily be discovered in a large library.

The bibliography on Rome and the Roman world is quite extensive. Of especial interest is the important work edited by Tenney Frank, *An Economic Survey of Ancient Rome* (6 vols. ; Baltimore, 1933–40).

For the city of Rome in the first and subsequent centuries A.D. see among others A. G. Mackinnon, *The Rome of Saint Paul* (London, 1930) ; and *The Rome of the Early Church* (London, 1933). A most detailed and informative work is that of Ludwig Friedländer, *Roman Life and Manners under the Early Empire*, Vols. I–IV (7th ed. tr. by A. B. Gough ; London, 1913). Volume III, pp. 84–214, contains an interesting treatment of religion, including Judaism and Christianity, in the empire. See also the excellent volume by Jerome Carcopino, *Daily Life in Ancient Rome* (ed. by Henry T. Rowell, tr. by E. O. Lorimer ; New Haven, 1940). Perhaps the best survey of the victory of Christianity over the thought-world of ancient Rome is C. N. Cochrane, *Christianity and Classical Culture : A Study of Thought and Action from Augustus to Augustine* (London, 1940).

There are, of course, many aspects of the subject of this chapter which are omitted. For example, a great deal more could be made of the Greek papyri and their meaning for New Testament times : see Adolf Deissmann, *Light from the Ancient East* (tr. by L. R. M. Strahan ; New York, 1927).

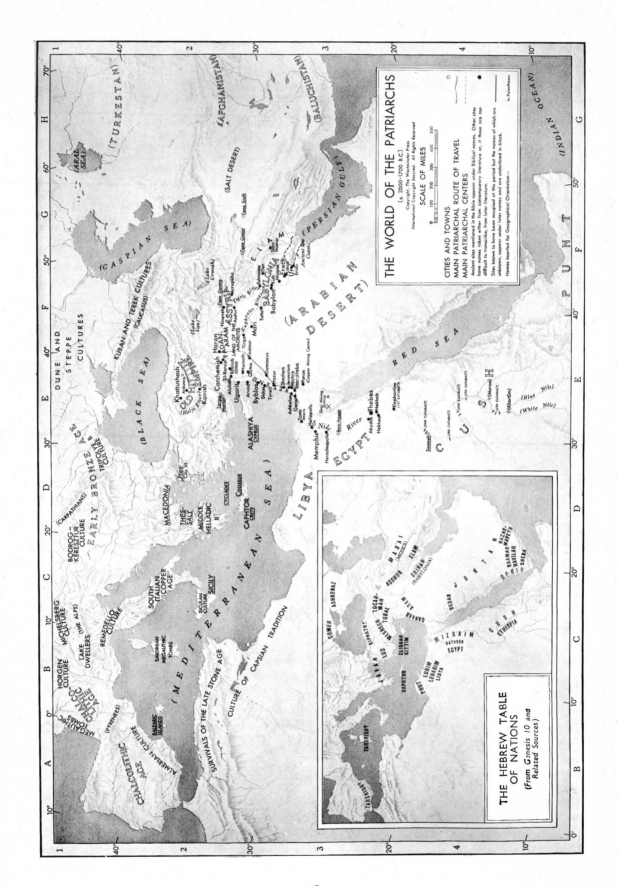

THE WORLD OF THE PATRIARCHS

(c. 2000–1700 B.C.)

Copyright, The Westminster Press
International Copyright Secured. All Rights Reserved

SCALE OF MILES

0   100   200   300   400   500

CITIES AND TOWNS
MAIN PATRIARCHAL ROUTE OF TRAVEL
MAIN PATRIARCHAL CENTERS

Ancient sites mentioned in the Bible appear under Biblical names. Other sites
have names taken either from contemporary literature or, if these are too
difficult to transcribe, from later literature.

Sites known to have been occupied at this period but the names of which are
unknown, appear under later names and are underlined in block.

Names inserted for Geographical Orientation—   in Parentheses

THE HEBREW TABLE OF NATIONS

(From Genesis 10 and
Related Sources)

278

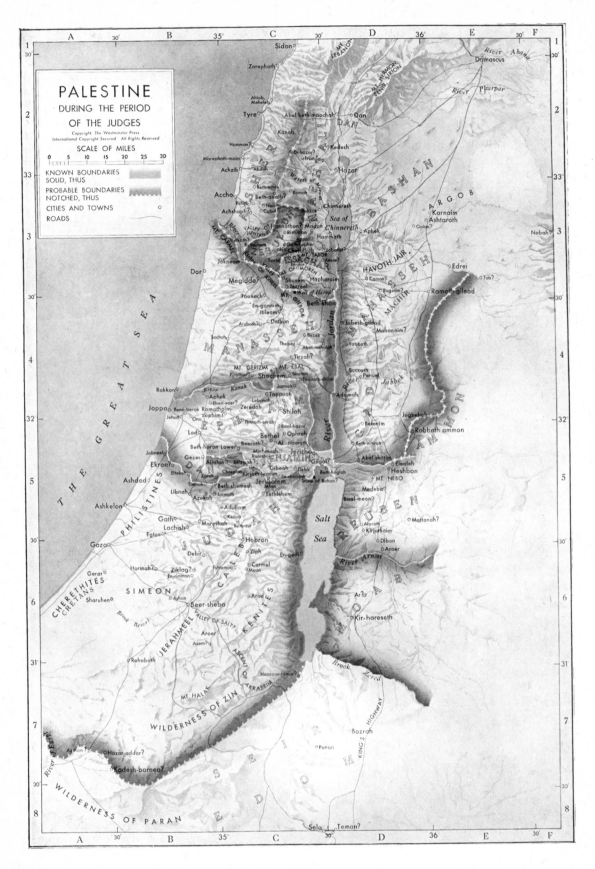

PALESTINE
DURING THE PERIOD
OF THE JUDGES

Copyright, The Westminster Press
International Copyright Secured All Rights Reserved

SCALE OF MILES
0 5 10 15 20 25 30

KNOWN BOUNDARIES
SOLID, THUS
PROBABLE BOUNDARIES
NOTCHED, THUS
CITIES AND TOWNS
ROADS

Sidon

Zarephath

MT. LEBANON

River Abana

Damascus

River Pharpar

Ahlab,
Meheleb

Tyre

Abel-beth-maachah   Dan

MT. HERMON,
SENIR-SIRION

Kanah

En-hazor?   Kedesh

Hammon?

Misrephoth-maim

Achzib   Abdon

Waters of Merom

Iron?

Hazor

BASHAN

Accho   Beth-anath?   Ramah

Achshaph?   Cabul   Rukkoh

Chinnereth

ARGOB

Karnaim
Ashtaroth

Golan?   Nobah?

Dor

VALLEY   Hannathon?   Madon

Shechem   Rimmon?

Japhia   Chesulloth   Gath-hepher

MT. TABOR   Anem?

HAVOTH-JAIR.

Sea of
Chinnereth

Hammath

Aphek

Jokneam

MT. CARMEL

Sarid

En-dor

MOREH

Edrei   Tob?

Megiddo

Shunem   Hapharaim

Jezreel   Camon?   Rogelim?

Ramoth-gilead

MT. GILBOA   Well of Harod

Taanach

Beth-shan

Jabesh-gilead

MACHIR

En-gannim   Ibleam

Dothan   Bezek

Mahanaim?

Tabbath

Arubboth?   MANASSEH

Thebez   Abel-meholah

Sochoh   Tirzah?   Succoth   Penuel

Jabbok

MT. GERIZIM   MT. EBAL

Pirathon?   Shechem   Shalem

Rakkon   Kanah   Janoah?   Teonath-shiloh

River   Aphek   Lebonah?   Tappuah   Adamah

Joppa   Eben-ezer?   Zeredah   SHILOH   Betonim   Jogbehah

Bene-berak   Ramathaim-   EPHRAIM   Rabbath-ammon

Jehud   zophim?   Timnath-serah   Baal-hazor

Ono   Bethel   Ophrah

Lod   Beeroth?   Naaram   Beth-nimrah

Jabneel?   Gezer   Michmash   Jericho   Abel-shittim

Ekron   Beth-horon Lower   Ai   Gilgal?   AMMON

Aijalon   Mizpah?   BENJAMIN   Beth-hoglah   Elealeh

Ashdod   Eltekeh?   Kirjath-jearim   Gibeah   Debir   Heshbon

Timnah   Zorah   En-shemesh   Stone of Bohan?   MT. NEBO

Beth-shemesh   Jerusalem   Medeba

Ashkelon   Libnah   Jarmuth   Jebus   Baal-meon?

Azekah   Bethlehem

Adullam   Ataroth?

PHILISTINES   Gath   Keilah   Kirjathaim?

Mareshah   Beth-zur?   Dibon

Lachish   Eglon   Hebron   Aroer

Gaza   Ziph

Debir   Carmel   En-gedi   River Arnon

Gerar   Hormah?   Eshtemoa?   Maon

Ziklag?   MOAB

En-rimmon?   Arad?   Ar?

CHERETHITES   Sharuhen?   Ashan   KENITES   Kir-haresheth

CRETANS   SIMEON   Beer-sheba   JERAHMEEL

Bozrah

VALLEY OF SALT?   Aroer

Azem?   Punon

Rehoboth   EDOM

Hazezon-tamar?

MT. HALAK   Brook Zered

WILDERNESS OF ZIN

River of Egypt   ASCENT OF AKRABBIM

Azmon?   Hazar-addar?

Kadesh-barnea?   KING'S HIGHWAY

WILDERNESS OF PARAN

Sela?   Teman?

THE GREAT SEA

Salt
Sea

REUBEN

GAD

DAN

ASHER

NAPHTALI

ZEBULUN

ISSACHAR

JUDAH

CALEB

279

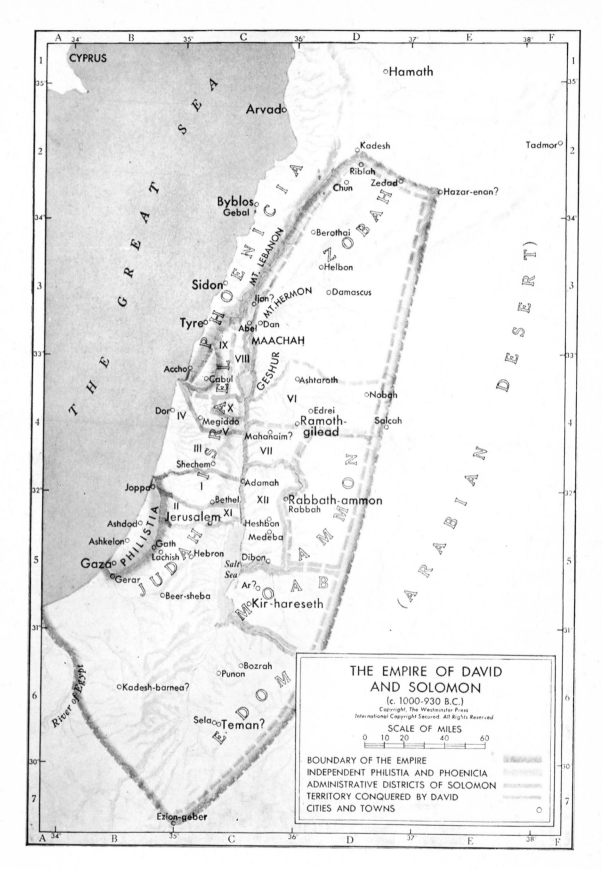

THE EMPIRE OF DAVID
AND SOLOMON
(c. 1000-930 B.C.)
Copyright, The Westminster Press
International Copyright Secured. All Rights Reserved.

SCALE OF MILES
0   10 20   40   60

BOUNDARY OF THE EMPIRE
INDEPENDENT PHILISTIA AND PHOENICIA
ADMINISTRATIVE DISTRICTS OF SOLOMON
TERRITORY CONQUERED BY DAVID
CITIES AND TOWNS

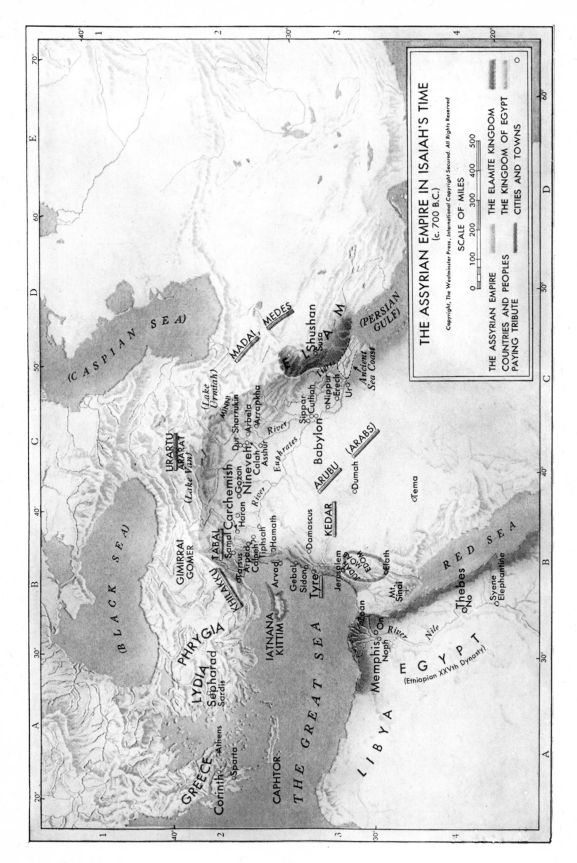

THE ASSYRIAN EMPIRE IN ISAIAH'S TIME
(c. 700 B.C.)

Copyright, The Westminster Press, International Copyright Secured. All Rights Reserved

SCALE OF MILES
0   100   200   300   400   500

THE ASSYRIAN EMPIRE   THE ELAMITE KINGDOM
COUNTRIES AND PEOPLES   THE KINGDOM OF EGYPT
PAYING TRIBUTE   CITIES AND TOWNS

(CASPIAN SEA)

(BLACK SEA)

(PERSIAN GULF)

RED SEA

THE GREAT SEA

GREECE
Athens
Corinth
Sparta

LYDIA
Sepharad
Sardis

PHRYGIA

CAPHTOR

GIMIRRAI
GOMER

TABAL

URARTU
ARARAT
(Lake Van)

(Lake Urmiah)

MADAI, MEDES

KHILAKKU

IATNANA
KITTIM

Arvad

Gebal
Sidon
Tyre

Carchemish
Samal
Tarsus
Arpad
Calneh
Tiphsah

Haran
Gozan
Nineveh
Calah
Asshur

Milinni
Dur Sharrukin
Arbela
Arrapkha

River
Euphrates
River

Hamath
Damascus

Jerusalem
JUDAH
EDOM
Elath

Mt.
Sinai

Zoan
On
Noph
Memphis
Naph

Nile River

LIBYA

EGYPT
(Ethiopian XXVth Dynasty)

Thebes
No

Syene
Elephantine

Babylon
Sippar
Cuthah
Nippur
Erech
Ur
Uruk

ELAM
Shushan
Susa
Tigris
Ancient
Sea Coast

ARUBU
(ARABS)
KEDAR
Dumah
Tema

S*   281

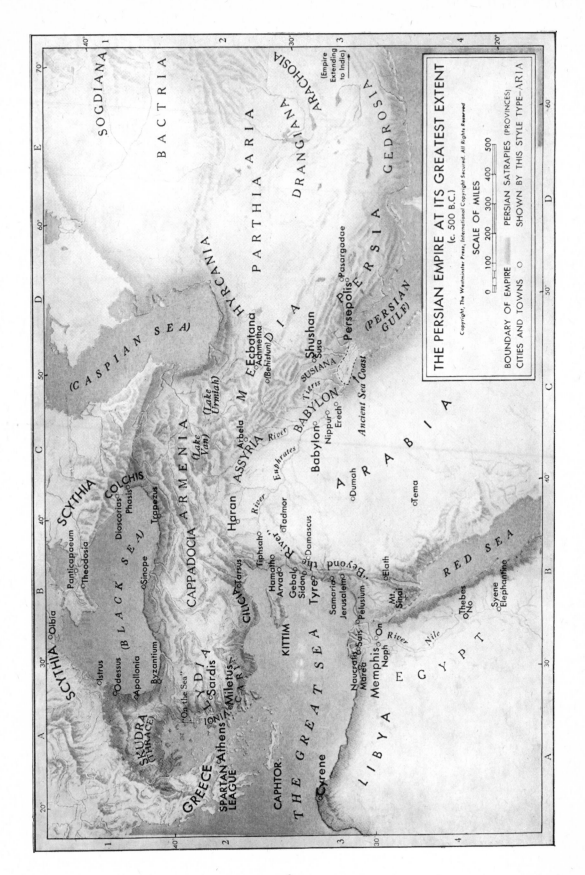

THE PERSIAN EMPIRE AT ITS GREATEST EXTENT

(c. 500 B.C.)

Copyright, The Westminster Press, International Copyright Secured. All Rights Reserved

SCALE OF MILES

0   100   200   300   400   500

BOUNDARY OF EMPIRE   PERSIAN SATRAPIES (PROVINCES)

CITIES AND TOWNS o   SHOWN BY THIS STYLE TYPE—ARIA

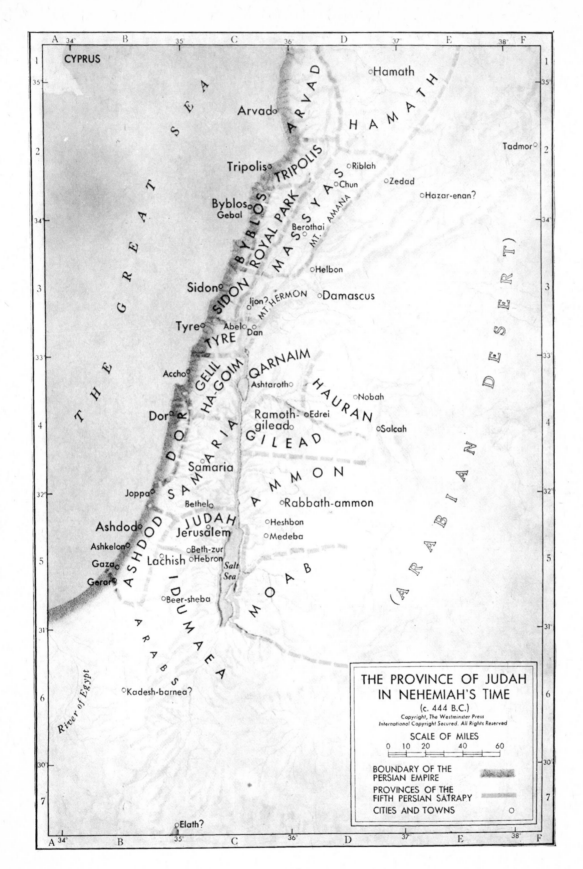

CYPRUS

A 34° B 35° C 36° D 37° E 38° F

THE GREAT SEA

River of Egypt

ARVAD

Hamath

Arvad

Tadmor

TRIPOLIS

Tripolis

Riblah

Chun

Zedad

Hazar-enan?

MASSYAS

BYBLOS

Byblos
Gebal

ROYAL PARK

Berothai

MT. AMANA

Helbon

HAMATH

Sidon

SIDON

Ijon?

MT. HERMON

Damascus

Tyre

Abel

Dan

TYRE

GELIL HA-GOIM

Accho

QARNAIM

Ashtaroth

Nobah

HAURAN

Dor

DOR

Ramoth-
gilead

Edrei

Salcah

GILEAD

SAMARIA

Samaria

AMMON

Joppa

Bethel

Rabbath-ammon

Ashdod

JUDAH

Jerusalem

Heshbon

Medeba

Ashkelon

Beth-zur

ASHDOD

Lachish

Hebron

Salt
Sea

Gaza

MOAB

Gerar

IDUMAEA

Beer-sheba

ARABS

(ARABIAN DESERT)

Kadesh-barnea?

Elath?

THE PROVINCE OF JUDAH
IN NEHEMIAH'S TIME
(c. 444 B.C.)
Copyright, The Westminster Press
International Copyright Secured. All Rights Reserved
SCALE OF MILES
0 10 20 40 60

BOUNDARY OF THE
PERSIAN EMPIRE
PROVINCES OF THE
FIFTH PERSIAN SATRAPY
CITIES AND TOWNS

283

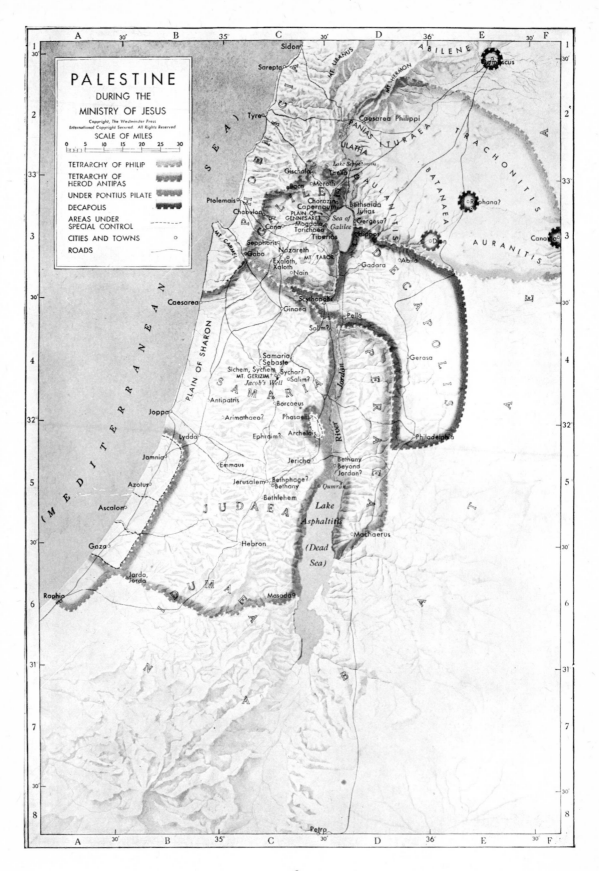

PALESTINE
DURING THE
MINISTRY OF JESUS

Copyright, The Westminster Press
International Copyright Secured. All Rights Reserved

SCALE OF MILES
0 5 10 15 20 25 30

TETRARCHY OF PHILIP
TETRARCHY OF
HEROD ANTIPAS
UNDER PONTIUS PILATE
DECAPOLIS
AREAS UNDER
SPECIAL CONTROL
CITIES AND TOWNS   o
ROADS

Sidon
Sarepta
MT. LIBANUS
ABILENE
MT. HERMON
Damascus

Tyre
Caesarea Philippi
PANIAS
ITURAEA
TRACHONITIS
ULATHA

Gischala
Giscala
Meroth
Lake Semechonitis
GAULANITIS
BATANAEA

Ptolemais
Chorazin
Capernaum
Bethsaida
Julias
Raphana?

Chabulon
PLAIN OF
GENNESARET
Magdala
Tarichaea
Gergesa?
Hippos
AURANITIS

Cana
Sea of
Galilee
Tiberias
Adippos
Dion
Canatha

Sepphoris
Gaba
Nazareth
MT. TABOR
Gadara
Abila

Exaloth
Xaloth
Nain
DECAPOLIS

Caesarea
Scythopolis
Ginaea
Pella
Salim?
Gerasa

Samaria
Sebaste
Sichem, Sychem
MT. GERIZIM
Sychar?
Salim?
Jacob's Well
PERAEA

Antipatris
Borcaeus

Joppa
Arimathaea?
Phasaelis
River Jordan

Lydda
Ephraim?
Archelais
Philadelphia

Jamnia
Emmaus
Jericho
Bethany
Beyond
Jordan?

Azotus
Jerusalem
Bethphage
Bethany
Qumran

Ascalon
Bethlehem
Lake
Asphaltitis

Gaza
Hebron
Machaerus
(Dead
Sea)

Raphia
Jarda,
Jorda
Masada

PLAIN OF SHARON
MT. CARMEL
(PHOENICE SEA)
GALILEE
SAMARIA
JUDAEA
IDUMAEA
NABA
(MEDITERRANEAN SEA)

Petra

284

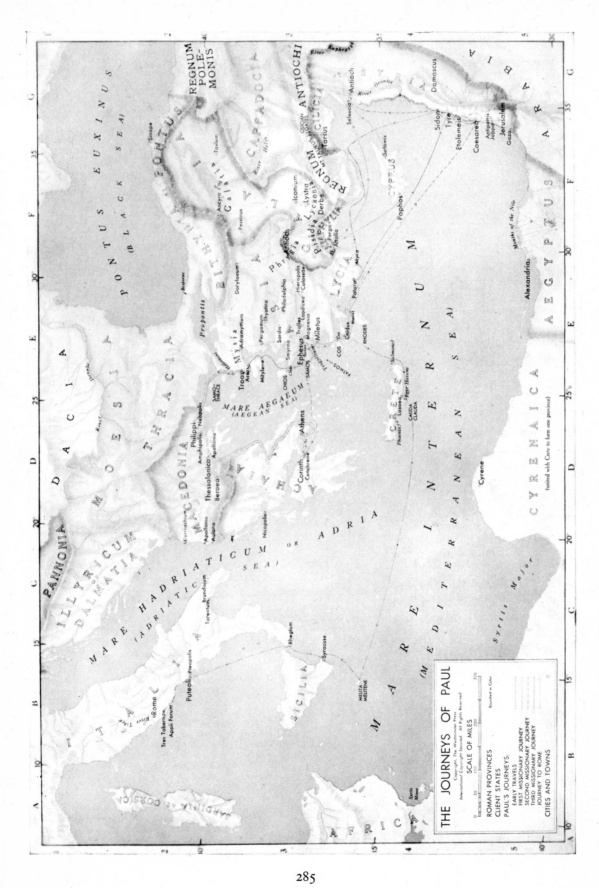

THE JOURNEYS OF PAUL

Copyright, The Westminster Press
International Copyright Secured   All Rights Reserved

SCALE OF MILES

ROMAN PROVINCES   Bounded in Color
CLIENT STATES
PAUL'S JOURNEYS:
    EARLY TRAVELS
    FIRST MISSIONARY JOURNEY
    SECOND MISSIONARY JOURNEY
    THIRD MISSIONARY JOURNEY
    JOURNEY TO ROME
CITIES AND TOWNS

INDEX

I. INDEX OF MODERN NAMES

II. INDEX OF BIBLICAL NAMES

III. INDEX OF BIBLICAL PLACES

IV. INDEX OF SUBJECTS

V. INDEX OF BIBLE REFERENCES